D1061788

*Praise for Books by Douglas Gray*

### The Canadian Guide to Will and Estate Planning (with John Budd)

"The authors have done a masterful job.... This is a shelf reference every Canadian taxpayer and every Canadian family should have."
—*The Globe and Mail*

"An informative, practical guide ... The authors ... cover all the bases."
—*National Post*

"This guide promises a general, practical, and objective overview of the issues, options, and terminology involved in estate planning. Fortunately, it delivers on all counts."
—*CAmagazine*

### The Canadian Snowbird Guide

". . . an invaluable guide to worry-free part-time living in the U.S. . . . by one of Canada's bestselling authors of business and personal finance books . . . most comprehensive book to address issues for retired part-time residents of the United States . . ."
—*The Globe and Mail*

". . . I hate to sound like a cheerleader for Gray and his *Canadian Snowbird Guide*, but RAH! RAH! RAH! Regardless . . . the book is a complete how-to—written in his characteristically thorough style . . . Gray delivers the goods right where the Snowbirds live. If you or someone close to you winters in the U.S., you should have this book . . ."
—*Business in Vancouver*

". . . Gray has written a reference book, thoughtful and complete, and prepared with the authoritative research skills and knowledge of a fastidious solicitor . . . as practical as a sunhat on a Tampa afternoon, and that alone warrants it a place on every southbound RV's bookshelf."
—*Quill and Quire*

### Mortgages Made Easy

". . . Gray's latest endeavour is a good educational tool . . . no legalese here, just some good ol' street-level English that explains—mostly for the benefit of novices—all the real and perceived complexities of mortgages . . ."
—*Calgary Herald*

**Making Money in Real Estate, 1st Edition**

"Gray delivers the goods. It is all-Canadian, and not a retread book full of tips that are worthless north of the U.S. border. It's chock-full of practical street smart strategies and advice, pitfalls to avoid, samples, what-to-look-out-for checklists and information."
—*Business in Vancouver*

**The Complete Canadian Small Business Guide (with Diana Gray)**

"... This guide is truly a gold mine ... taps into the authors' extensive expertise ... an encyclopedic compendium ... the bible of Canadian small business."
—*Profit Magazine*

"...Detailed, very informative, scrupulously objective as well as being written in a style that is refreshingly clear of jargon ... This one is a 'must-buy' ..."
—*BCBusiness*

**Home Inc.: The Canadian Home-Based Business Guide (with Diana Gray)**

"Should be required reading for all potential home-basers . . . authoritative, current and comprehensive."
—*The Edmonton Journal*

**The Complete Canadian Franchise Guide (with Norman Friend)**

"... This book tells it like it is, a realistic look at franchising and what it takes to be successful. The information provided is clear, concise, practical and easy to apply..."
—*Canadian Franchise Association*

**Raising Money: The Canadian Guide to Successful Business Financing
(with Brian Nattrass)**

"... The authors have combined their formidable talents to produce what may be the definitive work on raising money in the Canadian marketplace ... written in plain language, with a user-friendly question and answer format and contains invaluable checklists, appendices and information sources ... a definite keeper for potential and practicing entrepreneurs alike ..."
—*Canadian Business Franchise*

**Risk-Free Retirement: The Complete Canadian Planning Guide (with Graham Cunningham, Tom Delaney, Les Solomon, and Dr. Des Dwyer)**

"... This book is a classic ... will be invaluable for years to come ... it is arguably the most comprehensive guide to retirement planning in Canada today ..."
—*The Vancouver Sun*

# Making Money
## in
## Real Estate

# BOOKS BY DOUGLAS GRAY

## Real Estate Titles

*Making Money in Real Estate: The Canadian Guide to Profitable Investment in Residential Property*

*Real Estate Investing for Canadians for Dummies* (with Peter Mitham)

*The Canadian Guide to Buying and Owning Recreational Property in Canada*

*The Canadian Landlord's Guide* (with Peter Mitham)

*101 Streetsmart Condo-Buying Tips for Canadians*

*Mortgages Made Easy: The All-Canadian Guide to Home Financing*

*Home Buying Made Easy: The Canadian Guide to Purchasing a Newly Built or Pre-Owned Home*

*Condo Buying Made Easy: The Canadian Guide to Apartment and Townhouse Condos, Co-ops and Timeshares*

*Mortgage Payment Tables Made Easy*

*The Complete Canadian Home Inspection Guide* (with Ed Witzke)

## Small Business Titles

*Start and Run a Profitable Consulting Business*

*Start and Run a Profitable Business Using Your Computer*

*Have You Got What It Takes? The Entrepreneur's Complete Self-Assessment Guide*

*Marketing Your Product* (with Donald Cyr)

*The Complete Canadian Small Business Guide* (with Diana Gray)

*Home Inc.: The Canadian Home-Based Business Guide* (with Diana Gray)

*Raising Money: The Canadian Guide to Successful Business Financing* (with Brian Nattrass)

*The Complete Canadian Franchise Guide* (with Norman Friend)

*So You Want to Buy a Franchise?* (with Norman Friend)

*Be Your Own Boss: The Ultimate Guide to Buying a Small Business or Franchise in Canada* (with Norman Friend)

*The Canadian Small Business Legal Guide*

## Personal Finance/Retirement Planning Titles

*The Canadian Snowbird Guide: Everything You Need to Know about Living Part-time in the USA & Mexico*

*The Canadian Guide to Will and Estate Planning* (with John Budd)

*Risk-Free Retirement: The Complete Canadian Planning Guide* (with Tom Delaney, Graham Cunningham, Les Solomon, and Dr. Des Dwyer)

## Software Programs

*Making Money in Real Estate* (jointly developed by Douglas Gray and Phoenix Accrual Corporation)

# Making Money in Real Estate

## THE ESSENTIAL CANADIAN GUIDE TO INVESTING IN RESIDENTIAL PROPERTY

Third Edition

### DOUGLAS GRAY

John Wiley & Sons Canada, Ltd.

Library and Archives Canada Cataloguing in Publication

Gray, Douglas A.
    Making money in real estate : the essential Canadian guide to investing in residential property / Douglas Gray. — 3rd ed.

Includes index.
Issued also in electronic formats.
ISBN 978-1-118-11594-7

    1. Real estate investment.    2. Real estate investment—Canada.
I. Title.

HD1382.5.G73 2012          332.63'24          C2011-907373-0

ISBN  978-1-118-11594-7  (pbk);  ISBN  978-1-118-12203-7  (ebk);  ISBN  978-1-118-12204-4  (ebk); ISBN 978-1-118-12205-1 (ebk)

The material in this publication is provided for information purposes only. Laws, regulations, and procedures are constantly changing, and the examples given are intended to be general guidelines only. This book is sold with the understanding that neither the author nor the publisher is engaged in rendering professional advice. It is strongly recommended that legal, accounting, tax, financial, insurance, and other advice or assistance be obtained before acting on any information contained in this book. If such advice or other assistance is required, the personal services of a competent professional should be sought.

**Production Credits**
Managing Editor: Alison Maclean
Executive Editor: Don Loney
Production Editor: Pauline Ricablanca
Cover Design: Adrian So
Composition: Thomson Digital
Printer: Friesens Printing Ltd.

John Wiley & Sons Canada, Ltd.
6045 Freemont Blvd.
Mississauga, Ontario
L5R 4J3

Printed in Canada

1 2 3 4 5 FP 16 15 14 13 12

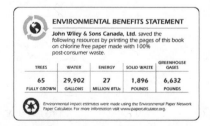

ENVIRONMENTAL BENEFITS STATEMENT

John Wiley & Sons Canada, Ltd. saved the following resources by printing the pages of this book on chlorine free paper made with 100% post-consumer waste.

| TREES | WATER | ENERGY | SOLID WASTE | GREENHOUSE GASES |
|---|---|---|---|---|
| 65 | 29,902 | 27 | 1,896 | 6,632 |
| FULLY GROWN | GALLONS | MILLION BTUs | POUNDS | POUNDS |

Environmental impact estimates were made using the Environmental Paper Network Paper Calculator. For more information visit www.papercalculator.org.

# Contents

# Preface

**The past decade** has seen one of the biggest real estate booms and busts in living memory. The boom times attracted many to become real estate investors, and the bust led to many more picking up bargain properties. And still others have hesitated due to concern over their lack of knowledge of just how to profit from the boom and bust periods. Others, of course, invested anyway, but lacked a due sense of caution or any clear plan or objective and lost money. The key to success is an approach that's ambitious and informed, prudent when it comes to sizing up the opportunities, and satisfied with the financial wealth and independence that prudence brings.

This book is a practical step-by-step guide designed to assist you in attaining your financial and investment objectives through real estate. It provides a realistic awareness of market conditions, and the basic knowledge for applying sound judgment to the opportunities that are available.

While sound judgment is always important, the information that makes it possible changes. This book appeared 20 years ago, in 1992, well before most investors were looking online for information: then again, in 2005, at the height of the real estate boom of the last decade. While it retained the core content of the original edition, it was revised to reflect the growth in popular interest in real estate investment and connected readers with the many new online sources of information.

This latest edition again updates the information regarding online sources, which have increased in scope and quality since 2005. Revised with the assistance of Peter Mitham, my co-author on *Real Estate Investing for Canadians for Dummies* (Wiley), it is designed as a reference to help you navigate the wealth of information now available while providing street-smart advice on investing in real estate in the post-boom era. Changes to lending practices, a more conservative attitude, and a focus on cash flow that will help reduce risk are all factors that contributed to this edition. Accordingly, the material in Chapter 5, "Understanding the Financing Aspects," is significantly updated while Chapter 10, "Managing Your Property," is expanded. Changes to tax policies, particularly the harmonization of federal and provincial sales taxes in Ontario, have prompted updates to Chapter 7, "Understanding the Tax Aspects." Chapter 9, which in previous editions was devoted to negotiating strategies, has been fleshed out as a full-fledged guide to buying a property.

These changes, and a comprehensive review of the entire text, are designed to fine-tune the content to today's reality. The hope is the new information and a clearer presentation will increase your confidence when sifting through information and making significant decisions regarding your real estate investment. Whether you've bought a property as a principal residence, a home with a secondary suite, or as straight-up investment, the guidance this book provides aims to boost the return you see on your investment.

I hope you enjoy this book and find the information helpful and encouraging. Your candid feedback on how this work can better meet your needs is welcomed and will assist in preparing future editions. Please refer to my contact information and website at the back of the book under "Further Education and Information."

Good luck and good fortune!
Douglas Gray
Vancouver, B.C.
www.homebuyer.ca

# Acknowledgments

**I am grateful** for the kind assistance given to me by many parties, including the Canada Mortgage and Housing Corporation and the Canadian Real Estate Association.

Thanks to Ken Chong of DMCL, chartered accountants, in Vancouver, B.C., for all his helpful assistance from time to time on tax implications of various business and investment scenarios.

I would like to express my appreciation to Don Loney, Executive Editor at John Wiley & Sons, for his patience, encouragement, and insightful suggestions in the development of this new edition. I have had the pleasure of working with Don for over 20 years, since the first edition of this book was published. I have indeed been fortunate to work with such a consummate professional in the publishing business.

Last but not least, I would like to thank Peter Mitham, a talented professional wordsmith and real estate expert, and collaborator on this new edition. Peter has been my co-author on two other Wiley publications—*Real Estate Investing for Canadians for Dummies* and *The Canadian Landlord Guide*.

# CHAPTER 1

# Understanding Real Estate Investment

**Many Canadians have** made a fortune in residential real estate and have become financially independent in the process. Many, even when financial markets plummeted on the back of U.S. housing woes in late 2008, didn't see the same sort of losses on real estate that their stock portfolios did. By following a prudent investment strategy, you can mitigate the risks of investing in real estate and come out a winner—even during a downturn. Since real estate is often a long-term investment, you have time to pursue a methodical approach that lets you do the necessary research and acquire the background knowledge that lets you feel comfortable with the decisions you're making. This book provides that knowledge, enabling you to make informed decisions that minimize the risks and maximize the profits possible from your real estate investment.

According to a recent survey by the wealth management division of Merrill Lynch and private consulting firm Capgemini, there are approximately 282,000 millionaires in Canada. But this number accounts for investable assets only—not those with cash in real estate assets. Add those whose total net worth, including real estate, is more than $1 million, and the number of millionaires would be far greater. Many ordinary Canadians have profited simply through long-term home ownership and regular contributions to their Registered Retirement Savings Plans (RRSPs), both of which yield tax-free gains.

There are distinct advantages to starting your real estate investment by purchasing a principal residence. A starter home—whether it's a studio apartment or an older, 750-square-foot bungalow in need of some TLC—gives you a foothold in the market and a chance to start building equity. Data from the Canadian Real Estate Association shows that between 1981 and 2010, sale prices for homes increased an average of 1 per cent a month nationally. Of course, not all months or geographic areas were equally favoured, but it is indicative of the long-term trend. Another Canadian study showed that residential real estate appreciates with an average margin of 4 to 5 per cent over the rate of inflation. Still, a third Canadian study demonstrated that the average return on residential real estate investment exceeded other forms of investment.

The key conclusion is that making money in real estate is not an impossible dream, one only for professional tycoons, but a realistic possibility for the average Joe. Sure, as with any investment, there are risks and pitfalls. But by learning some basic principles and applying the strategies outlined in this book, you can make a profit, build your personal wealth, and even ease your way into an early retirement. The tips in this book will also save you money in many different ways.

The preface gives you an overview of what to expect from this book. Although each chapter is self-contained, they should all be read thoroughly as the concepts, tips, strategies, and pitfalls are frequently interconnected in terms of the overall real estate investment environment. Look through the detailed table of contents, including the appendix material, to get an idea of what to expect.

This first chapter is an important foundation chapter to assist you in understanding the framework in which you will be operating. Whether you are buying your first home or other residential revenue property, you can't operate in a vacuum in terms of the market. Knowing how the market works will develop self-confidence, street smarts, and improve your chances of making the right choices. This chapter covers why you should consider investing in real estate, understanding the real estate market, establishing your investment strategies, buying with others, and avoiding the pitfalls.

## Why Consider Investing in Real Estate?

Before investing in real estate, it's worth considering the advantages and disadvantages. There are many advantages to a sound real estate investment. There are also risks that can make an otherwise sound investment a disadvantageous prospect, and personal factors may work against your investment plans, too. Nevertheless, here are some of the reasons why you should consider investing in real estate. (The disadvantages are outlined on page 7.)

### Advantages of Real Estate Investment

Here are the main advantages that make real estate investment attractive, compared to other types of investments. Many are interrelated and work together for the success of your investment.

- Low risk. Any investment has a potential risk, and you can indeed lose money in real estate (the reasons why are covered in this book to help you avoid them); however, real estate has traditionally been a secure, stable investment compared to other investments. Buying prudently and with a knowledgeable strategy helps reduce the risks you face as an investor. The strategies for mitigating risk vary depending on macro-economic factors, the geographic area, and stability of the local market, among other considerations. Some of the things to take into account include population changes and density, the amount of land available for development, the proportion of renters in a given area (it's usually higher in cities, which works in your favour), and the ease of financing in terms of availability and competition. Supporting these factors (and lowering your risk) is the intrinsic need and demand people have for a place to live and the consistent appreciation of land values over and above the inflation rate as land is developed to meet that need. The market is cyclic and, depending on location and so on, property values tend to eventually increase.

- Part-time involvement. Real estate investments require close attention, but they don't need to be a sinkhole for your time. Once you learn the techniques, you will be more efficient, selective, and confident in how you manage your investments. Many investors have been able to start with a single property or even a partial investment with others, and build a portfolio of properties while running their own businesses. The real estate is merely a place to invest savings. Determining how much time you are prepared to spend researching the market, negotiating, buying, managing, and selling properties at the outset will help you determine how deeply involved you want to be.

  Moreover, the skills required to be a successful investor can be learned—again, without taking up all your time. Naturally, if you are buying real estate for investment other than your principal residence, more knowledge and skills must be acquired. The essential knowledge is covered in this book.

- Low starting capital. Real estate allows you to take a minimum amount of money, sometimes as little as $10,000 to $20,000, and borrow the rest using the property itself as security—an infrequent strategy with most other kinds of investments. You might start off with a $150,000 condominium, for example, putting 10 per cent down, and obtain a mortgage for the remaining 90 per cent. This is considered high-ratio financing (a conventional mortgage requires a 20 per cent down payment; further details are discussed in Chapter 5, "Understanding the Financing Aspects"), but the payoff to you can be just as great—with a wise strategy—as if you borrowed a smaller amount.

  The key is leverage. Take the example of the $150,000 condominium. You borrowed 90 per cent ($135,000) and put in 10 per cent of your own money ($15,000). Perhaps the property's value increased by 10 per cent over the course of a year. What would be the return on your original investment of $15,000? The answer is 100 per cent. In other words, the increase in value of your home of $15,000 (10 per cent appreciation of the $150,000 original price) is a 100 per cent return on your down payment of $15,000. Conversely, if you had put all your own money into the home—that is, $150,000—your return would have been merely 10 per cent.

By the same token, the condominium is a highly leveraged investment; nine times as much money was borrowed as invested. But the risk to the lender is low or non-existent, as the property is the security. If the lender has to sell, the net proceeds from the sale should cover the amount of the mortgage, given real estate's ability to maintain its value and even appreciate. And if the market enters a downturn, the requirement for high-ratio mortgages to carry insurance (provided in Canada primarily by the Canada Mortgage and Housing Corp. [www.cmhc.ca], Genworth Financial Canada [www.genworth.ca], and Canada Guaranty Mortgage Insurance [www.canadaguaranty.ca]) would cover your payments to the lender.

A concept related to the idea of leverage is pyramiding. This strategy involves borrowing on the increasing equity in your existing properties, applying the principal of leverage, to acquire additional properties over time. Done prudently, this strategy compounds the increase of equity in your portfolio and the potential accrual of considerable wealth.

- Appreciation. This simply means the increase in value of the property over time. It is the growth in value of your original capital investment. The national average has been approximately 10 per cent annually over the past 30 years. As a caution, it should be stressed that it is an average. Certain geographic areas or locations can have less than that, and some considerably less. Conversely, a well-selected, located, and maintained property in a growing community could be higher than the average. If the real estate cycle is going up in a high-demand area, the appreciation could increase as much as 25 to 50 per cent in one year. A basic axiom in real estate is that what goes up rapidly and in a sustained fashion tends to come down—sometimes rather suddenly.

- Equity buildup. When you make payments on your mortgage, you are paying down on the principal over time. As you reduce your debt, you are at the same time building up your equity—that is, the portion of your original house price on which you no longer owe any money. This is independent of the percentage increase in appreciation or value of the property. In practical usage, most people commonly refer to equity as the amount of clear value in the property that the investor owns, free and clear of any debt. It is the amount of equity that a lender will lend further money on and place a mortgage on as security. In realistic terms, your true equity is what you would net upon sale, after all real estate commissions and closing costs are taken into account. Lenders realize this as well, which is why they generally do not like to lend on 100 per cent of the equity in order to minimize risk and leave a margin for safety.

- Inflation hedge. You are probably well aware of the concept of inflation, a phenomenon that sees the cost of products and services increase over time and your own purchasing power decrease. Something that cost $5 three years ago might be priced at $10 today. People on fixed incomes that are not indexed to inflation are keenly aware of the loss of purchasing power that inflation inflicts. The inflation rate in Canada has been stable at about 2 per cent in recent years, but it varies seasonally and regionally. Canada experienced double-digit inflation in the 1980s, but current policies—set by the Bank of Canada (www.bankofcanada.ca)—aim to keep inflation as close as possible to 2 per cent.

  The appreciation of the value of property over time naturally accounts for inflation. Historically, land appreciation value for residential homes has been 4 to 5 per cent greater than the inflation rate. A benefit for real estate investors is that financing is repaid in inflated dollars. That is, you are probably getting more money now in terms of salary increases (and rental revenue) to repay a loan that's worth less in today's dollars than when you took out the original mortgage.

- Tax advantages. There are numerous types of tax advantages to investing in real estate, whether you have a principal residence or investment income property. For example, all the interest you receive from a savings account (even a tax-free savings account, or TFSA), term deposit, or a guaranteed investment certificate (GIC) is eroded by inflation. Savings that earn you 3 per cent when the inflation rate is 3 per cent will earn you an effective, or real, rate of return of 0 per cent. Deposits outside a TFSA that are subject to taxes push your return into negative territory. Real estate does not have this problem, so wisely investing in real estate—starting with a principal residence—is attractive.

Other tax advantages of real estate investing are discussed in Chapter 7, "Understanding the Tax Aspects." It's fair to say that few investments have as many benefits as real estate, some of which include:

- tax-free capital gain (on your principal residence);
- the ability to write off principal residence suite rental income against your home expenses;
- the ability to write off a portion of a home-based business income against your home expenses (the home-based business could even be to manage your residential investment income);
- lifetime personal capital gains exemption of $750,000;
- reduced tax rate of 75 per cent of capital gain from investment in real estate;
- flow through of losses from negative cash flow against other sources of income;
- deduction of real estate property investment expenses against income; and
- the ability to write off depreciation of the building against income.

- Income potential. A prudent real estate investment could result in a net positive cash flow income to you every month—that is, after all expenses and debt servicing have been taken into account. The income not only provides additional money, but the fact that you have a positive cash flow is a factor that automatically increases the value of your income-producing real estate. This is discussed in greater detail in Chapter 3, "Finding and Evaluating the Right Property."

- Attractive return on investment. For all the reasons outlined in earlier points, clearly the potential for an attractive return on your investment—not only before tax but after tax—is very high in real estate. Keep in mind that it is not what you make before tax, but what you can keep after tax that is the important investment criteria.

- Increasing demand for land. Land is a finite commodity. Due to the population increase and decreasing supply, real estate prices go up. Many communities have slow growth or no growth policies, due to rapidly expanding needs for community services. This restricts land availability for new development, causing existing land to go up in value. Real estate is a commodity that the public needs. Other investment commodities are not so reliable because they don't constitute a public need and therefore demand. In addition, many people want to have a second home, as a retreat, vacation property, or for retirement. This creates further demand on land.

## Disadvantages of Real Estate Investment

To provide some balance, there are some limitations to investing in real estate that may not be present in other forms of investment. But by being aware of these limitations, you are going into the investment realistically in terms of expectations and planning. Most of the limitations can be dealt with or eliminated satisfactorily. Here is a brief outline:

- Subjective feelings. This problem is particularly common when people buy their first home. Some people make decisions based on emotion, rather than sound preparation, knowledge, and objective assessment. Developing a sound investment strategy should help mitigate the role of emotions, while honing your knowledge to ensure you can trust your gut feelings when it comes to investment decisions.

- Lack of liquidity. A liquid investment doesn't always mean a bottle of wine or fine single-malt Scotch; rather, it refers to the ease with which you can realize its cash value via a sale. Several factors affect liquidity, but one of the most common is demand. The least liquid assets are often found in the least desirable locations. On the other hand, an asset that hasn't attracted demand might be your ticket into a market that's about to become one of the country's star investment areas (but always do your homework).

- Extended holding period. Many real estate investments are held for 5 to 10 years, or longer. This is often a wise strategy that helps avoid the cyclical nature of the market. You will have to wait, however, to see a return on your investment. You may wish to consider alternative investments if your investment time frame is short.

- Time expenditure. The investment could take a considerable amount of your time, but with advance planning, this should not happen unexpectedly. If it does, you have other options, as explained in Chapter 10, "Managing Your Property."

- Potential high risk. Again, the potential for loss exists, but with prudent and cautious decision making and following the tips and strategies outlined in this book, the risk should be minimal or non-existent, in practical terms.

- Lack of accurate comparisons. Real estate, by its nature, is a market of diverse assets, conditions, and buyers. This makes a standardized reference point for comparing two or more properties difficult. While rules of thumb and other formulas exist to help gauge value (see Chapter 3, "Finding and Evaluating the Right Property"), the only true determinant of value for your particular property is its sale under a given set of conditions. The other values are proxies for its true worth, making it difficult to know what a property is actually worth until it changes hands.

- Exposure to government control. All levels of government have an impact on real estate. There are laws and regulations covering a wide range of areas, including planning, zoning, property use, building codes and licences, rent controls, and environmental regulations. Some provinces have considered introducing a special real estate speculators tax. In addition, governments can expropriate and require rights of way. All these factors could certainly have an impact on your investment. The best way to eliminate a potential problem is to avoid it to begin with. That is why you have to do your research thoroughly and obtain expert legal advice, especially in the case of income real estate investment.

## Pitfalls to Avoid

It is probably timely, at this point in the book and in conjunction with a consideration of the disadvantages of real estate investment, to outline some of the classic pitfalls to avoid in buying real estate. In most cases, investors who have problems generally succumb to a combination of the following traps. By being aware of these problems at the outset, it should help you place the discussion and cautions in the rest of the book in context.

Some of the classic pitfalls that will exacerbate the disadvantages of your real estate investment and prevent you from enjoying its full advantages include not

- understanding how the real estate market works;
- understanding personal and financial needs;
- having a clear focus and a realistic real estate investment plan, with strategies and priorities;
- doing thorough market research and comparison shopping before making the purchase;

- selecting the right property considering the potential risks, money involved, and specific personal needs;
- verifying representations or assumptions beforehand;
- doing financial calculations beforehand;
- buying at a fair-market price;
- buying real estate at the right time in the market;
- buying within your debt-servicing capacity, comfort zone, and skills;
- understanding the financing game thoroughly, not comparison shopping, and not getting the best rates, terms, and right type of mortgage;
- making a decision based on an objective assessment but on an emotional one;
- determining the real reason why the vendor is selling;
- having the property inspected by a building inspector before purchasing;
- selecting an experienced real estate lawyer and obtaining advice beforehand;
- selecting an experienced professional tax accountant when selecting real estate property, and obtaining advice beforehand;
- selecting an experienced realtor with expertise in the type of real estate and geographic location you are considering;
- negotiating effectively;
- putting the appropriate conditions or "subject clauses" in the offer;
- buying for the right reasons, in other words buying for a tax shelter rather than for the inherent value, potential, and viability of the investment property;
- verifying financial information beforehand, including rental income, expenses, and property taxes;
- obtaining and reviewing all the necessary documentation appropriate for a given property before making a final decision to buy;
- selecting real estate investment partners carefully;
- having a written agreement with real estate investment partners, prepared by a lawyer;
- detailing precisely what chattels are included in the purchase price;

- seeing the property before buying it, but relying on pictures and/or the representations of others;
- managing property well, or not selecting the right property management company; or
- selling the property at the right time in the market or for the right reasons.

# Understanding the Real Estate Market

You need to understand the cycles and factors that influence prices to have a better appreciation of how the real estate market operates, and how to operate prudently within it. The market is a dynamic entity, and no buying or selling decisions should be made without first assessing its conditions.

## The Real Estate Cycle

Real estate is cyclical, which means there will be good and bad times, shortages of supply relative to demand (and vice versa), and fluctuations in property values: too many available properties of a given type reduce values, too few increase them. It is essential to know where you are in the economic cycle and appreciate that different provinces, regions, and communities may be at different stages of the cycle. Therefore, timing is important when making buying or selling decisions.

One of the reasons for the cycle is that many developers are entrepreneurial by nature and operate primarily by short-term planning. If financing and credit are available, developers tend to build without regard for the overall supply and demand. If a glut occurs and the demand is not there, prices drop as houses and condominiums go unsold. The phases of the real estate cycle will be discussed later in the chapter.

External economic cycles that can affect the real estate cycle include:

- General economic cycle. The economy goes through periods of growth followed by recessions. The impact is greater, of course, in certain parts of the country than in others in any given cycle. During a recession, people lose their jobs and have to sell their houses. Real estate prices drop as potential purchasers decide to wait until the economy is more secure.

  It is difficult to know for certain when the economy will turn around, but various indicators should give you some insight. (Chapter 3, "Finding and Evaluating the Right Property," provides sources of information about particular markets.) However, if the economy has been in a recession for a sustained period of time, there could be definite opportunities to buy. Once the economy emerges from a recession (a recovery is deemed to have occurred after two consecutive quarters of economic growth), prices tend to climb. Conversely, if the economy has been on a growth trend for an extended period of time, be very cautious about your purchase decision because a change in the cycle, and therefore a drop in real estate prices, could be imminent.

- Local economic cycle. A local economy, such as a city or province, has its own cycle and factors that have impacts on real estate prices. Some factors are related to the general cycle above; others may be related to local events such as business closures, natural disasters, and the like.

- Community economic cycle. Specific communities within a city can have their own economic cycles, as well as particular issues affecting supply and demand, all of which affect real estate prices. In addition, a community has its own life cycle from growth to decline to stagnation to recovery. When investing in real estate, it's wise to find areas of future growth and be ahead of a market upswing.

Awareness of economic, business, and community cycles is critical to prudent decision making. Before buying or selling real estate in a certain area, determine what external factors are prevalent and how they impact the cycle of the real estate market. Different types of real estate, such as condominiums, new homes, resale houses, and small apartment buildings, can be in different parts of a cycle.

A real estate cycle has four distinct stages. Each segment exhibits characteristics that are helpful in assessing market conditions and determining at what stage the real estate cycle is. (Refer to Chart 1 in the Appendix.)

The real estate market is commonly described in three ways:

- Seller's market. In a seller's market the demand, or number of buyers wanting homes, exceeds the supply, or number of homes on the market. It is characterized by homes that sell quickly, a low inventory of homes, and an increase in prices. These characteristics have implications for the buyer, who has to make decisions quickly, pay more, and frequently has his or her conditional offers rejected.

- Buyer's market. In a buyer's market, the supply of homes exceeds the demand. Characteristics of this type of market include: homes that are on the market longer, high inventory, and a reduction in prices.

The implications for buyers are: favourable negotiating leverage, more time to search for a home, and better prices.

- Balanced market. In a balanced market, supply equals demand. The characteristics of this type of market include: houses selling within a reasonable period, stabilized prices, and sellers accepting reasonable offers. The implications for the buyer are that the atmosphere is more relaxed and that there are a reasonable number of homes from which to choose.

## Factors that Affect Real Estate Prices

Many factors influence real estate prices. Whether you are a buyer or seller, you need to understand what factors are having an impact on the market, so you can make the right decisions at the right time and in the right location. Many of these factors are interconnected.

- Position in real estate cycle. The position of any particular real estate market in the cycle—whether at the general, local, or community level— will have a bearing on prices. During a seller's market, prices will be high; during a buyer's market, prices will be low, and a balanced market will offer no distinct advantage to buyers or sellers in terms of pricing.

- Interest rates. There is a direct connection between interest rates and prices. High interest rates typically mean lower prices because buyers have to allocate more cash to financing their purchase than to actually buying it. When interest rates are low and financing is cheap, prices climb. The cost of financing and the price of properties will influence buyer demand and overall market health.

- Taxes. High property taxes can be a disincentive to a purchaser, contributing to a drop in real estate prices. Provincial taxes, such as a property transfer tax or speculators tax, will restrict some buyers. Changes in sales taxes, such as the harmonized sales tax (HST) in place in many provinces or the goods and services tax (GST), may influence buyers of new homes or building lots. Federal tax legislation on real estate, such as changes in capital gains taxes or the personal lifetime capital gains exemption (currently set at $750,000 for eligible property), could have a negative influence on investors. All these factors would affect the overall amount of real estate activity, including prices.

- Rent controls. Provinces have the power to establish rent controls in Canada, which limit the scale and frequency of rent increases landlords can levy on tenants. Rent controls, and similar legislation governing landlord-tenant relations, could have a limiting effect on investor real estate activity. This could lead to fewer buyers in the market for certain types of properties. Alternatively, the removal of rent controls may provoke an investment surge.

- Economy. Confidence in the economy is important to stimulate home-buyer and investor activity. If the economy is buoyant and the mood is positive, more market activity will occur, generally resulting in price increases. Conversely, if the economy is stagnant and the mood is negative, less market activity occurs, resulting in price decreases. If real estate purchasers are concerned about the same problems, a predictable loss of confidence occurs in the market.

- Population shifts. Geographic locations with attractive business, employment, tourism, and retirement opportunities will attract people from across the country and around the world. This increased demand will increase prices. Conversely, if there is net migration out of the area due to closure or potential closure of industry, environmental problems, or other factors, real estate demand and prices will decrease.

- Vacancy levels. High vacancy levels could reduce investor confidence due to the potential risk, and real estate sales could go down. Competition for tenants increases, creating more favourable conditions for renters. On the other hand, low vacancy levels could stimulate activity among investors and first-home buyers. Renters who can't find a place to rent may borrow from relatives or find other creative ways to enable them to purchase a home.

- Location. A highly desirable location will generally see steadier and faster increases in price versus a less desirable location, or one that has fallen out of favour.

- Land availability. A natural shortage of land because of barriers including rivers, mountains and oceans, municipal zoning restrictions, and other regulations that restrict its use for housing and development will generally cause prices to increase. This occurs because the stock of developable land is limited relative to the existing and long-term demand.

- Public image. The public perception of a certain location, type of residential property, or developer of a specific building will affect demand and, in turn, price. Some areas or types of properties are hot and some are not at any given time.

- Political factors. Provincial or municipal government policy concerning real estate development will naturally have a positive or negative effect on supply and demand and therefore prices. A potential change of government, particularly in an election year, may affect market activity depending on whether market participants expect a change of government to be positive or negative for real estate sales and development.

- Seasonal factors. Certain times of year—such as winter and summer vacation times—are traditionally slow months for residential real estate sales, hence prices decline. The same seasonal factor impacts on recreational property. There are ideal seasons for purchase and sale, the most common being spring.

# Establishing Your Investment Strategies

To attain the maximum financial benefit from real estate investment with a minimum of risk, you need to have clearly defined goals and objectives, and a plan for achieving them. There are four steps in the process of determining your plan.

## Step 1: Self-Assessment of Skills and Attributes

Your success in real estate investment has a lot to do with the qualities that you bring to the process. It is important to know your strengths and weaknesses so that you can capitalize on your strengths and compensate for your weaknesses. This self-assessment is particularly important if you are considering group investments or owning several properties. It will help you identify your interests as well as your skills, attributes, and talents that are relevant to the business of real estate investing.

## Step 2: Determine Your Current Financial Status and Needs

Start by completing Form 1, "Personal Cost-of-Living Budget (Monthly)," and Form 2, "Personal Net-Worth Statement" (see pages 333 and 336 in the Appendix). Then fill out Forms 3 and 4, in which you will calculate your gross debt-service ratio and total debt-service ratio, respectively. Forms 3 and 4 will give you some guidelines in terms of mortgage eligibility. Keep in mind that these are only guidelines. There are exceptions, and there are other creative ways of achieving your financial objectives. This is explained in more detail in Chapter 5, "Understanding the Financing Aspects."

## Step 3: Determine Your Future Personal and Financial Needs

This essential step gives you an idea of the degree of risk you are prepared to take. It will also clarify your time commitment, financial involvement, and realistic short-, medium-, and long-term goals and objectives. For example, maybe you want to be financially independent, primarily through real estate investment, in 10 or 15 years.

## Step 4: Plan Your Investment Strategies

Take the time to develop your investment program thoroughly. Like any plan, you will need to monitor and possibly modify it regularly due to changing circumstances. The safest way to make money in real estate is through prudent and cautious investment.

Don't look on real estate as a "get-rich-quick" scheme. There are many who have adopted that attitude, to their misfortune. Avoid the prophets of profit—that is, the self-styled gurus and pitchmen touting U.S.-oriented real estate investment programs. In many cases these real estate investment programs are not directly applicable to the Canadian context (due to differences in legal and tax matters). Some programs are barely ethical or unrealistic. Some real estate seminars and books promote the concept of becoming rich through property tax sales, foreclosure sales, quick flips of property, or the selling (assigning) of the agreement of purchase and sale before closing. In most cases in the Canadian context these options are not applicable or applicable only with considerable difficulty, risk, and skill, so considerable caution is advised.

# Key Investment Strategies to Consider

Here are some the key real estate investment strategies to consider:

- Research the market thoroughly before making any decisions. Consider at least three potential investment opportunities, if possible.
- Give yourself a realistic time frame to achieve your investment objectives. For example, normal real estate cycles are 5 to 8 years and in some cases 10 to 12 years.
- Buy specific types of revenue property that are in demand and are easy to maintain and/or manage; for example, a single-family house (ideally with a basement suite for separate revenue), a condominium, duplex, triplex, or fourplex. Don't buy an apartment building until you have

experience as a landlord with several smaller properties, or unless you are going in with experienced investors.

- Attempt to make a low down payment (for example, 5 to 10 per cent) unless, of course, you can only obtain a maximum of 75 per cent financing. If you can make a purchase with a low down payment, this frees up your available cash for the purchase of additional properties. Offset a low down payment with a vendor-take-back mortgage, high-ratio financing, or a second mortgage.

- Strive to have a break-even cash flow. In other words, try to avoid debt servicing the property because of a shortfall of rental income over expenses. Make sure you cover all expenses from cash flow such as mortgage payments, taxes, property management, condominium fees, insurance, repairs and maintenance, and allowance for vacancies.

- Ensure that you have competent property management, whether you do it yourself or hire an expert.

- Rely on professionals—including a lawyer, accountant, financial planner, building inspector, appraiser, contractor, realtor, property manager—at all times for peace of mind, enhanced revenue potential, reduced risk, and realistic budgetary projections.

- Never pay more than fair market value unless there are other collateral benefits to you that you have identified. These types of potential benefits are discussed in more detail in Chapter 9, "Buying Your Property."

- Use all the tax-planning strategies available to you after receiving expert tax advice. These options are explained in Chapter 7, "Understanding the Tax Aspects."

- Keep rents at market maximums and manage expenses to keep at market minimums.

- Buy when no one else is buying and sell when everyone else is buying. This is the so-called contrarian view of investment, which is the opposite of conventional wisdom.

- Always view and inspect property before you buy. Verify all financial information. Obtain your advisers' guidance.

- Have a minimum three-month contingency reserve fund for unexpected expenses (repairs) or a reduction in cash flow (vacancies).

- Buy investment properties within a four-hour drive from where you live, so you can easily monitor your investment. There are exceptions to this general principle, of course.

- Consider applying the principle of pyramiding—that is, purchasing selected real estate on a systematic basis. For example, you may purchase one or two or more properties a year—when the cycle is in your favour, of course.

For additional guidance, refer to Checklist 6, "Master Checklist for Successful Real Estate Investing," on page 376 in the Appendix.

# Buying with Partners

Investing with others is not for everyone. Most people prefer to invest on their own, if possible. Occasionally, people may choose to buy in a group. On the one hand, some people prefer to start out investing with a group as it may provide mutual support; shared (and therefore reduced) risk; pooled skills and expertise; greater investment opportunities; shared responsibility and time; and collective energy, synergy, and momentum. On the other hand, if you do not select your group investment wisely, it could be a financial and emotional nightmare. The key is to know the benefits and limitations of the various group investment options and the pitfalls to avoid. Never go into a real estate purchase with others without obtaining prior professional advice from your lawyer and accountant. Always make sure that you have a written agreement in advance.

## Factors to Consider When Buying Real Estate with Others

It is important to remember that approximately 80 per cent of business partnerships don't work out. The statistical odds, therefore, are very high that any real estate group relationship in which you are involved may not survive. By cautiously assessing the individuals who will make up a potential group, you can minimize the risk immensely. Here are some key factors to consider:

### Goals and Objectives

Ensure that your goals and objectives are consistent with those of the rest of the group. For example, some members may want a long-term investment (say, five years) with positive cash flow from rents; others may want a medium-term investment (perhaps three years) and be prepared to subsidize the negative cash flow in the hope that the property value will appreciate due to rezoning or subdivision potential; still others may want to flip the property within a few months of purchase because of its desirability or a because of a rapid increase in property values in a hot market.

## Expertise

You know what skills you can bring to an investment partnership, and if your partners are friends and relatives, you probably have a clear idea as to what skills they bring to the table. But if you are joining an investment group of strangers or people you know only casually, it is important to clarify exactly what, if any, skills they will bring to the group investment. It may not matter, if they are silent investors—that is, if the investors are just putting their money in and are not actively involved. Sometimes these types of investors are also referred to as passive investors.

If they are active investors and it is a small group, you need to determine what skills they will contribute and in what form. If you are buying into an investment group that will be totally managed by one of the group members, make sure you know the person's credentials and track record, and get it in writing. If you are going to rely on the person to protect your investment, it would be prudent for you to be careful and cautious.

## Liquidity

Basically, this means how easily and quickly you can get your money out of the investment. Your financial resources and needs will determine your liquidity needs. For example, if you need to get your investment capital back quickly, then you probably won't want a long-term investment. In addition, you should reconsider the investment if you would suffer if your money was tied up or put at risk. You should not invest money you cannot afford to lose. Therefore, be cautious about investing retirement money or contingency reserve funds if you need immediate liquidity.

In practical terms, most investments are tied up for the duration of the deal. That relates back to the investment group's goals and objectives. If you are buying shares in a real estate investment on the public stock exchange, you may have liquidity, but not necessarily at an attractive price. Also, consider having a buy-out clause in the investment group agreement. This means the group would buy you out within a fixed period, although normally at a discount price, to discourage investors from leaving the group early.

## Liability

This issue is, of course, a critical one to consider. Make sure, if at all possible, that your risk is limited to the amount of your investment. You want to avoid personal liability for any financial problems that occur, either to mortgage companies, other investors, or the investment group as such. For example, if you are investing in a corporation that is holding the property for the group and the corporation has taken out a mortgage with a lender, the lender may require personal guarantees from the shareholders of the corporation. Another example of risk would be a partnership. If you went into a general partnership with two other investors whose actions resulted in financial problems, you would still be liable for the full amount of the debt if the other two couldn't pay.

A third example of risk would be if you signed an investment group agreement and it stated that any shortfall of funds would have to be paid by the investors on a basis proportional to the percentage interest. A last example of risk would be in a limited partnership. If you stopped being an inactive partner and started to actively manage the investment, you could be liable. Also, some limited partners are asked to sign personal guarantees up to a certain limit. Avoid this scenario. You can see why you need a lawyer to look at the agreement and advise you of the implications and ways of limiting or eliminating personal liability risk.

## Legal Structure

There are several types of legal structures: a general partnership, limited partnership, corporation, or joint venture agreement. Group investments fall into these categories or variations of them. Some legal structures allow more flexibility than others. The degree of personal liability exposure varies depending on the structure and the group investment agreement. Some of these were discussed in the previous point. Obtain advice from your lawyer. Also, refer to the sections on legal structures on pages 190–3 in Chapter 6, "Understanding the Legal Aspects."

## Control Issues

Certain types of investment groups allow for more investor control than others. Control relates to the degree of influence that you have on the management of the investment and related decision making. Obviously, smaller groups tend to allow more individual control than others. For example, in some cases, unanimous consent is required for major decisions; in other cases, 75 per cent consent is needed; and in still other cases, a simple 51 per cent majority vote of investors will do. In some instances you do not have any vote at all. You put your money in and hope for the best. If you are buying into a limited partnership or other form of investment that is being touted to you, make sure you thoroughly check out the promoter's previous history, experience, and reputation. You can see why management and quality of management are so important.

## Tax Considerations

One of the main reasons for investing in real estate would be for the tax benefits in your given situation. Certain types of investments are more attractive than others from a tax perspective. Be very wary of salespeople or financial advisers who attempt to induce you into buying a tax shelter. That area is fraught with pitfalls and risks. You can see why you need objective and impartial advice in advance from your lawyer and professional tax accountant before making your investment decision. The property should be inherently viable from an investment viewpoint first, with tax benefits then taken into account. Refer to Chapter 7, "Understanding the Tax Aspects," for a more detailed discussion.

## Compatibility

Look at the other people in your investment group. Are there similarities in personality, age, financial position, and investment objectives? What do the other group members think about issues such as control, management, and liability? What contributions, if any, are the other people making to the success of the investment? If the people in the group have diversified skills, this could save the group money and make the investment more secure. In general, people you know are safer than people you don't know. Ego, power, greed, arrogance, and unrealistic expectations are common causes of group stress or disintegration. You can't afford the risk, so be selective with your investment partners.

## Risk Assessment

As discussed throughout this section, you need to look objectively at the potential risks: the nature of the investment, the potential for profit, the degree of potential personal liability, the type of legal structure, the nature and degree of control, the quality of management, and the compatibility of other investment group members.

## Contribution

Find out what contribution is expected of you in terms of money, time, expertise, management, personal guarantee, and contingency backup capital. Do you feel comfortable with others' expectations of you?

## Percentage of Investment

Do you feel comfortable with the percentage of investment that you are getting, relative to the contribution you noted in the above point? For example, let's say that there are four people in an investment who incorporate a holding company. One is an active partner and finds and manages the property, and the other three are silent investors. The active partner has 55 per cent of the investment, did not invest any money, and did not sign any personal guarantees. The three silent partners invested all the money equally, signed personal guarantees to the bank for the mortgage, and hold 15 per cent of the investment each. Would you feel comfortable with that investment percentage if you were a silent partner? What if you were the active partner?

## Getting Out or Buying Others Out

One of the important things to consider when investing with a group is getting out. What if you want to leave for any number of reasons? Is there a procedure to follow? What penalty do you pay, how is it calculated, and how long will it take to get your money? Conversely, what if you want to buy out the other investors because of a personality conflict or some other reasons? Can you do so? If there is nothing in the agreement outlining how an investor can leave the group before the property is sold, you could have a problem.

## Management

How will the group investment be managed? Will it be managed by a professional management company, a resident manager, a group of investors, one of the investors, or the original promoter? How confident do you feel about the issue of management? What are the management fees? Are they reasonable under the circumstances?

## Profits and Losses

Determine how these aspects are to be dealt with. For example, what about excess revenue from the income property? Will that be kept in a contingency fund, or will a portion of it be paid to the investors? What about decisions such as selling the shares of a corporation holding the property or the property itself? How will those decisions be made and who will make them? These decisions have tax implications that will affect you. What about losses? Will the shortfall be covered by a bank loan, or by remortgaging the property, or by the group investors? In practical terms, how will that be done?

Now that some of the key factors have been discussed, you can see why you have to be careful and selective before going into a group investment.

## Types of Group Investments

There are many options available in terms of group investing. The most common options are co-tenancy, general partnership, limited partnership, joint venture, syndication, and equity sharing. (See also Chapter 6, "Understanding the Legal Aspects," and Chapter 7, "Understanding the Tax Aspects.") The following discussion will explain how these types of group investments operate.

## Co-tenancy

Each co-tenant has a proportional interest reflected in the title to the property filed in the land title office. For example, if three people decide to invest together on an equal basis, the title to the property would show that each party has "an undivided one-third interest each, tenants in common," or other such variation. In law, co-tenants or tenants in common can generally deal with the property without the consent of the other co-tenant(s). In addition, if a co-tenant dies, his or her interest in the title to the property goes to the estate; it does not go to the surviving co-tenants, as it does in a joint tenancy type of legal ownership.

When people buy for investment purposes or buy a property together to live in, but are not living together in a common-law or legal marriage, tenancy in common is often the way they hold the property.

The ownership of the land through tenancy in common reflects percentage ownership on title; it does not involve partnership-type obligations to third parties. To make sure that there will be no misunderstanding on the issue of partnership in case of a co-tenant dispute or creditor problems, a co-tenancy agreement should be prepared and signed. Again, make sure you have your lawyer prepare it or review it carefully if another lawyer prepares it.

### Co-tenancy Cautions

In addition to the types of issues discussed in a group investment agreement, which is explained later in this chapter, consider including in an agreement that the co-tenants:

- are not partners of each other, as set out in the provincial partnership act;

- do not have the power to act for each other, except as outlined in the co-tenant agreement;
- are not agents of each other;
- can compete with each other in other real estate investments;
- are responsible for their own tax or other financial liability relating to his or her percentage interest in the property; and
- can make money from the co-tenancy without it being considered a conflict of interest; in other words, there are no fiduciary duties.

In addition, the co-tenant agreement should set out the living accommodation rights, duties, and responsibilities if the parties are living in the same dwelling. A sketch map showing the living area should be attached.

It is common for friends or relatives to invest in real estate through a co-tenant arrangement. It is also common for people who cannot afford to buy a principal residence with their own income or down payment to buy with someone else, either a parent, relative, or friend.

One of the key advantages of a co-tenancy is that it is a reasonably simple structure and relatively easy to get out of.

## General Partnership

You should be very cautious about going into a general partnership. There are many potential liability risks involved, as well as investment limitations. Never go into one without competent legal and tax advice. A general partnership is governed by the partnership act of each province. The disadvantages of this type of relationship are covered on page 192 in Chapter 6, "Understanding the Legal Aspects." In brief, the risks involve individual liability for all the debts or liability of the partnership, regardless of how many other partners there are. For example, if the partnership owes $50,000 and the other two investors do not have any money or assets and you do, creditors will go after you for the full amount. Many people don't realize that, and assume that if there are three partners, the liability will be split three ways.

In addition, there are other aspects governed by the provincial partnership act. There are automatic rights that each partner has in law, tax, control, and ownership implications; non-competitive provisions; fiduciary duties (explained in an earlier point); dissolution rights; automatic breakup of the partnership on death of a partner; and inability to pledge the partnership interest as security to a lender. Lack of control and limited management and investor options make the general partnership option an inflexible one, and the implications can be onerous for most investors. Although a partnership agreement can mitigate some of the limitations of a general partnership, it does not eliminate them. General partnerships normally only involve a few people.

## Limited Partnership

This is a variation of a general partnership and a corporation. It has fewer of the legal disadvantages of a general partnership, but maintains the tax advantages. For example, the rights and liabilities of the partners are set out in the limited partnership agreement. The liability of each partner is limited to the amount of his or her investment, which is why the partner is referred to as a limited partner. The limited partner is an inactive partner, and has no control over management of the limited partnership, other than voting on the issue of who should be the manager. The general partner is normally a corporation and is responsible for the active management of the limited partnership investment. The general partner can be sued, but usually is operated by a corporation without assets.

It is important that a limited partner not be involved in any fashion with the management and decision making of the limited partnership. To do so could expose the limited partner to unlimited liability as a general partner.

The operation of a limited partnership is governed by various regulations, including a limited partnership agreement, the provincial limited partnership legislation, and possibly the provincial securities legislation. Limited partners hold their interest in the partnership in the form of "units" issued by the limited partnership. These units are similar to shares in a corporation and represent the proportionate share in the limited partnership held by the investor. Units can be sold to other group investors or outsiders, subject to the policies and restrictions set out in the limited partnership document. Many limited partnerships have a large number of investors, as the financial cost of the project can be considerable.

There can be many risks to limited partnerships. Keep in mind that the promoter is out to make a personal profit. This may or may not be consistent with making money for you from the investment. There can be many representations by the promoter (general partner) and agents of the promoter. Minimize the risk by requesting cash flow guarantees from the promoter, secured against assets of the promoter.

Attempt to get a written commitment from the promoter to purchase your unit, if you so wish, after a period of time. Make sure that long-term financing is in place, so that you don't have to come up with more money in a short time. Finally, make sure that your lawyer and tax accountant review the project and documentation, and advise you in advance as to the legitimate tax benefits, degree of risk, and reliability of the financial and operating projections.

## Corporation

You may wish to hold real estate by owning shares with others in a corporation. A corporation is usually governed by the provincial company legislation for most real estate investments, rather than a federally incorporated company. A corporation is a separate legal entity and can sue and be sued, but its liability is limited to the assets of the corporation. Individual shareholders are not personally liable for corporate liability, unless personal guarantees of the corporation were signed by the shareholders. Refer to page 192 in Chapter 6, "Understanding the Legal Aspects," for a more detailed description of corporations.

It is important to make sure that you sign a shareholders' agreement with the other investors. This agreement contains various provisions, as discussed later.

A corporation can be a convenient vehicle for real estate group investments. It is structured in such a way as to make it easy to sell or transfer shares, subject to the articles of incorporation and shareholders' agreement. If a shareholder dies, the corporation and its investment continue. The shares would go to the estate of the deceased or be purchased by the corporation, depending on the terms of the shareholders' agreement. Generally speaking, there is a limit on the number of shareholders in a corporation, beyond which the corporation could be governed by provincial securities legislation. This would involve stringent public reporting requirements and accountability, as well as limitations in the management of the corporation. For this reason, you have to be cautious and obtain legal advice to ensure that you are not covered by securities legislation. Many holding corporation investments consist of a small number of people, generally not more than 10.

Corporations are a popular means of holding revenue property such as apartment buildings. Income from the corporation is tabulated and taxed in the corporation. Investors pay taxes on income only if they receive money by means of dividends or salaries from the corporation. Otherwise, investors have to wait until the property is sold. If the shares of the company are sold to a new owner, the investor could therefore have a taxable gain on those shares. Refer to Chapter 7, "Understanding the Tax Aspects," for a further discussion.

## Joint Venture

A joint venture may involve individuals or corporations who want to pool money, resources, skills, expertise, land, or other assets to make a profit by means of development or investment. Generally it is one specific project. Joint ventures can be formed in different ways, such as a co-tenancy, general partnership, limited partnership, or holding corporation, in which the shareholders are the joint venturers. It is also possible for a corporation to be formed to hold the property in trust for the joint venturers.

The nature and form of joint venture structure depends on various considerations, such as legal, tax, and financial issues, as well as the purpose of the joint venture. Most joint venture groups are small. It is essential to have a joint venture agreement drawn up and signed. Make sure that the agreement makes it clear that the relationship is not one of a general partnership, due to the tax and legal implications. Get advice from your lawyer and tax accountant before committing yourself.

## Syndication

This is usually in the form of a limited partnership and is designed to provide silent investors with limited liability, capital appreciation, and tax deferral. The promoter of the syndicate or the company contracted by the syndicate undertakes management of the project. The syndicate makes money from the investors as well as from the investment itself. Generally, the cost to the investor is directly related to the degree of risk and the degree of financial and performance guarantees by the syndicate promoter. As with any investment, there is risk. Have your lawyer and tax accountant give you their unbiased professional opinions before signing any documentation or paying any money. Many syndicates have a large number of investors and are therefore governed by provincial security legislation.

## Equity Sharing

There are many variations to this method of investment. In a way, it is a combination of a partnership and co-tenancy. For example, one approach is for an investor to look for a tenant who wants to buy a house but doesn't have the down payment. The investor buys the house and the tenant moves in and pays slightly more than fair market rent. The rent is sufficient to cover all mortgage debt-servicing costs, property taxes, utilities, insurance, and maintenance. Therefore, there is no negative cash flow. The tenants have a place to live and a house to maintain with pride.

The above parties sign an agreement setting out the arrangement. Generally speaking, the investor has title to the property with a stipulation that if the tenant remains for, say, three years, the tenant has the option of purchasing the house for the appraised value minus the normal real estate commission that would otherwise be paid, minus an agreed-upon percentage for the equity increase over the three-year period (perhaps 10 to 25 per cent). This could bring the house price down sufficiently that the tenant would be able to get financing and buy it. If the tenant can't or doesn't want to purchase at the end of the term, the tenant loses the option and all equity-sharing and purchase rights.

The secret of a successful equity-sharing plan is the selection of the right property at the right price and terms, the right investor-tenant match, and a well-written agreement that is fair to both parties. The agreement should be drawn up by your lawyer and cover important potential problems such as the following: the tenant stops paying, breaches other terms of the agreement, or dies; the investor declares personal bankruptcy; a disagreement occurs over the appraised value of the property; or the investor does not want to sell after three years because the market is depressed.

Equity sharing can also mean including the tenant on the title for an agreed percentage interest at the outset. This approach is not recommended as it would be difficult for the investor to get the full title back without paying considerable legal fees if a falling-out occurs with the tenant.

From an investor's viewpoint, the equity-sharing concept has some advantages as well as disadvantages. The advantages include the benefits of ideally assured positive cash flow, a committed tenant, and no management problems. From the tenant's viewpoint, the arrangement allows the tenant to choose a house of his or her own and provides a financial backer to get into the market, as well as a share of the equity buildup with an option to buy at a discounted price (net after real estate commission savings are deducted). One of the main disadvantages to an investor, though, is sharing the equity buildup. This has to be weighed against the advantages. You can do equity-sharing arrangements yourself, or invest in companies that offer the service. The problem is that you lose control in these companies, as groups of 8 to 10 investors are put together. In addition, you will have to pay the equity-sharing management company an administrative fee.

You now have a better idea of real estate group investment options. The smaller the group, the more control and involvement; the larger the group, the less control or no control, and lack of individual identity or involvement with the investment. In some large groups, investors are detached from any involvement or input. Consult your legal and tax advisers before venturing into these waters.

## Putting the Arrangement in Writing

After you have considered all the factors outlined above and decided which type of group investment you prefer, the next step is to set out a written agreement. As mentioned earlier, make sure that your lawyer prepares the agreement or reviews an agreement prepared by someone else. Each type of group investment group necessitates a different form of agreement. The agreement you sign should be customized for the specific type of investment in which you're involved, and it should take into account the factors discussed earlier.

The main points and procedures that are common to, although not necessarily all included in, group investment agreements consist of the following:

- type of legal structure;
- name and location of investment group;
- goals and objectives of group;
- duration of agreement;
- names and categories of investors (general, limited, active, silent);
- financial contribution by investors;
- procedure for obtaining additional capital;
- role of individual investors in the investment management;
- authority of any investor in the conduct of the investment group;
- nature and degree of each investor's contribution to the investment group;
- how operating expenses will be handled;
- how operating income will be handled;
- debts of investment group separate from individual investor;
- separate bank account;
- signing of cheques;
- division of profits and losses;
- books, records, and method of accounting;
- draws or salaries;
- absence and disability of investor;

- death of an investor;
- bringing in other investors;
- rights of the investors;
- withdrawal of an investor;
- buying out other investors;
- management of employees;
- sale of investor interest;
- restrictions on the transfer, assignment, or pledging of the investor's interest;
- release of debts;
- settlement of investor disputes and arbitration procedures;
- additions, alterations, or modifications to investment group agreement;
- non-competition with the investment group in the event of an investor's departure.

## Summary

This chapter has provided a general introduction to the benefits of real estate investment, how the real estate market works, determining your investment strategies, avoiding the classic pitfalls, and buying with others. Now it's time to look at specific types of residential real estate.

# CHAPTER 2

# Types of Residential Real Estate

**There are many types** of residential real estate. Deciding which type to buy depends on many factors, such as your budget, how much risk you are willing to take, the amount and speed of return desired, the amount of involvement in managing the investment, whether you are buying property as a principal residence, your past experience (if any) in real estate investment, whether you are buying property with others, and your personal needs and investment goals.

Many people already own a principal residence, such as a house or condominium, and may wish to rent out a suite to experience being a landlord before buying investment in real estate. Some people may not have a principal residence and want to purchase one as an investment for the financial, tax, and other benefits. Others may want to invest jointly with several friends or relatives to buy houses or an apartment building.

This chapter discusses the seven main types of residential investment properties, as well as some commercial investment options. Types of properties addressed include condominiums, single-family properties (including new and resale houses, and building lots), properties for renovation, recreational properties, multi-unit buildings, apartment buildings, and raw land. Within many of these main categories, there are several options.

## Condominium

Canada is an increasingly urban nation. A shift in favour of cities has been driven by the loss of rural employment opportunities and a corresponding increase of urban opportunities and services. In addition, many newcomers to Canada are opting to be in major centres where amenities and cheap housing are both readily available. Condominiums are cheaper than detached homes, for example, and a reflection of the greater demand for housing in Canada's urban centres.

Canada's first residential condominium was registered in Edmonton in 1967. By 1990, approximately 4 per cent of Canadians lived in condos. Today, that figure is more than 15 per cent and rising.

## What Is a Condominium?

Condominiums are an attractive option for home buyers, either as a primary residence or an investment. A condominium will not suit everyone, however, as it combines individual ownership of a unit (the home) and shared ownership in other property. There are also rules and regulations to be respected, and shared management. On the other hand, many people prefer condominium living to the alternatives because it reduces yardwork and very often places them at the centre of any given community with all the amenities an area can bring.

The word *condominium* refers to a specific legal form of ownership rather than the kind of structure actually owned. Condominiums (called co-proprietorships in Quebec, and often referred to in British Columbia as strata-titled property) may be detached, semi-detached, row houses, stack townhouses, duplexes, or apartments. They can even be building lots, subdivisions, or mobile-home parks. Whatever the style, a residential unit is specified and owned by an individual in a freehold or leasehold format. *Freehold* means that you own the title to the property outright. *Leasehold* means that you don't have any ownership rights to the land, only the leasing rights. (These formats are described in more detail on page 167 in Chapter 6, "Understanding the Legal Aspects.") The rest of the property, including land, which is called the common elements in most provinces, is owned in common with the other owners. For example, an owner would own a fractional share of the common elements in the development. If there were 50 condominium owners, then each owner would own one-fiftieth as a tenant of the common elements. Provincial legislation can vary, but it is always designed to provide the legal and structural framework for the efficient management and administration of each condominium project. Once the condominium project documents are registered, the project is brought into legal being.

The part of the condominium that you will own outright is referred to as the unit in most provinces. You will have full and clear title to this unit when you purchase it (assuming you are buying a freehold, not a leasehold, property), which will be legally registered in your name in the land registry office in your province. The precise description of the common elements, and exactly what you own as part of your unit, may differ from development to development, but in any event it will be provided for in the documents prepared and registered for each condominium.

Common elements generally include walkways, driveways, lawns and gardens, lobbies, elevators, parking areas, recreational facilities, storage areas, laundry rooms, stairways, plumbing, electrical systems and portions of walls, ceilings, floors, and other items. Parts of the common elements may be designated for the exclusive use of one or more of the individual unit owners, in which case these are called limited common elements. In other words, they are limited for the use of only specific owners. Examples would include parking spaces, storage lockers, roof gardens, balconies, patios, and front and backyards.

Condominiums can be built on freehold or leasehold properties. A condominium can also be in a stratified format, where a legal description for the unit is allocated in a vertical dimension. In other words, if you live in a condominium apartment on the thirtieth floor, there is a precise legal description in the land titles office for that specific unit in the complex. Another format is a bare-land condominium. In this example, it is similar to a building lot subdivision with individual units owned by the unit holders, although the units appear as detached homes. The rest of the land is considered a common element.

A condominium development is administered by various legal structures set out in provincial legislation.

## Types of Condominiums

There are numerous types of condominium formats, including residential, recreational or resort, and commercial or industrial. Here is an overview of the most common options.

### Residential Condominiums

Residential condominiums are found in metropolitan and suburban settings. In a metropolitan setting the most common formats are as follows:

- high-rise apartment building;
- three- to five-storey new mid-rise building;
- converted older building that formerly consisted of rental apartments;
- building where the street-level floor is owned jointly by the condominium corporation members (the unit owners) and rented out to retailers to help offset the common maintenance fees of the residential condominiums in the rest of the building;
- same format as the previous one, except that the retail space is sold as condominiums.

Suburban condominiums tend to be different and are most often found in the following formats:

- cluster housing consisting of multi-unit structures of two or four units apiece, each with its own private entranceway;
- townhouse-type single-family homes distributed in rows;
- garden apartments consisting of a group of apartment buildings surrounding a common green, frequently with each of the floors held by separate condominium owners;
- a series of detached single-family homes in a subdivision format, all utilizing the same land and parking areas;
- duplexes, triplexes, or fourplexes.

The suburban condominium format tends to make maximum use of the land while creating attractive views, private driveways, and common recreational facilities, such as swimming pools, tennis courts, saunas, and playgrounds.

Many residential condominium developments, offering conveniences and amenities, have created a complete lifestyle experience. The purpose of these separate developments—restaurants, shopping centres, recreational and entertainment facilities, and care facilities for seniors—is to make the condominium community a very distinct and self-contained environment for many people.

## Recreational/Resort Condominiums

Recreational condominiums can take various formats, including mobile-home parks where the "pad" with utility hookups is owned in fee simple—that is, freehold or the right to the property—with a share in the common property of the rest of the park. Alternatively, it could be in a leasehold format. Another option is a bare-land condominium in rural, wilderness, or waterfront areas. In these examples an owner could build a cabin with fee simple ownership to the land underneath and own a partial interest in the common elements, which could include a marina, beach, farm, or forest. Common recreational facilities could include a playground or community centre, and assets could include boats or farm animals.

The development of condominiums in resort areas is extensive, and condominiums are frequently built on lakeshores, seacoasts or island resorts, or in ski country. There are two main types of resort condominiums: those developed for warm climates and those developed for cold ones.

The warm-climate type is generally built around a common recreational facility, such as a seashore, lake, marina, or golf course, which the owners can enjoy throughout the year. The buildings tend to range from high-rise apartments to cluster housing.

The cold-climate type is often built near a popular ski-resort development. Many provide recreational facilities for the summer season as well, such as golf courses, tennis courts, and swimming pools, so that it is a year-round resort. The buildings tend to be cluster housing, modular housing, or attached townhouses.

People who purchase a recreational or resort condominium tend to own:

- it outright and use it throughout the year;
- it outright and rent it out when not it is in use by using the condominium corporation or management company as an agent, using a real estate agent, or renting it independently; or
- a portion as a time-share and use it for one week or more a year; normally each one-week block purchased is equivalent to approximately one-fiftieth ownership in the condominium.

## Commercial or Industrial Condominiums

Ownership of a commercial or an industrial condominium is similar in concept to the ownership of a residential one. There are various reasons why condominiums for commercial purposes are an attractive alternative to renting space, buying land with a building on it, or buying land and building on it. Some of the benefits include:

- tax advantages for the owner-occupier of business premises, including depreciation, and expense deductions for mortgage interest;
- a limit on monthly costs by carefully regulating costs through the condominium corporation policies;
- no rent increases;
- shared contribution of costs for features such as maintenance, security, common facilities, and advertising;
- appreciation in value of the condominium over time;
- right to participate in the decision making relating to the condominium development;
- assurance of a unique, commercially attractive location;

- no financial risk of owning in a unique, commercially attractive location; and

- provision of an alternative if there is a lack of financial capability or desire to own the whole building.

The three main types of commercial-use condominiums are office buildings, professional buildings, and industrial parks.

## Office Buildings

The concept of condominium office buildings is not new. For example, Brazil was the first Western country to pass condominium ownership legislation in 1928, and most office buildings in that country are now owned in that manner. In Canada, it is a popular concept in many major cities, and involves a cross-section of retail and service businesses operating through the condominium structure.

## Professional Buildings

A familiar form of office use is the dental or medical condominium, where each dentist or doctor owns a suite. Dental and medical offices do not expand as other businesses do. Another advantage for the professional is the possibility of sharing reception areas, a central telephone-answering service, accounting services, and expensive equipment. It is fairly common in this type of building to sell or lease the street-level condominiums to retail outlets such as pharmacies, laboratory or X-ray services, magazine stands, and restaurants. Lawyers also own offices in condominium buildings and take the same approach in terms of sharing office space, boardrooms, reception areas, library areas, and so on.

## Industrial Parks

Industrial parks established on a bare-land condominium format are a popular development. They can be advantageous because a business can have an individual unit for its industrial or manufacturing needs, but can share in the common elements such as docks, loading areas, rail sidings, and so on.

# Additional Expenses Relating to Condominium Ownership

Once you have completed the purchase transaction and are now an owner of a condominium unit, you have to plan for ongoing monthly or annual expenses and other potential expenses. People often don't realize the extra expenses involved in owning a condominium, which is very different from a owning a single-family home. The most common additional expenses, other than mortgage payments, are as follows.

## Property Taxes

The municipality assesses each individual condominium unit and the owner has to make an annual payment to cover property taxes. If you have a mortgage, the lender may or may not have required you to include monthly property-tax payments in your mortgage payment. These payments are held in a property-tax account so that the lender can pay your municipal property taxes. If you do not have a mortgage, you will have to pay property taxes separately. The common elements are assessed for property tax as well, but that tax is covered in your monthly maintenance payments.

## Maintenance Payments

Maintenance payments or "assessments for common expenses" cover all the operating costs of the common elements and are adjusted for any increase or decrease in expenses. You are responsible for a portion of the development's total operating costs. Use the formula below to calculate your portion:

Unit entitlement is the basis on which the owner's contribution to the common expenses or maintenance fees of the condominium corporation is calculated. Various formulas are used for the calculation. In some developments the percentage calculated for the unit's share is determined by the original purchase price of each unit in relation to the value of the total property. Another method is to apportion costs on the basis of the number of units in equal proportion, regardless of unit size. But the most common formula is to calculate the unit entitlement by dividing the number of square feet in all the units by the number of square feet in an owner's unit. For example, let's say a condominium development contains 15 condominium units, the total area of all units is 15,680 square feet, your individual unit is 784 square feet, and the annual cost to maintain the common elements and other related expenses is $40,000. To calculate your monthly financial commitment, you would go through the following steps:

1. Calculate the unit entitlement (15,680 ÷ 784 = 1/20 share in the common property).
2. Calculate the annual share of maintenance costs (1/20 × $40,000 = $2,000 per year).

3. Calculate the monthly share of maintenance costs ($1/12 \times \$2{,}000 =$ $166.66 per month).

Payments for common expenses are made directly to the condominium corporation and generally cover the following items:

- Maintenance and Repair of Common Property. This includes maintenance, landscaping, building repairs, recreational facilities, equipment, and other expenses.

- Operating and Service Costs. Operating and servicing costs typically include services such as garbage removal, heat, water, and electricity.

- Contingency Reserve Fund. The contingency reserve fund is maintained to cover unforeseen problems and expenses such as replacing the roof or repairing the swimming pool or heating system. These expenses are typically not factored into the condominium building's annual budget. Owners contribute to this fund as part of the monthly maintenance fee. Condominium legislation in most provinces requires owners to contribute a minimum amount to the contingency reserve fund, which will sometimes account for 10 per cent of the annual budget. When purchasing an older condominium, you should verify what percentage of the monthly payments is allocated toward the contingency reserve fund, as an older building typically requires more funds to cover repairs and other contingencies than a newer development. In older buildings, the fund will possibly be 25 per cent or more, depending on the circumstances. In most cases you are not entitled to a refund of your contribution to the reserve fund when you sell your unit.

- Management Costs. Management costs cover the cost of hiring private individuals or professional management firms to administer all or part of the condominium development's daily functions.

- Insurance. Condominium legislation requires a development to carry sufficient fire and related insurance to replace the common property in the event of fire or other damage. Condominium corporations generally obtain additional insurance to cover other payables and liabilities. This insurance does not cover damages to the interior of an individual unit (condominium owner insurance is discussed on page 39).

## Special Assessment

There could be situations in which 75 per cent or more of the condominium members want to raise funds for special purposes. These funds would not come from the contingency reserve fund or from the regular monthly assessments. Perhaps there is an interest in building a swimming pool or tennis courts, or it may be necessary to cover the cost of repairs that will exceed the money available in the contingency reserve fund. Once the decision is made to assess members, you cannot refuse to pay the special assessment if it has been approved according to condominium bylaws, even though you might not agree with its purpose.

## Condominium Owner Insurance

As mentioned on page 38, the insurance on the areas of the building that are covered by the condominium development does not include the interior of your unit. Therefore, you will need to obtain your own insurance to cover the contents as well as damage to the inside of your unit, including walls, windows, and doors. There are several types of insurance, including replacement cost, all-risk comprehensive, and personal liability. It is also common to get insurance to cover deficiencies in the condominium corporation's insurance coverage in the event of fire so that any damage to your unit could be repaired in full; otherwise, the unit owners would have to pay on a proportional basis any deficiency by means of a special assessment. Most insurance companies offer a condominium homeowner's insurance package. Consult the Insurance Brokers Association of Canada (www.ibac.ca) for a list of local members and shop around for a package that suits your needs, including earthquake coverage (some policies are more favourable than others).

## Lease Payments

If you have a leasehold condominium, you will be required to make monthly lease payments in addition to many of the other costs outlined in this section.

## Utilities

You are responsible for the utilities you use in your unit, including hydro, water, and heat. In apartment condominiums, these expenses are usually included in the maintenance fee, whereas townhouse condominiums tend to have individual meters. You would be billed directly and individually by the utility companies.

## Unit Repair and Maintenance Costs

You will have to allocate a certain amount of your financial budget for repair and maintenance needs relating to the inside of your unit. Your monthly assessment fee would cover common elements outside your unit only.

## Advantages and Disadvantages of Condominium Ownership

There are advantages and disadvantages in any situation where ownership and living arrangements are shared. Someone who buys a condominium solely as an investment won't enjoy the full advantages and disadvantages of condominium ownership, but the following points are still relevant as you consider your investment.

### Advantages

The advantages of condominium ownership include:

- ready availability of financing as a single-family home;
- range of prices, locations, types of structures, sizes, and architectural features;
- availability of amenities such as swimming pools, tennis courts, health clubs, community centres, saunas, hot tubs, exercise rooms, and sun decks;
- participation in the real estate market and potential growth in equity;
- enables people with moderate income to own their own homes;
- freedom to decorate the interior of the unit to suit personal tastes;
- security of mid- to long-term neighbours and, in many cases, controlled entrances;
- little or no maintenance responsibilities associated with home ownership, since issues outside the individual unit, such as landscaping and window washing, are delegated to a professional management company or manager;
- often considerably less expensive than buying a single-family home because of more efficient use of land and economy of scale;
- profitable investment opportunity if selected carefully;
- good transitional type of home between rental apartments and single-family houses for growing families or singles or couples; conversely, good transition for "empty nesters" who wish to give up their larger family house;
- lower costs due to shared repair and maintenance responsibilities;
- social activities and sense of community with other mid- to long-term neighbours;
- elected council is responsible for making many business and management decisions;

- owners participate in the operation of the development, such as setting and approving budgets; making decisions; determining rules, regulations, and bylaws; and other matters affecting the democratic operation of the condominium community.

## Disadvantages

The disadvantages of condominium ownership include:

- appreciation is generally not as high as for a single-family house, due to the total ownership of land when owning a house; it is the land that goes up in value;
- difficulty assessing the worth of the project's construction;
- restrictions on matters such as rentals or the kind and number of pets allowed;
- close proximity to neighbours, potentially creating occasional problems with parking, parties, people, and personalities;
- condominiums may be slower to sell than single-family houses in some markets;
- paying for maintenance and operation of amenities that you don't want or use;
- condominium councils are made up of volunteers, who may or may not have the appropriate abilities and skills;
- owners might be unwilling or unable to join the council, so that the same people remain on it for a long time; and
- some elected councils behave in an autocratic fashion, reducing the control you have over your investment.

## Investing in a Condominium

The first-time real estate investor could find buying a condominium unit as a rental property an attractive option for several reasons. If you are considering investing in a condominium, consider the advantages and disadvantages of the different types of condominiums—for example, an apartment, townhouse, or hybrid mix, or a conversion of a former rental apartment building to a condominium. Check on whether rental units are permitted in the development before finalizing any offer, and get it confirmed in writing in advance. (This is particularly important, and is covered in Chapter 6, "Understanding the Legal Aspects.") You don't want to buy a condo only to find out that the bylaws permit rentals, but the quota has been reached. Check on the current mix of tenants and owner-occupiers.

Here are some of the benefits to consider:

- Condominiums generally appreciate in value at a rate that is higher than the rate of inflation because it is a newer form of property catering to a growing demand.

- A lack of new, purpose-built rental buildings in many Canadian cities mean apartment condominiums enjoy strong demand from renters.

- There is an increasing demand for the condominium lifestyle and the convenience that it provides.

- Because a minimal amount of upkeep is involved, the economic benefits are more attractive for the first-time investor.

- Many of the management and maintenance problems are taken care of by the condominium corporation and the professional management company.

- Facilities such as tennis courts and swimming pools are maintained by the condominium corporation, thereby freeing the new investor from the responsibilities of upkeep.

- The owner is protected by the bylaws, rules, and regulations set by provincial condominium legislation, by the original project documents, or by the condominium council. For example, many condominiums do not allow pets in the building because of the potential wear and tear on the apartment. This type of rule protects and benefits the investor.

If you are looking for higher appreciation (resale value), compare the purchase of the least expensive unit in a luxury condominium townhouse complex versus the largest unit in a modestly priced development, assuming the purchase price is the same. Your research will provide you with the necessary background statistics in your market interest area to determine which of the above options might provide the most attractive return.

Additional tips to look for when selecting a condominium are covered in Chapter 3, "Finding and Evaluating the Right Property."

## Dealing with Condominium Disputes

In the condominium community there is always the possibility that a problem or dispute may not be resolved quickly and easily. It is important to know your rights and options in that event. This section will cover the most common types of disputes and the means of resolving them.

## Nature of Common Disputes

Problems tend to fall into the following general categories:

### The Five P's, "Pets, Parking, Parties, People, Personalities"

The five P's tend to be the most common problems. Some pets can be noisy, roam the property, scare children, or foul the common property. Members or guests can be selfish and irresponsible when using parking spaces. People and parties are too loud for too long too late at night. Personalities may clash when people live in close proximity; some owners get annoyed when people use or abuse the common elements, and some people can irritate others with their attitude, arrogance, indifference, or lack of courtesy.

### Decisions of the Condominium Corporation or Council

Disputes with the condominium corporation or council can occur, for example, if you believe that the conduct of the corporation or council is oppressive and unfairly prejudicial toward your rights; if you believe that a decision relating to a special assessment was unnecessary and irresponsible; if you were fined for allegedly breaching the bylaws or rules and regulations and you believe the fine was unfair and unwarranted.

## Resolving Disputes

The means for resolving disputes, in ascending order of complexity, are negotiation, mediation, arbitration, and litigation.

### Negotiation

It is always best to try to resolve the dispute by discussing the matter directly with the person concerned. That may be all that is necessary, so it is worthwhile to make the attempt.

### Mediation

If the negotiation does not work, you may complain to the condominium council outlining your dispute. If another owner's conduct has contravened the bylaws or rules and regulations, bring those points to the attention of the council, which has the authority in most cases to deal with infringements.

## Arbitration

If mediation through the condominium council is unsuccessful, you may consider arbitration. Condominium legislation of most provinces sets out the procedures for arbitration. Normally the process is not available if litigation has commenced. Matters that may require arbitration include disputes about contributions to common expenses; fines for breach of bylaws or rules and regulations; damage to common elements, common facilities, and other assets of the condominium corporation; and council or corporation decisions.

The parties should agree on a single arbitrator, but if that is not possible, each party selects its own arbitrator and the two arbitrators select a third who acts as a chairperson. Unless the parties agree otherwise, each arbitrator must have been an owner and occupier of a condominium unit in another development for at least one year, but may not be an owner in the condominium corporation affected by the arbitration. The arbitrators may accept evidence under oath and may make whatever decision they consider just and equitable. The arbitrators' decision is entered into court as if it were an order of the court. This is a common procedure set out in most provincial condominium legislation, although the procedures may vary in individual provinces.

A list of arbitrators is available upon request from most professional condominium-management companies or provincial condominium owners associations, if one exists in your province.

## Litigation

If all else fails, you have rights in common law, as well as under most provincial condominium legislation, to commence an action in court. You can proceed against a condominium corporation or council to rectify what you believe is a failure to meet their obligations under the condominium legislation or bylaws, or because you feel that their actions toward you have been oppressive. The court can make any order it considers appropriate, depending on the circumstances.

The difficulty in the litigation process, of course, is that it can be very expensive, stressful, uncertain, and lengthy. If you have a problem and are wondering whether you should choose arbitration or litigation, you should seek a legal opinion from a lawyer who specializes in condominium law. Ideally it would be helpful to obtain a second opinion from another lawyer who specializes in condominium law in order to confirm that the legal advice is consistent.

How to select a lawyer is covered on page 110 in Chapter 4, "Selecting Your Advisory Team." Also, refer to Chapter 6, "Understanding the Legal Aspects."

# Single-Family House

A single-family house is one of the most attractive investments beginning investors can make because they are generally more familiar with a house as often they already live in one or have done so. Finding tenants is usually not a problem. In fact, if you have a self-contained suite in the basement, you could rent it out to one or two tenants.

There is generally a wide selection of single-family houses from which to select. Land value goes up over time. The price is lower than it is for other types of residential real estate (such as duplexes or apartments). Also, financing is easier to obtain, and management effort and time are minimal. You can see why a single-family house is attractive as a principal residence.

However, there are some disadvantages to investing in a single-family house compared to other investments. If a tenant vacancy occurs, you will have to cover the expenses yourself. The small yield in terms of cash flow is lower. You would therefore be relying primarily on resale of the property to make a profit. The opportunity of making a large profit is less than with a multi-unit building. These are general observations, and there are many exceptions.

Among single-family houses, there are various choices available: you could buy a resale house, a new house, a lot and build a house yourself or with a builder, or you can assemble a prefabricated house. There are advantages and disadvantages to each option. Note, the terms *builder* and *contractor* are essentially interchangeable. If you are buying a newly built home, the term *builder* is frequently used. When contracting for someone to build you a house on a lot you bought, the term *contractor* is common.

## Buying a Resale House

Many people prefer to buy a resale house when purchasing for personal use or as an investment. Here are some of the advantages and disadvantages of buying a resale rather than a new house. These are general guidelines and do not necessarily apply in every case.

### Advantages

- A resale house is generally less expensive than a new house.
- An older home may have architectural styles and elements that are no longer in common use, giving it a retro cachet.
- Mature landscaping enhances the comfort and ambience of the property.

- The neighbourhood is established and has developed its own character and community services.

- Some older resale properties are available in or near the centre of the city, giving access to urban amenities and services.

- A resale house may include extras not normally included in a new home purchase, such as customized features that previous owners have built or installed.

- The purchase isn't subject to GST or, where applicable, harmonized sales tax (HST) (refer to Chapter 7, "Understanding the Tax Aspects").

## Disadvantages

- A resale property may not have been built to current building standards, so it might not meet electrical or insulation codes. It might have lead rather than copper pipes, for example, inefficient insulation, or worse, asbestos or urea formaldehyde foam insulation (UFFI).

- Defects in the construction may not be visible or identified unless a thorough inspection is done by a professional building inspector.

- Buyers may not be protected by a new home warranty program (NHWP), which typically applies only to newly built homes for a set length of time and may expire prior to a second owner taking possession.

- Resale homes in established metropolitan areas may be more expensive because the land has a greater value, whereas a new house in a suburban area could be less expensive due to lower land costs.

- An older home may have been renovated without a building permit, which may render it noncompliant with municipal codes and regulations, or worse, prove a safety risk.

- Some older homes simply lack an attractive or functional design, including small rooms, unfinished or non-functional basements, low ceilings, or other unattractive features that would require a substantial investment of time and money on your part to upgrade.

- Heating systems and other equipment may be outdated and in need of repair.

On the plus side, many of the disadvantages related to the purchase of an older property can be identified by a certified professional building inspector (listings for your area are available through www.cahpi.ca).

## *Buying a New House*

You may wish to purchase a new house for your principal residence or investment needs. Here are some of the advantages and disadvantages of buying a new house over an older resale house.

### Advantages

- New houses tend to be better designed and have modern features, such as larger kitchens, more appliances, more windows, or better functionality, such as higher ceilings in the basement or opportunities to finish the basement to create a small apartment.

- A builder often offers several house models. You can generally select certain features to customize your needs—such as carpeting, kitchen appliances, kitchen and bathroom floor coverings, paint colours—if you contract the builder and build from plans or before the house is fully completed.

- New houses are constructed in compliance with current building code standards with respect to plumbing, electrical, heating, insulation, and the like.

- It looks clean, modern, fresh, and smells new.

- You are the first occupant in the house, which is an advantage because you can personalize the house to meet your own or your family's needs rather than remodelling.

- Market evaluation of the house is easier because of similar, comparable houses built in the same area.

- The price of the house could be lower or the house could be larger (compared to a similar resale house) if a new house is built in a suburb with lower land costs.

- Many new homes are built by builders registered with the NHWP in their respective province, protecting buyers in the event of problems following the sale. Check the terms of the program in your province and read the fine print of the coverage (this varies from province to province).

### Disadvantages

- The builder may not be registered with the NHWP, raising the purchaser's liability if problems occur following passion of the property.

- Due to land availability and cost savings, many builders construct new houses a considerable distance from the city core, which means an increase in commuting time and fewer services than are available in more built-up metropolitan areas.

- It is common to have delays in paving, landscaping, and finishing touches, not to mention defects, which can be frustrating and expensive.

- Many new houses are purchased prior to construction and are selected based on an artist's sketch or various model plans. The property may appear and feel quite different upon construction and not meet your expectations.

- Purchase documents prepared by the builder tend to be more complex and detailed than resale-house contracts. (Purchase documents are discussed at greater length in Chapter 6, "Understanding the Legal Aspects.")

- You might lose your deposit if the builder ceases to operate. In some provinces there is consumer protection legislation that protects these funds. Unless you put the funds in a lawyer's or realtor's trust account, though, you could lose your deposit. It is important to check the builder's reputation through the following:

- If the builder is registered with the NHWP, in some provinces the deposit funds are protected up to a maximum amount. If the builder is not registered with a NHWP, be very cautious and don't pay any money or sign a builder's contract without your lawyer's advice. The NHWP of each province is similar, but there are some differences. The builder adds the fee for NHWP coverage to the house price or builds it into the price. Coverage generally includes buyer protection for the deposit, incomplete work allowance, warranty protection up to a year, basement protection for two years, and major structural defect protection for five years. Although the NHWP was designed to protect purchasers of newly constructed houses (condominiums can also be covered) against defects in construction, there are limitations in coverage. These limitations and exclusions could cost you a lot of money. That is why you need to check out the NHWP and builder thoroughly.

- The local or provincial home builders' association will be able to confirm whether a contractor is a member or not.

- The local Better Business Bureau will have a record of any complaints against the contractor.

- Purchasers of houses from other developments the contractor has built are good sources of information. Also ask the contractor for names and locations of previous development projects. You can then knock on doors and ask the owners if they would give you their candid opinion as to the quality of the house and the builder's responsiveness to correcting any problems. Ask if they got what they bargained for and would they buy from the same builder again, and why.
- The local (municipal) business licensing office can verify if the contractor is licensed.

If the contractor has no previous history in the industry, be very cautious. The contractor could have been operating under a previous company name but went under, and is now operating under a different company name. Alternatively, the contractor could be a first-timer and be learning at your expense. Take the time to check out the contractor's background and reputation. It will save you time, frustration, and money later on.

Make sure that you take the contract supplied by the house builder to your lawyer before you sign it. Builder's contracts tend to be customized and are designed primarily for the benefit of the builder. Sometimes you can negotiate changes to the contract, but sometimes you cannot; it depends on the builder, the changes, and the market. A builder must occasionally be flexible in terms of the contract, especially if an experienced lawyer who is acting on behalf of the purchaser finds them to be unfair. The builder would not insist on retaining these clauses if it would stop the deal from proceeding.

You should have your lawyer advise you in general about the contract, as well as specifically on issues such as the following:

## Deposit

Will the deposit be held in trust and, if so, where? Will interest be paid on the deposit to the credit of the purchaser? There is a risk if the money is going directly to the builder and not being held in trust by a lawyer or real estate company.

## Financing

Will the builder arrange financing at a fixed rate through a lender or carry the financing himself? Make sure the payment terms are clearly spelled out. Make sure the rates and terms are competitive and that the financing package is attractive. For example, the builder could provide or arrange for a discounted interest rate for a year. The rate could be artificially low, rather than a prevailing market rate, to attract buyers who might not otherwise be interested or qualify for financing. What if interest rates go up at the end of the year when you have to refinance? Can you handle the increased monthly payments?

### Assigning or Selling

Does the builder's contract have a restriction to prevent you from assigning your interest in the contract to someone else before the closing date, or selling your property to someone else after closing, within a certain period of time? Some builders don't want you to assign before closing so that you make potential profit in an increasing market. Other builders don't want you to resell your property after closing and before they have sold out the rest of the project, because they could lose a potential sale, or you could offer your house for sale at a lower price, thereby affecting their pricing structure.

### Closing Date

What if the builder does not close on the agreed date? Consider adding clauses to the effect that the house price will be reduced by an agreed sum for a late closing, giving the purchaser the option to back out of the contract and get the deposit money back, plus accrued interest, if the purchaser so wishes (you might not want to exercise this option with a fixed sale price in an escalating market), or adding your own penalty clause that the builder has to pay you a penalty if the building is not completed on time. All these options are negotiable depending on the nature of the circumstances. There is no set formula. An example of a penalty could be a reduction of the purchase price, such as 1 per cent, for every week of delay.

Depending on your needs and objectives, you should ask your lawyer for advice. Attempt to negotiate a better deal by yourself or through your lawyer. If you are not satisfied with the outcome, consider buying from a different builder.

## Buying a Lot and Building a House

Some people prefer this arrangement and want to hire a contractor to build the house, build it themselves, or buy a prepackaged type of house (such as a log cabin or ski chalet) and have it constructed.

If you are building your own house, make sure that you know what you are doing, otherwise it could be very time consuming, frustrating, and expensive.

An alternative is to take a school board or college course on building your own house, and then hire a trustworthy contractor on an hourly basis to advise you. Check with your municipal planning department on the steps, building codes, permits, and inspections required. There are many regulations involved. Read how-to books on building your own house. You could save money and obtain personal satisfaction by doing it yourself, but don't overestimate your abilities or the amount of time you have available. Do-it-yourself construction almost always turns out to be more complicated and time consuming than initially expected.

Many of the problems that owners have in their dealings with contractors are due to misunderstanding of the rights, responsibilities, and functions of the various people who are involved in the work.

## Homeowner's Responsibilities

Homeowner's responsibilities generally include the following:

- Decide what is to be done. Write a description of the work and provide as much detail as possible.
- Obtain blueprints from an architect or a "stock" blueprint plan.
- Decide on all the features of the house in detail.
- Make arrangements with a lender for construction financing.
- Select a contractor.
- Make sure the written contract describes the job completely, thoroughly, and correctly.
- Obtain zoning approval and building permits, if required.
- Provide the space and freedom that the workers need to do their work.
- Inform the contractor about deficiencies or mistakes as quickly as possible, preferably in writing, so there is no misunderstanding and you will have a dated record.
- Pay for the work as required by the contract, holding back a portion to comply with provincial builder's lien legislation (normally 10 per cent).
- Make the final decision as to whether or not the job has been done satisfactorily.
- Release the builder's lien holdback.

## Contractor's Responsibilities

Contractor's responsibilities generally include the following:

- Carry out the work described in the contract.
- Follow the details in the blueprint (architect or "stock").
- Decline to do any work that is not covered in the contract without written authorization from the owner for the changes.
- Maintain public liability and property damage insurance, and workers' compensation coverage for workers. Ensure that the subcontractors carry the same for their workers.
- Obtain any permits, licences, and certificates required by the municipality, unless there is a written agreement that the homeowner is responsible for them.
- Adhere to all building codes (federal, provincial, and municipal) and other government construction regulations.
- Supervise the quality of all work carried out by the contractor, including work done by subcontractors.
- Pay all workers, suppliers, and subcontractors.
- Remove construction debris upon completion of the job.
- Provide warranties on all work and materials (in addition to manufacturer's warranties) for a period of at least one year if possible.

## Finding the Right Contractor

It is important to clearly define your needs before you commit yourself. You should have at least three competitive bids (written, fixed-price quotes) from contractors before selecting the one you want. There are various ways of finding names of contractors:

- recommendations from friends or neighbours;
- local building-material suppliers or hardware stores;
- local or provincial home builders' associations;
- provincial NHWP offices for names of contractors registered with them;
- search online or via your local home builders' association, which often list renovators as well as builders.

Before finalizing your decision, check on the reputation and past performance of the contractor, using the cautions listed on page 48 under "Buying a New House." This is very important. Also, consider the advantages of hiring a contractor who is registered with the NHWP. You will pay an extra amount for this coverage, but the protection could save you thousands in the event something goes wrong within the first 5, 10, or 15 years of the building's life. (See the discussion of the NHWP on pages 47–48, "Buying a New House.") Contractors should be able to name the insurance company backing their work. A contractor should also be able to provide written verification of adequate public liability and property damage insurance; ask the insurance company for confirmation if you have any doubts or concerns. If the contractor is doing a remodelling job rather than the whole house, ask for the following:

- plans and/or sketches of the work to be done;
- samples and literature showing different products that could be used;
- photographs of previous work completed.

As mentioned earlier, a written contract with the contractor is essential. Many home builders' associations provide sample contracts for members to use, so check with them. Have your lawyer look at the contract, and involve him or her in the release of any progress draws (payment to the contractor of an agreed portion of the total contract price) as the work progresses. Depending on the nature of the house construction, there could be from three to five different payments at various stages of construction or it could be every week. At each stage, confirm that the work is complete, that subcontractors, suppliers, and other creditors on the job have been paid, and that there is nothing outstanding from the previous draw. It is not uncommon for contractors to use progress draws to pay for subcontractors' services or for supplies. Often lawyers will do lien searches to make sure that no liens have been filed against the contractor before the payment is made.

Your lender will normally require you to make progress draws. If you pay a lot of money to the builder and the work has not been performed or if the contractor goes out of business, you could lose the money you advanced.

## Key Contents of a Construction Contract

A construction contract usually includes the following:

- date of agreement;
- correct and complete address of the property where the work will be done;

- your name and address;
- contractor's name, address, telephone number, cell number, fax number, e-mail address; if a company name is used, the name of the company's official on-site representative should be indicated;
- detailed description of the work, sketches, and list of materials to be used;
- type of work that will be subcontracted;
- the right to retain a builder's lien holdback as specified under provincial law;
- a clause stating that work will conform to the requirements of all applicable federal, provincial, or municipal building codes;
- start and completion dates;
- the contracted price and payment schedule (remember the lien holdback, which is normally 10 per cent);
- an agreement on who is responsible for obtaining all necessary permits, licences, and certificates;
- a clause setting out the procedures for confirming in writing any "extras" to the contract requested by the owner;
- signatures of the parties to the contract.

# Property for Renovation

Many types of residential properties would be profitable after they are renovated. Generally, single-family houses, multi-unit dwellings, and apartment buildings are the most common choices.

When considering a property for investment, the main strategic plan is to locate the right property, improve the property, raise rents to increase the value, and sell at the right time for maximum profit.

## Key Factors When Looking for a Property to Renovate

The factors to look for in selecting a real estate investment property are covered later in this chapter. When selecting a property for renovation, though, also consider some of the following factors:

- Look for a neighbourhood where people are renovating older houses. This will create a positive image that rejuvenation is taking place.
- The property should be readily accessible by various forms of transportation and not be isolated.

- It should be an attractive, high- or middle-income neighbourhood with a low crime rate.

- The neighbourhood should have more owner-occupiers than tenants and absentee landlords.

- The property to be renovated should be in a neighbourhood that is not yet in high demand.

- New residential construction implies that others consider this a growing neighbourhood.

- New commercial construction such as shops or offices, or other nearby existing commercial areas, is a positive sign.

- The property should have some character and quality construction and craftsmanship.

- The property should be close to other attractive amenities, such as public transit, a college or university, park, downtown area, and proximity to lake or ocean view.

- The property should have potential for renovation without problems from city hall such as a "non-conforming use" under current bylaws that would require correction if the property is renovated. If you decide to renovate, you could be obliged to make adjustments to the property to make it conform to the current municipal requirements. This could be unappealing to you from an investment perspective.

- If the neighbourhood has a community organization to improve the quality of the area, that is a positive sign in terms of pride and initiative.

Other factors to consider when finding and selecting a property are covered in Chapter 3, "Finding and Evaluating the Right Property."

## Steps to Follow before You Buy a Property to Renovate

Before you buy a property for renovation, review the following:

- Familiarize yourself with the renovation process. If you are inexperienced, consider taking courses, reading books and magazines, and getting expert advice.

- Be realistic and focused on the types of renovations and types of renovation properties you are considering. Certain types of renovations get a better return on your investment in terms of price and general saleability. The highest return generally comes from renovating the kitchen and bathrooms.

- Make sure that your personal goals and investment goals are clear. Do you intend to purchase a property for a principal residence and then renovate it throughout the year and sell it? If so, you would normally be exempt from paying any capital gains tax on the sale because it would be deemed your principal residence. Or, is it your objective to rent out the property after the renovation?

- Compare various properties and shortlist them to two or three that have good potential profit return. That way you can negotiate with more leverage because you are considering more than one property.

- Consider having an architect view the property and give you ideas on how it can be improved. The Royal Architectural Institute of Canada (www.raic.org) and its provincial affiliates maintain a list of members, and many architects (or the firms to which they belong) also have websites where you can review their work. Websites of the professional associations typically have sections on how to choose an architect and other helpful information.

- Have a professional appraiser give you an idea of the property's current market value. Consult the Appraisal Institute of Canada (www.aicanada.ca) for a directory of appraisers, as well as consumer information.

- Have a professional building inspector give you a report on the physical aspects, internal and external, of the building, including what changes would be possible. (Refer to page 123 in Chapter 4, "Selecting Your Advisory Team," for tips on how to select a building or home inspector.) Check out the Canadian Association of Building and Property Inspectors website (www.cahpi.ca), which has a list of members in your area.

- Have at least three contractors give you written quotes on the cost of the renovations. Refer to "Buying a New House" (page 47) and "Buying a Lot and Building a House" (page 50) for tips on selecting a contractor. Visit the Canadian Home Builders' Association (CHBA) webpage (www.chba.ca) to find provincial associations and a list of members in your area. It also has excellent information and tips.

- The Canada Mortgage and Housing Corporation (CMHC) (www.cmhc.ca) offers excellent information on home renovations, as well as various incentive programs for certain types of projects.

- Do a feasibility study to determine if the whole exercise makes financial sense. If the property is already a revenue property, analyze the previous expense history and do projections of future expenses. Prepare an income-and-expense statement and a cash flow projection of income to be derived from increased rents over time. Do a projected budget. You can find sample forms for these types of projections in the appendix under Forms 5, 6, and 7.

- Apply the capitalization of net income formula after the projected renovation to determine what the property value would be compared to the present market value, plus the cost of renovations. Will you make money? This formula will be covered on page 99 in Chapter 3, "Finding and Evaluating the Right Property."

- If the property still looks attractive after you have followed the previous steps, then have your potential investment objectively reviewed by your accountant and lawyer before you make your final decision.

# Recreational Property

For many reasons, the demand for recreational property has increased. You may wish to consider buying recreational property for personal use or investment purposes. Depending on your choices, the purchase could result in an attractive financial return and personal enjoyment over time. The term *recreational property* refers to a range of options, including an existing home (chalet, cabin, or cottage), a condominium, a townhouse, a building lot, or a hobby farm, with recreational amenities nearby, such as fields, mountains, rivers, lakes, the ocean, a ski hill, golf courses, campsites, and recreational vehicle parks. Activities could include snowmobiling, hunting, hiking, climbing, boating, canoeing, sailing, fishing, downhill or cross-country skiing, or other recreational pursuits.

## Trends Generating Interest in Recreational Property

Various trends and other motivating factors that are generating an interest in rural and recreational property include:

- having more leisure time;
- balancing a hectic career with quality of life;
- combining the best aspects of country and city life;
- seeking a simpler existence;
- needing to be close to recreational interests;
- operating a home-based business, commuting to the city only as required; this could also include telecommuting (being an employee,

but working primarily from home and using various online services to interact with the employer);

- wanting a family retreat, which could be passed on to succeeding generations;
- planning for a retirement home;
- buying a lot in the desired area, and building when savings are sufficient; in the meantime, the land could be used with a mobile home or recreational vehicle;
- buying recreational properties is less expensive than buying urban ones;
- increasing demand for (and therefore value of) recreational or rural properties that are within a four-hour driving distance to metropolitan areas;
- financing through a vendor-take-back mortgage to the purchaser;
- optioning to purchase the property for a period of time—say, one to two years—at an agreed price. The option fee itself is normally nominal.

## Potential Downsides of Purchasing Recreational Property

There are some potential downsides to purchasing recreational property. These are general comments, however, and there are many exceptions.

- Lenders are sometimes reluctant to lend money or approve a mortgage for recreational property, especially raw land.
- There may be some restrictions on land use (which will be discussed on page 59).
- If you have a seasonal property and intend to rent it out, you could have a negative cash flow (shortage in revenue to offset expenses) that you would have to subsidize.
- Maintaining the property could be frustrating if you are far from home.
- Vandalism is more likely if the property is in a remote location or is only used seasonally.
- If the economy is in a recession, the property's value can diminish considerably (along with demand) if you need to sell; a recreational property is generally considered a luxury, not a necessity.

## *Special Considerations When Selecting a Recreational or Rural Property*

There are special cautions when assessing a recreational or rural property for purchase. Chapter 3, "Finding and Evaluating the Right Property," which includes a section on "Important Factors to Consider" (on page 77), deals with the general aspects, although primarily in an urban or metropolitan setting. It is important, though, to read that section thoroughly. Here are some issues that are specific to recreational or rural property.

### Location

This is one of the most important points. You want to consider proximity to an urban area, what unique features are present (such as tourist attractions or the area's natural beauty), desirability of location relative to other areas, and whether the area has seasonal or year-round usage. If you are buying property in a subdivision, try to be among the first to buy, so you can get the best location.

### Accessibility

The area should be easily and quickly accessible by ferry, boat, plane, or car.

### Restrictions on Use

There are various forms of legal restrictions that could affect your land and its use. Your lawyer can search the title of the property in the land titles office to see what encumbrances are on title as a condition of any offer you make.

### Right of Way

This generally means a statutory (legal) right for certain companies, Crown corporations, or government departments to use or have access to part of your property for hydro, telephone, sewer, drainage, dike, or public-access purposes.

### Easement

An easement is similar to a right of way, but is the term used when one neighbour gives another the right to use or have access to a piece of land, such as permission to reach a waterfront by crossing the neighbour's land. This agreement is put into writing and filed in the local land titles office.

## Restrictive Covenant

In this situation, a developer in a subdivision could make any purchase subject to an ongoing restriction in certain areas, such as requiring that all roofs be covered by shakes rather than shingles. The purpose would be for aesthetic uniformity. A document setting out the restrictions would be filed in the land titles office.

## Zoning

There could be restrictions on how your property could be used—exclusively for seasonal use, no mobile homes, or no other buildings or uses permitted for the property.

## Water Availability

Check on this critical issue. Do you have well water? Is it safe to drink? Is it sufficient for your needs? Do you have a water system, private or local, available to you? If you don't have a well, what would it cost to drill one?

## Waste Disposal

What type of system is required or available? Is it a septic tank or other type of system? Is the soil suitable for a septic field? What about other types of waste disposal, such as garbage?

## Crime

Check with the local police division regarding crime rates in the area, including theft, arson, and vandalism.

## Land Boundary

Make sure that the property boundaries have been clearly marked and pegged by a qualified surveyor. This is especially important with acreage or waterfront property. You don't want to have disputes with your neighbours.

## Amenities

What types of public or private recreational facilities are near the area you are considering? If the developer is establishing facilities, check out the developer's other projects to determine quality and residents' satisfaction.

## Local Government

Find out the local government's attitude toward seasonal residents. It might assess higher taxes on seasonal residents to keep the tax base of year-round residents lower.

## Existing Building

If you are buying a property with an existing building on it (a home, chalet, or cottage), have the building's structural condition inspected. Rural or recreational properties are particularly susceptible to the elements—wind, sun, ice, rain, and snow—depending on the location. If the building is not regularly or properly maintained, it can deteriorate rapidly. Also check for infestation, wood rot, and other damage.

## *Time-Share Properties*

You may also want to consider purchasing a recreational condominium or time-share property. If you are interested in such a property, see the section "Investing in a Condominium," on page 41. If you are interested in time-share properties, there are two main categories: fee simple ownership and right to use.

## Fee Simple Ownership

In this situation you would own a portion of the condominium or cabin, for example, one-fiftieth of the property. Each portion would entitle you to one week's use of the premises. Other people would also invest in the property. Often you would be allocated a fixed week every year. In other instances, it could be a flexible arrangement, with the exact dates to be agreed upon, depending on availability. If the whole property is sold, you would receive your proportional share of any increase in net after-sale proceeds. You would also be able to usually rent, sell, or give your ownership portion to anyone you wished.

## Right to Use

This concept is much like having a long-term lease, but with use for just one-week intervals a year. It is similar to prepaying for a hotel room for a fixed period every year for 20 years in advance. In other words, you don't have any portion of ownership in the property; you only have a right to use it for a fixed or floating time period every year. The right-to-use concept involves condominiums, cabins, chalets, recreational vehicle parks, and other types of properties.

From a real estate investment viewpoint, the opportunity for return on your money is limited or non-existent, especially in the right-to-use case. In practical terms, it is primarily a lifestyle choice. Here are some of the disadvantages and cautions of which you should be aware.

## Disadvantages of Time-Share Properties

- You may tire of going to the same location every year, as your needs change over time.

- The time-share programs that include an exchange option (such as switching for a week in a different location) are not always as anticipated in terms of availability, flexibility, and convenience, or there may be an upgrade fee.

- Make sure you know what you are getting. Some people who purchase the right-to-use type think they are buying a fee simple ownership portion.

- Be wary of hard-sell marketing techniques. Many time-share promotions, especially the right-to-use type, use aggressive and unethical strategies to get you to sign up. In most instances, the dream fantasy is heavily reinforced and there are so-called free inducements such as a meal or cruise to entice you to hear a sales pitch.

- High-pressure sales pitches, with teams of salespeople, can go on for hours. They can be very persuasive, if not aggressive, and often use very manipulative techniques to get you to sign a credit-card slip as a deposit. The so-called freebies are generally worth from $5 to $10. It is an illusion to think you will get something for nothing. At best, you will only be subjected to an intense one-on-one sales approach. At worst, you will be out a $5,000 to $10,000 deposit charged to your credit card, plus monthly payments over time. Trying to get your money back afterwards, if you suffer from "buyer's remorse," is extremely difficult, if not impossible.

- Time-share sales in Canada are sometimes covered by provincial consumer protection, in terms of your right to get your money back by rescinding (cancelling) the contract within a certain time period. If you are buying in certain American states, in Mexico, or in other destination resort areas, you could have no rights at all if you change your mind. The hard-sell promoters will generally require you to bring your spouse and show your credit card before agreeing to let you into the sales pitch room to be "eligible" for the "freebie." This is a danger sign for you to stay away. Remember: act in haste, repent at leisure.

- The legal aspects are generally more complex and expensive when dealing with time-shares outside Canada.

- There is usually an ongoing management fee for maintaining the premises.

- Speak to at least three other time-share owners in the project you are considering to get their candid opinions before you decide to buy. Never give out your credit card as a deposit or for any reason, or sign any documents requested of you, without first speaking with a local real estate lawyer. Don't let yourself be pressured. Check with the local Better Business Bureau.

## Multi-unit Dwelling

These types of dwellings can range from a duplex (two-family house, either side by side or one above the other) to an eight-unit building. Generally, each housing unit is separate, each with exterior access, so you don't need to go through a central lobby to reach each unit. Normally each unit is self-contained with its own bathroom and kitchen. If they were shared, the building would be more like a rooming house.

The multi-unit investment can be ideal for investors who intend to live in one of the units and perform much of the maintenance and repair themselves. This, of course, can also result in tenants bothering you if maintenance problems arise. Multi-unit dwellings are also ideal for splitting into smaller units and renting to singles to maximize the overall income. The return on investment (ROI) in a multi-unit dwelling can be quite attractive as financing is frequently easier to obtain and cash outlays are low or non-existent, compared to larger buildings. Conversely, if a single vacancy occurs, and there is a maximum of eight tenants, for example, the proportional impact on the total rent income will be greater than it would be for a larger building.

## Apartment Building

This is not typically the type of purchase for a first-time investor. The usual pattern is to start with a single-family house or condominium, duplex, triplex, or multi-unit dwelling before considering an apartment building. You want to start your learning experience as an investor and landlord slowly and cautiously before taking on more challenging investments. You may decide to restrict your investments to single-family homes, for example, for many logical reasons. Frequently an investor in an apartment building joins an investment group to share the risk, experience, management, responsibility, financing, and profit. (Refer to the section "Buying with Partners" on page 17.)

For the purpose of this discussion, an apartment building is defined as a building with 8 or more housing units having interior access (one enters the building first before entering any individual unit). The previous point covered multi-unit buildings up to 8 units. In practical language, though, any building with between 6 and 20 units is referred to as a small apartment building.

Here are some of the advantages and disadvantages, in general terms, of apartment buildings as an investment.

## Advantages

- Cash flows from medium or large apartments are relatively stable and not as sensitive to tenant vacancies as small buildings such as duplexes and fourplexes.
- There is usually a good resale market, depending, of course, on location, vacancy rates, cash flow, expenses, and the economy.
- Opportunity for profit is generally good, depending on the variables noted above.
- Financial leverage in terms of borrowing on equity and cash flow is generally good.
- Rents and, therefore, profits are often responsive to upgrades and renovations; if you buy an apartment building at a price based on its expected return, then upgrade the building or improve its profitability, the new sale price would reflect the more attractive net revenue figure and justify an attractive profit on sale.
- A well-located and well-maintained apartment building generally appreciates in value at least with the inflation rate. However, the potential for appreciation is related to an anticipated cash flow increase in the future (no rent control) or land value increase due to an attractive location.

## Disadvantages

- Rents may be subject to provincial rent-control legislation, thereby limiting increases in cash flow. This has a more significant impact in a large apartment building than a single-family home or small, multi-unit dwelling.

- Apartment buildings require more extensive management than other types of properties. Inferior management can quickly lead to increased turnover and rising vacancies.

- Maintenance costs (elevators, swimming pools, heating systems) can be expensive.

- If construction quality is poor, the apartment can deteriorate rapidly, thereby increasing operating expenses. If rent control exists, revenue may not be increased sufficiently to offset increased expenses. A related factor is the risk of considerable depreciation of the building, which reduces the refinancing and sale potential.

- If the local market changes (say, significant unemployment), vacancy rates may increase. This risk is particularly great in a single-industry community.

- If interest rates drop, many renters will opt to become first-time home-buyers due to the increased amount of mortgage funds available and attractive rates. This would especially be so in a buyer's market. The practical effect is that there could be a sharp drop in apartment occupancy rates, resulting in negative cash flow.

- New construction of apartment buildings can create competition for tenants due to an oversupply of units on the market.

- Increased property tax assessments on apartment buildings as a result of a change in municipal tax-base policy or new zoning regulations can result in increased expenses and decreased operating profit.

## Factors to Consider When Selecting an Apartment Building

There are many factors to consider when selecting an apartment building, most of which will be covered in the next chapter. Others include:

- monthly net income (after expenses);
- quality of construction and condition of the building (affects operating expenses); a detailed property inspection report is a must;
- quality of existing management;
- potential for increased revenue and reduced expenses;
- physical attractiveness of property (affects rent levels and demand);
- amenities;

- mix of apartment units (studio, one, and two bedrooms) will affect demand and whether the apartments attract singles, couples, or families;

- rent control or the prospect of rent control;

- overall real estate investment climate;

- degree and type of competition;

- history of vacancy and occupancy rates among buildings in the community generally and in the specific building in particular;

- demographics and trends in the community, including where tenants come from;

- federal and provincial tax incentives or tax policies favourable to apartment investment, not only in terms of annual net profit but capital gains on resale; and

- availability and attractiveness of financing terms and rates, including the possibility of vendor-take-back mortgage.

Make sure that you get competent professional legal and tax advice before signing any agreement of purchase and sale. Buying an apartment building is a complex business and real estate investment decision, and the potential pitfalls are many. (Refer to Chapter 7, "Understanding the Tax Aspects," and the section on tax tips on page 226 when purchasing a revenue property.)

## Raw Land

Possibly you are buying raw land so you can build a year-round house or a vacation cottage. If so, take into account many factors, including the cost of servicing the land in order to prepare it for construction, assuming the land is not already in a subdivision. (See also the sections "Single-Family House" on page 45 and "Recreational Property" on page 57.)

If you are buying raw land with no building on it, however, for the purpose of holding it as a future investment, you should be aware that it is one of the most speculative and risky types of real estate investment. On the other hand, if you are purchasing the land at a reasonable price and you can afford (preferably with cash or a large down payment) to reduce any monthly debt servicing, or if the land is attractive to you and is purchased as a long-term investment without any expectation of profit in the near future, then purchasing raw land might be an appropriate option to consider. In addition, if the land is large enough and has good soil, you may be able to generate some revenue by leasing it out to a farmer.

Those who buy raw land and profit from it tend to be sophisticated investors who tie up the property with an option-to-purchase agreement (with a nominal amount paid for the option), spread the risks by going into the purchase with a group of other investors, do their research beforehand, know that the property will increase in value due to rezoning or subdivision potential, or plan to hold it for future development or sale. In other words, you need to be clear and objective about your goals and the degree of risk you are willing to take.

There are inherent problems, though, if you are intending to buy raw land for investment purposes. Due to the risks involved, you should expect a higher rate of return on your investment. Here are some of the advantages and disadvantages.

## Advantages

- Raw land is available at a relatively low cost.
- There is high potential gain if the land is rezoned, subdivided, developed, or if it increases in value for other reasons such as the building of a road, highway, public transit, or if sewers are installed proximate to the property.
- Diversification of real estate investments—that is, by investing in different types of real estate, you are spreading your risk and therefore minimizing your overall financial and investment risk.

## Disadvantages

- No income will be generated, so there will be a negative cash flow. You have to subsidize the debt servicing of expenses such as a mortgage, interest, and property taxes yourself, unless you paid the entire cost in cash.
- If the land cannot be converted to a better use or if prospects, such as the expansion of the community, do not materialize, the investment could lose money through debt-servicing costs, real estate sales commission fees, reductions in value to other prospective purchasers, or lack of interest by other investors.
- The municipality may place zoning or environmental restrictions on the use of land, such as restricting uses to agriculture only.
- The municipality might expropriate the land to expand a highway, designate the land as green space, or request a right of way over part of the land.

- Financing from banks and other lending institutions to purchase the land is more difficult to obtain because of the speculative nature of raw land and the lack of income to service the debt.

- Using raw land as security or collateral for raising money for other investment purposes is difficult for the same reasons as noted earlier, so using leverage (borrowing on equity of property) on raw land is reduced.

- The Canada Revenue Agency (CRA) generally considers the profit obtained from the sale of raw land as income from speculation, not a capital gain from an investment. The result is that you will pay more tax. If it were considered a capital gain, you would be taxed on 50 per cent of the net profit. (Refer to Chapter 7, "Understanding the Tax Aspects.")

## Summary

This chapter discussed the main categories of property available when deciding to invest in condominiums, houses, property for renovation, recreational property, multi-unit buildings, apartment buildings, and raw land. The various options available within many of these main categories were also explained. The next chapter deals with how to find and evaluate a property.

# CHAPTER 3

# Finding and Evaluating the Right Property

**Whether you are** buying a principal residence or investment property, you want to make money on resale and avoid problems and expenses during the interim. Ideally, you want to buy low and sell high. You also want to minimize stress and inconvenience, and maximize tax-free or after-tax profit. There is a good prospect of doing so if you follow the guidelines outlined in this chapter and the rest of the book. This chapter explains the main factors to consider when selecting a property, where to find a property for sale, and how to determine its value.

## What to Consider When Selecting a Property

There are many factors to consider when selecting real estate for use as a principal residence or for investment purposes. In general, a combination of factors will determine your decision to buy in a particular area. It is important to make a final assessment based on an objective review of the realistic investment potential, taking into account the various factors. This section discusses where to get general and specific real estate information, and the types of issues to consider. Refer to Checklist 1 on page 356 of the Appendix for an outline of many of the factors you should consider and compare in properties that interest you.

### Researching a Property

The quality of the investment decision you make will depend on your understanding of both the general and specific trends and economic factors affecting a given property. There are many sources of information, depending on your available time, personal priorities, and the amount of effort you are willing to expend. The saying "knowledge is power" holds true; the more information you have, both general and specific, the more you'll know about the opportunities and make the right decision. Since each market is different, general trends may or may not have a direct bearing, but they will give indications.

Other factors in your specific geographic area will influence demand and prices. The sources discussed here are arranged under four headings: general information, statistical information, neighbourhood information, and other sources.

## General Information

### Newspapers

Online publications haven't completely displaced the humble newspaper. The best publishers have adapted to the new online environment, and some have even formed alliances with publishers of online databases and newsletters. Canada's two national papers—the *Globe and Mail* (www.theglobeandmail.com) and the *National Post* (www.nationalpost.com)—provide coverage of financial and economic issues and trends, as well as regular features and reports on real estate. Subscribing to them is worthwhile, and, remember, the subscription fee qualifies as a tax-deductible expense against any income from your business or investment.

The same holds true for many of the several city papers, daily and weekly, as well as real estate–oriented papers serving specific communities and regions. In addition to market information, they may also highlight social or economic issues affecting the specific neighbourhood in which you hope to invest. Many of the smaller publications are available free of charge, while the best of the bunch are typically available by subscription. Scout the options and find which ones best serve your needs. Many will be available online or at your local library if you want to check out the content before subscribing.

### Books

While this book will get you started, a number of other titles on general investing practices, the responsibilities of a landlord, and business and economic issues will help you hone your investment activities. Public libraries as well as your local independent bookshop, Indigo (www.chapters.indigo.ca), and Amazon (www.amazon.ca) will give you an idea of what's available. Some titles are available as e-books.

### Online Sources

The Internet is a valuable research tool, and with a few clicks of a mouse you can set up Google (www.google.ca) to send you daily alerts delivering news that may be pertinent to your investment plans and existing portfolio. In addition, online data is a valuable complement to libraries. You may want to double-check the sources you find online, but with some discernment, you will be able to tap into a wealth of information that will serve your needs as an investor.

## Courses and Seminars

Courses and seminars provide other ways to increase your awareness and enhance your decision making. Continuing studies programs at schools, colleges, and universities offer real estate and general business management courses from time to time. Also, practical courses on home buying, building, and renovating are offered to the general public by homebuilder industry associations. (For a list of local associations, check the CHBA [www.chba.ca] and the CMHC [www.cmhc.ca] sites).

## Trade Shows

Local home or renovation shows, where you can pick up ideas and contacts and attend seminars, are excellent sources of information.

## *Statistical Information*

Knowing what other people think about the economic situation is good. Being able to look at the raw data yourself and understand what it's saying to your specific situation is even better. The following resources will put many of the common sources of market statistics at your fingertips, and allow you to judge for yourself what the market is doing. Being able to trot out key numbers can help you make a case for yourself, or drive a hard—but fair—bargain when it comes to buying or selling properties.

## Statistics Canada

Statistics Canada (www.statcan.gc.ca) is the federal government department that collects, crunches, and circulates information relating to population movements, general trends, census details, socio-economic profiles, and other demographic data. The Daily is a daily summary of the latest statistical information from Stats Can, which also makes a wealth of information available online for free. Other information is available for a fee. If you take time to familiarize yourself with their site you'll find much of what you need, from neighbourhood-specific demographic data to big-picture industry analyses.

## Canada Mortgage and Housing Corporation

Canada Mortgage and Housing Corporation (www.cmhc.ca), also known as CMHC, is a federal Crown corporation whose main business is guaranteeing mortgages and providing support to home owners and developers. It also collects and distributes invaluable historical data and analyses of housing trends including starts, completions, vacancies in rental housing, and renovation intentions. It has superb sources of information, and can provide personalized research consulting services for a fee if you need information about a specific area. Many of the free publications are downloadable from their website or available upon request. Other publications are available at market cost. Some of the most valuable CMHC publications for investors include:

- *The Housing Market Outlook* (semi-annual), which covers projections of market activity in communities with a population of 100,000 or more;
- *Rental Market Reports* (annual) for all areas with a population of 100,000 or more, and has stats for communities of 10,000 or more;
- *Local Housing Now* (monthly) covers new and resale home stats for the same type of community populations as noted above; and
- *National Housing Observer* (annual) for new and resale homes.

## Real Estate Associations

Typically, local real estate activity is monitored by a board representing local real estate offices and their agents. Most boards keep statistics on historical prices in their geographic area and release this information on a regular basis. This information is also supplied to the provincial association made up of all the boards in the province. Nationally, the Canadian Real Estate Association (www.crea.ca) represents the various provincial real estate associations and local boards.

The information contained in the boards' and associations' reports will give you insight into local market conditions, including the number of listings available in a given month, sale times, and pricing information. This will help you determine where a particular market is in a cycle, and whether or not the area is ripe for investment.

Here are the real estate associations for the various provinces and territories:

- Alberta Real Estate Association (www.areahub.ca)
- British Columbia Real Estate Association (www.bcrea.bc.ca)
- Manitoba Real Estate Association (www.realestatemanitoba.com)

- Newfoundland and Labrador Association of Realtors (http://boards. mls.ca/nl/)
- New Brunswick Real Estate Association (www.nbrea.ca)
- Nova Scotia Association of Realtors (www.nsar-mls.ca)
- Ontario Real Estate Association (www.orea.com)
- Prince Edward Island Real Estate Association (www.peirea.com)
- Quebec Federation of Real Estate Boards (www.fciq.ca)
- Association of Saskatchewan Realtors (www.saskatchewanrealestate.com)
- Yukon Real Estate Association (www.yrea.ca)

Websites for each association should include links to recent statistics, typically in reports, publications, or press releases.

## Real Estate Firms

Associations have a mandate to provide unbiased information, but individual real estate offices and brokerage houses also track market activity and produce reports. The information may also be unbiased, but each office may have variations in the methodologies used for compiling the data. Some firms produce more detailed reports than others; some examine specific trends while overlooking others. Tapping into these reports' insights and collating them with what the associations provide as the official line will broaden your knowledge of the market, and give you a perspective you wouldn't have otherwise considered.

Both residential and commercial real estate firms produce reports, usually on a quarterly and annual basis. Most reports are available for the asking because they're a good way for the brokerage to keep its name in front of potential clients; they'll often be available for free download from the brokerage's website, too.

Some of the firms to contact for reports for residential properties include:

- Century 21 Canada (www.century21.ca)
- Coldwell Banker Canada (www.coldwellbanker.ca)
- RE/MAX Canada (www.remax.ca)
- Royal LePage (www.royallepage.ca)

For commercial offerings, contact:

- Avison Young (www.avisonyoung.com)
- Colliers International (www.colliers.com)

- CB Richard Ellis (www.cbre.com)
- Cushman & Wakefield (www.cushmanwakefield.com)
- DTZ Barnicke Ltd. (www.dtzbarnicke.com)

A key report is the *Royal LePage House Price Survey*. It provides information on the current estimated fair market value of homes, the prices three months earlier and one year earlier, and the year-to-year percentage change. Estimated average taxes and average monthly rentals are also indicated. Four different categories of single-family housing are surveyed, together with a standard and luxury condominium high-rise apartment. Each housing type and its amenities are specifically described, permitting value comparisons across the country. This includes many regional construction variances for which adjustments have been applied. Naturally, the quality of location has a major influence on real estate values. The properties surveyed are deemed to be within average commuting distance to the city centre and are typical of other housing in the neighbourhood. The survey will also give you an idea of price and rental trends in a particular location.

Royal LePage also produces a biannual recreational property report that reviews key destination locations across Canada. Its summer report typically reviews cottage and lakefront properties, while the winter report rounds up ski hill properties and chalets.

## Real Estate Agents

Agents are a vital source of housing information in the geographic area of interest that you are considering. (How to select and effectively use an agent is covered on page 106 in Chapter 4, "Selecting Your Advisory Team.") A real estate agent can locate a great deal of information for you through the multiple listing service (MLS) system, such as price comparisons, historical data and trends, listing profile of property, and more. You can also do your research on the www.mls.ca site.

## Banks and Credit Unions

Banks and credit unions often produce reports examining both general and sector-specific trends relating to real estate. RBC Royal Bank (www.rbc.com/economics/) and Scotiabank (www.scotiacapital.com) are two key and respected sources of information, particularly with respect to affordability and long-term trends. The research typically looks at both national and provincial trends, and sometimes includes sections focusing on larger metropolitan areas. To access the reports, simply go to the publications section of the banks' websites.

## Neighbourhood Information

Real estate investing is more than a numbers game. It's also a question of location and the social activities and policies that affect that location. This is why it's important to consult information available through city hall and municipal agencies if you're unfamiliar with a particular location, or want to know more about the neighbourhood in which you're considering an investment.

## Municipal Planning Department

The municipal planning department should be able to advise you if there is a development planned in the community of interest to you. This includes apartment buildings, condominium complexes, shopping centres, or highway expansions, for example. You could also enquire if there is any potential rezoning that might affect the property you are considering. Check to see if there have been any natural disasters such as flooding or mudslides that could affect your property. Also, find out how many building permits have been issued. Which areas have the greatest new construction and renovation activities? If you are interested in applying for rezoning, building a new house, or renovating an old house, ask for the following material as your circumstances dictate: zoning maps and regulations; building codes, permit application forms, and instructions; municipal codes; and regional master plans.

## Economic Development Department

The economic development department is normally associated with the municipality or regional district. Its function is to stimulate economic activity and employment in the area. The department should have information about long-term growth plans that will have a positive economic impact on the community. This includes the locations of the growth. Purchasing a residential property near a future growth area could enhance your financial return (e.g., public transit, major shopping malls, or office development).

## Municipal Tax Department

Find out how property taxes are calculated. Your municipality might have a high commercial tax base, which effectively subsidizes the residential tax base, thereby keeping residential taxes down. Maybe your municipality is growing rapidly and is becoming, in effect, a bedroom community with lots of families. If the supply of schools and teachers in the municipality is low and the demand is increasing, property taxes could go up to finance the school construction and teacher recruitment.

If you are buying for retirement purposes, you may not want to pay property taxes for services you will not use immediately. Check to see if there are any major property tax increases planned in general and why, and specifically for the property you are considering. In the latter case, a new drainage system or lane paving could be passed on directly to the property owners affected.

## Municipal Police Department

Check with the local police department for statistics related to crime in the neighbourhood you are considering. Compare the crime rate with other communities. Determine if it is increasing or decreasing. An increasing rate may indicate buying opportunities, or a deteriorating neighbourhood where there could be little draw for tenants and increasing management issues. A declining crime rate might also indicate buying opportunities, and the possible gentrification and ascendancy of the neighbourhood.

## Municipal Fire Department

Ask the fire department about the frequency of fires in the neighbourhood you are considering, relative to other areas in the general community. If there are a high number of fires, the neighbourhood could be a risk area, especially if arson is suspected. Also ask about the incidence of false alarms in the neighbourhood you are considering. This also gives an indication of potential problems.

## Other Sources of Information

### Neighbours

Don't forget to ask the people in the area you are considering how they enjoy the neighbourhood. Would they buy there again? Which specific features about the neighbourhood do they like or dislike? What is the ratio of owners to renters? Ask for feedback that gives you some feeling for the quality and stability of the community. Whether you are thinking of buying a principal residence or an investment property, these issues are important for peace of mind as well as resale potential.

## Professional Associations

The several professions and trade associations that work with real estate in Canada may also have insights regarding the neighbourhood and properties you're considering for your investment portfolio. Many professional associations are happy to provide referrals to accredited members in your specific area, or a directory you can consult to make your own choice. Some key associations include:

- Appraisal Institute of Canada (www.aicanada.ca)
- Canadian Association of Home and Property Inspectors (www.cahpi.ca)
- Canadian Home Builders' Association (www.chba.ca)
- Royal Architectural Institute of Canada (www.raic.org)

## Important Factors to Consider

Some of general features and factors are discussed below. Certain issues might be more important if you are buying for personal use (principal residence) rather than as a revenue real estate investment. Remember to refer to Checklist 1 on page 356 of the Appendix when you are making your selection.

## Location

One of the prime considerations is the location. How close is the property to schools, cultural attractions, shopping centres, recreational facilities, work, and transportation? How attractive is the present and future development of the area surrounding the property? You could invest in a property and six months later discover a high-rise complex being built across the street from you, blocking your view and decreasing the resale value of your property. The location should have ample access to parking and other attractive features. Check on the amount of traffic on the streets in your area. Heavy traffic can be a noise nuisance as well as a hazard for young children.

## Noise

Thoroughly assess the noise level. Consider the proximity of the property to roads, highways, driveways, parking lots, playgrounds, and businesses. If you are buying a condominium, also consider the location of the garage doors, elevators, garbage chutes, and the heating and air conditioning plant or equipment.

## Privacy

Privacy is an important consideration and has to be thoroughly assessed. For example, ensure that the sound insulation between the walls, floors, and ceilings of your property is sufficient to enable you to live comfortably without annoying your neighbours or having your neighbours annoy you. If you have a condominium or townhouse unit, such factors as the distance between your unit and other common areas, including walkways, roads, and fences, is important.

## Price

The price of the property you are considering should be competitive with that of other, similar offerings. On the other hand, if you are purchasing a condominium unit, it is sometimes difficult to compare prices accurately without taking into account the different amenities, such as tennis courts, swimming pools, and recreation centres, that may be available in one condominium but not available in another. You may decide that you do not want these extra facilities in view of your lifestyle needs, in which case paying extra for the unit because of these features would be unattractive. On the other hand, you have to look at the resale potential, so check with your realtor. He or she can obtain accurate information on comparative pricing and cost per square foot for similar properties.

## Common Elements and Facilities

If you are buying a condominium unit, review all the common elements that make up the condominium development. Are they relevant to your needs? What are the maintenance or operating costs required to service these features?

## Parking Facilities

Is the parking outdoors or underground? Is there sufficient lighting for security protection? Is it a long distance from the parking spot to your home? Is there parking space available for a boat, trailer, or second car, and is there ample visitor parking?

## Storage Facilities

Check out the type of storage space available, including its location and size. Is there sufficient storage space for your needs, or will you have to rent a mini-locker to store excess items?

## Quality of Construction Materials

Look thoroughly at your building and the surrounding development to assess the overall quality of the development. If you are buying a condominium, keep in mind that you are responsible for paying a portion of the maintenance costs for the common elements. You may wish to hire a contractor or building inspector whom you trust to give you an opinion on the quality and condition of the construction before committing yourself. An older building will obviously cost money to repair, possibly a considerable amount of money over a short time.

## Design and Layout

When looking at a building, consider your present and future needs. For example, if you are buying a condominium, although you are entitled to use the interior of your unit as you wish, there are restrictions relating to the exterior of your unit or any structural changes that you may make to the unit. If you intend to add a separate room for an expanded family, in-laws, or an office, if that is possible, you should consider the implications beforehand.

For example, you may find that the balcony is very windy and you would like to build a solarium. There is a very good chance that you would not be able to do so without the consent of the condominium council because it would affect the exterior appearance of the development.

## Neighbours

Look at the surrounding area and determine whether the value of the residences in the neighbourhood will affect the property value. For example, are the homes in the area well maintained? Are there children in the same age group as your own? Who lives in the neighbourhood? Are they single adults, young couples, families, or retired people? Chatting with the people neighbouring the property you're considering buying may also provide insights into the area, and how they'll respond to the plans you have for your investment.

## Owner-Occupiers versus Tenants

If you are buying a condominium, ask how many tenants as opposed to owners there are or will be in the condominium complex, and the maximum number of tenants allowed; the higher the percentage of owner-occupiers, the better the chance that there will be more pride of ownership and therefore more responsible treatment of common elements and amenities. If you are purchasing a house, the same principle applies. Generally you should be concerned if the tenant percentage in the condominium complex or residential area is 25 per cent or more and is increasing.

## Management

If you are buying a condominium unit or apartment building, find out whether the building is being operated by a professional management company, a resident manager, or if it is self-managed. (This is discussed in more detail in Chapter 10, "Managing Your Property.") Ideally, you should check out the condominium unit or property that you are interested in at three different times before you decide to purchase: in the day, in the evening, and on the weekend. That should give you a better idea of noise level, children, or parties, and the effectiveness of the management control.

## Property Taxes

Compare the costs of taxes in the area that you are considering with those of other areas equally attractive to you. Different municipalities have different tax rates and there could be a considerable cost saving or expense. Also, find out if there is any anticipated tax increase and why.

## Local Restrictions and Opportunities

Check if there are restrictions on use and other matters. For example, is there a community plan? What type of bylaw zoning is there, and is it changing? Is there a rezoning potential for higher or different use? Is there a land-use contract? What about non-conforming use of older or revenue buildings?

## Rental Situation in the Area

If you are thinking of purchasing a revenue property, find an area that enjoys high rental demand. This will minimize the risk of vacancies, both short- and long-term. The twice-yearly rental reports from CMHC (www.cmhc.ca) are especially helpful, while the *Royal LePage House Prices Survey* (available at www.royallepage.ca) details average house rentals in the area. Census data also provides a snapshot of the proportion of owned versus rental households in an area (visit www.statcan.gc.ca). Too many rental households in a given area will not only increase competition, it may reduce the overall desirability of the neighbourhood for homeowners; conversely, a neighbourhood with a high proportion of homeowners may be this way because it lacks features that attract renters, such as nearby services and amenities including shops, laudromats, and transit.

## Stage of Development

A geographic area will typically go through a series of stages, phases, and plateaus over time. For example, the normal stages are development (growth), stabilization (maturing, plateauing), conversions (from apartments to condos), improvements of existing properties, decline of improvements (deterioration), and redevelopment (tearing down of older buildings and new construction, with more efficient use of space).

## Economic Climate

The economic climate is a major factor to consider. What is stimulating the economy, not only in terms of renters but actual homebuyers? Is there new development such as shopping centres, house and condo construction, office buildings, franchise outlets, and other commercial activity? Will the provincial or federal government construct or move offices to the community? Is a major single-industry employer the main source of economic activity in the area? In the latter case, you can appreciate the risk involved if the industry or main employer has financial problems or decides to close down or move away.

Conversely, in many major Canadian cities, the high commercial and residential rent in the downtown and long commute times to and from the suburbs inhibit employee retention. For this reason, many companies are moving their operations to the suburbs, where rent and land costs are cheaper and commute times are shorter.

## Employment

Employment is, of course, related to the economic climate. The closer the tenants live to their workplace, the lower the turnover will be. The closer the workplace to the employee, the higher the demand will be if you sell your property.

## Population Trends

Look for the trends in the community you are considering. Who is moving in or out, and why? What is the average age? Type of employment? Income level? Family size? Ethnic origins? Marital status? Many of these demographic statistics can be obtained from Statistics Canada or from your provincial or municipal government. If the population is increasing, it will generally create more demand for rental and resale housing. Conversely, if it is decreasing, the opposite will occur. If the population is older, people may prefer down-sizing to condominiums rather than buying smaller houses. There are many variables to consider.

## Size and Shape of Lot

The size and shape of a lot may affect the opportunities you have as an owner to subdivide and rezone the property, its marketability at resale, and its enjoyment by current users (a tiny lot with no yard may be a disincentive, for example, to a family with young children).

## Transportation

A prospective tenant or homebuyer will want to have convenient transporta-tion routes. Whether it's a bus, subway, rapid transit, freeway, ferry, or other mode of transportation, the quality of transportation will have a bearing on your rental or resale price.

## Topography

The lay of the land is an important consideration. If the property is low-lying (adjacent to a rise or hill), water drainage problems could result. Water could collect under the foundation of the house, thereby causing settling, assuming there is only soil under the foundation. Maintaining the property in terms of cutting the grass could be more difficult if the ground is uneven rather than level. These are just some of the issues to consider.

## Appearance

Look at the appearance of the property you are interested in. Would it be attrac-tive to someone else if it is resold? Is it well maintained, or does it need repair? What do the other buildings in the neighbourhood look like? Are they new, renovated, or attractive? Or are they poorly maintained with peeling paint, uncut grass, broken windows, and trash lying about?

## Services in the Community

Different services available in the community—for example, shopping, churches, community and recreational facilities, playgrounds or parks, and schools—will attract different types of tenants or purchasers, depending on their needs.

## Climate

If you are buying for personal use and eventual resale or buying as an investment, climate is an important consideration. Certain areas of the city or community may have more rain, snow, and wind than others, depending on historical climate patterns.

## Unattractive Features

Look for factors that will have a negative influence on a prospective tenant or purchaser: unpleasant odours from an industrial plant; overgrown trees blocking the sun; a lack of street lighting that impairs safety; inadequate municipal services such as septic tanks rather than sewer facilities, unrepaired roads, or open drainage ditches. Being aware of these negative features will also assist you in your decision making and negotiating approach. (This is covered in more detail in Chapter 9, "Buying Your Property.")

## Convenient Proximity

If you are buying real estate as an investment, it is prudent to purchase within a four-hour drive of your principal residence so you can conveniently monitor and/or maintain your property. This is just a general guideline, of course.

## Reasons for Sale

It is important to determine is why the property is for sale. Maybe the vendor knows something you don't, which will have a bearing on your further interest. On the other hand, maybe the vendor wants to move to a larger home or downsize to a smaller home or condo, plans to separate or divorce and move out, has lost employment, needs to relocate for a job, or is seriously ill or incapacitated. (A more detailed discussion of a vendor's motives is covered in Chapter 9, "Buying Your Property.")

# Where to Find a Property for Sale

Discovering the right property doesn't only require you to understand the market and the kinds of listings that are available in a given neighbourhood. You also have to have a strategic plan in hand that will guide your decision-making process:

- Be clear about what type of real estate you want and which area you are interested in; this will save time and stress. (Chapter 1, "Understanding Real Estate Investment," deals with determining your real estate strategies.)

- Target specific geographic area(s). This makes your selection process much simpler and gives you an opportunity to get to know specific areas thoroughly. Obtain street maps of the area as well as a zoning map from city hall.

- Know your price range based on your available financing and real estate needs.

- Determine the type of ideal purchase package that you want (the price and terms) as well as your bottom-line fallback position. What is the maximum you are willing to pay, and what are the most restrictive terms with which you are comfortable? Make sure that you don't compromise your own position.

- Do comparisons and shortlist choices. That way you can ensure you get the best deal, in comparative terms.

- Be realistic in terms of your purchase conditions in accord with the current market situation. Many people fantasize about buying investment real estate for 20 per cent or more below the fair market value and keep searching for this elusive purchase. The reality is such a purchase is very difficult to find.

- Don't wait for mortgage rates to go down before looking. Higher mortgage rates generally mean less demand in the market and therefore lower prices and more negotiating leverage for the purchaser. Conversely, lower mortgage rates generally mean more demand in the market and therefore higher prices and less negotiating leverage. These are guidelines only. The key is to buy at the right price, taking all the factors outlined in this book into consideration. If mortgage rates come down, you can renegotiate a lower mortgage rate with or without a penalty, depending on the mortgage you originally negotiated.

- Remember, the location of a property is very important, especially for a principal residence. Location is, of course, also important for investment property, but it has to be balanced against overall investment goals such as tax benefits, appreciation, resale potential, and net revenue.

- Consider the issue of distance between your prospective investment property and where you reside. It really depends on several factors, such as type of investment, size of investment, and amount of management required. If it is a small investment, you may want to be close to the property so that you can visit it, manage it, attend to any problems, and show vacant suites. If it is a large investment, you may consider hiring a resident manager or professional management company. In this situation, you could live a considerable distance away, even in a different province.

Once you've reviewed these points and established a plan relative to your broader investment strategy, dig into the many sources of information that will let you know what properties are available and will let potential vendors know you're interested in buying what they have to offer.

## Real Estate Agent

An experienced real estate agent is an invaluable asset. A realtor can save you time, expense, and frustration, and provide advice and expertise. Remember that the vendor pays the real estate commission whether the agent is a listing or selling broker. (Refer to page 170 in Chapter 6, "Understanding the Legal Aspects," for a discussion of real estate listing agreements. Refer to page 106 in Chapter 4, "Selecting Your Advisory Team," for a discussion on selecting realtors.)

There are many advantages to using realtors. You can use their services to source properties listed on multiple or exclusive listings, or for property being sold by the owner. You can also use them to contact owners who wish to sell a property, but who haven't listed it yet. The advantage of using realtors to source unlisted properties is that they might be able to negotiate a better deal for you than you could get yourself.

There are strategic benefits to having an agent present the offer and negotiate on your behalf. Frequently, the owner will agree to pay a commission to the realtor if you buy, although the commission for an unlisted sale would generally be less because the realtor has not spent money or time actively promoting it. Alternatively, you could arrange to pay the realtor a negotiated fee if he or she arranges a sale at a price attractive to you.

If you use a realtor to assist your search, be loyal to him or her if you purchase the property. On the other hand, if the realtor is disinterested, then find another. Give your agent a list of your requirements so the agent can refine the search for you. For example, if you want to buy a house, give the agent information such as:

- price;
- location;
- style of house;
- age of house;

- number of bedrooms;
- square footage;
- basement or non-basement;
- self-contained suite with its own kitchen and bathroom suitable for rentals, or no self-contained suite;
- lot size;
- exposure of lot;
- fireplace;
- ensuite bathrooms or laundry facilities;
- zoning.

## Multiple Listing Service

Multiple listing service (MLS) data provides excellent information about residential properties. Current listings are posted on the MLS website (www.mls.ca); a sister site lists commercial properties (www.icx.ca). However, a real estate agent would be able to assist you in your historical or comparative research by accessing the source MLS database, which is unavailable to the general public. When reviewing listings, you should be alert to clues regarding vendor motivation or the appropriateness of the property for your purposes. This could assist you in negotiating a lower price. For example, look for the exact area; when the property was listed (how long ago); if it has been relisted; whether the property is vacant; if any price reductions have occurred (for how much and when); and whether there has been a previous collapsed sale. Remarks with the listing may indicate why the property is for sale, such as a court-ordered sale/power of sale action (or simply note that the vendor "must sell"), a relocation, or something as simple as "vendor bought another house." All this information is important.

With respect to court-ordered sale proceedings, commonly known as foreclosures, a keen investor may wish to connect with real estate agents or lawyers who keep abreast of such opportunities. This will keep you alert to what is moving through the courts, as well as opportunities listed for sale through MLS.

## Newspaper Ads

Despite the rise of online venues, newspapers continue to host a wide range of ads for new and resale properties. The classified section of your local daily or community newspaper will features listings under the headings "Houses for

Sale," "Homes for Sale," "Condominiums for Sale," "Revenue Property for Sale," or "Apartments for Sale." The weekend section tends to have the most listings, but almost all the ads will also be posted to the newspaper's website and potentially shared with other online publishers. Many regions and cities in Canada also have papers geared to real estate sales, making them a treasure trove for serious buyers and sellers.

Many ads are designed to entice you with the impression the owner is anxious, implying that you may be able to get a better price. This may or may not be the case, so approach listings with a critical eye and ask questions if you follow up. Watch for ads that imply the offering is subject to time pressures, such as "estate sale," "owner transferred," or "foreclosure sale."

Develop an organized system when reviewing ads. You may wish to clip or print copies of ads that interest you, writing relevant notes and questions on the back. Your checklist of questions will keep you on track so that you have information for comparative purposes. Retaining the listings for properties that interest you may be wise, as some properties may rise or fall in price, helping you to gauge not only where the market is heading but what you're willing to pay.

Many newspaper ads for real estate will be the "sale by owner" type, allowing you to deal directly with the vendor. On the other hand, you may wish to advertise your interest in buying properties. Some property owners will be watching the market to know when it is a time good to sell, and if you're in the game then you stand a chance of being considered first. An ad in the "Real Estate Wanted" or "Property Wanted" section of the daily or community newspaper serving the area you're considering may net you some offers, either by the owner or their real estate agent. Be precise about your needs in the ad, or many people may waste your time phoning you for clarification. Develop a standard checklist of questions to ask the callers. That will save you time and frustration. Get right to the point to obtain the information you need.

## Direct Offer to Owner

In the process of becoming familiar with a particular neighbourhood, you might see a property that is not currently for sale but whose owner might be interested in selling. Look for clues that the property is vacant—uncut lawns, peeling paint, broken windows or fences. A weathered for-rent sign may signal a long-term vacancy and an owner keen to sell the underperforming property—one that you might be able to turn around.

Once you have determined which properties might seriously interest you, identify the owner by searching land title records and the local registry office. These documents are a matter of public record. You could do the search yourself or through a lawyer or realtor. You may discover other information in your search, such as when the existing owner bought it and for how much, the nature and amount of mortgage financing, and if there are any legal problems relating to the property such as liens, judgments, foreclosures, or power of sale. If you want to pursue it further, you could contact the owner yourself, or preferably have your lawyer or realtor contact the owner.

During boom times, some potential purchasers or their realtors engage in targeted mailings or distribution of leaflets in areas where they think owners might be willing to sell. The leaflets often state what the prospective purchaser is willing to pay, in order to attract interest. This strategy is worth considering, but the effort and cost may outweigh the results because the recipients of the notice may not have any intention of selling at any price.

## Drive through the Neighbourhood

As mentioned earlier, it is important to become familiar with the area you are interested in. Drive through the area regularly and look for for-sale signs, both properties listed with a realtor and for sale by owner. Note addresses, names, telephone numbers, and other contact information.

## Word of Mouth

Tell your friends, neighbours, relatives, or business associates that you want to buy property, the type of property you are looking for, and the area where you are interested. They might hear of someone who is thinking of selling or see a property for sale in their neighbourhood that might interest you.

# Determining the Value of the Property

One of the most important steps is determining the value of the property you are considering. In other words, how much should you pay for it? In theory, a property is worth whatever a buyer is prepared to pay for it. There are various appraisal techniques that you can use, and that are used by professionally qualified appraisers. In addition, there are rules of thumb that real estate investors often use with revenue property. These rules of thumb are guidelines only. There are limitations to some of them, in terms of their accuracy or acceptance.

Appraising a property value is more an art than a science. Two pieces of property are seldom identical. When a professional appraiser writes a report, the estimate of value is given as an opinion, not a scientific fact. This is helpful to you as a basis for negotiation with the owner. Anyone can have an opinion as to value. The appraisal, though, is only as reliable as the competence, integrity, experience, and objectivity of the appraiser and the accuracy of information obtained. Real estate appraisal is only as reliable as the assumptions that are made. There are distinct benefits to having a professional appraisal. The main reasons for an appraisal would be to determine the following:

- a reasonable offering price for purchase purposes;
- allocation of the purchase price to the land and building (revenue property);
- a property's value for financing purposes (your lender will require this);
- a property's value at death for estate purposes;
- a property's value when converting the use from principal residence to investment (rental) use, or vice versa, which would be for CRA capital gains determination purposes, unless you are exempt from this provision (more detail is covered in Chapter 7, "Understanding the Tax Aspects");
- a reasonable asking price for sale purposes;
- the amount of insurance to carry;
- a feasibility study of a purchase;
- property-assessment appeal preparation;
- litigation preparation;
- expropriation negotiations;
- taxation records or appeal preparation.

There are several professional designations for property appraisers in Canada. They subscribe to uniform academic, professional, and ethical standards, and are regulated by their professional associations. The most common national designations are Accredited Appraiser Canadian Institute (AACI) and Canadian Residential Appraiser (CRA). There are other national and provincial appraisal designations as well as specialty appraisal areas, such as industrial and commercial. The Appraisal Institute of Canada (www.aicanada.ca) offers more information.

Here are some of the basic methods or rules of thumb that professional appraisers, real estate investment lenders, and homebuyers use. Even if you just use the market-comparison approach initially, you should be familiar with the other methods and their limitations, especially if you intend to invest in revenue real estate.

## Market-Comparison Approach

This approach is probably the most easily understood concept for a first-time homebuyer or investor. It is also the most common approach that real estate agents use for single-family dwellings. In effect, it is comparison shopping— comparing properties that are similar to the one you are considering.

Because no two properties are exactly the same due to age, location, lay-out, size, features, and quality differences, you need close variables with which to work. Compare properties whose sale dates are as current as possible so that they reflect the same market conditions. To make more realistic comparisons when you determine prices of comparable properties, you may have to take into consideration such matters as the circumstances of the sale (such as a forced sale due to financial problems, order for sale, or foreclosure), special features of the property (including flower garden, shrubs, arboretum), and location of property if it offers special views or exclusive privacy.

The market-comparison approach lends itself to situations where the properties are more numerous; there are more frequent sales, so they are easier to compare. Condominiums, single-family houses, and raw land are the most common types of properties for which to use the market-comparison method. At least it gives you a general sense of the appropriate value.

See Checklist 1 (page 356) and Form 9 (page 350) in the Appendix as guides for comparing properties. Generally, when an appraiser is doing a market comparison, he or she compares recent sales of similar properties, similar properties currently listed for sale on the market, and properties that did not sell (listings expired). The limitation of the market-comparison approach is that similar properties may not be available for comparison in a particular situation. Also, it is difficult to know the vendors' motivations, so in some cases the sale price might not reflect the fair market price.

For example, if you are comparing a condominium for sale against two other identical condos in the same complex that have sold very recently, the data will give you a fairly close comparison. You could calculate the cost per square foot of the two recent condo sales and compare these costs against the cost per square foot of the one you are considering.

If that latter price is higher, you need to know why. Perhaps it has a better view, is on a higher floor, or maybe the previous owner made many interior decorating changes to improve the condo. The point is that the market-comparison approach does have its limitations and provides general guidelines only.

If you are buying an apartment revenue property, some appraisers use various market-comparison approaches to determine value.

- One approach is to calculate the average price per unit for comparison. For example, if the "average" price of comparables were $50,000 per apartment and the property you were considering had 10 apartments, the purchase price in theory would be $500,000. The problem with this price-per-unit rule of thumb is that it is probably the least reliable in determining the value of a revenue property. When the appraiser researches the area and prepares a list of comparable revenue properties, the following types of factors are, ideally, similar amenities, appearance, size, location, rent structure, condition, and dates of sale. The problem is that it is difficult to find similar comparables in apartment buildings that are reliable. There can be so many variables. The result in terms of estimated market value can therefore be artificial and unreliable. There are more reliable methods for estimating value that will be discussed later.

- Another approach to determining the value of an income property involves calculating the income per square foot of the building, and comparing this figure with comparable properties. To do this, you calculate the amount of income-generating square footage in the building (excluding square footage of common areas, hallways, and lobbies). Once you have this figure, you can divide it by the gross revenue from rents to end up with the income per square foot. This approach also has some of the limitations mentioned in the point above.

## Cost Approach

This approach involves calculating the cost to buy the land and construct an equivalent type of building on the property you are considering with appropriate adjustments, and then comparing the end prices. If you calculate that the replacement cost is below market value, you might want to seriously consider the benefits of buying a lot and building on it, in terms of cost savings. This approach comes, of course, with its own advantages and disadvantages. There are various steps involved in arriving at a figure using the cost approach.

## Step 1

Estimate the land value, using the market-comparison approach discussed earlier. The sale price of similar vacant residential lots in the area should be determined, with adjustments made for such factors as use (zoning), size, location, and features (view).

## Step 2

Estimate the cost to construct a new building that is comparable in square footage, features, and quality to the one you are considering. For example, a modest-quality construction could be $100 per square foot to replace, whereas a luxury-quality construction could be $200 per square foot to replace.

## Step 3

If the house you are considering is not new, you will have to calculate a depreciation factor, that is, the reduced value of the building as it wears out over time. Calculating the depreciation adjustment factor depends on the building's condition, age, and estimated useful life. Estimated useful life means the point beyond which the building is not economical to repair or maintain. In effect, it would have no market value. If that is the case, you might be buying primarily for lot value and intend to tear down the building or substantially renovate it. A professional appraiser is usually required to calculate this depreciation factor.

## Step 4

To determine estimated property value, add the depreciated cost of the building (Steps 2 and 3) to the cost of the land (Step 1).

For single-family houses and condominiums, the appraiser normally arrives at an estimate of value as of a certain date by adding the market and cost approach values, and dividing by two. An example of this is shown below.

## Example of Estimate of Market Value

This estimate uses market and cost approaches, which is the usual formula for evaluating properties such as houses and condominiums. If you were buying a revenue property (such as an apartment building), you would normally add the income approach and then take an average of all three approaches.

1. Market-Comparison Approach

   Compare four similar properties whose prices were $150,000, $155,000, $160,000, and $157,500. The average price is therefore $155,625.

   | | |
   |---|---|
   | Market approach estimate: | $    155,625 |

2. Cost Approach for Land

   30-foot × 150-foot lot =

   | | |
   |---|---|
   | 4,500 square feet at $10 per square foot | $  45,000.00 |
   | Value of improvements on land, such as shrubs, trees, fence, garden, tool shed | $    7,500.00 |
   | Construction of building is 1,000 square feet at $100 per square foot construction cost (new) | $    100,000 |

   Less 5 per cent depreciation per year because building being purchased is two years old:

   $100,000 − 5% = $95,000 (Year 1), and

   $95,000 − 5% = $90,250 (Year 2)

   | | |
   |---|---|
   | Therefore, depreciated value of building | $  90,250.00 |
   | Cost approach estimate: | $ 142,750.00 |
   | Final estimate of market value: | $ 149,187.50 |

   (Market value is determined by the following formula.: Market approach estimate of $155,625 plus cost estimate of $142,750 divided by two equals $149,187.50.)

The limitation of the cost approach is that depreciation might be difficult to correctly estimate. In addition, construction costs vary, depending on location, supply and demand, and inflation. Again, the cost approach value is only an estimate.

## Income Approach

This approach is the most common one used when estimating the value of income property. In practical terms, though, you will probably use a combination of all three approaches to determine the value of a revenue property. In addition, there are other rules of thumb for revenue investment property that will be discussed later.

Basically, the income approach assumes that the value of the property is the present worth of the future cash flow that the property is expected to generate. For example, the property is worth X times its annual net operating income.

As mentioned, the income approach cannot be viewed in isolation. It is important to use it in conjunction with the previous two approaches so you can consider factors affecting the overall investment climate, such as interest rates, taxes (municipal, provincial, and federal), rent controls, inflation, cost of land, cost of construction and materials, comparative property prices, and supply and demand (of tenants and competitive rental buildings). When you calculate the value of income property for your own investment purposes, be conservative and use the lowest evaluation. Depending, however, on the nature of the property, your investment goals, and the objective of the appraisal, one approach may be better than another.

The most common income approach used by lenders and appraisers to determine a fair market value is the capitalization method. The purpose is to project the value of a property based on the amount, certainty, and length of time of future flow of income (income stream), and then place a dollar value on that future income stream by applying a capitalization rate. The capitalization (or "cap rate," as it is commonly known) is a rate of return used to derive the capital value (total value) of an income stream.

For example, the net operating income (NOI), which is the amount remaining after all expenses of the property have been met but before taxes, is "capitalized" at a certain percentage (say, 10 per cent) to determine a value of a property. If a building is producing an NOI of $30,000 and that is capitalized at 10 per cent (or sometimes referred to as "cap rate of 10"), then the fair market value would be $300,000. In other words, to achieve a cap rate of 10, the property would deliver an NOI of $30,000 relative to the $300,000 paid for the property.

This formula that every investor should understand is commonly known as the IRV formula:

$I$ = Income or, more specifically, net operating income (NOI)

$R$ = Rate or, more specifically, capitalization (or cap) rate

$V$ = Value or, more specifically, fair market value (FMV)

The basic formula is $I \div R \times V$

As long as you know at least two of the three items in the formula, you can determine the third item by removing it from the formula and calculating out the remaining item; in other words, rearranging the components of the formula. For example, the values of $I$, $R$, and $V$ can be obtained as follows:

net operating income (I) = cap rate × market value, or I = R × V

*Question:* If you are prepared to pay $245,000 for an income property and you want a 9.5 per cent return on your investment, what net operating income would be required?

*Answer:* Separate out the unknown factor and fill in the other two letters (factors) with the known information:

I = R × V = .095 (9.5%) × $245,000 = $23,275

Therefore, you would need a net operating income of $23,275.

capitalization rate (R) = net operating income divided by market value,
   or R = I ÷ V

*Question:* A property generating a net operating revenue of $25,000 a year is priced at $220,000. What is the cap rate on the investment?

*Answer:* Separate out the unknown factor.

R = I ÷ V = $25,000 ÷ $220,000 = 11.3%

Therefore, the cap rate is 11.3 per cent. In other words, as an investor, you will earn an 11.3 per cent return on your $220,000 investment (ROI).

market value (V) = net operating income divided by cap rate,
   or V = I ÷ R

*Question:* A property is to be capitalized at 11.5 per cent. It has a net operating income of $16,000. How much can you justify paying for it if you want to obtain an 11.5 per cent return on your investment (ROI)?

*Answer:* Separate out the unknown factor.

V = I ÷ R = $16,000 ÷ .115 (11.5%) = $139,130.43

The most you could justify paying will therefore be $139,130.43.

You can see the benefit of the IRV formula in terms of a quick analysis of the key factors. It is important to remember that the formula does not take financing or mortgages into account. All the results obtained are based on the assumption that the property is clear of all financing.

The IRV formula is also helpful when comparing similar properties. When deciding what cap rate to use for your investment purposes, remember your investment objectives and the degree of risk you are prepared to take. Ideally you will want at least a cap rate of 10 per cent (higher than that is better) in terms of your return on your investment. Different investors have different cap rate criteria.

The factors taken into account include the type of property (small or large apartment building); age (the older the building, the less future income can be derived from it in its present state); location (the closer the building to the tenant base, the better); and quality of tenancies (long-term leases are preferable to month-to-month). As a rough rule of thumb, a low-risk investment or area (or anticipated low inflation in the area) should have a minimum 8 per cent cap rate; a medium-risk investment or area (or anticipated medium inflation in the area) should have a minimum 10 per cent cap rate; and a high-risk investment or area (or anticipated high inflation in the area) should have a minimum 12 per cent cap rate. The greater the risk, the greater the premium you will want in terms of a higher cap rate.

Another method of estimating the approximate cap rate value for a building you are interested in is taking the average of the cap rates of comparable properties in the same geographic area. You can also contact a professional appraiser familiar with the area and type of income property, and request approximate cap rates.

Remember, if you can get a totally risk-free investment return from Canada Savings Bonds, Treasury bills, or term deposits of 6 per cent (or whatever the prevailing rate would be at any given time), for example, you will want to buffer your risk by ensuring the overall income property package is attractive. (Refer to Form 8, which is an income approach worksheet, as well as Form 9, which is an investment property analysis worksheet, on pages 348 and 350 in the Appendix.)

## Percentage of Operating Expenses

Once you start comparing various revenue properties in your area, you will see an average overall pattern in terms of the proportion of the various operating expenses relative to the gross income. In Canada, apartment-building expenses tend to be between 35 and 45 per cent of the gross income. That can vary, of course, depending on the circumstances. If you see that the percentage reflected by the vendor's information supplied to you is less than 35 per cent or more than 45 per cent, for example, you should thoroughly verify the data independently.

You should also confirm the accuracy of the information. Some vendors can be less than forthright in order to make the investment picture appear more attractive. If you rely solely on the vendor's information and it turns out you were misled because it was inaccurate or incomplete, you could lose a lot of money.

Look for individual expense variances from the norm. For example, if the insurance cost is 2 per cent when the norm should be 5 per cent, then the building might be underinsured, and you will have to pay more in insurance premiums to protect your investment. If the property-management-fee percentage is lower than normal, the management company may not be providing adequate management, or is new and inexperienced and gave a low quote to get the contract.

If the resident manager's costs are too low compared to the normal percentage, possibly the reason is that the costs are artificial. The real costs to hire someone if you buy the building could cost more because the owner's family is performing all the on-site management and not taking a fair market payment for the services provided.

Again, refer to Form 8, which is an income approach worksheet showing the various categories of expenses, and Form 9, which is an investment property analysis worksheet. Before you make any final decision to purchase a particular revenue property, do a projected cash flow statement (Form 5 on page 344), a projected income and expense statement (Form 6 on page 346), and a projected balance sheet (Form 7 on page 347). In other words, you need an accurate idea of what you can make from the property based on realistic projections. The initial analysis you did of the property just dealt with the current situation. Realistic projections will tell you if the current financial analysis will improve or worsen over time. Of course, your professional accountant should thoroughly review all the financial statements of the revenue property for inaccuracies, inconsistencies, shortcomings, and false or unrealistic assumptions.

## Gross Income Multiplier

You may hear of real estate investors who use the gross income multiplier (GIM) formula. You should understand how it works. It is an inaccurate method of determining a property value, not only in absolute terms, but in relative terms to other properties. You may wish to use it, but only in combination with the other more realistic rules of thumb described.

Investors use different GIM multipliers, depending on their investment objectives and other factors. For example, if an investor uses a GIM of 6, the annual gross income (say $40,000) would be multiplied by 6 to determine the maximum value of the property. In this example, it would be $240,000. The problem is that the GIM method does not take into account such critical factors as mortgage payments or operating expenses, so the formula is rather artificial. Say the average range of operating expenses for the type of income property in the geographic area you are considering is 35 to 45 per cent, as discussed in the previous section. The GIM formula does not take into account that the property you are looking at could have costly operating expenses, at 70 per cent, for example. Therefore, the GIM of 6 would arrive at a greater value than the property is really worth. Also, you could be locked into a long-term, high-interest closed mortgage with a six-month interest penalty or cancellation. Current mortgage rates could be 4 per cent lower, for example. The GIM does not reflect these factors. On the other hand, the property could be very efficiently operated and have operating expenses of 30 per cent and a long-term, low-interest mortgage. The property could therefore be worth more than six times the gross income. Remember, from an income property purchase viewpoint, the lower the GIM, the better.

The GIM basic formula is:

gross income multiplier = market value ÷ effective gross income

or GIM = MV ÷ EGI

or MV = GIM × EGI

or EGI = GIM × MV

Effective gross income means the actual current income, not a projected or potential income.

Another application of the GIM usage is to determine the amount of time it would take to pay back the investment. The GIM calculated tells the investor how many years it would take to recover the total investment costs (purchase price) if all the gross income were allocated to pay off the purchase price. Again, this formula has limitations, of course, because it is rather artificial in that you would, in reality, be paying operating costs from the gross income. It is just another yardstick to use. For example, if an investor is considering an investment with an asking price of $700,000, and the effective gross income in the first year is $100,000, the GIM would be 7:

GIM = $700,000 ÷ $100,000 = 7

Therefore, in theory, if all the gross income were used to pay for the original total property cost, it would take seven years to recover the total cost of the investment.

## Net Income Multiplier

The net income multiplier (NIM) is a more reliable way to determine the number of years it will take to recover the initial investment outlay from the future net income from operating the revenue property. Conversely, the formula will help you determine the maximum price an investor would be prepared to pay for the property.

Net operating income (NOI) is a frequently used term in investment real estate. It is basically income produced by the property after all operating expenses and allowances for vacancies have been removed, but before mortgage payments.

For example, if you apply an NIM of 10 as your investment formula, and the NOI of a property is $30,000, you would place a maximum value that you would pay of $300,000 for the property. The formula is:

$$MV = NIM \times NOI$$
$$MV = 10 \times \$30,000 = \$300,000$$

The NOI formula is more accurate because all the variables in the building operation, such as rental income, vacancies, and operating expenses, have been accounted for. The only variable that has not been accounted for—because it varies, of course—is the cost of mortgage financing. This is the one factor that can affect the accuracy of the NIM rule of thumb, in terms of the bottom-line income. For example, what may appear to be a good investment because of the NOI would not be so attractive if there was a high-interest, long-term closed mortgage with a large penalty clause. That is why you have to consider the limitations of the NOI multiplier formula and make allowances for it.

The basic formula for determining the NIM is:

$$\text{net income multiplier} = \text{market value} \div \text{net operating income or}$$
$$NIM = MV \div NOI$$

For example, if an investment property has a purchase price of $600,000 and the net operating income is $60,000, the NIM multiplier would be 10. This number is also used for payback calculation purposes; for example, it would take 10 years to recover the total investment cost if all the net operating income was applied for that purpose. Conversely, the overall capitalization rate is the reciprocal of the NIM (10)—that is, 10 per cent. In other words, you would be receiving a 10 per cent return on your initial purchase price outlay relative to the NOI.

## Internal Rate of Return

The internal rate of return, sometimes referred to as the IRR, is a calculation that some investors use to determine how much they will make annually on their investment. There are many factors that have to be taken into account to increase the accuracy of the results; for example, mortgage principal reduction, anticipated property appreciation, anticipated inflation, and after-tax cash flow.

Realistically, when you are projecting your final return on your investment upon sale, that is your true net profit. You also have to take into account such additional factors as the amount of capital gains tax on sale of the property, closing costs on sale, legal fees, real estate commissions, and mortgage penalty if there is a closed mortgage at the time of the sale. In addition, you have to calculate any projected interest you might be able to earn on the excess cash flow, if it is a positive cash flow. Such factors as your projected personal income tax rate also have to be estimated. This can vary, of course, but for projection purposes you have to make certain assumptions, such as percentage of appreciation and inflation.

Most IRR calculations are done on a computer spreadsheet program. At the bottom of the printout you will see the IRR percentage. For example, the IRR might show an annual return of 25 per cent. You might intend to keep the investment for five years and sell it, assuming the market conditions are favourable. Normally, the IRR figure would initially exclude the inflation factor. You will also want a calculation with inflation projected to make sure that your intended investment, in real value of money terms over time, exceeded inflation as much as possible. It does have some limitations as well, in terms of assumptions. As the IRR calculation is initially based on estimates, the IRR itself is only an estimate of the expected return on your investment capital. Your professional tax adviser can tell you more.

This section has covered some of the most common types of techniques for establishing the value of a property purchase. There are many others that experienced or sophisticated investors may use in addition to the ones noted. Some of the techniques described are easier to calculate than others. Some are more accurate and reliable than others. Some require computer spreadsheet analysis. The important point is to understand the basic concepts and to know when to apply them, to know their limitations, and to use several different formulas to provide some balance when comparing other properties as well as the property itself. The key benefit of these methods is that they can often be quickly calculated to determine if the owner is asking too much, if a property meets your personal investment criteria, or to determine if the property is a bargain. Remember, the rules of thumb are only guidelines. The calculations could also provide you with negotiating leverage to have the purchase price reduced. You will, of course, want to consider other factors before making your final decision.

Also keep in mind that the values are only estimates. You may not be prepared to pay the estimated price for various reasons, such as:

- price is more than you can afford;
- price is higher than your comfort level in terms of risk;
- market is starting to decline;
- economic turndown; or
- you are waiting for more attractive property in which to invest.

Conversely, you might be prepared to pay more than the estimates suggest. Here are some of the factors that might lead you to pay more than the estimates indicate:

- Confidential Information. You might be aware of a possible zoning change, subdivision potential, or proposed development nearby.
- Financing. You might be able to obtain favourable financial terms, such as a low-interest, vendor-take-back mortgage or high-ratio financing.
- Potential for Income. The property could have a basement suite.
- Attractive Closing Date. You could get a long closing date, enabling you to get funds that you are expecting from various sources, or to get access to higher mortgage financing by closing, or to sell the agreement of purchase and sale to someone else (almost like having an option).
- Your Income Tax Bracket. Depending on your personal situation, you may be able to offset a negative cash flow against your other income and thus buy the property at a discount price because of the negative cash flow. You would then be relying on the factor of appreciation and a capital gain over time. You might also have a lower return on investment benchmark.

## Summary

This chapter discussed the many factors to consider when selecting a property, as well as where to find a property for sale. The various methods and formulas for determining the value of a property were explained. Now that you know the type of property that interests you and how to evaluate it, it's time to introduce you to the team of professionals you will need.

# 4

# Selecting Your Advisory Team

**When starting out** in real estate investment, whether you are purchasing a principal residence or an investment property, it is important to have a team of experts and professionals to assist you in achieving your goals. The team should consist of a realtor, lawyer, accountant, lender, financial planner, mortgage broker, building inspector, and insurance broker. Common selection criteria for each will be covered first, followed by specific selection criteria. At the end of this chapter is a list of useful websites of interest.

## Common Selection Criteria

You should be very selective in your screening process. The right selection will enhance your prospects for profit and growth; the wrong selection will be costly in terms of time, money, and stress.

There are many factors you should consider when selecting advisers. For example, the person's professional qualifications, experience in real estate investment, and the fee for services are factors you need to consider. It is helpful to prepare a list of such questions, plus others relating to your specific needs, to ask the prospective advisers. Some people may feel awkward discussing fees and qualifications with a lawyer, for instance, but it is important to establish these matters at the outset before you decide to use that person's services. The most common selection criteria include qualifications, experience, compatibility, confidence, competence, communication skills, accessibility, objectivity, trust, integrity, references, and fees. It is best to interview and compare at least three candidates before you select the one suitable for your needs.

### Qualifications

Before you entrust an adviser with your work, you will want to know that he or she has the appropriate qualifications. These may include a professional degree in the case of a lawyer or accountant, or some other professional training or qualifications relative to the area of work.

## Experience

When assessing the adviser's experience, it's important to consider the degree of expertise, the number of years of experience, and the percentage of time spent offering a service in that area. How much you rely on a lawyer's advice and insights, for example, is obviously related to his or her experience; just because a lawyer has been practising for 10 years does not necessarily mean that her or she has expertise in real estate. Perhaps only 10 per cent of the practice has been spent in that specific area. An accountant who has had 15 years of experience in small-business accounting and tax advice will certainly provide you with a depth of expertise about small business in general. If that accountant has experience in the real estate investment area, this is an important factor. Inquire about the adviser's degree of expertise and length of experience in real estate deals. If you don't ask the question, you won't get the answer, which may make the difference between mediocre and in-depth advice.

## Compatibility

When selecting an adviser, make certain that you feel comfortable with the individual's personality. If you are going to have an ongoing relationship with the adviser, it is important that you feel comfortable with the person's degree of communication, attitude, approach, candour, and commitment to your real estate investment. A healthy respect and rapport will put you more at ease when discussing business matters and thereby enhance your further understanding.

## Confidence

You must have confidence in your adviser if you are going to rely on his or her advice to enhance the quality of your decision making and minimize your risk. After considering the person's qualifications, experience, and personality, you may have considerable confidence in the individual. If you do not, don't use the person as an adviser because there is a very good chance that you will not use him or her as extensively as you should or when you need to. This in itself could have a serious negative impact on your decision making.

## Communication Skills

You want an adviser who is a good listener, who elicits your responses, and provides feedback in understandable layperson's terms. Any issues and options should be fully disclosed, with pros, cons, and recommendations.

Your adviser should return your phone calls promptly and keep you regularly informed in writing. Some people and situations require more frequent communication than others.

## Accessibility

If your adviser becomes too busy for you, reconsider the relationship. Your needs should be a priority. If you are shunted to a junior adviser against your wishes, your original adviser may be culling clientele to concentrate on more lucrative clients.

## Objectivity

If advice is tainted in any way by bias or personal financial benefit, obviously it is unreliable and self-serving. Get a minimum of three opinions on your particular situation before carefully deciding which professionals to select.

## Trust

Whether the person is a lawyer, accountant, financial planner, or other adviser, if you don't intuitively trust the advice as being solely in your best interests, never use that person again. You have far too much to lose, in terms of your financial security and peace of mind, to have any doubts whatsoever. You cannot risk the chance that advice is governed primarily by the adviser's financial self-interest, with your interests as a secondary consideration.

## Integrity

Your adviser should have a high standard of personal and professional integrity. The adviser's reputation with other professional colleagues is one reference point. Maintaining the confidentiality of information is another.

Depending on the nature of the advisory relationship, you may disclose your personal needs, wants, hopes, and dreams, as well as concerns. This puts you in a potentially vulnerable position.

## References

References and word-of-mouth referrals are particularly important when selecting any adviser who will be taking an overall holistic approach to your financial affairs. Ask for professional references, contact those professionals, and ask about the adviser's strong attributes and any professional weak points. Also, ask how long they have been dealing with each other. Don't feel embarrassed to ask the tough questions—candid feedback can provide you with a revealing reality check.

Don't ask for or expect an adviser to provide you with a list of clients as this would normally breach confidentiality.

## Fees

It is important to feel comfortable with the fee being charged and the payment terms. Are they fair, competitive, and affordable? Do they match the person's qualifications and experience? For instance, if you need a good tax accountant to advise you on minimizing taxes, you may have to pay a higher hourly rate for the quality of advice that will save you several thousands of dollars. On the other hand, if what you require is the preparation of annual financial statements, perhaps a junior accountant can do the job competently at a more affordable rate. You may want to hire a bookkeeper to do your books, or do them yourself. There are some excellent accounting software programs to manage your real estate investments. (This is covered on page 272 in Chapter 10, "Managing Your Property.") Be certain the rate is within your budget, or you may not fully use the adviser effectively because of the expense. Not using available professional advice when you need it is poor management. Ask about the estimated fee at the outset.

## Comparison

It is a good rule of thumb to see at least three advisers before deciding which one is right for you. The more exacting you are in your selection criteria, the more likely it will be that you will find a good match and the more beneficial that adviser will be to your real estate investment goals. It is a competitive market in the advisory business, and you can afford to be extremely selective when choosing advisers to complement your real estate team.

# Selecting a Realtor

There are distinct advantages to having a realtor act on your behalf when buying or selling a property. As in any profession, there is a range of competence among the many real estate salespeople throughout Canada, but with careful due diligence you can minimize the risk and benefit greatly from the skills of a knowledgeable and sincere realtor.

Over the past several years, a new relationship structure, sometimes referred to as agency disclosure, has replaced the old system. Many people assumed that if they found a realtor and the house was listed on the multiple listing service (MLS), for example, the realtor would represent their interests exclusively when an offer was presented and through negotiation.

The new system spells out the respective roles and responsibilities of each realtor involved. The seller still pays the real estate commission, which is shared with any other realtor involved. All disclosure of who is acting for whom is spelled out in the agreement of purchase and sale. Some agents working with the buyer may also enter into a buyer agency contract. In other words, each realtor is acting exclusively for the benefit of the buyer or seller. However, if the listing realtor is also the selling realtor (double-end deal), the agent has to enter into a limited dual agency agreement. This is agreed upon and signed by both the buyer and seller. The agent modifies his or her exclusive obligations to both the buyer and the seller by limiting it primarily to confidentiality as to each party's motivation and personal information.

You can get more information from any real estate agent, real estate company, or your local real estate board.

## Qualifications

Real estate agents are regulated by provincial government real estate legislation. Agents have to successfully complete an approved real estate agent licensing course and renew their licence annually.

## How to Select a Realtor

There are a number of approaches to finding a good real estate agent:

- Ask friends, neighbours, and relatives for the names of agents they have dealt with, and why they would recommend them.
- Go to open houses for an opportunity to meet realtors.
- Check newspaper ads that list the names and phone numbers of agents who are active in your area.
- Check for-sale signs for agents' names and phone numbers.
- Check the Internet.
- Contact real estate firms in your area; speak to an agent who specializes or deals with the type of property you want and is an experienced salesperson.

After you have met several agents who could potentially meet your needs, there are a number of guidelines to assist you with your selection. Look for an agent who is:

- knowledgeable about the neighbourhood where you are interested. Such an agent will be on top of the available listings, will know comparable market prices, and can target the types of property that meet your needs as you have explained them;

- familiar with the buying and selling of residential and revenue properties;

- experienced and knowledgeable in the real estate industry;

- prepared to prescreen properties so that you are informed only of those that conform to your guidelines for viewing purposes;

- familiar with the various conventional and creative methods of financing, including the effective use of mortgage brokers;

- thorough on properties you are interested in, in terms of background information such as length of time on the market, reason for sale, and price comparisons among similar properties. An agent who is familiar with the MLS can find out a great amount of information in a short time, assuming the property is listed on the MLS;

- candid with you in suggesting a real estate offer price and explaining the reasons for the recommendation;

- effective at negotiating to ensure that your wishes are presented as clearly and persuasively as possible;

- working on a full-time basis, not dabbling part-time;

- attempts to upgrade his or her professional skills and expertise;

- good with numbers; in other words, one who is familiar with the use of financial calculations and can therefore assist in clarifying the revenue property analysis aspects; and

- highly effective with the Internet when acting for a vendor or purchaser.

You should give the agent your exclusive business if you have confidence in him or her because the agent will devote considerable time and energy to your needs. Keep the agent informed of any open houses in which you are interested. Advise any other agents that you have one working for you. Review the section about listing agreements on page 170 in Chapter 6, "Understanding the Legal Aspects." Focus clearly on your needs and provide the agent with a written outline of your specific criteria to assist in shortlisting potential prospects. If for any reason you are dissatisfied with the agent who is assisting you, find another agent as quickly as possible.

## Benefits of a Realtor to the Purchaser

There are obvious benefits to the buyer of using a realtor as outlined in the previous points. One of the key benefits is that the realtor can act as an intermediary between you and the listing broker. That way, the listing broker may never meet you and therefore cannot exert any influence on you with aggressive salesmanship, or otherwise make an assessment of you that could compromise your negotiating position. The agent who has the listing agreement with the vendor would know you only through discussions with the realtor you are dealing with and through any offer that you might present. This arm's-length negotiating position is an important strategic tactic that will benefit you. This is discussed further on page 255 in Chapter 9, "Buying Your Property."

Another advantage to a buyer is the opportunity for the realtor to access a multiple listing service, which can provide instant, thorough, and accurate information on properties that might interest you. Without an agent searching for you, you seriously minimize your range of selection and the prospect of concluding the deal at an attractive price.

## Benefits of a Realtor to the Vendor

There are extensive benefits to listing your property with a realtor rather than attempting to sell it on your own. A realtor can:

- list your property on the multiple listing service as well as the Internet, which provides extensive exposure throughout and beyond your market area;

- prequalify and prescreen potential homebuyers so that only serious buyers who have the interest and financial resources present an offer;

- provide information to the purchaser on matters such as financing and other assistance programs that could facilitate the sale of your property;

- suggest methods of improving the appearance of your property in order to maximize the positive impression and therefore the potential buyer's interest and sale price;

- explain the real estate market in your area, and can provide you with MLS reports on comparable listings or sales patterns in your area; they can also supply other facts and figures to assist you in realistically establishing a market price;

- free up your own time, using all their contacts and marketing techniques in order to effect the sale of your property;

- negotiate an agreement on your behalf and according to your instructions, while you remain at arm's length from the one-on-one negotiating. This improves your negotiating position.

## How Realtors Are Compensated

Traditionally the vendor pays the realtor a commission, which is negotiable. Some are fixed percentages and some are variable, depending on the price involved. Some commissions are a negotiated flat rate, regardless of the sale price. There are different commission structures for residential and commercial properties.

If there is more than one realtor involved, for example, a listing broker and a selling broker, then the commission is normally split based on an agreed formula, such as 55 per cent to the listing broker because he or she incurs more expenses to sell the property, and 45 per cent to the selling broker.

## Resolving Disputes

If you have a dispute with a realtor, keep a record of all your correspondence outlining the complaint. Speak to the realtor first, followed by his or her manager, then the regional, provincial, and national managers. If the complaint is more serious, complain to the local real estate board or provincial agency that licenses realtors.

# Selecting a Lawyer

Whether you are the buyer or the seller of real estate, it is essential that you obtain a lawyer to represent your interests—a standard precaution with any real estate transaction. As you will realize by the time you have finished reading this book, there are many potential legal pitfalls for the unwary when buying real estate. The agreement for purchase and sale and related documents are complex. For most people, the purchase of a home or other investment property is the largest investment of their life, and the agreement for purchase and sale is the most important legal contract they will ever sign.

## The Selection Process

There are a number of ways to select the right lawyer for your needs:

- Ask friends who have purchased real estate which lawyer they used, whether they were satisfied, and why.

- Contact the lawyer referral service in your community. Under this service, sponsored by the provincial law society or a provincial division of the Canadian Bar Association, you can have a half-hour consultation with a lawyer for a nominal fee (usually $10), which lawyers generally waive to facilitate bookkeeping and PR. To obtain contact information for the lawyer referral service in your province, look in your phone book or search for "lawyer referral service" on the Internet. Make sure you specify that you want a lawyer who specializes in real estate. Contact the law society in your province for further information.

- An online search for specialty lawyers in your area may highlight the best-known firms that address issues like the ones you're facing. For example, "Toronto mortgage lawyers" or "Saskatoon apartment lawyers" will yield some relevant leads.

- If you are obtaining a mortgage, speak to the lawyer who is preparing the mortgage documents on behalf of the lender. If the lawyer you choose is also preparing the mortgage documents, you could save on some duplicated disbursement costs and negotiate a package price. Be cautious, though, to avoid conflict; ensure that the lawyer provides you with a full explanation of the mortgage terms and conditions that might affect your interests. Keep in mind that the mortgage is being prepared on behalf of the bank, but at your expense. If you have any concerns in this area, retain a separate lawyer to do the non-mortgage legal work and explain the contents of the mortgage to you. Alternatively, ask the lender to let you see a lawyer of your choice from the lender's list of approved lawyers.

You may have heard the term *notary public* and assumed that it means the same as *lawyers*. This is not necessarily so. In most provinces a lawyer is also automatically a notary public, but a notary public is not necessarily a lawyer. Make sure you know the difference. A notary public is not formally trained, qualified, or permitted by law to provide a legal opinion on any subject. He or she can only prepare the required transfer of title documentation, necessary affidavit material, and other related documentary material, and file the documents in the land registry office. In other words, the services provided are primarily technical and procedural; therefore, the buyer or seller of a property is advised to consult a lawyer. In matters relating to properties, you need a lawyer to avoid the potential risk and pitfalls involved, and to deal with the matter for you if a legal problem occurs.

In Quebec, lawyers are referred to as *notaries* (non-courtroom lawyers) or *advocates* (courtroom lawyers). Therefore, in Quebec you would use a notary for your property purchase or sale transaction.

Once you have contacted the lawyer over the phone, ask about the areas of his or her real estate interest and expertise. Tell the lawyer that you are looking for a person with expert knowledge in property law. If the lawyer cannot offer this, ask for a recommendation.

If you did not obtain the referral through the lawyer referral service, ask the lawyer over the phone what a half-hour initial consultation would cost. (In many cases it is free.)

Have all your questions and concerns prepared in writing so that you won't forget any. If you wish to make an offer to purchase, bring your offer-to-purchase document with you, and the details about the new, resale, or revenue project you are considering. Ask about anticipated fee and disbursement costs. If you are not pleased with the outcome of the interview for any reason, move on to another lawyer.

## Legal Fee Arrangements

Here are the most common fee arrangements and the types of costs you might encounter.

### Hourly Fee

A lawyer bills a fixed rate per hour for all work done. The fee could range between $100 and $300 or more per hour, depending on specialty expertise, experience, and so on.

### Fixed Fee

If you hire a lawyer to provide a routine service such as a conveyance (transfer of property to your name) or a will, the lawyer may be able to quote a flat fee, regardless of how much work might be involved. For example, a simple will may cost from $200 to $300. A straightforward conveyance could start at $500. Fees can vary based on geographic location, size of community, and so on.

## Percentage Fee

Sometimes fees are calculated as a percentage of the value of the subject matter. This approach is often used when probating an estate. Most provinces have legislation that limits the maximum percentage that can be charged, regardless of the time spent.

## Contingency Fee

Many provinces allow lawyers to charge on a contingency-fee basis, that is, for a percentage of the total amount awarded if the case is won. This is negotiable, but can vary from 25 to 50 per cent depending on the nature of what is being done. For example, let's say that you have a strong case, but do not have the funds to pay your lawyer at the outset. Your lawyer may agree to act for you and charge a percentage of the amount that you eventually receive, either at trial or settlement. If you lose or the matter is not settled, the lawyer gets nothing for the time spent; however, you would be responsible for paying the lawyer's disbursements.

## *Factors that Affect Legal Fees*

A lawyer considers many factors when setting fees such as the:

- degree of specialization in the specific area;
- number of years in practice;
- amount of time spent on your behalf;
- legal complexity of the matter;
- monetary value of the matter;
- degree of responsibility;
- importance of the matter to the client;
- degree of difficulty in dealing with the issue;
- degree of skill and competence;
- results obtained on the client's behalf; and
- client's ability to pay.

In many cases the legal-fee structure is based on what other lawyers are charging. Although competition in the legal profession is obviously a factor in keeping fees competitive, there are many circumstances when two lawyers will charge a different fee for performing the same routine or specialized service. Always clarify the fee arrangement in writing in advance.

As in any other business relationship, in order to maintain an effective rapport with your legal adviser, good communication is essential. Be certain that you and your lawyer keep each other informed of important matters, so neither is operating without complete information. If you are in doubt about the particular advice you are being given, you may prefer to get a second opinion. This is reassurance that you are following the best advice for your business.

## Resolving Disputes

Misunderstandings on fees or other matters should be immediately clarified to prevent them from becoming serious problems. You may decide at any time to have the working file transferred to a new lawyer. If you have serious doubts about a lawyer's invoice, you can have it "taxed" or reviewed by a court registrar. This is an informal procedure and results in the fee being upheld or reduced. Your local court office will be able to provide further information.

If you feel that the lawyer acted improperly or incompetently, you have other forms of recourse. All provincial law societies require that their members have a certain minimum coverage for professional liability insurance to cover negligence suits. Individual law firms could have additional coverage. If trust funds go missing, the law society allocates funds to cover that situation. Suing your lawyer is an option, but certainly the last resort.

If you have complaints such as possible conflict of interest, poor advice, or other forms of professional misconduct or incompetence, you can file a formal complaint with the provincial law society. The complaints committee has many forms of discipline.

In summary, make sure that you select a lawyer and consult with that lawyer before you commit yourself to any final agreement for purchase and sale.

## Selecting an Accountant

An accountant's chief role is to monitor the financial health of your investment and reduce the subsequent risks and tax payable. Along with your lawyer, your accountant will complement your real estate team to ensure that your investment decisions are based on sound advice and good planning. Some accountants have also obtained their certified financial planner (CFP) certification, in order to offer their clients more comprehensive consulting advice. Refer to the section on "Selecting a Financial Planner" on page 117.

An accountant can help you right from the pre–real estate investment phase. The wide range of services includes:

- setting up a manual or computerized bookkeeping system that both the investor and accountant can work with efficiently;
- setting up a customized software program for real estate investment and management of the properties;
- setting up systems for the control of cash and the handling of funds;
- preparing or evaluating budgets, forecasts, and investment plans;
- assessing your break-even point and improving your profitability;
- preparing and interpreting financial statements;
- providing tax- and financial-planning advice; and
- preparing corporate and individual tax returns.

## Qualifications

Since the term accountant isn't regulated in Canada, anyone can adopt the title without training, qualifications, experience, or accountability to a professional association. It's therefore very important that you select an accountant who has a formal designation. There are three main designations of qualified professional accountants in Canada: chartered accountant (CA), certified general accountant (CGA), and certified management accountant (CMA). Accountants with the above designations are governed by provincial statutes. The conduct, professional standards, training, qualifications, professional development, and discipline of these professionals are regulated by their respective institutes or associations. Rely on the advice of an accountant, therefore, only after you have satisfied yourself that he or she meets the professional qualifications that you require for your real estate investment needs.

There are differences in the educational requirements, training, experience, and nature of practice of the accounting designations mentioned above. Some accountants, such as CAs and CGAs, have public practices that serve specific sectors (such as real estate investors). Other accountants work in industry, education, or government, or specialize in the areas of management, cost, financial, or tax accounting. For further information, contact the professional institution or association for the specific accounting designation and request an explanatory brochure. The professional governing bodies are the Institute of Chartered Accountants (www.cica.ca), the Certified

General Accountants Association (www.cga-canada.org), and the Society of Management Accountants (www.cma-canada.org).

## How to Find an Accountant

- Referrals: Often a banker, lawyer, or business associate will be pleased to recommend an accountant who has expertise in real estate investment. Such referrals are valuable since these individuals are probably aware of your area of interest and would recommend an accountant only if they felt he or she was well qualified and had a good track record in assisting real estate investors.

- Professional Associations: The professional institute that governs CAs, CGAs, and CMAs may be a source of leads. You can contact the institute or association with a request for the names of three accountants who provide public accounting services to real estate investors within your geographic area. Also, check out the provincial associations' websites. Often an initial consultation is free of charge. Always find out before you confirm the appointment.

## Preparing for the Meeting

Prior to a meeting with your accountant, make a written list of your questions and concerns in order of priority. As noted earlier, you will want to know the person's qualifications, areas of expertise, and method of record keeping, such as what type of computer system is used. Ask the accountant what his or her range of experience is in your type of investment—tax, business management advice, accessing financing, and so on. Ask about fees, how they are determined, how accounts are rendered, and what retainer may be required. Ask who will be working on your file—the accountant, a junior accountant, or a bookkeeper. It is common for accountants to delegate routine work to junior staff and keep more complex matters for their own review.

## Understanding Fees and Costs

Accountants' fees vary according to experience, specialty, type of service provided, size of firm, and other considerations. They can range from $40 to $150 or more per hour. A highly skilled tax accountant could charge considerably more. It is common for an accountant to have different charge-out rates for the various activities performed: bookkeeping, preparation of financial statements, tax consultation, and advice. For example, if an accountant is doing bookkeeping, it will be at a lower rate scale; complex tax advice is charged at the high end of the range. Accountants generally charge for their time plus additional costs for a bookkeeper, a secretary, and other expenses. The bill-out rates for these staff members vary and you should ask in advance exactly what you will be charged.

As with your lawyer, a good level of rapport and communication with your accountant will enhance the quality of advice and the effectiveness of your use of that advice. Openly discuss your concerns and questions with your accountant. You may from time to time wish to seek a second opinion on advice you have been given. If you are not satisfied with your accountant for any reason, you should promptly find another accountant who could better meet your needs.

## Resolving Disputes

If you have complaints about fees, service, or conduct, attempt to resolve the dispute directly with the accountant concerned. If that doesn't work, complain to the manager of the firm. Depending on the issues, you can also complain to the provincial professional accounting association. The association can investigate and discipline members. In addition, these provincial professional associations will have a basic insurance package to cover professional liability for negligence or incompetence, as well as missing trust funds. Individual accounting firms may have supplemental professional liability insurance coverage.

## Selecting a Lender

When deciding which bank, credit union, or trust company to deal with for your real estate investment affairs, it is advisable to shop around, especially if you need bank financing. Services and rates vary among branches of the same bank. It is helpful to have a lender who has had experience in the area of real estate investment. As a lender's loan-approval limit will vary from branch to branch, you will ideally want a lender who has a loan-approval level greater than the amount of money that you need to borrow. (More information on dealing with lenders is given in Chapter 5, "Understanding the Financing Aspects.")

## Selecting a Financial Planner

Everyone's financial planning needs are different. The process should take into account all the psychological and financial factors that affect your financial goals and objectives and provide a short-term and long-term strategy. Some financial planners liaise with other professionals—for example, with lawyers, accountants, and insurance brokers—to make sure that the overall plan is integrated. (Refer to Chapter 12, "Understanding Financial and Estate Planning.")

## Qualifications

Anyone can call himself or herself a financial planner; there are no federal, provincial (except in Quebec), or local laws that require certain qualifications, such as those imposed upon lawyers. However, several associations grant credentials that signify a planner's level of education, although criteria can change from time to time, so check with the association. These are some of the most commonly recognized designations:

### Certified Financial Planner (CFP)

CFP is an internationally recognized designation first introduced into Canada by the Financial Planning Standards Council (FPSC). Their website is www.fpsc.ca.

### Chartered Life Underwriter (CLU)

A chartered life underwriter is a financial adviser with advanced knowledge in life and health insurance and estate planning. An adviser with a CLU specializes in advice on insurance and related tax- and estate-planning integration. The CLU designation is awarded by the Financial Advisors Association of Canada. For more information, visit their website at www.advocis.ca.

## How to Find a Financial Planner

Canada does not regulate financial planners, nor have they organized themselves as formally as accountants have. This makes it especially important that you review and interview candidates closely to ensure that they understand your needs and you know what they're able to do for you. Here are some tips for finding a competent financial planner:

- Get referrals from friends, accountants, or lawyers. Do they currently use the planner's services? How long has he or she known the person professionally? What are the planner's strengths and weaknesses?
- The Financial Planning Standards Council (www.fpsc.ca) maintains a directory of those with the CFP designation in your area.
- The Financial Advisors Association of Canada (www.advocis.ca) maintains a directory of its members, who may hold any one of several industry-sponsored designations including the CFP and CLU.

## How to Select a Financial Planner

Once you've made the decision to seek the services of a financial planner, you may have many more questions: Which professional is right for me? How do I identify a competent financial planner who can coordinate all aspects of my financial life?

Just as when you select a lawyer or accountant, base your decision on a number of factors—education, qualifications, experience, and reputation.

When selecting your financial planner, choose one you can work with confidently. It is your responsibility and right to fully inquire about the practitioner's background, years in practice, credentials, client references, and other relevant information. Meet with the practitioner to determine compatibility and financial-planning style. Interview at least three planners before you make your final selection. To work together effectively, it's important to find someone with whom you feel completely comfortable.

## How a Financial Planner Is Compensated

It is important to understand, and be comfortable with, the way your financial planner gets paid. Financial advisers are compensated in one of four ways: solely by fees, a combination of fees and commissions, solely by commissions, or through a salary paid by an organization that receives fees. In some cases, financial advisers may offer more than one payment option. Here is how these different methods work.

### Fee Only

Many lawyers, accountants, and fee-only financial planners charge an hourly rate, including time spent in research, reviewing the plan with you, and discussing implementation options. Others charge a flat amount, but usually offer a free, no-obligation initial consultation. Some will do a computerized profile and assessment of your situation for a fee that can range from $200 to $500 or more.

Fee-only financial advisers typically advise you on investments, insurance, and other financial vehicles, but do not benefit from commissions. The planner has no vested interest in having you buy one financial services product over another. Some fee-only financial planners will help you follow through on their recommendations using mutual funds and other investments. Otherwise, you will have to take your own initiative.

## Commission Only

Some financial advisers are compensated solely through commissions earned by selling investments and insurance, including life insurance, annuities, or mutual funds. A commission-only adviser will develop recommendations for your situation and goals, review the recommendations with you, and discuss implementation.

In some cases, commissions are clearly disclosed, for example, a percentage front-end load commission on a mutual fund. In other cases, the fees are lumped into the general expenses of the product, as with life insurance, so you won't know how much your planner makes unless you ask. When you interview potential candidates, ask about the relative percentages of commission revenues from annuities, insurance products, mutual funds, stocks, bonds, and other products. The candidates' answers will give you a sense of the kind of advice the firm usually gives.

You could also pay ongoing charges that apply as long as you hold an investment. Some insurance companies pay planners trailer fees for each year a client pays premiums. In other situations, you must pay a fee if you sell a product before a set period of time has elapsed. These surrender charges, a percentage of your investment, reimburse the insurer for the commissions it has paid your planner. Some mutual funds require a back-end load fee on early sale. These are usually applied on a sliding scale. After the set time period, you will not be charged. Some companies entice commission-motivated planners with free travel, merchandise, or investment research if their sales of a particular product reach a target level. Your planner might not like your questioning of his or her cash payment and perks; however, it is your right to know whether the products you buy generate direct fees and indirect benefits for the planner in order to decide whether the advice is self-serving or objective.

## Fee Plus Commission

Some planners charge a fee for assessing your financial situation and making recommendations, and also earn a commission on the sale of some of those products.

Some planners are "captives" of one company, so they recommend only its product line. Others are independent and can recommend the mutual funds or insurance policies of any company with which they are affiliated.

Another form of compensation, called fee offset, involves a reduction in fees for every product purchased. If you buy so many products that your entire fee is covered, request a refund of the fee you paid for your basic plan.

## Salary

In most instances, the staff financial advisers at many banks, trust companies, and credit unions are paid by salary, and earn neither fees nor commissions. Of course, there could be other monetary incentives based on the volume and value of the business done or quotas. Career advancement could also be tied to sales performance.

If an adviser helps you select and monitor the purchase of investments or insurance, there will be some cost to you and/or payment to the adviser. This could be in the form of a commission, redemption fees, trailer fees, or asset management fees.

Also, many investments charge annual management and transaction fees. For example, if you open an RRSP, the company that serves as trustee may charge an annual custodial fee for the service. Weekly comparisons of the management-expense ratios of various funds are available in newspapers. These costs will be in addition to the fee for advice.

## What to Know about a Financial Planner

Compensation is just one important element that you should consider when hiring a financial adviser. Be sure that the planner you choose has a defined financial-planning process that addresses your current situation, sets goals, identifies alternatives, selects and implements a course of action, and calls for periodical reviews. It should be a client-centred process. Education, credentials, references, trust, and rapport are also important.

Choose the compensation method that best meets your needs. As a smart consumer, you want to know what you're buying and how much you're paying for it, and you're entitled to that information. Do not consider hiring a financial planner who is reluctant to disclose how he or she is compensated.

Research shows that consumers rate "trust" and "ethics" as the most important elements in their relationship with financial advisers. In fact, survey respondents gave this response twice as often as they mentioned good advice and expertise.

## Resolving Disputes

If you have any complaints about fees, service, or conduct, first attempt to deal directly with the person concerned. If that does not resolve the matter, you can complain to management, the professional association that the adviser may belong to, the national industry association, the provincial regulatory associa-tion, and the provincial securities commission with which the adviser may be registered. Avoid potential advisory problems by pre-empting them through careful selection.

## Selecting a Mortgage Broker

Mortgage brokers are shepherds for investors seeking to navigate their way through the complex landscape of real estate financing. They're familiar with the constantly changing rates, terms, and conditions, and know where to find and secure good deals. Moreover, each lending institution has its own criteria that apply to potential borrowers. Some insist on a particular type of property as security, while others require a certain type of applicant. In the latter case, factors such as type of employment, job stability, income, and credit background are weighed. Lending institutions have a broad range of philosophies and policies on the issue of security and applicant qualifica-tions in order for a lender to advance mortgage funds. (For further informa-tion, refer to Chapter 5, "Understanding the Financing Aspects.")

These factors, among others, affect mortgage approval. The availability or shortage of funds, past experience in a specific area, the perceived resale potential of a particular property, and the attitude of the lending committee (especially if the lender is a credit union) are additional issues that could affect approval of a mortgage.

Mortgage brokers make it their business to know all the various plans and lending policies, as well as the lender's attitude on various aspects of mortgage security and covenants. A mortgage broker is in effect a matchmaker, attempt-ing to introduce the appropriate lender to the purchaser.

Mortgage brokers have access to numerous sources of funds, including:

- conventional lenders such as banks and trust companies (RBC Royal Bank, however, does not work with mortgage brokers);
- credit unions;
- CMHC;
- Genworth Financial Canada;
- private pension funds;
- union pension funds;
- real estate syndication funds;
- foreign bank subsidiaries;

- insurance companies;
- private lenders.

The broker knows all the lenders' objectives; the broker is therefore capable of matching the applicant and his or her property with the appropriate plan and lender. Alternatively, the broker can provide a series of mortgage plans from which the borrower may select the one that best suits his or her needs.

Mortgage brokers offer two types of services:

- They arrange a simple mortgage that will get automatic approval in your particular circumstance, which saves you a lot of time searching. The broker generally receives a commission directly from the lender as a "finder" or "referral" fee. You don't pay any extra money or higher interest. Lenders do this because the mortgage market is so competitive.

- They arrange a more complex mortgage that would not be automatically approved. This takes more time, skill, and persuasion on the part of the broker to source out a lender or number of lenders who will provide the funds you need. For example, if you are unable to provide a conventional down payment, have a negative credit rating, are highly leveraged, or do not have a sufficiently high or stable income, you would probably be turned down by a conventional lender such as a bank, credit union, or trust company.

If a mortgage broker succeeds in arranging your complex mortgage financing, you would pay a commission. The commission could be from 1 to 5 per cent or more of the amount of the mortgage arranged, depending on the degree of difficulty, the urgency of the need for funds, and other factors.

To find a mortgage broker, ask your real estate lawyer or your realtor. You can also obtain the names of mortgage brokers from their provincial association, the Canadian Association of Accredited Mortgage Professionals (www.caamp.org).

## Selecting a Building or Home Inspector

### Qualifications

One of the most important aspects of purchasing your principal residence or investment property is to know the condition of the property in advance. It is a small expense for peace of mind. You don't want to have problems after you buy that will cost you money to repair. You could lose all your potential profit and put your investment at risk.

Make sure when you obtain an inspection that the person doing it is qualified and independent. Ask what association he or she belongs to, if any, and, if not, why not. One of the main associations in Canada is the Canadian Association of Home and Property Inspectors (CAHPI), with various provincial chapters. To become a member of CAHPI, an inspector must meet various professional and educational requirements, successfully complete a training course and write exams, and practise professionally for a trial period before being considered by the association. In addition, there are annual continuing education requirements to ensure that their industry knowledge is kept current. You can check out the CAHPI website (www.cahpi.ca) to get names of members in your area.

The terms *home inspector* and *building inspector* are used interchangeably in terms of independent fee-for-service inspections. These services are different from municipal building inspectors, who approve various stages of a new home construction or renovation as staff of the local government.

## Services Provided by a Building Inspector

A home inspector is an objective expert who examines the home and gives you a written opinion of its condition and, ideally, the approximate range of costs to repair the problems. Home inspectors look at all the key parts of the building, such as condition of the roof, siding, foundation, basement, flooring, walls, windows, doors, garage, drainage, electrical, heating, cooling, ventilation, plumbing, insulation, and so on. They should also look for signs of wood rot, mould, and insects.

The older the building, the more potential problems, but new buildings can have serious problems as well. If the new building is covered by a new home warranty program, then you have some protection. However, that program does have some exclusions, and you don't need the hassle of rectifying a problem. If a new home is not covered by the NHWP, or is not a new property, you definitely want a home inspection; otherwise, you might have to pay to repair the problem if the builder refuses to do so or goes out of business. You can have an inspection done of a house, townhouse, or apartment condominium, or any residential building.

Older homes present a more challenging inspection process, for example, to check for aluminum wiring, asbestos, urea formaldehyde foam insulation (UFFI), lead paint, and termites or carpenter ants.

Quite apart from avoiding expensive surprises, using a home inspector has another potential benefit. If the report shows problems with a quantifiable cost to rectify it, you could use that information to negotiate a reduction in the property's price to reflect the estimated cost of repair. You may not want to buy the home, even if problems can be rectified. At least the report gives some objective professional's opinion on the condition of the home to discuss with the vendor.

Make sure that you put a condition in your offer that says "subject to purchaser obtaining a home inspection satisfactory to the purchaser within X days of acceptance of the offer." This way it will be your discretion as to whether you want to complete the deal or not. In addition to the need for a home inspection, you might also be able to obtain a "vendor's disclosure statement." Real estate boards in some provinces have prepared such a form for vendors to sign, disclosing any known problems with the home. As this is a voluntary program in many cases, ask for the reasons if a vendor refuses to complete the form. Have a professional home inspection done anyway, for obvious reasons. The owner may honestly not be aware of serious problems with the home if they are not visible or obvious.

## How to Select a Building or Home Inspector

It is important to obtain a qualified and independent inspector (see "Qualifications" on page 123). Avoid someone who has a contractor business on the side and may hope to get the repair business from you. Their advice could be self-serving and biased. Apply the same selection criteria discussed earlier in this chapter for other advisers. Search online. Ask friends, relatives, neighbours, or your real estate agent for names of inspection companies they know and recommend. Call several inspectors in your area and interview them. Check with your local Better Business Bureau to see if there have been any complaints against the company that you are considering. Ask for references and check them out.

Home-inspection fees range from approximately $200 to $400 or more depending on the expertise required and the nature of the inspection, the size of the home, its age and condition, your geographic area, the nature of inspection services requested, and other variables. It normally takes a minimum of three hours to do a thorough inspection.

Here are the questions that you should ask when deciding which inspection company to select:

- What does the inspection include? Inspections should include the areas previously discussed under "Services Provided by a Building

Inspector" on page 124. Always make sure that you get a written report and ask for a sample of a report and what will be covered.

- How much will it cost? Determine the fees up front.

- How long will the inspection take?

- Does the inspector encourage the client to attend the inspection? This is a valuable educational opportunity. You will have a chance to see the problems first-hand. You will also learn various helpful maintenance tips. If an inspector refuses to have you attend the inspection, this should raise a red flag.

- How long has the inspector been in the business as a home-inspection firm and what type of work was the inspector doing before inspecting homes?

- Is the inspector specifically experienced in residential construction?

- What and where was the inspector's training? Does the inspector participate in continuing education programs to keep his or her expertise up to date?

- Does the company offer to do any repairs or improvements based on its inspection? This might cause a conflict of interest.

- Does the inspector carry errors and omission insurance? This means that if the inspector makes a mistake in the inspection and you have to pay to rectify the problem, the insurance will cover it. How much insurance does the inspector have and are there any restrictions or exceptions? Will the inspector confirm all that in writing before you make a decision to have the inspection done?

- Does the inspector belong to an association that will investigate any consumer complaint? This is an important point and was covered earlier under "Qualifications."

## Selecting an Insurance Broker

An insurance broker is not committed to any particular company and therefore can compare and contrast the different policies, coverage, and premiums from a wide range of companies that relate to the type of insurance coverage that you are looking for. Also, insurance brokers can obtain a premium quotation for you and coverage availability from insurance company underwriters if the particular investment you have is unique or difficult to cover by other existing policies. Insurance brokers generally have a wide range of types of insurance available. Ensure that the broker is affiliated with a reputable firm.

When selecting an insurance broker, you should ask about the person's professional credentials, expertise, and experience. It is important to have confidence in the broker's background and skills.

Every real estate investment building needs insurance. Creditors such as banks often require insurance. Ask the insurance broker for brochures describing the main type of insurance and an explanation of each. (The main categories and types of insurance that you should consider and discuss with your insurance broker are discussed on page 237 in Chapter 8, "Understanding the Insurance Aspects.")

## Qualifications

Insurance agents are licensed and regulated by the provincial governments. Some agents are tied to a particular insurance company, and will sell only the insurance products offered by that company. However, it has become far more common for property or life insurance agents to operate as brokers and to deal with any number of insurance companies, although officially licensed by one company. If you want a broker for property insurance, make sure they are a member of the Insurance Brokers Association of Canada. If you want life or health insurance, make sure they are members of the Financial Advisors Association of Canada.

## How to Find an Insurance Broker

There are several ways to find an insurance broker:

- Ask your accountant, lawyer, business associates, and friends for a recommendation.
- Ask your business, trade, or professional association whom they would recommend.
- Check with the Insurance Brokers Association of Canada (www.ibac.ca) for names of members in your area.
- Check with the Financial Advisors Association of Canada (www.advocis.ca) for names of members in your area.

## How to Select an Insurance Broker

Choose an agent you can trust, one who will take the time to listen to you and understand your needs. Ask the agent how long he or she has been in the business, and consider asking for references or a recommendation from one of the agent's other clients.

Your insurance agent should be willing to work with your accountant, lawyer, investment adviser, and tax adviser to develop the optimum estate-planning strategy. Check with your business association, local chamber of commerce, and provincial retail merchants association for special rates.

## How Insurance Brokers Are Compensated

Insurance agents earn their income in commissions on the insurance policies they sell. Commission rates vary from company to company, and from one life insurance product to another, and recommendations should be evaluated as objectively as possible.

However, despite this apparent built-in lack of objectivity, most life insurance agents are people of integrity who will not recommend the purchase of life insurance unless it is clearly warranted under particular circumstances. They know that their recommendations must be able to withstand scrutiny by the client's accountant or financial adviser, and their reputations are at stake.

## Resolving Disputes

If you have a problem with an insurance broker, deal with it directly, assertively, and candidly. Put your concerns in writing so you have a record. If this approach does not work, talk to the manager, the regional or provincial manager, and even the national head office if necessary. Always keep copies of your correspondence.

# Summary

You need to have a minimum benchmark comparison of three advisers in each area of your interest before you can make a reasonable decision in selecting one (if any) of them. As expert advice is critical to your personal, investment, and financial well-being, the selection process has to be thorough. This process will also greatly accelerate your learning curve, and raise your confidence level and the quality of your decision making.

Now that you know how to select your team, it's time to learn about the ins and outs of financing a purchase.

# CHAPTER 5

# Understanding the Financing Aspects

**If you have been** considering the purchase of a house, condominium, or any sort of real estate investment for some time, you probably have some savings set aside for a down payment. You will, however, probably require a mortgage to afford the purchase. The amount of mortgage a lender is willing to grant you will depend not only on the savings you're able to put toward the down payment, but also how much money you can raise from other sources. Your personal financial needs and the financial demands of your investment strategy will complete the information you need to narrow your property search to a realistic and affordable price range. (Chapter 1, "Understanding Real Estate Investment," also discusses financial planning issues related to a property purchase.)

This chapter addresses the issues you need to consider when obtaining property financing. It demystifies the jargon and concepts you'll encounter when researching financing and selecting the option that's right for you. Topics include the types and sources of financing, how to calculate the amount of your mortgage eligibility, applying for a mortgage, costs of a mortgage, and what happens if you default on a mortgage. In addition, this chapter explains creative financing, dealing with negative cash flow, and tips on negotiating financing.

## What Is a Mortgage?

A mortgage is a contract between one party who wants to borrow money and another party who wants to lend it. The borrower is referred to as the *mortgagor*, and the lender is referred to as the *mortgagee*. These terms can sometimes be confusing. The terms *borrower* and *lender* are also used. The mortgage agreement states that in exchange for the money that the lender provides, the borrower will provide security to the lender in the form of a mortgage document to be filed against the property. For the purposes of this book, the term *property* will refer to the purchase you are considering, whether it is a condominium, house, multi-unit dwelling (such as duplex, fourplex, apartment), or raw land. The mortgage document specifies the rights that the lender has to the property in the event the borrower defaults on the terms of the mortgage. The types of remedies that the mortgagee has against the mortgagor are covered later in this chapter.

A mortgage document filed against the title of the property in the appropriate provincial land registry provides security to the mortgagee against other creditors that the mortgagor may have. If a first mortgage is filed against the property and there are no other encumbrances or charges against the property, then the amount outstanding on the first mortgage takes priority over any and all other creditors; that is, it is paid off first from the sale of the property on default. Additional loans could be obtained by the mortgagor that take the form of second and third mortgages, which are also filed against the property.

Each more recent loan ranks lower in priority than the previous one, as the date of registration is the criterion that determines priority. Because of the increasing risk involved for subsequent mortgages, higher interest rates are charged. For example, the first mortgage interest rate may be 6 per cent, the second 8 per cent, the third 12 per cent, and the fourth 18 per cent. The first mortgage would be paid out in full from any proceeds of sale, followed by the second mortgage, and so on. It is possible that the price that a home would sell for would cover only the first and second mortgages, leaving no funds available to pay off the third and fourth mortgages.

Mortgages are regulated by federal and provincial law. Although the laws may differ from one province to another, the description of a mortgage outlined in this book applies to most mortgages. The methods of mortgage registration and the enforcement laws vary among provinces. Some of the common clauses in a mortgage are discussed later in this chapter.

The difference between the amount the property could be sold for (less all costs) and the amount owed on the property's mortgage is referred to as the equity in the property.

## Types of Mortgages

There are several types of mortgages available. Banks, credit unions, trust companies, mortgage companies, private lenders, the government, and even the vendor of a property can provide you with a mortgage. While most residential property borrowers obtain financing through a conventional mortgage, it is good to know the alternatives. The following is a brief discussion of the main types of mortgages.

## Conventional Mortgage

The conventional mortgage is the traditional means of financing a property purchase, whether a principal residence or residential investment property. It is fairly standard in its terms and conditions, although there can be variations. The loan cannot exceed 80 per cent of the appraised value or purchase price of the property, whichever is the lesser of the two. Under the Bank Act, the federal government requires all first mortgages greater than 80 per cent to be insured against loss in the event of default. High-ratio insurance is designed to protect the lender and encourage lenders to provide money when the potential risk might otherwise be considered too great. The federal government, as a matter of public policy, encourages people to buy homes and provides incentives to lenders to provide the mortgage money through the National Housing Act. A federal Crown corporation, the CMHC (www.cmhc.ca), is the federal organization charged with insuring high-ratio home financing. The purchaser is responsible for raising the remaining 20 per cent, either through a down payment, vendor-backed mortgage, or other means.

Conventional mortgages are available through most financial institutions, including banks and credit unions. In most cases, these mortgages do not have to be insured, but a lender may require it if the property is older or if it is located in a rural or rundown area or otherwise considered a higher risk in the event that the borrower defaults and the lender has to sell the property to recoup the loan. In addition to CMHC, Genworth Financial Canada (www.genworth.ca) provides approximately 20 per cent of the current market and is the largest private mortgage insurer in the country. Canada Guaranty Mortgage Insurance (www.canadaguaranty.ca), formerly known as AIG, also insures a small volume of mortgages.

## High-Ratio/Insured Mortgage

If you are unable to raise the necessary 20 per cent funding to complete the purchase of the property, then a high-ratio mortgage may be available to you. These are conventional mortgages that exceed the 80 per cent referred to earlier. By law, these mortgages must be insured, and they are available only through approved lenders that are accepted by CMHC, Genworth, or Canada Guaranty. These organizations have specific guidelines for qualifying, but the administration is done through the bank, trust company, or credit union.

High-ratio mortgages are available for up to 95 per cent of the purchase price or appraised value of a property, whichever is less. The amortization term of government-insured mortgage—one insured by CMHC—is limited by law to 30 years. Private brokers and insurers may offer different terms. Given ongoing turbulence in housing and financial markets, it is wise to obtain the most recent information regarding restrictions and opportunities directly from one of the insurers, your mortgage broker, banker, or realtor. The federal government, for example, imposed new rules in March 2011 that limited refinancing against government-insured mortgages to just 85 per cent of the value of a home.

## Collateral Mortgage

In a collateral mortgage, the mortgage security is secondary, or collateral, to some other main form of security taken by the lender. This main security may take the form of a promissory note, personal guarantee, or assignment of some other form of security that the lender may require. A collateral mortgage is therefore a backup protection of the loan that is filed against the property. The payment requirements on the loan are covered in the promissory note, and once the promissory note has been paid off in full, the collateral mortgage will automatically be paid off. You would then be entitled to have the collateral mortgage discharged from the title of the property.

One of the main differences between a collateral and a conventional mortgage is that a conventional mortgage may be assumed, whereas a collateral mortgage cannot be, as it is subject to some other form of security between the parties. Otherwise, the terms of the collateral mortgage could be very similar to the terms of a conventional one. The money borrowed on a collateral mortgage could be used for the purchase of the property itself, or for other purposes such as home improvements or other real estate investments.

## Government-Assisted Mortgage

National Housing Act (NHA) mortgages are loans granted under the provisions of this federal act. The loans are administered through CMHC. You can apply for an NHA loan at any chartered bank, trust company, or credit union. Borrowers must pay an application fee to CMHC that usually includes the cost of a property appraisal and an insurance fee. The latter is usually added to the principal amount of the mortgage, though it may be paid at the time of closing. Contact CMHC or your financial institution for the most current information on borrowing requirements.

In addition, some provinces have second mortgage funding or funding guarantees available for principal residence home purchases. Generally there is a limit on the amount of the purchase price of the home and a ceiling on the amount of the mortgage. Obtain further information from your realtor or lending institution.

## Secondary Financing

Secondary financing generally consists of a second mortgage and possibly a third. You may wish to take out a second mortgage because the existing first mortgage (which you plan to assume) has an attractive interest rate or other desirable features, and because there will be a shortfall between the amount of your available down payment and the amount of the first mortgage. You therefore need to obtain funds. Chartered banks will usually provide money for second mortgages up to a limit of 80 per cent of the lower of the purchase price or appraised value. You can also obtain second mortgages through mortgage brokers or other sources that could go as high as 90 per cent, or sometimes higher, of the lower of the purchase price or appraised value. If the second mortgage has a term that is longer than that of the first mortgage you assume, make sure you have a postponement clause put into the second mortgage. With this clause, you would be able to automatically renew or replace the first mortgage when it becomes due without having to obtain permission from the second mortgage lender to do so. In other words, if you renewed the first mortgage or obtained a replacement first mortgage, that mortgage would still be in first position, ahead of the second mortgage. Your lawyer will advise you.

## Assumed Mortgage

In the case of an assumed mortgage, the lender qualifies you to assume an existing mortgage on the property. In some instances mortgages can be assumed without qualifications. If you assume the existing mortgage, it will save you the cost of legal fees and disbursements for registering the mortgage, obtaining an appraisal, and other expenses. Whenever you are assuming an existing mortgage, it is important that your lawyer obtain a mortgage assumption statement showing the principal balance outstanding, the method of paying taxes, the remaining term on the mortgage, and a copy of the mortgage that shows other features, such as prepayment privileges, and other details.

If you are a seller of the property, you should be very cautious about someone assuming your mortgage unless you obtain a release in writing from the lender that you will not be liable under the mortgage, in the event that the person assuming it defaults on his or her obligations. In the event of default, the lender would be entitled to go after the original mortgagor, as well as the person who assumed the mortgage, for the full amount of the debt outstanding or any mortgage shortfall after sale of the property due to mortgage default. Make sure that you obtain legal advice before permitting any buyer to assume your mortgage.

## Builder's Mortgage

If purchasing a new house or building, you may be able to assume the builder's mortgage. Make sure that you obtain legal advice before signing any such mortgage to ensure that the provisions in the mortgage are acceptable to you. If you are building the house, the lender may approve a mortgage for construction purposes, but will advance mortgage draws based on the various stages of construction, such as foundation, framing, and roofing. There could be three or more stages. It depends on the nature of the construction and the policy of the lender.

## Discounted Mortgage

Another possibility is that the vendor will offer you a discounted mortgage. In other words, to make the house price attractive, the mortgage rate might be reduced to 2 per cent, for example, whereas the prevailing interest rate for a first mortgage could be 5 per cent. (The interest rates given in the examples throughout this book will obviously vary depending on the marketplace at any given time.) The builder is able to "buy down" a mortgage from a lender at an attractive rate by paying a discount—the difference in financial terms between what the lender would make on a 2 per cent mortgage and what he would make on a 5 per cent one. However, vendors frequently add this discount onto the purchase price of the home; you could be paying a lower interest rate because you are paying a higher price for the property than you would otherwise pay. The discounted mortgage may also last only for a short time, say, six months or a year. After that period you will have to obtain your own mortgage at the prevailing rate. Thus, although a discounted mortgage could initially appear attractive, over the long term it could be a false economy.

## Vendor Mortgage

A vendor mortgage is sometimes referred to as a vendor-back or vendor-take-back mortgage. Here, the vendor encourages the sale of the property by giving the purchaser a loan on the purchase of the property. For example, if the purchaser is able to get 80 per cent conventional financing, but does not have sufficient funds for a down payment of 20 per cent, the vendor may be prepared to give, in effect, a second mortgage for 10 per cent of the purchase price. That way, the purchaser would need to come up with only a 10 per cent down payment. The purchaser would then make mortgage payments to the vendor as if a normal commercial lender held the second mortgage. If you are the vendor, for obvious due diligence reasons, you should make sure that there is a provision in the offer to purchase that it is conditional upon a satisfactory credit check of the purchaser before deciding on granting the second mortgage, and also that any second mortgage is subject to your lawyer's approval as to the contents. When doing a credit check, either of yourself or a prospective tenant if you are a landlord, you can obtain that credit-report information from Equifax over the Internet. For more information, check out their site at www.equifax.ca.

Sometimes the vendor makes arrangements through a mortgage broker for the second mortgage to be sold at a discount as soon as the transaction is completed. This way, the vendor gets cash immediately, minus, of course, the cost required to discount the mortgage and the broker's fee. Generally speaking the mortgage has to have a fixed and not a floating rate if it is to be sold; the terms should be at least a year to be attractive to a purchaser of the mortgage; and the mortgage is generally not assumable. If the vendor intends to sell the vendor-back mortgage, there is usually a precondition in it that the purchaser will co-operate with any credit checks and will agree to the mortgage being assigned. Also, that acceptance of the offer to purchase is based on a commitment from a mortgage broker that there is a purchaser for the second mortgage as soon as the sale is completed.

If you are considering providing a vendor-take-back mortgage, again it is important to be cautious and obtain legal advice in advance. There is a risk that the purchaser will refuse to pay on the second mortgage if there appears to be any problem with the condition of the property after the sale. Naturally the vendor or the assignee of the vendor's second mortgage could commence foreclosure or order for-sale proceedings, but in practical terms it is possible that the purchaser could attempt to raise defences. Discussion in any detail of these types of problems is outside the scope of this book. They are raised merely to alert you to the need for competent legal advice in these unique situations.

## Blanket Mortgage

A blanket mortgage is a type of mortgage registered over two or more properties. The purpose behind the mortgage is to provide the lender with additional property as security. It is normally used when a borrower wants more money than the lender is prepared to provide on the basis of one property alone. That property may not have sufficient equity and, for example, the amount of money that is being requested could constitute 90 or 95 per cent of the value of the first property. If the second property has attractive equity, the lender may be prepared to advance the funds to the borrower, but have one mortgage filed against both properties. In the event of default, the lender could proceed against one or both of the properties in order to get sufficient proceeds from the sale to satisfy the outstanding debt.

Blanket mortgages are very common in cases when someone invests in or owns several properties. They are also common in real estate development. The developer normally has a blanket mortgage over all the properties. As soon as a property is sold, the lender releases the portion of the blanket mortgage that was filed on that property in order for the purchaser of the property to place his own mortgage. The developer normally has a requirement with its lender that all or a portion (for example, 50 or 75 per cent) of the purchase price of the property has to be paid to the lender to reduce the blanket mortgage as a condition for the lender's releasing the encumbrance on the individual property.

## Leasehold Mortgage

A leasehold mortgage is a mortgage on a house, condominium, or other property where the land is leased rather than owned. The mortgage must be amortized over a period that is shorter than the length of the land lease. Normally a lender will not grant a mortgage on leasehold property unless the duration of the lease is of sufficient length that the risk is fairly minimal to the lender. For example, if a condominium is on leasehold land with a 99-year lease and there are 85 years left on the lease, then there is relatively little risk to the lender. On the other hand, if the leasehold is for 30 years and there are 5 years left on the lease, the lender may consider the risk too high because the lease expires in just 5 years. Any right or entitlement to the property reverts to the original owner of the land (the lessor). The loss of rights eliminates the condominium's value, leaving the lender at risk if the buyer defaults on the mortgage. (Chapter 6, "Understanding the Legal Aspects," includes a discussion of leasehold interest in property on page 167.)

## Condominium Mortgage

In many cases condominium mortgages are identical to any of the other mortgages discussed in terms of the provisions, except for a few special provisions because of the unique nature of a condominium. Although a purchaser of a condominium receives a legal title to one individual unit, the purchaser also has an undivided interest in the common elements of the development.

Some of the special clauses contained in most condominium mortgages that distinguish this type of mortgage from a conventional house mortgage are as follows:

- The lender has the right to use the unit owner's vote or consent in the condominium corporation. In other words, the lender has a proxy to vote in place of the borrower. In practical terms, the lender does not usually vote on any and all decisions in normal circumstances. The lender, though, can require that the borrower provide notice of all condominium corporation meetings, including special or extraordinary meetings announced by the condominium corporation, and receive copies of minutes and information.

- The lender requires the borrower to comply with all the terms of the bylaws, rules, and regulations of the condominium corporation. Any default on the borrower's part will constitute default under the mortgage.

- The lender requires the borrower to pay the appropriate portion of maintenance costs of the common elements. In the event that the borrower fails to do so, the lender is entitled to pay the costs on behalf of the borrower and add these onto the principal amount outstanding on the mortgage, with interest charged to this amount.

## Agreement for Sale

An agreement for sale is not actually a mortgage, but another way of financing a sale. It should not be confused with an agreement for purchase and sale. An agreement for sale is normally used in a situation when the buyer of the property does not have sufficient funds for a down payment and the vendor wishes to dispose of the property. In an agreement for sale, the vendor finances the purchase of the property in a fashion similar to that of a vendor-take-back mortgage. The purchaser, though, does not become the legal owner of the property until the agreement for sale has been paid in full. At that time, the purchaser is legally entitled to have the conveyance of the legal interest of the property transferred over to the purchaser. In the meantime, the vendor remains the registered owner on title of the property. The purchaser has the legal right of possession and makes regular payments to the vendor under the terms of the agreement between the vendor and the purchaser. The purchaser has a legal "right to purchase" that is registered against the title of the property in the provincial land registry office.

The terms of an agreement for sale are in many ways very similar to the terms of a mortgage. The agreement for sale may have a five-year term, for example, after which time the full amount is due and payable. At that time either the purchaser has to arrange conventional mortgage financing or another form of financing to pay off the vendor, or else make an agreement with the vendor for an extension of the agreement for sale for another term. Agreements for sale are frequently used where the purchaser cannot qualify to assume the existing mortgage or to obtain a new mortgage; in effect, the purchaser assumes a mortgage that would otherwise be unassumable. The purchaser pays the vendor and the vendor maintains payments on the underlying mortgage.

## Sources of Mortgages

Keep in mind that competition among mortgage lenders is extremely intense, and they are all trying to attract customers. You should therefore do thorough research before deciding on which mortgage lender to use. Major city newspapers publish comparisons of the prevailing mortgage rates by institution in the real estate section of the weekend editions.

Banks, credit unions, mortgage companies, and mortgage brokers post current rates online. The mortgage brokers serving your community will be happy to discuss the rates they're seeing, and the ones they can offer you, if you give them a call or e-mail them. Search online for mortgage brokers in your community or visit the Canadian Association of Accredited Mortgage Professionals website (www.caamp.org). (Selecting a mortgage broker is discussed on page 122 in Chapter 4, "Selecting Your Advisory Team.") Some mortgage brokers and lenders will also offer mortgage approvals directly to you via online applications.

These are the main sources of mortgage funds available for residential or investment purchases:

- banks;
- trust companies;
- credit unions;
- federal government, through the CMHC;

- provincial governments;
- a vendor-take-back mortgage;
- an existing mortgage that you assume;
- personal sources, including family, relatives, friends, and business associates;
- mortgage companies;
- real estate companies;
- mortgage brokers.

# Key Factors to Consider When Selecting a Mortgage

There are many factors to consider before finalizing your mortgage decision, the key ones being amortization, term of the mortgage, open or closed mortgage, interest rate, payment schedules, prepayment privilege, and assumability. Each of these concepts is briefly explained below along with hints on where to find mortgage calculators on the Internet.

## Amortization

Amortization is the length of time over which the regular (usually monthly) payments have been calculated, on the assumption that the mortgage will be fully paid over that period. The usual amortization period is 25 years, although there is a wide range of options available from 5 to 35 years. The shorter the amortization period, the more money you save on interest (see Chart 5 on page 354 of the Appendix).

## Term of the Mortgage

The term of the mortgage is the length of time for which the mortgagee will lend you the money. Terms may vary from 6 months to 10 years. If the amortization period was 25 years, that would mean that you would have several different mortgages, possibly 10 to 20 separate terms, before you have completely paid off the loan. In reality, many people sell their principal residence or investment property after 5 to 10 years of ownership, depending on needs and circumstances; for example, illness, death, divorce, job loss or a new job, increasing or decreasing size of family.

At the end of each term, the principal and unpaid interest of the mortgage becomes due and payable. Unless you are able to repay the entire mortgage at this time, you would normally either renew the mortgage with the same lender on the same terms, renegotiate the mortgage, depending on the options available to you at that time, or refinance the mortgage through a different lending institution. If you renew with a different mortgage lender, there could be extra administrative charges involved. As there is considerable competition among lenders, often there is no administrative fee if you are transferring a mortgage to another institution. In some cases the other institution will absorb the legal fees and costs and still offer an inducement for you to take the business away from a competitive lender and bring it to them.

Some people take out short-term mortgages for as little as six months, anticipating a lower drop in interest rate that will mean lower borrowing costs when the time comes to renew the mortgage. But if rates have gone up instead of down at the end of the six months, the monthly mortgage payment will increase and you may not be able to afford, or want to pay, the higher rate. The other option you have is to negotiate a long-term mortgage—a standard term is five years—so that you can budget for the future over five years without worrying about interest rates. The lender is not obliged to renew the mortgage at the end of a term, but in practical terms it will do so as long as you have met your payment terms. An administration fee of $100 to $250 is often charged on renewal.

## Interest Rate

There are various ways to calculate interest on a mortgage. A fixed-rate mortgage will charge a constant interest rate on the loan over the term of the mortgage. A variable-rate mortgage allows the lender to change the monthly interest rate, according to the premium interest rate set by the lender every month. While the actual monthly payments you make would typically stay the same, the proportion of each monthly payment allocated to paying down the principal and interest of the mortgage will vary with each month's rate.

How often interest is compounded—in other words, the interest charged on interest—will determine the total amount of interest that you actually pay on your mortgage. Obviously, the more frequent the compounding of interest, the more interest you will pay. The lender can charge any rate of interest, within the law, and compound that at any frequency desired. That is why it is important for you to check on the nature of the compounding interest.

By law, mortgages have to contain a statement showing the basis on which the interest rate is calculated. Mortgage interest has traditionally been compounded on a half-yearly basis. If a mortgage is calculated on the basis of straight interest, there is no compounding, but just the running total of the interest outstanding at any point in time. Some mortgages, such as variable-rate mortgages, may be compounded monthly. The initial rate quoted for a mortgage is called a nominal rate, whereas the real interest rate for a mortgage compounded semi-annually, for instance, is called the effective rate. As an example, a mortgage that quotes a nominal rate of 10 per cent has an effective rate of interest of 10 per cent when compounded yearly, 10.25 per cent when compounded half-yearly, and 10.47 per cent when compounded monthly.

An interest average calculation is useful if you're assessing your financing options. You may want to assume an existing first mortgage with an attractive rate and term, but are concerned about the rate of interest on a second mortgage or other financing. By calculating the average interest on the two loans, you might find the deal to be in your favour. Here is an example of how you calculate it:

First mortgage: $60,000 \times 5\% = \$3,000$

Second mortgage: $30,000 \times 8\% = \$2,400$

$$\$90,000 \times X\% = \$5,400$$

Average interest rate: $X\% = \$5,400 \div \$90,000 = 6\%$

## Open or Closed Mortgage

An open mortgage allows you to increase the payment of the principal at any time. You could pay off the mortgage in full at any time before the term is over without any penalty or extra charges. Because of this flexibility, open mortgages cost more than standard closed mortgages.

A closed mortgage locks you in for the term of the mortgage. There is a penalty fee for any advance payment. A straight closed mortgage will normally have a provision that if it is prepaid because the property is sold, a three-month interest penalty will be applied, or the penalty will be waived entirely if the new purchaser of the property takes out a new mortgage with the lending institution. Most closed mortgages have a prepayment feature. This will be discussed shortly.

## Payment Schedules

As to payment schedules, there are many options available in the marketplace, including weekly, biweekly (every two weeks), monthly, semi-annually, annually, and other variations. Naturally, the more frequently you make payments, the lower the interest that you pay (see Chart 5 on page 354 in the Appendix).

Depending on your negotiations with the lender, you may make payments on interest only or have a graduated-payment schedule. This would mean that at the beginning of the term of the mortgage, your payments would be lower and would increase over time, so that at the end of the term the payments would be considerably higher. The reason for this arrangement is that the borrower's ability to make the payment may increase over time, and the payment schedules are graduated to accommodate that. This could be an advantage with revenue real estate purchases.

Usually payments made on the mortgage are a blend of principal and interest. These have traditionally been amortized, assuming a monthly payment basis.

## Prepayment Privilege

This is a very important feature to have in your mortgage if it is a fixed mortgage. If it is an open mortgage, you can pay the balance outstanding on the mortgage in part or in full at any time without penalty. If, on the other hand, you have a closed mortgage that does not have any prepayment privileges, you are locked in for the term of the mortgage without the privilege of prepaying without penalty.

You may therefore wish to have a mortgage that, though called a closed mortgage, is in fact partly open, permitting prepayment at certain stages and in a certain manner, but not at other times. For example, you may be permitted to make a prepayment of between 10 and 20 per cent annually on the principal amount outstanding. This could be made once a year at the end of each year of the mortgage, or at your choice any time during the year.

Another variation would also give you the option of increasing the amount of your monthly payment by 10 to 20 per cent once a year. The results are impressive in terms of saving interest and reducing the amortization period. Every time a prepayment is made, or every time you increase your monthly payments, the balance owing and thus the monthly interest are reduced. (For a graphic illustration, see Chart 5 on page 354 in the Appendix.) The net effect is that a larger portion of each payment is applied toward the principal, since monthly (or other agreed-upon, regular) payments usually remain the same. Make sure you completely understand your prepayment options, as they could save you a lot of money.

## Assumability

Assumability means that the buyer takes over the obligation and payments under the vendor's mortgage. Most mortgage contracts deal with the issue of assumability very clearly. The lender can agree to full assumability without qualifications, assumability with qualifications, or no assumability. For example, if a vendor reluctantly gave a vendor-back second mortgage for $50,000 for two years, the vendor (the lender) may not want to have that mortgage assumed by anyone else because the vendor would prefer to be paid out in full in the event that the property is sold, rather than carry the mortgage any longer.

The assumability issue is important to consider. You would have a wider range of potential purchasers interested in buying your property if purchasers who may not otherwise qualify for your mortgage are able to assume it without qualifications. Most mortgages, though, generally have a clause that says the mortgage is assumable with qualification by the lender. While a negotiable item, lenders typically check out the creditworthiness and debt-servicing capability of the new owner.

Also, there is a risk if someone assumes your mortgage and you are still on the mortgage document. For example, what if the new owner defaults on the mortgage and the lender has to foreclose? Your name would be added onto the court documents. That is why you don't want to have anyone assume your mortgage unless you obtain a release of any liability from the lender at the same time. It would be prudent to get your lawyer's assistance to ensure that your interests are properly protected.

## Portability

Some lenders offer a feature called portability, which means that if you sell one home and buy another during the term of your mortgage, you can transfer the mortgage from one property to the other. In practical terms, you could save money if interest rates have gone up during the term of your present mortgage. Thus you would not have to take out a new mortgage for your new home at current, higher mortgage rates, thereby decreasing the amount of mortgage money available to you. Remember, the higher the interest rate, the lower the mortgage amount for which you can qualify. Conversely, if mortgage rates have gone down since your current mortgage took effect, you would probably not be interested in continuing your existing mortgage. You must take into consideration the costs of terminating your mortgage early.

# General Contents of a Mortgage

Most mortgage documents are in fine print and fairly detailed. There are no so-called standard clauses in a mortgage. The only way you can fully understand your mortgage is to have a competent and experienced real estate lawyer review it and explain the key areas to you. In addition to differences in mortgage contracts, the laws change constantly. Many people sign mortgages without having any idea of what is in them. This section outlines some of the common terms with which you should be familiar.

In any mortgage, there are these basic provisions: the date of the mortgage, the names of the parties who are signing, a legal description of the property, the amount of the loan, the payment terms including interest and frequency, the respective obligations of the lender and the borrower, and the signatures of all the parties. There are also some terms common to mortgages related to condominiums, but these are discussed elsewhere in this chapter in the section related to condominium mortgages.

## Personal Liability

Under a mortgage, the borrower is personally liable for the debt to the lender, assuming the mortgage is in an individual's name rather than a corporate name. In the event of default, the lender can sue the borrower for the full amount of the mortgage. While the lender *is not obliged* to commence foreclosure or power-of-sale proceedings, and take over or sell the property, the lender usually commences a form of foreclosure or power-of-sale action to protect its interest, in addition to suing the borrower personally. If the property is sold, then the borrower would be responsible for the shortfall, plus all the associated legal and other costs that the lender has incurred.

If there is a co-covenantor on the mortgage—someone else who covenants or promises that he or she will meet all the obligations of the mortgage—the lender can sue both the borrower and the co-covenantor for the debt under the mortgage. (Sometimes the term *guarantor* is used instead of *co-covenantor*. In practical terms, they are interchangeable.)

The lender may refuse to give funds covered by a mortgage without extra security protection by means of an additional guarantor or co-covenantor. If you are married and are purchasing the property under your personal name, the lender will almost always insist that your spouse sign as a guarantor or co-covenantor, regardless of your creditworthiness. This is to protect the lender under the matrimonial or family-relations legislation of the province in the event that a separation or divorce occurs. The lender does not want its property security to be compromised by a marital dispute.

If you have an incorporated company to purchase real estate and take out a mortgage in that name, in most cases the lender will ask you for a personal guarantee of the corporate mortgage. This makes you personally liable, of course.

## Insurance

This clause requires that the mortgagor insure the building against fire. The insurance policy must show that the mortgagee is entitled to be paid first (if a first mortgage) from the mortgage proceeds in the event of a claim on the policy.

There is also a provision in the mortgage that sets out the amount of the insurance (replacement). It states that if you fail to pay the premium, the mortgagee can do so, or if you fail to get sufficient insurance, the mortgagee can do so. Also, all the additional premium costs can be added on to the principal amount of debt of your mortgage.

## Requirement to Pay Taxes

This clause states that you are obliged to pay all property taxes when they come due, and that if you do not do so, the lender is entitled to pay the taxes. The lender would then add the amount paid in taxes to the principal amount of the mortgage. Some lenders attempt to avoid any problem with taxes by having a separate tax account set up at the time you take out the mortgage. This means that you pay an extra amount every month on your payment to the bank for a tax portion that goes into that account, and once a year the lender pays the property taxes directly. Attempt to negotiate your way out of this prepayment provision and look after the taxes yourself. Some lenders require proof that taxes are current and have been paid every year.

## Maintain Property

This clause in the mortgage states that you are required to keep the property in good repair. The reason for this provision is that the lender obviously does not want the property to deteriorate through neglect and therefore reduce its property value, compromising the value of the security.

## Requirement to Keep Any Subsequent Mortgages in Good Standing

This provision states that you must maintain all your financial obligations on the second and third mortgages so that they do not go into default. If they do go into default, foreclosure proceedings could occur. If the property were sold, the first mortgage would be paid off first, followed by the second and the third, etc.

## No Urea Formaldehyde Foam Insulation (UFFI)

Many mortgages state that no UFFI is permitted in the premises at the time the mortgage is granted. UFFI is a known carcinogen and causes breathing problems. It is banned in Canada, and lenders will typically not provide financing for purchase of a property with UFFI due to the liability it poses. The prohibition typically extends to UFFI's installation as well, but since it is no longer sold in Canada its installation is no longer a concern.

## Prohibition against Renting Out Premises

Some mortgage documents state very clearly that the premises cannot be rented out, but can only be used as your principal residence. This can occur with some residential mortgages that are granted for the benefit of the owner-occupier and not for investment or rental purposes.

Having said this, almost all lenders permit "mortgage-helper" rental suites in your home. In fact, most lenders will include the revenue you receive from your rental suite as part of your overall personal income for calculating the maximum amount of mortgage for which you are eligible.

Due to the realities of the competitive mortgage marketplace and demand, you can readily get mortgages for properties used for rental purposes.

## Assignment of Rents

If you are purchasing a revenue house or building, the lender may request that you sign a document entitled "Assignment of Rents." In the event that you fail to make your monthly payments to the lender, the lender can formally notify the tenants that you have assigned the rent payments directly to the lender.

## Must Comply with All Laws

This provision advises that the use and occupancy of the property must comply with all federal, provincial, and municipal laws, which is important if you intend to rent out the property. Although there may not be a strict prohibition against rentals, there could be an indirect one if municipal zoning bylaws prohibit the rental of residential premises. In practical terms, most mortgage companies don't care if you rent out part of your home as a mortgage helper, even though it does not technically comply with existing municipal bylaws. On the other hand, there is a trend in many municipalities to permit illegal suites, as it is serving a community and social need.

## Quiet Possession

This provision states that unless the mortgagor defaults, the mortgagee will not interfere in any way with the peaceful enjoyment of the property by the mortgagor. In practical terms, this means that the mortgagee cannot enter the premises.

## Prepayment Privileges

It is important that the prepayment privileges are set out clearly in the agreement. The various types of prepayment privileges have been previously discussed.

## Assumption of Mortgage Privileges

Assumption of mortgage privileges should be set out clearly in the mortgage document. This subject also has been discussed earlier.

## Acceleration Clause

This clause states that if the mortgagor defaults on any of the terms of the mortgage agreement, then, at the option of the mortgagee, the full amount outstanding on the principal of the mortgage plus interest is immediately due and payable. In some provinces, legislation restricts the mortgagee from exercising the right of acceleration, even though it may be in the mortgage document.

## Default

This section of the mortgage deals with the type of matters that could place the mortgage in default of the agreement, and sets out the rights of the mortgagee in the event of default. This is discussed elsewhere in this chapter.

Refer to Checklist 2 on page 364 in the Appendix when negotiating with a lender. Again, have your lawyer advise you on the contents of the mortgage before signing it.

# Determining the Amount of Mortgage Available

Different lenders have different criteria for approving the amount of mortgage funds available. There is considerable flexibility with many lenders and it is important to compare or have a mortgage broker do so on your behalf in order to get the maximum amount of mortgage funds possible in your situation. Lenders use the gross debt-service ratio and total debt-service ratio as standard formulas for determining mortgage qualification. There are also other calculations to determine the data relating to mortgages.

In calculating matters of principal and interest relating to mortgages and other factors, such as different pay periods and options, there are various sources of information. This will be covered at the end of this section.

## Gross Debt-Service (GDS) Ratio

The GDS ratio is used to calculate the amount you can afford to spend for mortgage principal (P) and interest (I) payments. Some lenders also include property taxes (T) as part of this formula, and possibly heating costs (H) as well. All these expenses are added together. Under the GDS ratio, payments generally should not exceed 30 per cent of your income. There is flexibility in lending criteria, though, as some lenders will go up to 32 per cent and in some cases 35 per cent or more of your income and only include P and I rather than PIT or PITH. Refer to Form 3 on page 341 in the Appendix to calculate your own mortgage eligibility.

## Total Debt-Service (TDS) Ratio

Many people have monthly financial obligations other than mortgage and taxes, which lenders want to know about in order to determine ability to debt service the mortgage. Using the TDS ratio, the bank wants to know your fixed monthly debts such as credit-card payments, car payments, other loans, and condominium maintenance fees. In general terms, no more than 40 per cent of your gross family income can be used when calculating the amount you can afford to pay for principal interest and taxes, plus your fixed monthly debts. The lender is naturally concerned about minimizing the risk that you will be unable to meet your financial obligations relating to the mortgage if the ratio is too high. Refer to Form 4 on page 342 in the Appendix.

It is important to consider all your monthly obligations (such as insurance and electricity costs), some of which may not be taken into account by the lender, so that you get a good sense of your financial standing. Complete your personal cost-of-living budget (Form 1 on page 333 in the Appendix). This should give you some idea of what your monthly income is (net after tax) and what your monthly debt-servicing charges will be on the mortgage, plus other expenses.

## Obtaining Mortgage Amortization Tables

There are different ways that you can access information to obtain free amortization tables customized for your needs. Books of amortization and mortgage interest charts were once commonplace, but the same information is now available online. Comparing mortgage and amortization terms will help you reduce the interest you pay, boosting the speed with which you build equity in your property.

Chart 6 on page 354 in the Appendix provides a sample mortgage amortization schedule; Chart 7 (page 355) shows what monthly mortgage payments are like for a given term. These examples illustrate the point. The information you get from the online charts will provide you with information customized to your situation, and allow you to weigh the benefits of particular terms and interest rates.

# Applying for a Mortgage

There are several steps you should follow to ensure you obtain the funds you need on the terms and conditions you want. Some of these steps may not be required if you use a mortgage broker, but the preparation is worthwhile nevertheless. They will help you to understand the jargon, and help you decide what to ask a potential lender (Checklist 2 on page 364 in the Appendix is also a helpful guide).

## Preparing to Obtain a Mortgage at the Best Rate

Here is a summary of the steps that you should follow prior to an interview with a lender:

- Comparison shop among all of the lending institutions from which you could get a mortgage. Contact a mortgage broker and check newspapers to compare interest rates. The mortgage market is highly competitive, and lenders often offer incentives such as free legal fees, free appraisal, free home inspection, and so on.
- You may want to do a personal credit check, especially if your credit history might show any cause for concern for the lender. Alternatively,

you might just be curious and want to know what others know, or just see that the information is accurate and that nothing negative appears on your record. You are entitled to know this information, and can obtain it online. Check with your local credit bureau, if you have one, or visit Equifax (www.equifax.ca), the credit-reporting company that lenders frequently use.

- Prepare for the negotiation with questions such as, "What incentives do you offer potential borrowers?" and "What is the best discount that you can give me on the posted (displayed or published) rate for the mortgage I want?" Try to get at least a 1 per cent discount off the posted rate. Many banks and credit unions will provide this if you have several accounts with them, including a chequing account, credit card or other personal loan, and investment accounts such as a TFSA or RRSP. Mortgage brokers may also be able to secure a better-than-posted rate from a lender because of the volume of business they do (RBC Royal Bank does not work with mortgage brokers, however).

- Prepare a statement of your assets, liabilities, and net worth (refer to Form 2 on page 336 in the Appendix), and determine your financial needs (see Form 1 on page 333 in the Appendix).

- Calculate the maximum amount of mortgage available that you might be able to expect from a lender (see pages 341 and 342 for the formulas). Remember, these are only guides.

- Use the mortgage calculators available online to get a sense of the options available, the benefits, and the probable maximum amount that might be available to you. These, however, can depend on the lender. Some are more generous in their criteria and formulas than others. The last part of this section discusses these websites.

- Obtain an employment confirmation letter from your employer (if you are employed) that confirms your salary, position, and the length of time you have been with that company. If you are self-employed, you are required to produce copies of recent financial statements and/or income tax returns (usually the last three years). Because so many people are self-employed and because of the competitive mortgage marketplace, lenders are generally more accommodating and understanding of the variable income cycles of self-employment, and therefore are more flexible than they have been in the past.

- Confirm the details and source(s) of your down payment. This last step could include savings accounts, term deposits, Canada Savings

Bonds, RRSPs, a family loan, an inheritance, a divorce settlement, proceeds from the sale of a house, or other sources.

- Obtain a copy of the purchase-and-sale agreement, though in many cases you may be pre-approved for a mortgage.

## The Mortgage Application Process

There are various ways of obtaining a mortgage: by speaking with your existing lender, by comparing various lenders to get the best deal, by applying online, or by using a mortgage broker. The following overview describes the usual approval process:

- Visit a lending institution with your spouse, partner, and any co-applicant or guarantor. The process from this point on is basically the same as it would be if you applied for a mortgage online or through a broker.

- Complete a formal mortgage application, which is typically divided into three main sections: description of the property, financial details relating to the purchase of the property, and personal financial information.

Processing the application normally takes between one and five business days. During that time the lender will:

- check your credit references and credit rating;
- verify your financial information;
- have the property appraised (at your cost or theirs);
- assess your application within the lender's approval guidelines; and
- issue a formal commitment of approval in writing.

## Guidelines for Assessing Mortgage Applications

Different lenders have different guidelines when assessing mortgage applications, but generally there are three main criteria: character, capacity, and collateral.

### Character

The lender will assess your credit history and other factors to predict how you will meet your obligations. For example, do you regularly pay your bills on time? What is your credit rating in terms of your credit history in previous loans that you have had? (See page 135 to learn how to obtain a copy of your own credit report.) Do you seem to be dependable in terms of your length of employment? Or have you had a different job every three or four months?

## Capacity

The lender is concerned about your ability to meet your financial obligation and will ask the following questions:

- Does your GDS ratio come within their guidelines?
- What are your other debts and obligations?
- Is your income sufficient to handle the mortgage payments?
- Is your income stable and does it appear as though it will continue to be so?
- Is there a mortgage-helper rental suite in the home?
- Are you self-employed, for how long, and in what industry?

## Collateral

Lenders want to know that the security that has been provided for a loan is sufficient to cover the loan if it is not repaid. That is why they use their own appraisers to assess property value; generally they want to have a conservative appraisal as an extra precaution. The lender wants to be satisfied that the property being offered as security could be readily sold if necessary. When making an appraisal and therefore determining the value of the security that is being pledged as collateral, the following factors are considered: location, price, zoning, condition of the housing unit, quality of neighbourhood, size, appearance, municipal services available, and comparative sales in the same area.

## Pre-approved Mortgage

The pre-approved mortgage is fairly popular with most conventional lending institutions, trust companies, and credit unions. The purpose is to give you a precise amount of money on which you can rely for mortgage purposes when you are out searching to buy a property and negotiating a purchase. You are given a fixed amount of mortgage for a period of time, for example, $100,000 with an interest rate that would be guaranteed for 60 to 120 days, depending on the relative stability of mortgage rates at the time. There is always a condition, of course, that the lender must approve the actual property being purchased before you can enact a final contractual offer to purchase. This provides the lender with an opportunity to make sure that the security is suitable.

## Loan Approval

When the lender is in the process of approving the loan, the amount requested is an important consideration. As discussed earlier, if the loan exceeds 80 per cent of the appraised value or the purchase price, whichever is lower, the mortgage normally has to be insured as a high-ratio mortgage.

Once the lender has granted approval for the mortgage, the lender will generally appoint its own lawyer to protect its interests by checking on the title of the property to make sure that it is clear, and to perform any necessary duties, including filing the mortgage. Alternatively, the lender may allow the borrower's lawyer to perform the mortgage work. In either case, the borrower customarily pays all the legal fees and disbursements. If you are required, or prefer, to use the lender's lawyer for preparing the mortgage documents, obtain independent legal advice about the provisions of the mortgage to make sure that the document sets out your intended deal. (Other legal aspects relating to the transfer of title of the property and the filing of a mortgage are covered in Chapter 6, "Understanding the Legal Aspects.")

# Cost of Obtaining a Mortgage

There are numerous direct and indirect expenses related to obtaining a mortgage. Not all the following expenses will be applicable in your case, but it is helpful to be aware of them. There are also additional expenses that are not covered in this chapter as they relate to purchasing a property and having the title of the property transferred over to your name. They include legal fees and disbursements, provincial land-transfer filing fees, and property-purchase tax. (These will be discussed in Chapter 6, "Understanding the Legal Aspects.") Other expenses that may be involved include a new-home warranty fee, condominium-maintenance fee adjustment, utility connection charges, cost of repairs required prior to occupancy, and moving expenses (see Checklist 3, "Real Estate Purchase Expenses," on page 368 in the Appendix).

Costs will vary considerably from one lender to another. The type of financing that you obtain will be a factor. The following sections discuss some of the most common expenses for which you should budget.

## Appraisal Fee

The lender will obtain its own appraiser to determine the value of the security for mortgage purposes. The necessary fee is either paid by the borrower to the lender (generally in advance) at the time of application or is taken from the mortgage proceeds by the lender. In any event, the borrower generally pays the cost of the appraisal. Lenders usually will not give you a copy of the appraisal, although you should attempt to get it by requesting it in advance. In a competitive marketplace, ask the lender to assume the cost of the appraisal as part of your negotiation. This is a fairly common request, and often the lender will automatically assume the cost. If you use the services of a mortgage broker, the broker will know which lenders are providing incentives, including assumption of the appraisal fee.

You might save on the appraisal fee under certain circumstances. For example, if a vendor or purchaser has already arranged for a professional appraiser to evaluate the property, and the appraisal is not over 60 to 90 days old, the lender may be prepared to accept the appraisal if it approves of the appraiser, and if property values have remained the same or increased since the appraisal was made.

## Mortgage-Application Fee

Some lenders charge a processing or set-up fee for their administrative expenses to process your mortgage application. Avoid paying this type of fee if possible. Due to the highly competitive nature of the mortgage industry, many lenders do not charge any application fee for residential mortgage purposes. If you are borrowing money for real estate investment, this fee is fairly common because of the extra work required to assess the loan application. Normally, though, when purchasing a single-family dwelling for rental purposes, such as a house or condominium, the mortgage-application fee is waived.

## Standby Fee

Some lenders charge the borrower a fee for setting aside and reserving the money that the borrower requires until the money is advanced. The rationale is that the mortgage company will lose revenue on this money in the interim. It is uncommon to apply this fee to a principal-residence mortgage; however, it is a common fee on money committed for real estate investment purposes or for new construction.

## Credit-Investigation-Report Fee

The lender may charge this fee to the borrower for the expense the lender incurs for doing credit investigation on the borrower. The fee may be separate or included in the mortgage-application fee. Many institutions absorb it as a cost of doing business, as they hope to make money from you on the interest that you pay on your mortgage.

## Survey Fee

You will be required to obtain a property survey before the mortgage funds are paid out. A qualified professional will do the survey to make sure that the lender knows the exact dimensions of the property that it is using as security. The lender may also want to be satisfied that the building meets the requirements for setbacks as required by the municipal bylaws, or that any additions to the building comply with the bylaws. The cost of the survey could be deducted from the mortgage funds that have been advanced to you, or you could pay for it directly. Your lawyer normally arranges this survey for you. Sometimes this expense is negotiable with the lender, who might absorb the cost to obtain your business. If you don't ask for concessions, you don't automatically get them. This negotiating attitude and style should be an automatic part of your approach to business or real estate investment.

## Mortgage-Broker Fee

If you use a mortgage broker, you may have to pay a fee of 1 to 2 per cent or more of the amount of mortgage that was raised for you. This is paid at the time of closing. Alternatively you may not have to pay any fee. There is generally no fee charged for principal-residence purposes, and a small fee for investment real estate that is more complex or difficult to obtain. (This was discussed in Chapter 4, "Selecting Your Advisory Team.") Most mortgage brokers will require an advance fee from you for appraisal costs and out-of-pocket costs incurred in advance. This is not the same as an application or administration fee, but could be included within such fees if they are charged.

## Mortgage-Insurance Fees

If you are obtaining a high-ratio mortgage or the lender requires you to obtain mortgage insurance for other reasons, then you will pay a mortgage-insurance fee, which ranges between 0.5 and 4.25 per cent of the amount of the mortgage that is being insured. The premium depends upon various risk factors and whether the home is a new purchase or is being re-financed. It is either added onto the mortgage total or paid by you in a lump sum at the time of closing the mortgage transaction. Mortgage insurance was discussed on page 131 under "High-Ratio/Insured Mortgages."

## Mortgage Life Insurance

Mortgage life insurance is not the same as mortgage insurance. Many lending institutions provide an option for you to purchase insurance that will pay off the mortgage in the event of your death, the premium for which is generally loaded into your monthly payments. You should compare the cost with term insurance from private insurance carriers to see if the rates are competitive. Generally term insurance is cheaper.

As an option you may prefer to protect yourself by taking out your own term insurance, which would be payable to your estate in the event of your death. Your estate would then have sufficient proceeds to pay off the mortgage. An additional benefit of this option is that the insurance policy is portable— that is, you (not the lender) would have control over it. You can obtain competitive term life insurance rates from an insurance broker. You can get names of insurance brokers from a mortgage broker, your accountant or financial planner, or check online. The Canadian Life and Health Insurance Association's website has excellent consumer information and member brokers in your area (www.clhia.ca). (Refer to page 126 in Chapter 4, "Selecting Your Advisory Team," for the process of selecting an insurance broker. Also, see Chapter 8, "Understanding the Insurance Aspects.")

In certain circumstances, as a condition of mortgage approval, a lender may require that you take out mortgage life insurance. Usually this would be if the lender considered your health to be a risk factor. Again, you could purchase your own term or other type of life insurance and verify to the lender that you had such coverage. The lender may require it to be shown on the insurance policy as being paid first from the proceeds, but this would be an unusual request for a principal-residence deal. It might be more common if you were borrowing money for real estate investment purposes.

## Home Fire Insurance

Lenders require borrowers to carry sufficient fire insurance to cover the amount of the mortgage, and that they be paid off first. The second mortgage lenders would want the same type of coverage and have it shown that they would be paid off second, and so on. It is necessary for the borrower to purchase sufficient replacement insurance. The borrower is responsible for making insurance arrangements and paying the costs of the policy, which would show that the lender would be paid first or second, as the case may be. This must be provided to the lender's lawyer before any mortgage funds are advanced.

## Property Tax-Adjustment Holdback

If the lender requires you to pay a portion of the property taxes every month, and if you purchase the property on April 1 with property taxes due in July, obviously there will be a shortfall in the tax account. In other words, if the property taxes are due and payable in full on July 1 and you have made payments each month of one-twelfth of the projected annual tax, then by July 1 the tax account set up by the lender will be short by nine-twelfths of the amount required to pay the taxes. The lender may require that you pay nine-twelfths of the projected annual tax into the tax account at the time of closing the mortgage transaction. Either you would have to come up with these additional funds or the lender would subtract that amount of money from the mortgage proceeds being made available to you. Alternatively you may be required to pay four-twelfths of the projected property tax to the lender for each of the three months of April, May, and June prior to the tax payment deadline of July 1.

## Contribution to Property Tax Account

Some lenders require that you pay one-twelfth of the projected annual taxes each month. This payment would be built into your monthly mortgage obligations, and the lender would set up a separate tax account and remit the funds directly to the municipality at the appropriate time each year. Normally taxes are payable in June or by July 1 each year, although they are calculated on the calendar year, i.e., January 1 to December 31. Some municipalities require an advance part-payment in February of each year and the balance in July of that year. If the lender makes the automatic monthly property tax payment a condition of mortgage approval, ask whether interest will be credited to your tax account and, if so, what the interest rate would be. The interest paid is normally lower than the interest paid on deposit accounts. Some lenders require monthly payments to minimize the risk that you will not have sufficient funds to pay the taxes every year. If this happened, the property could conceivably be put up for tax sale and jeopardize the lender's security.

In most cases lenders will give you the option to be responsible for paying your own taxes directly once a year. Try to negotiate this option. If you are paying a portion of the projected property tax every month, you will have to build that expense into the costs related to your mortgage.

## Interest Adjustment

When you pay rent, you are paying in advance. When you are paying mortgage payments to the lender for principal and interest, you are paying in arrears. In other words, if you make a mortgage payment on March 1, it is to cover the use of the funds and the interest on those funds for the month of February.

Because the lender's internal system runs on a monthly payment basis, assuming that it is a fixed interest rate, the lender will want to be paid in advance for the use of the funds from February 15 to March 1. This interest adjustment is then advanced from the mortgage funds provided to you on February 15 so that the interest is prepaid up to March 1. When your normal mortgage payment is made on April 1, it would cover the one-month interest for the month of March, plus a small repayment of the principal. Not all lenders require this arrangement, but you should know in advance so that you are aware of the net proceeds that you will receive on the mortgage.

## Interest

Interest is, of course, the cost of having the funds paid to you under a mortgage. What you will have to pay to the lender in interest, and the steps you should go through to obtain the most attractive interest rate, have been discussed.

## Provincial Mortgage Filing Tax

Most provinces charge a tax or a fee for filing a mortgage in the land registry.

## Provincial Property Purchase Tax

Some provinces charge a tax for transferring title in property. The tax formula varies, depending on the province.

## Legal Fees and Disbursements

You are responsible for paying the lawyer's legal fees as well as out-of-pocket disbursements that he or she incurs relating to the preparation and filing of the mortgage documentation. Disbursements would cover such things as property search, photocopy expenses, courier costs, and other costs associated with the preparation and registration of the mortgage. The disbursement costs would normally include the provincial mortgage-filing tax or fee referred to earlier. It is usual for lawyers to deduct the legal fees and disbursements directly from the money to be advanced under the mortgage.

Sometimes lenders require that you use a particular law firm. Alternatively, they might provide you with a list of approved law firms from which you can select your preference. At other times the lender will permit you to use a lawyer of your choice. In all cases you are responsible for the legal fees and disbursements. Due to the competitive nature of the marketplace, some lenders will offer to pay all your legal costs and disbursements related to the mortgage, and sometimes the transfer of title as well.

## Defaulting on Your Mortgage

As long as you meet the payments and the terms as agreed with the mortgage company, it cannot commence any action to foreclose on the property or obtain an order for sale. On the other hand, if you have difficulty with your payments or breach any terms of the mortgage, the lender can resort to severe measures to protect its security. Defaulting on a mortgage has potentially serious consequences. If you are consistently late, this could affect your credit rating, and also your ability to renew your mortgage or obtain other mortgages in the future.

This section will cover factors that constitute default, the borrower's (mortgagor's) options, and the lender's (mortgagee's) options. It is beyond the scope of this book to go into any more detail on mortgage default or foreclosure other than to give an overview of the issues to consider.

### Factors that Constitute Default under a Mortgage

The mortgage agreement sets out in considerable detail what is required of the borrower. Some of the most common clauses were discussed on page 144. The main areas of default are:

- failure to make your mortgage payments;
- failure to pay your taxes;
- failure to have insurance, or sufficient insurance;
- failure to obey municipal, provincial, or federal law as it relates to the premises that you have mortgaged;

- failure to maintain the premises in a habitable condition;
- failure to keep the premises in proper repair; and
- deliberately damaging the property that secures the mortgage.

## Borrower's Options on Default

A borrower who is having difficulty making mortgage payments has a few options to consider, which include:

- Making arrangements with the lender for a waiver of payments for a period of time—say, three or six months—or arranging for partial payments to be made, a common practice if a borrower is sick, injured, laid off, or has a reduced monthly income to service the mortgage due to a marital separation, or other such factors.

- Rescheduling the debt and making new payment arrangements.

- Refinancing the mortgage with another lender on terms that are more flexible and appropriate in the circumstances.

- Providing additional security to the lender in order to negotiate concessions.

- Listing the property for sale.

- Transferring the property to the lender. This is not always feasible or desirable from the owner's or the lender's perspectives.

- Exercising a right of redemption. This privilege, which allows a borrower to pay the arrears outstanding on a mortgage, is usually enshrined in law. It prevents the mortgagee from commencing power-of-sale or foreclosure proceedings. An exception occurs when the mortgage includes an acceleration clause. The lender is then entitled to deem the full amount of the mortgage immediately due and payable. In that event you would have to pay the full amount of the mortgage in order to stop foreclosure proceedings.

  Some provinces have legislation restricting the application of acceleration clauses. In many provinces you have a right of redemption of from one to six months in order to pay the lender, or the lender would be entitled to take over the property or sell it, among other measures.

- Asking the court for more time. If a borrower knows that funds to repay a lender will not be available within the right-of-redemption period, he or she is entitled to request an extension. Whether or not the court grants an extension depends on the circumstances.

For example, a borrower who recently emerged from a period of unemployment and is now being paid regularly, or who expects to receive an inheritance, may be able to successfully petition a court for an extension. These factors support the request because they indicate a reasonable ability to make the necessary payment. Substantial equity in the property would also assist an effort by the borrower to extend the right of redemption period.

## Mortgagee's (Lender's) Options on Default

If you are in default and, despite all your efforts, are unable to come to terms with the lender, the lender has various options. Generally the last thing lenders want to do is take over the property, as there are other options that are more appropriate, depending on the circumstances. The lender is required to go to court and get approval for most of the main measures available. That gives you an opportunity to present your side of the situation and reveal unique circumstances if you so wish.

Legislation governing the mortgage is provincial and can vary between the provinces. For the most part, though, the following measures would be available to the lender:

- Pay taxes, maintenance fees, or insurance premiums on your behalf. The lender then adds these payments onto your total mortgage debt and charges interest on the amount.

- Get an injunction from the court that you stop carrying on some improper or illegal activity. In addition, the order could require you to perform some specific obligation under the mortgage document to protect the mortgage security. You would have to pay the lender's costs of obtaining the injunction.

- Obtain a court order to appoint a receiver of the rents to pay the mortgage payments. This procedure is not often utilized except in serious situations involving revenue property. In reality, if you have borrowed money for revenue property, the lender will probably have asked you to sign an assignment of rents at the outset. The lender then can automatically notify all tenants to direct the rent payments to the lender if you default on the payment terms in the mortgage.

- Get a court order to put the property into receivership. In this case an independent party, called a receiver-manager or receiver, takes possession of the property on behalf of the lender and maintains it. This procedure is usually utilized in the case of revenue property if other remedies are not more efficient, and if the property is held in a corporate (rather than a personal) name, which has given the bank a debenture (a security document).

- Accelerate the mortgage. The lender can either request the arrears under the mortgage, or deem the full amount of the balance outstanding on the mortgage as immediately due and payable. The lender cannot request this latter course unless there is an acceleration clause in the mortgage. Some provincial legislation restricts the use of acceleration clauses, as noted earlier.

- Sell the property. The lender would be able to put your property up for sale and sell it if you are in default in your payments over a set period of time. The period of time depends on the province. In many cases the lender will go through the court to get a court order for a sale so that the court can monitor the sale price and therefore minimize the risk of a borrower's claim that the house was undersold. In other cases the lender does not have to go to court to list it for sale.

- Sue the borrower personally for the debt outstanding. The borrower's liability under the terms of the mortgage remains an option for the lender whether or not the property has been sold. If it is sold, the borrower is responsible for any shortfall. If the property is being held in a corporate name, the lender usually requests a personal guarantee of the people behind the corporation. The lender is not required to commence other actions such as foreclosure or sale of the property.

- Foreclose against the property. In a foreclosure, the lender requests that the court extinguish your property rights and transfer all legal interest that you have, including the right of possession and legal title, to the lender. In this situation the lender is entitled to all the equity in the property. The courts are generally involved in this procedure and your rights are protected in that regard. For example, the court would consider it unfair to you if you had considerable equity in the property. It would probably advise the lender that instead of foreclosure, there should be an order for sale. In that event, the equity in the mortgage property would be able to go to the mortgagor after all the costs associated with the sale had been paid off. These costs would include the sales commission, the lender's legal expenses and disbursements, plus any principal and interest outstanding.

In practical terms, therefore, lenders foreclose probably less than 1 per cent of the time. The most common method of recovery is sale of the property.

As you can see, there are many factors to consider if you are having financial difficulties with your mortgage. The circumstances of your default will make a difference in terms of what steps you wish to take. Contacting the lender and attempting to negotiate a resolution is clearly the first step toward resolving the problem. If that is unsatisfactory, it would be prudent to seek advice from a lawyer specializing in foreclosure matters so that you are fully aware of your available rights and options. Your lawyer could also negotiate with the bank on your behalf.

## Creative Financing

Sometimes the only way to make a particular deal work is with creative financing. This simply means that financing is arranged legally, but in non-traditional ways. The standard fixed-payment bank mortgage, for example, would be considered traditional financing. A regular payment is made monthly, with the interest due applied first and the balance to the reduction of the principal. Here are some alternative creative-financing techniques:

- Interest deferral. Interest is still calculated as usual, but payment of the interest is delayed. This is sometimes referred to as a balloon-payment mortgage.

- Equity participation. In exchange for lending money with attractive terms, the lender shares in the increase of equity (net worth) of the property.

- Mortgage assumption. Rather than taking out a new mortgage, the purchaser assumes the vendor's existing mortgage. The vendor should normally negotiate a full release of any future obligations under the mortgage.

- Variable-rate mortgage. The interest rate on a variable-rate mortgage fluctuates according to an index, usually the Bank of Canada's prime rate or the lender's own best rate, but at certain intervals and with a limit on the amount of interest. Terms and payment may be adjusted. Many lenders have the option that you can quickly convert your variable-rate into a fixed-term mortgage if you think interest rates are going to rise.

- Reverse mortgage. Owners of a property with substantial equity can receive regular monthly payments that have to be repaid at a later time, generally at the time of the house's sale or the debtor's death. It is very similar to an annuity. Retired people tend to find this strategy appealing. A minimum age of 62 is generally required. There are drawbacks to a reverse mortgage, the main one being a rapid increase in interest, diluting the accumulated equity in the property over time. As with any financial decision, you need to analyze the pros and cons. In some cases, it may be a better alternative to simply borrow money on a line of credit secured by your home.

- Graduated-payment mortgage. In this example, the payments start at a lower monthly amount and gradually increase over time. The monthly payments may average out over the term of the mortgage. This mortgage is common for people who have investment property, but don't want to have negative cash flow. The monthly payments therefore increase with the monthly cash flow over time. Review this option carefully, however, to ensure cash flow projections are solid and won't leave you paying financing costs that outstrip revenue projections! A graduated payment mortgage is also a method for working with negative cash flow, a topic discussed in the next section.

## Dealing with Negative Cash Flow

Negative cash flow simply means a shortfall every month when it comes to satisfying your monthly financial obligations. You would normally have to subsidize the shortfall yourself. However, negative cash flow could be temporary and a justifiable expense in relation to the potential of the property. There are different ways of avoiding, or addressing, a situation presenting negative cash flow:

- Rent with an option to buy. A renter pays an extra premium every month over the base rent, along with an option to purchase. The vendor would deem the overage to be a down payment on eventual sale. In the meantime, the vendor has eliminated the cash flow shortage. If the renter does not exercise the option, the overage is deemed a fee for the option and is not returned to the renter.

- Equity sharing. Equity sharing was discussed previously in Chapter 1, "Understanding Real Estate Investment," on page 26 under "Buying with

Partners." Basically, it means the renter pays a monthly premium and shares in the equity buildup when the property is sold. Generally the renters also have a first option to buy.

- Purchase lower-priced home. One way of dealing with negative cash flow is to purchase a property at a lower price that requires lower monthly payments. The property may still have significant investment potential, allowing you to launch your portfolio and work your way up to bigger investments.

- Refinance the property. If interest rates have dropped, you may be able to refinance the property. Even if you have to pay a penalty on a closed mortgage, you could still be further ahead over time in terms of the savings. Your calculations will tell you the cost/benefit. Also, consider locking in a long-term, fixed-rate mortgage——five years or more——if interest rates are at an attractive level.

- Boost property income. Take a close look at the configuration of your rental property. You can probably generate more revenue by renting the house to six individuals rather than a married couple with a family. This is a smart option if the building has a self-contained basement suite separate from the main level. The extra revenue each tenant provides could eliminate negative cash flow from the property, allowing you to service a larger mortgage. While it means more tenants to manage, and greater potential for wear and tear, careful selection of your tenants should minimize the risk. See "Improving the Bottom Line" on page 293 in Chapter 10, "Managing Your Property," for more suggestions for boosting property income.

- Obtain a longer amortization period. The longer the amortization period, the lower the monthly rates. A 30-year amortization will ensure lower payments than a 20-year period.

- Reduce expenses. Review all the expenses that are being incurred and look for ways to reduce them. (Chapter 10, "Managing Your Property," includes a section on minimizing expenses on page 297.)

- Negotiate a lower purchase price. If you know in advance that you will have a shortfall (which you normally should, of course), use that as leverage to reduce the price.

- Pay a larger amount down. A larger down payment will reduce your monthly debt-servicing charges and close the gap in monthly cash flow.

## Summary

This chapter provided a detailed overview of locating, selecting, and negotiating mortgage financing. It covered the various types and sources of financing, and tips on determining your needs and successfully attaining your objectives. More information is available in my book, *Mortgages Made Easy: The All-Canadian Guide to Home Financing.*

Financing goes hand-in-hand with understanding the legal issues of property ownership, which are discussed next.

# Understanding the Legal Aspects

**It is important** to understand the legal issues and terminology in order to discuss the appropriate matters clearly with your lawyer and make the correct decisions. Every aspect of a real estate purchase for personal use or investment involves legal implications, so you want to avoid legal problems.

This chapter explains different kinds of property ownership, the legal documents involved in the purchase and sale of real estate, the implications of backing out of an agreement, services provided by a lawyer, types of listing agreements, and legal structures to hold revenue property.

## Types of Ownership of Property

### Types of Interest in Land

There are several types of legal interests in land, the most common being free-hold and leasehold.

### Freehold Interest

Freehold interest entitles the owner to use the land for an indefinite period and to deal with the land in any way desired, subject to municipal bylaws; hydro utility easements or rights of way; provincial mineral rights or legislation; contractual obligations, including subdivision restrictive covenants; and any charges that encumber the title of the property and are filed in the provincial land titles office, such as mortgages, liens, and court judgments. Another term for freehold is *fee simple*.

### Leasehold Interest

In a leasehold interest, the holder of the interest in land has the right to use the land for a fixed period, say, 50 or 99 years. The owner of the property (landlord or lessor) signs an agreement with the owner of the leasehold interest (tenant or lessee) that sets out various terms and conditions of the relationship. The leasehold interest can be bought and sold, but the leaseholder can sell only the right to use the land for the time that is remaining in the lease, subject, of course, to any conditions contained in the original lease.

Both freehold and leasehold interests can be left in your will as an asset of your estate, or specifically bequeathed in your will.

## Types of Joint Ownership in Property

You may wish to have shared ownership in the property with one or more other people. There are two main types of legal joint ownership: joint tenancy and tenancy in common. (Chapter 1, "Understanding Real Estate Investment," has a section on "Buying with Partners" on page 17.)

### Joint Tenancy

In a joint tenancy, an owner has an undivided but equal share with all the other owners. No one person has a part of the property that is specifically his or hers because all the property belongs to all of the owners. At the time of purchasing the property, all the people who are joint tenants will be listed on the title of the property equally and each of the joint tenants has the right in law to possession of the whole property. These are the essential conditions involved in joint tenancy, and if any of these conditions are not met, then the ownership is deemed to be a tenancy in common and not joint tenancy.

One of the main features of a joint tenancy is the right of survivorship. This means that if one of the joint tenants dies, the others automatically and immediately receive the deceased person's share, equally divided. In other words, the deceased person's share in the joint tenancy is not passed on as an asset of his or her estate to beneficiaries, whether or not a will exists. It is fairly common for a couple to hold the legal interest in the property by means of a joint tenancy. Thus, you should consider tenancy in common if you do not want to have your interest go automatically to other parties.

### Tenancy in Common

In this form of ownership, the tenants can hold equal or unequal shares in the property. Each party owns an undivided share in the property and therefore is entitled to possession of the whole property. For example, there could be five people who are tenants in common, but four of them could own one-tenth of the property each, and the fifth person could own six-tenths of the property.

If the holder of a tenancy in common wishes to sell or mortgage his interest in the property, that can be done. If a buyer cannot be found and the tenant in common wants to get his money out of the property, he can go to court and, under a legal procedure called partition, request that the court order the property to be sold and that it distribute the net proceeds of sale proportionately.

Tenancy in common does not carry an automatic right of survivorship as joint tenancy does. In other words, if one of the tenants in common dies, the interest does not go to the other tenant(s), but to the estate of the deceased. If there is a will, the interest is distributed under the terms of the will. If the deceased person does not have a will, there is provincial legislation to deal with that type of situation, and the person's assets, which would include the tenancy interest, would be distributed to relatives according to the legislation.

There are various reasons why some people prefer tenancy in common to joint tenancy.

- If you are purchasing property for investment purposes with people who are not relatives, you may not want them to automatically have your interest in the property in the event of your death.

- If you have been previously married, have children from a previous relationship, and have since remarried, or are living in a common-law relationship, you may want to specify in your will that a certain portion of the value of the estate goes to your children individually or collectively. The only way this can be dealt with is in a tenancy-in-common situation because the interest would be deemed to be an asset of one's estate.

- If you are putting unequal amounts of money in the property, a tenancy-in-common structure would reflect those different contributions in terms of the percentage interest in the property.

Written agreements should be signed by tenants in common, setting out the procedures if one of them wants to get out of the situation. This is a prudent procedure that can be accomplished by giving the others the first right of refusal on a proportional basis to buy out the interest, or there could be a clause requiring the consent of the other tenants in common for approving a potential purchaser, or there could be a provision requiring a certain period of notice to the other tenants before the property is sold. Another case when tenancy in common might be preferable would be when one of the property owners wishes to have the personal independence to raise money for other outside interests, such as a business. In many cases the tenancy-in-common portion could be mortgaged without the consent of the other parties.

# Understanding the Purchase-and-Sale Agreement

The most important document you will sign will be the offer to purchase, which, if accepted, becomes the purchase-and-sale agreement. It sets out the terms and conditions between the parties and, as in any contract, it is legally binding if there are no conditions in the contract that have to be met before it becomes binding. Of course, there can be verbal contracts, but all contracts dealing with land must be in writing to be enforceable. That includes a purchase-and-sale agreement or a lease, which, of course, is also a contract.

This section covers the elements that make up a contract, legal implications of backing out of the agreement, and how to understand the contents of a purchase-and-sale agreement.

## Elements of a Contract

In order for a contract to be valid, five main elements have to be present: mutual agreement, legal capacity, exchange of consideration, intention to be bound, and compliance with the law.

### Mutual Agreement

There must be an offer and an acceptance. The terms and conditions of the bargain must be specific, complete, clear, and unambiguous. The parties to the contract must be sufficiently identifiable.

An offer may be withdrawn (revoked) any time before acceptance by either party as long as that revocation is transmitted to the other party—ideally in writing so you have proof. If the offer has already been accepted without condition and signed to that effect before receipt of the revocation, a binding contract has occurred.

### Legal Capacity

The parties to a contract must have the capacity to enter into a legally binding contract; otherwise the contract cannot be enforced. Each party to a contract must:

- be an adult, which in most provinces means 19 years of age or older;
- not have impaired judgment and must understand the nature and quality of what is involved in signing the contract. If it can be proven that a person is impaired by drugs, alcohol, stroke, or mental infirmity (diminished capacity), it would invalidate the contract;

- not be insane in medical and legal terms; and
- be able to act with free will, that is, not under duress, threat, or intimidation.

## Exchange of Consideration

This concept means that "something of value" must be exchanged by the parties in order to bind the contract. Usually money changes hands, but "consideration" could mean another property by exchange, something of value to the other side such as a service or product or other benefit, or a promise to do something in exchange for a promise to do something.

## Intention to Be Bound

The parties must have the intention of being bound by the agreement and its commitments, and they must expect that it will be a bargain that could be enforced by the courts.

## Compliance with the Law

A contract, to be enforceable, must be legal in its purpose and intent. The courts will not enforce a contract that is intended to, or has the effect of, breaching federal, provincial, or municipal legislation.

## Legal Options and Implications of Getting Out of a Signed Contract

There are instances where either the vendor or the purchaser may wish to back out of an agreement. You have to be careful because legal problems can result in litigation, which is expensive, time-consuming, stressful, protracted, and uncertain in outcome. Get legal advice before you act. Some examples are discussed below.

## Rescission

In several provinces and states there is a rescission or "cooling-off" period, whereby the purchaser of a new property has a period of time (usually from 3 days to 30 days) to back out of the contract by giving notice to the vendor in writing before the deadline. The vendor is obliged to pay back without penalty all the money that the purchaser has placed on deposit. In cases where legislation does not give an automatic right to rescission, the documents that are a part of the property package may have a rescission period built in. If you do not have a statutory (by law) right to rescission and it is not part of the documents relating to the purchase of a new property, then you may want to make it a condition of your offer.

## Specific Performance

If the vendor or purchaser refuses to go through with a purchase-and-sale agreement when there are no unfulfilled conditions attached to the agreement, the other party is entitled to go to court and request the court to order that the breaching party specifically perform the terms of the agreement—in plain language, complete the transaction. The party who succeeds in obtaining the court order would be entitled to ask for the costs of the application from the court. Generally, court costs awarded represent about 25 to 40 per cent of the actual legal costs incurred; therefore, those who win at court ultimately lose financially in terms of total cost recovery of legal costs expended.

## Damages

If one party refuses to complete the agreement, instead of suing for specific performance of the terms of the agreement, the other party can sue for damages. Damages mean the financial losses that have been incurred because the other party failed to complete the bargain. There is a basic legal maxim that says "to get financial damages [compensation], you have to prove you have suffered financial damages." For example, if a vendor refused to complete the deal because he thought he could make $50,000 more on the sale of the house (if the price had gone up considerably), and if in fact it could be shown that he did sell it for $50,000 more after refusing to go through with your signed commitment, then you could claim $50,000 damages plus court costs. Your loss could be quantified, assuming that there were no other reasons that could explain the differential in price. Alternatively, if the purchaser fails to complete and the vendor can show that he was relying on those funds and therefore the purchase he had planned failed to occur, and so on down the line with various back-to-back purchases and sales that were all relying on the first, there could be considerable damages for which the purchaser may possibly be liable. These are called "consequential" and "foreseeable" damages. Skilled legal advice is critical in this complex area of law.

   If the house value has not gone up or down by the purchase date, and if, for example, another purchaser was found and no other losses occurred, the vendor (in this example) could attempt to claim the deposit funds as "liquidated damages." This is generally negotiable unless it states clearly in the agreement of purchase and sale that the deposit funds automatically and irrevocably go to the vendor.

## Conditional Contract

If the vendor or purchaser has preliminary conditions built into the purchase-and-sale agreement ("subject" clauses), and those conditions cannot be met, no valid binding contract exists and neither party is liable to the other.

## Void Contracts

A contract is void and unenforceable if the required elements that make up a contract (see page 170) are not present, or if the contract is prohibited by statute (municipal, provincial, or federal law).

## Voidable Contracts

If one of the parties has been induced to enter into the contract on the basis of misrepresentation—whether innocent, negligent, or fraudulent—that party may be entitled to void the contract. If the misrepresentation was innocent, generally only the contract can be cancelled and any money returned, and no damages can be recovered in court. If there is negligent or fraudulent misrepresentation, however, not only can the contract be cancelled, but damages can also be recovered in court. For example, if the vendor was going to provide vendor-back financing and relied on the purchaser's representations concerning his creditworthiness and ability to pay, but prior to completion of the transaction (by doing a credit check and/or other investigation) the vendor finds out that the purchaser is a terrible credit risk, then that could be deemed to be negligent or fraudulent misrepresentation. For that reason the contract could be cancelled. To give another example, if the purchaser finds out before completion that the representation of the vendor or the vendor's agent is grossly untrue—that zoning has been approved for subdivision purposes, and investigation shows that no application has been made for subdivision purposes—then the purchaser could get out of the contract and sue to recover damages, if any can be proven.

These are just some examples of things that could affect the validity or enforceability of a contract. Competent legal advice in advance from a skilled real estate lawyer is needed to minimize potential problems.

## *Understanding the Purchase-and-Sale Agreement*

Most purchase-and-sale agreements come in standard formats, with standard clauses, and are drafted by the builder, the local real estate board, or commercial stationers. There are generally spaces throughout the agreement for additional, customized clauses. A contract prepared by a builder has distinctly different clauses from those of a standard form for resales, and there are considerable differences in the standard contract clauses among builders and among real estate boards.

There is a high risk that the standard clauses, or additional ones that you may choose to insert, will not be comprehensive enough for your needs; you may not even understand them or their implications, and may sign the agreement nevertheless. That is why it is so important to have a lawyer review your offer to purchase before you sign it. Regrettably, only a small percentage of people do this, because they either don't realize they should, perceive it will be an unnecessary or costly legal expense, or are naive or too trusting. It would be a false economy to save on a legal consultation, as the costs to obtain a legal opinion are very reasonable relative to the risk involved in signing a bad contract. Alternatively, rather than seeing a lawyer before submitting an offer to purchase, some people may wish to insert a condition that states the offer is "subject to approval as to form and contents by the purchaser's solicitor; such approval to be communicated to vendor within X days of acceptance, or to be deemed to be withheld."

There are many common clauses and features contained in the purchase-and-sale agreement, many of which vary from contract to contract according to various circumstances—whether one is purchasing a new or a resale property, type of property, revenue property, etc. Here is a brief overview of some of the common features of the agreement for purchase and sale.

## Amount of Deposit

A deposit serves various purposes. It is a partial payment on the purchase price, a good-faith indication of seriousness, and an assurance of performance if all the conditions in the offer to purchase have been fulfilled. The deposit is generally 5 to 10 per cent of the purchase price. If there were conditions in the offer, and these conditions were not met, then the purchaser is entitled to receive a refund of the full amount of the deposit. This is one reason why it is important to have conditions or "subject" clauses in the offer to protect one's interests fully. Most agreements for purchase and sale have a provision that gives the vendor the option of keeping the deposit as "liquidated damages," in the event that the purchaser fails to complete the terms of the agreement and pay the balance of money on the closing date.

When making a deposit, it is very important to be careful to whom you pay the funds. If you are purchasing on a private sale and no realtor is involved, never pay the funds directly to the vendor; pay them to your own lawyer in trust. If a realtor is involved, the funds can be paid to the realtor's trust account or your own lawyer's trust account, as the situation dictates. If you are purchasing a new property from the builder, do not pay a deposit directly to the builder. The money should go to your lawyer's trust account, or some other system should be set up for your protection to ensure that your funds cannot be used except under certain conditions based on those that are clearly set out in the agreement. The risk is high in paying your money directly to a builder because if the builder does not complete the project and goes bankrupt, you could lose all your money and, in practical terms, could have great difficulty getting it back. Although several provincial governments have brought in legislation dealing with new property projects to protect the public on the issue of deposits—as well as many other property risk areas—legislation provides only partial protection.

Another matter you have to consider is interest. If you are paying a deposit, you want to ensure that interest at the appropriate rate or based on the appropriate formula is credited to you. In many cases, deposit monies can be tied up for many months, and that could represent considerable interest.

## Conditions and Warranties

It is important to understand the distinction between conditions and warranties, as it is very critical to the wording used in the agreement.

A condition is a requirement that is fundamental to the very existence of the offer. A breach of condition allows the buyer to get out of the contract and obtain a refund of the full amount of the deposit. A buyer's inability to meet the condition set by a vendor permits the vendor to get out of the contract.

A warranty is a minor promise that does not go to the heart of the contract. If there is a breach of warranty, the purchaser cannot cancel, but must complete the contract and sue for damages. Therefore, if a particular requirement on your part is pivotal to your decision to purchase the property, it is important to frame your requirement as a condition rather than as a warranty. Both vendor and purchaser frequently insert conditions into the agreement. These conditions are also referred to as subject clauses and should:

- be precise and clearly detailed;
- have specific time allocated for conditions that have to be removed, for example, within 2 days, 30 days, or some other appropriate time frame. It is preferable to put in the precise date that a condition has to be removed, rather than merely refer to the number of days involved; and
- have a clause that specifically says that the conditions are for the sole benefit of the vendor or purchaser, as the case may be, and that they can be waived at any time by the party requiring the condition. This is important because you may wish to remove a condition even though it has not been fulfilled, in order for the contract to be completed.

Here is just a sampling of some of the common subject clauses. There are many others possible that you or your lawyer may feel it appropriate to insert.

### For Benefit of Purchaser

- title being conveyed free and clear of any and all encumbrances or charges registered against the property on or before the closing date at the expense of the vendor, either from the proceeds of the sale or by solicitor's undertaking;
- inspection being satisfactory to purchaser by relative, spouse, partner, etc. (specify name);
- inspection being satisfactory to purchaser by house inspector/contractor selected by purchaser;
- sale of purchaser's other property being made;
- confirmation of mortgage financing;
- deposit funds to be placed in an interest-bearing trust account with the interest to accrue to the benefit of the purchaser;
- approval of assumption of existing mortgage;
- granting of vendor-take-back mortgage or builder's mortgage;
- removal of existing tenancies (vacant possession) by completion date;
- existing tenancies conforming to prevailing municipal bylaws;

- interim occupancy payments being credited to purchase price;
- review and satisfactory approval by purchaser's lawyer of the contents of the agreement of purchase and sale;
- warranties, representations, promises, guarantees, and agreements shall survive the completion date;
- no UFFI having ever been in the building;
- vendor's warranty that no work orders or deficiency notices are outstanding against the property or, if there are, that they will be complied with at the vendor's expense before closing.

## Additional Clauses If Purchasing a Condominium

- receipt and satisfactory review by purchaser (and/or purchaser's lawyer) of project documents, such as disclosure, declaration, articles, rules and regulations, financial statements, project budget, minutes of condominium corporation for past two years, management contract, estoppel certificate, etc.;
- confirmation by condominium corporation that the condominium unit being purchased will be able to be rented.

## Additional Clauses If Purchasing a Revenue Property

- review and satisfactory approval of financial statements, balance sheet, income-and-expense statement, list of chattels, list of inventory, names of tenants, amount of deposits and monthly rents, dates of occupancy, list of receivables and payables, list and dates of equipment safety inspections, list of repairs and dates, service contracts, leases, warranties, property plans, and surveys.

## For Benefit of Vendor

- removal of all subject clauses by purchaser within 72 hours upon written notice by vendor of a backup bona fide (legitimate) offer;
- confirmation of purchase of vendor-take-back mortgage through vendor's mortgage broker;
- confirmation of purchaser's creditworthiness by vendor or vendor's lawyer;
- issuance of building permit;

- builder receiving confirmation of construction financing;
- registration of a subdivision plan;
- deposit funds non-refundable and to be released directly to the vendor once all conditions of the purchaser have been met;
- review and satisfactory approval by vendor's lawyer of the contents of the agreement of purchase and sale.

## Risk and Insurance

It is important that the parties agree to an exact date when risk will pass from the vendor to the purchaser. In some cases the agreement will state that the risk will pass at the time that there is a firm, binding, unconditional purchase-and-sale agreement. In other cases the contract states that the risk will pass on the completion or the possession dates. In any event, make sure that you have adequate insurance coverage taking effect as of and including the date that you assume the risk. The vendor should wait until after the risk date before terminating insurance.

## Fixtures and Chattels

This is an area of potential dispute between the purchaser and vendor unless it is sufficiently clarified. A fixture is technically something permanently affixed to the property; therefore, when the property is conveyed, the fixtures are conveyed with it. A chattel is an object that is moveable; in other words, it is not permanently affixed. Common examples of chattels are washer and dryer, refrigerator, stove, microwave, and drapes.

A problem can arise when there is a question of whether an item is a fixture or a chattel. For example, an expensive chandelier hanging from the dining room ceiling, gold-plated bathroom fixtures, drape racks, or television satellite dish on the roof might be questionable items. One of the key tests is whether the item was intended to be attached on a permanent basis to the property and therefore should be transferred with the property, or whether it was the vendor's intention to remove these items and/or replace them with cheaper versions before closing the real estate transaction.

In general legal terms, if it is a fixture and it is not mentioned in the agreement, it is included in the purchase price. On the other hand, if it is not a fixture and no reference is made to it in the agreement, then it is not included in the purchase price. To eliminate conflict, most agreements for purchase and sale have standard clauses built into them stating that all existing fixtures are included in the purchase price except those listed specifically in the agreement. In addition, a clause should list any chattels specifically included in the purchase price, and they should be clearly described.

## Adjustment Date

This is the date used for calculating and adjusting such factors as taxes, maintenance fees, rentals, and other such matters. As of the adjustment date, all expenses and benefits go to the purchaser. For example, if the vendor has paid the maintenance fee for March and the purchaser takes over with an adjustment date as of March 15, there will be an adjustment on the closing documents showing that the purchaser owes half of the amount of the prepaid maintenance fee to the vendor for the month. (A discussion of adjustments for property tax is included on page 157 in Chapter 5, "Understanding the Financing Aspects.")

## Completion Date

This is the date when all documentation is completed and filed in the appropriate registry and all monies are paid out. The normal custom is for all the closing funds to be paid to the purchaser's solicitor a few days prior to closing. As soon as all the documents have been filed in the land registry office and confirmation has been obtained that everything is in order, the purchaser's solicitor releases the funds to the vendor's solicitor. The steps taken by the lawyers for the vendor and purchaser relating to the closing date are further discussed later in this chapter. The adjustment date and the completion date are frequently the same.

## Possession Date

This is the date on which you are legally entitled to move into the premises. It is usually the same date as the adjustment and completion date. Sometimes the possession date is a day later in order for the vendor to be able to move out; in practical terms, though, many purchasers prefer the adjustment, completion, and possession dates to be the same, and make prior arrangements in terms of the logistics, if it is possible. One of the reasons is that the risks of the purchaser take effect as of the completion date, and there is always a risk that the vendor could cause damage or create other problems in the premises if he or she remains there beyond the completion date. As soon as your lawyer has advised you that all the documents have been filed and money has changed hands, the realtor or lawyer with whom you have been dealing arranges for you to receive the keys to the premises.

## Merger

This is a legal principle to the effect that if the agreement for purchase and sale is to be "merged" into a deed or other document, the real contract between the parties is in the document filed with the land registry. To protect you, it should be stated in the agreement for purchase and sale that the "warranties, representations, promises, guarantees, and agreements shall survive the completion date." There are exceptions to the document of merger in cases of mistake or fraud, technical areas that require your lawyer's opinion, but it is important to understand the concept.

## Commissions

At the end of most purchase-and-sale agreements there is a section setting out the commission amount, which the vendor confirms when accepting an offer. The vendor should make sure the purchase-and-sale agreement states that, if the sale collapses, at the option of the vendor the deposit monies can be deemed liquidated damages and the full amount can go to the vendor. A discussion of the various types of agreements for listing and selling real estate through a realtor appears later in this chapter.

# Services Provided by the Purchaser's Lawyer

There are many services provided by your lawyer at various stages—before the agreement is signed, after the agreement is signed, just before closing the transaction on the closing day, and after closing the transaction. What follows is a partial summary of some of the matters discussed and services performed in a typical real estate transaction. Each situation will vary according to the complexity and nature of the transaction.

## Before the Agreement Is Signed

- Discuss the contents of the offer to purchase with your lawyer. If there is a counter-offer from the vendor, make sure that you continue your communication with your lawyer before accepting the counter-offer, unless it is simply a matter of the purchase price.
- Discuss with your lawyer the ways in which you intend to finance your purchase.
- Enquire about all the various legal fees and out-of-pocket disbursement costs that you will have to pay.

- Ask your lawyer about all the other costs related to purchasing the property of which you should be aware. The most common expenses are shown in Checklist 3 on page 368 in the Appendix.

- Address matters such as your choice of closing date, inspection of the property before closing, and any requirements that you want the vendor to fulfill.

## After the Agreement Is Signed

Once your lawyer has received a copy of the signed agreement, he or she will carry out a thorough investigation to ensure that all the terms of the contract are complied with and that you obtain clear title to the property without any problems. In other words, your lawyer will make sure that you are getting what you contracted for and that all your rights are protected. The areas that a lawyer will check include the items below.

## Title of Property

An agreement for purchase and sale normally states that the vendor will provide title free and clear of all encumbrances. Therefore, your lawyer has to make sure that there are no claims or other filings against the property that could impair the title that you are purchasing. When searching the title, you will discover the name of the registered owner, the legal description, the list of charges (matters affecting the property) registered against the property, and other documents that are filed against the property. The types of charges that may be shown against the property include the following (terminology may vary from province to province):

- mortgage;

- right to purchase (agreement for sale);

- restrictive covenant (discussed on page 60 in Chapter 2, "Types of Residential Real Estate");

- builder's lien (claim for money owing);

- easement and right of way (discussed on page 59 in Chapter 2, "Types of Residential Real Estate");

- right of way (discussed on page 59 in Chapter 2, "Types of Residential Real Estate");

- option to purchase;

- certificate under provincial family-relations legislation, restricting any dealing with the property;

- judgment;
- caveat (formal notice that someone has an interest in the property and the nature of that interest);
- *lis pendens* (an action pending relating to the property, such as foreclosure proceedings);
- lease or sublease, or option to lease;
- the government's mineral rights;
- condominium project documents;
- condominium bylaws.

The following documents and items are also generally reviewed:

- survey certificate;
- property taxes;
- outstanding utility accounts;
- zoning bylaws;
- status of mortgages being assumed or discharged;
- ensuring financing will be sufficient and in place on closing;
- compliance with restrictions, warranties, conditions, and agreements;
- fixtures and chattels that are included in the purchase price;
- documents prepared by solicitor acting for seller (if applicable);
- survey certificate;
- all documents required relating to property purchase (including building regulations, project documents, bylaws, rules and regulations, financial statements, disclosure statement, estoppel certificate, and other documents as required);
- insurance obtained;
- mortgage reviewed;
- benefits of title insurance are considered.

## Title Insurance

Your lawyer could also recommend the benefits of obtaining title insurance for your peace of mind. Sometimes lenders require it. This insurance protects you in the event that pre-existing property defects show up after you bought the property. You would be covered up to the amount of your policy for as long as you are still the property owner.

The types of risks that are usually covered include: claims due to fraud, forgery, or duress; work orders; zoning and setback non-compliance or deficiencies; survey irregularities; forced removal of existing structures; unregistered rights of way or easements; and lack of vehicular or pedestrian access to the property. Shop around for the best policy rates, features, and coverage. One of the largest title-insurance companies in Canada is First Canadian Title (www.firstcanadiantitle.ca). The site has extensive consumer information.

## Closing the Transaction

Just prior to closing, there are various steps that your lawyer will generally go through, including the following:

- preparing documents relating to any sales tax for the chattels that you may be purchasing;
- preparing any mortgage documents necessary and making arrangements for depositing funding to the lawyer's trust account from the mortgage proceeds on filing;
- showing you a purchaser's statement of adjustments, which gives the balance outstanding that you must come up with before closing the transaction; you normally have to provide these funds to your lawyer at least two days beforehand;
- preparing the vendor's statement of adjustments;
- receiving for forwarding any postdated cheques required for the mortgage lender; and
- preparing all documents for filing in the land registry office on the closing date. If a different lawyer is involved in preparing the mortgage, that has to be coordinated for concurrent registration.

## On the Closing Day

On the date of closing the transaction, your lawyer will perform various services, including the following:

- checking on the search of title of the property to make sure that there are no last-minute claims or charges against the title;
- releasing funds held in trust after receipt of mortgage proceeds from the lender if applicable, and sending an amount to the vendor's lawyer based on the amount the vendor is entitled to as outlined in the purchaser's statement of adjustments;

- receiving a copy of the certificate of possession from the NHWP, if applicable;

- paying any monies required on the date of closing as outlined in the purchaser's statement of adjustments, such as sales tax on chattels being purchased, land transfer tax as applicable, and balance of commission owing to the real estate company paid from the proceeds of the purchase funds due to the vendor, and as outlined in the purchaser's statement of adjustments; and

- holding back any non-resident withholding tax if you purchased the property from a non-resident of Canada. The withholding tax is 25 per cent of the purchase price. If you fail to have the appropriate funds held back from the purchase funds, the CRA could attempt to collect the appropriate taxes from you. The premise behind this requirement under the Income Tax Act is that if the vendor owes any taxes for capital gains from the sale of the property to you, the CRA would have difficulty collecting those taxes if the vendor does not live in Canada and has no other real property assets in Canada. That is why the onus is on you to collect and remit 25 per cent of the sale price to the CRA. Your lawyer can tell you more about this.

## After Closing the Transaction

Once your lawyer has confirmed that the purchase is complete, you can make arrangements with the realtor to obtain the keys to your home, or your lawyer will arrange to get the keys for you. Your lawyer will also:

- send you a reporting letter with all the filed documents and all the other related documents attached for your records, including an account for fees and disbursements that have been taken from the funds that you provided to your lawyer in trust prior to closing;

- arrange to obtain and register the appropriate discharges of mortgages that were paid off from the funds you paid for the purchase, unless the vendor's lawyer is attending to this obligation; and

- ensure that all the vendor's promises have been satisfied.

There are numerous costs involved in purchasing new property, as shown in Checklist 3 on page 368. As for legal fees, you should be able to calculate them accurately in advance by asking your lawyer, and budget for the costs. Most lawyers charge a fee based on a percentage of the purchase price. In the case of condominiums or revenue properties, there is a higher charge for the extra documentation and responsibility involved on the lawyer's part, due to the nature of a condominium or revenue-property transaction. Although fees can vary from place to place because of market competition and other factors, between 0.75 and 1 per cent of the purchase price is normal. This relates only to legal fees and not to disbursements, which can vary considerably according to the nature of your transaction. It helps to shop around for legal fees; a flat-rate quote could save you money, especially if the lawyer does both the transfer of title (conveyance) and the mortgage documentation preparation.

## Services Provided by the Vendor's Lawyer

If you are a vendor, it is important that you obtain a lawyer to represent your interests in the sale transaction. Whereas it is customary for the purchaser's lawyer to be paid a percentage of the purchase price, it is customary for the vendor's lawyer to be paid on an hourly basis for time actually expended. In view of the fact that condominium and revenue-property transactions are more complicated and therefore take longer, you can expect that they will be slightly more expensive than house purchases. The hourly bill-out rate is normally between $100 and $200 or more, depending on the regional location and the lawyer's experience and expertise.

The lawyer acting for the vendor performs a wide range of services, the extent of which depends on each transaction. Some of the services are discussed below.

### Before the Agreement Is Signed

Before you sign the agreement, you should have selected a lawyer to represent you, and discussed the contract with him or her to make sure that you are protecting your interests and not incurring any additional expense or unnecessary frustration. If you are presented with a written offer, there are three options open to you:

1. You can accept the offer in the form in which it is presented by signing. In this event there is a binding contract between you and the purchaser, once all conditions have been removed.

2. You can alter the offer by making changes that are more suitable to you and having the offer resubmitted to the purchaser. By making changes to the purchaser's offer, you are in effect rejecting the offer and countering with a new one. The purchaser can either accept your changes or

make further changes and return the agreement to you, which would constitute a new offer.

3. You can ignore the offer completely if you feel that it is unrealistic or otherwise unsatisfactory to you.

## After the Agreement Is Signed

Once the bargain has been reached in writing between the vendor and the purchaser, the vendor's lawyer will request various documents from the vendor in order to assist in completing the transaction. The type of material that you should obtain depends on what is customary in your area and on provincial jurisdiction. The documents may not all be easily obtained, but you should attempt to provide the following:

- real estate tax bills;
- hydro or other utility bills;
- copies of any insurance policies;
- a survey, if you have one available;
- a copy of the deed to your home, if you are in a province that has such a system;
- a copy of any outstanding mortgages, with the address of the mortgage company and, if possible, the mortgage account number and amortization schedule;
- if an existing tenancy is being assigned, details on the tenancy and on any security deposits;
- any condominium-related documents such as project documents, bylaws, rules and regulations, estoppel certificate, and others that may be required;
- any revenue-property-related documents such as financial statements, income-and-expense statement, balance sheet, list of chattels, names of tenants, and so on.

Prior to completion of the transaction, you should make arrangements to notify the utility, cable television, Internet, and telephone companies that you want service disconnected from your address as of a certain date. Also, advise your insurance company to cancel the insurance policy on the day after the closing date.

## *Just before Closing the Transaction*

Your lawyer will prepare a deed or transfer document that you must sign before title can be passed to the purchaser. Your lawyer will also review the vendor's statement of adjustments. In most provinces or regions the custom is for the purchaser's lawyer to prepare the conveyance (property transfer) documents for the vendor to sign and prepare the vendor's and the purchaser's statements of adjustments. These would then be forwarded to the vendor's lawyer for review before the vendor signs.

If there is a mortgage on your home, it is the vendor's responsibility to discharge the mortgage so that clear title to the property can be transferred. Your lawyer, after obtaining a copy of the mortgage statement showing the balance outstanding as of the closing date, would then undertake (legally promise) to the purchaser's lawyer that the mortgage would be paid off first from the proceeds of the purchase.

If you are a non-resident of Canada, there is a withholding tax that will be kept back from the sale proceeds and remitted to the CRA. This is because a non-resident could be making a profit or capital gain on the sale of the property, and is required to pay tax on that property, but the CRA could have difficulty collecting from someone outside of the country. That problem is prevented by having funds paid to the CRA directly from the sale proceeds. The withholding tax under the Income Tax Act is 25 per cent of the sale price. Your lawyer will advise you as to the correct amount of withholding tax.

## Title Insurance

Your lawyer could advise you to obtain title insurance coverage in case any defects with your property are discovered after the sale, and a claim is made against you. Title insurance would cover your liability up to the amount of your policy, and under the terms of the policy, as long as the risk existed as of the date of the policy. There are many different types of risks covered by title insurance, but you need to comparison shop for features, benefits, and costs.

## *On the Closing Day*

On the closing date, your lawyer or your lawyer's agent will meet the purchaser's lawyer or lawyer's agent at the land registry office so that the transfer documents can be filed, changing title.

## After Closing the Transaction

After the transaction has been completed, and your lawyer has received the appropriate money based on the vendor's statement of adjustments, he or she will clear off any existing mortgages with those funds and have the mortgages discharged from the title of the property. You will then receive the balance of funds after the legal fees and disbursements have been deducted.

Finally, your lawyer will send you a reporting letter setting out the services that were performed and enclose any appropriate documents for your files.

# The Listing Agreement

The real estate–listing agreement is usually a partially pre-printed form with standard clauses and wording. The balance of the agreement, completed by the agent and the vendor, covers the specific information with respect to the property being offered for sale and the nature of the contractual bargain between the agent and vendor. Because the listing agreement is a binding legal contract, you should be very cautious about signing it without fully understanding the implications of what you are signing. If in doubt, get advice from your lawyer beforehand. The following section covers the general contents and the types of listing agreements.

## Contents of a Listing Agreement

A listing agreement performs two main functions. First, you are giving the real estate agent the authority to act on your behalf to find a purchaser for your property. The agreement sets out the terms and conditions of this agency relationship, including the commission rate or method of compensation for the agent's services, the length of time of the appointment, when and how the fee or commission is earned, and how and when it will be paid to the agent.

Second, the agreement sets out the details of the property being offered for sale, including civic and legal address, list price, size of property, description of the type of property, number and size of rooms, number of bedrooms, type of heating system, main recreational features, and other amenities. Any chattels or extra features that are to be included in the list price should also be set out, such as appliances, draperies and drapery track, and carpeting.

You should also insert other particulars in the listing agreement relating to the property for sale, including details of existing financing, the balance on the mortgage, the amount of monthly payments, and the due date on the mortgage. Any other mortgages should be listed as well. Annual property taxes should be set out, as well as any liens, rights of way, easements, or other charges on the property.

Once you have come to an agreement on all the terms and you are satisfied with them, the agreement is signed and witnessed and you receive a copy.

## Types of Listing Agreements

There are three basic types of agreements that you may wish to consider when listing your property with a real estate agent: open, exclusive, and multiple listings.

### Open Listing

In an open listing, the real estate agent does not have an exclusive right to find a purchaser for the property; you can sign any number of open-listing agreements with as many different agents as you wish. Only the agent who sells the property earns a commission. The problem with an open listing is that many realtors don't spend a great deal of time on such a listing because, with so many other realtors also be looking for purchasers, they may not earn a commission.

Open listings are more common in commercial sales than in residential sales, and in any event you should obtain legal advice on drafting an open-listing agreement if you are considering such an option. To protect yourself, make sure that the agreement is in writing and the terms clearly spelled out. Commission rates could be similar to the "exclusive listing" below.

### Exclusive Listing

In this example, the vendor gives to the real estate agent an exclusive right to find a purchaser for the property. This right is given for a fixed period. The real estate agent is automatically entitled to receive a commission whether someone else sells the property, the vendor sells the property, or the property is sold at some future point to someone who was introduced to the property by the real estate agent during the listing period. The duration of an exclusive listing is normally 30, 60, or 90 days. In many ways the shorter the time period, the more energetically the realtor will have to work to achieve the sale. You can always extend the listing if you are satisfied with the realtor's performance and service. The range of commission is between 4 and 5 per cent on the first $100,000, and 2.5 per cent thereafter. If it is raw land, a 10 per cent commission is common. Commissions can vary and are generally negotiable, depending on the circumstances.

## Multiple Listing

With a multiple listing, a realtor is given an exclusive listing, in effect, for a fixed period of time, but also the right to list the property with the MLS. This highly sophisticated computerized database is available to all members of the real estate boards who participate in the service. In practical terms, this constitutes almost all real estate companies; the entire real estate network becomes like a group of subagents for the sale of your property. If another agent finds a buyer, the selling company and the listing company will split the commission equally. Multiple listings are generally offered for a minimum of 60 days, but this is negotiable. Commission rates vary between 5 and 7 per cent on the first $100,000, and 2.5 per cent thereafter. Commissions can vary and are negotiable, depending on the circumstances.

# Forms of Legal Structure to Hold Investment Property

One of the first issues you have to consider when buying investment real estate is deciding the form of legal structure in which to hold your property. This will be necessary before you set up a bank account or purchase the property. Your main alternatives are sole proprietorship, partnership, and corporation. A general description of each of these follows, along with advantages and disadvantages of each.

The type of legal structure you choose will depend upon the type of real estate investments you wish to acquire, your potential risk and liability, the amount of money needed to start, what you expect to earn, whether you have partners, and the tax implications. (See also Chapter 1, "Understanding Real Estate Investment," in the section on "Buying with Partners" on page 17.) If your risk and liability are high, the incorporation process will provide some protection. On the other hand, there may be tax advantages to having a sole proprietorship instead. Once you become familiar with the differences between each form, you should consult a lawyer and tax accountant. The decision is an important one.

## Sole Proprietorship

A sole proprietorship refers to an individual who owns an investment in his or her personal name. The real estate investment income (if it is a revenue business) and the owner's personal income are considered the same for tax purposes. Therefore, business profits are reported on the owner's personal income tax return and are based on federal and provincial income or loss schedules. Business expenses and losses are deductible. It is advisable, though, to keep personal and business bank accounts separate. For instance, you may wish to pay yourself a salary from your business account and deposit it into your personal account for your personal needs—food, clothing, lodging, personal savings, etc.

### Advantages:

- government regulations are minimal;
- ease of rolling over into an incorporated company if necessary or desired at some later point;
- owner has total control and gets all profits;
- capital gains or losses are easily calculated.

### Disadvantages:

- owner has unlimited liability; that is, he or she is personally liable for all debts and obligations of the business.

## Partnership

A partnership is a proprietorship with two or more owners. The owners may not necessarily be 50/50 partners; they may have whatever percentage reflects their investment and contribution to the partnership. The partners share profits and losses in proportion to their respective percentage interest. While the partnership has to file a tax return, it does not pay any tax. Instead, the partners pay tax on the basis of their portion of the net profit or loss. In a partnership, each partner is personally liable for the full amount of the debts and liabilities of the business. Each of the individuals is authorized to act on behalf of the company, and each can bind the partnership legally, except if stated otherwise, in a partnership agreement. It is sound business advice not to enter into any partnership arrangement without a written agreement between the partners regarding responsibilities for financing the business, sharing the profits and losses, working in the business, specific duties, and other important considerations. Partnerships are governed by provincial partnership legislation.

### Advantages:

- government regulations are minimal;
- ease of rolling over into an incorporated company if necessary or desired at some later point;
- joint responsibility; not everything rests on your shoulders;
- access to money and skills is greater;
- capital gains or losses are easily apportioned depending on your percentage interest.

### Disadvantages:

- potential for conflict between partners;
- unlimited liability; all the partners are individually and collectively liable for all the debts and liabilities of the business. Thus, if one person makes an error in judgment, all partners will be exposed;
- ownership and control must be shared, as well as the profits.

## Corporation (Limited Liability Company)

A corporation is a business that is a legal entity separate from the owner or owners of the business. After being incorporated with the provincial or federal registry, a business must file annual reports, submit regular tax returns, and pay tax on its profits. The owners are called shareholders and have no personal liability for the company's debts unless they have signed a personal guarantee. The liability of the company is limited to the assets of the company. You can have a single-shareholder corporation. If there are two or more shareholders, make sure you have a shareholders' agreement. This is similar to a partnership agreement. The shareholders elect directors (usually the shareholders) who are responsible for managing the affairs of the corporation. Directors have some potential liability to statutory creditors, such as the CRA, for the company's debts.

It is advisable to obtain legal and tax advice to assist with the preparation of the incorporation documents and shareholders' agreements.

### Advantages:

- The shareholders are not personally responsible for any of the debts or obligations of the corporation unless a shareholder has signed a personal guarantee.

- The corporation continues regardless of whether a shareholder dies or retires.

- There may be various business tax advantages not available to a proprietorship or partnership.

- The tax rate could be lower than for a proprietorship, up to a certain level of income.

- You should still be eligible for the personal lifetime capital gains tax exemption when the property is sold and you obtain a profit on your initial investment. Get your tax accountant's advice in advance to make sure the original deal is structured properly.

- There is increased business stability, in that while shareholders may come and go, the business continues uninterrupted and all property of the corporation remains intact.

- Share ownership interest is transferable.

- A corporation is a separate legal entity from an individual. It may sue or be sued in its own name.

## Disadvantages:

- Corporations are regulated by each province or the federal government. The regulations are more complex than those of the partnership legislation.

- The costs of incorporating are higher than costs relating to other business structures—approximately $400 to $700 plus the lawyer's out-of-pocket disbursements, which are approximately $300 to $400.

- The operating losses and tax credits remain within the corporate entity; they are not available to individual shareholders if the corporation is unable to utilize them.

# Other Legal Cautions and Protections to Consider

## Limiting Your Personal Liability Exposure

If you are operating a small business, or consider your real estate investments as a business, you also want to protect yourself and your family from creditors. Here are some techniques to discuss with your lawyer.

- Don't sign personal guarantees, or limit them. There is no point in going to the effort of incorporating a company if you nullify the personal protection by signing a personal guarantee of the corporate debts. Don't sign personal guarantees at all, for example, to suppliers, trade creditors, or landlords. Alternatively, only do so for a bank if absolutely necessary, and then limit the amount of liability. For example, if the company is borrowing $45,000, and there are three partners, agree to be liable for a maximum of only one-third. Get legal advice before you sign any personal guarantee to a lender. Use the competitive market-place as leverage when choosing one creditor over another.

- Never pledge personal security. Adopt a policy of not pledging any personal security—your personal car, house, or life insurance policy—under any circumstances.

- Transfer property and other assets to your spouse. You can transfer the ownership of your home and other personal assets, such as your car, to your spouse. That way, the assets are not in your personal name. In the event of a marital breakup, the matrimonial home is generally considered to be owned 50/50 in many situations anyway. Also, under family law legislation of most provinces, family assets are combined for calculation purposes and then divided in half. Speak to your lawyer about the laws in your province.

- Be aware of director liability. If you are a director of a corporation, you do have liability risks, particularly under provincial and federal government legislation. For example, there could be potential liability for corporate tax, GST/HST, provincial employment standards legis-lation, provincial sales tax, builder's lien legislation, etc. Therefore, if you are a director, consider not owning any personal assets of conse-quence to limit the potential risk.

- Don't have your spouse as guarantor or director. To limit the family's risk, you don't want to ask your spouse to act as a director or guarantor.

- Don't have joint accounts. If you have a joint account, and a creditor garnishees your bank account, they will seize all the funds in that account. By having separate accounts, you avoid that risk.

- Consider spousal RRSPs. If your spouse is earning less than you are, you may wish to contribute to his or her RRSP as a spousal RRSP. You get the RRSP tax deduction, but your spouse gets the money in his or her RRSP account. Therefore, if a creditor tries to collect on your RRSP with a court judgment, there will be less money available. If an RRSP is collapsed to pay the creditor, there will only be the amount left after federal tax is taken off the RRSP amount. This fact gives room for your lawyer to negotiate with the creditor for some creative compromise settlement—for example, a maximum of 10 to 25 cents on the dollar, with flexible payment terms over time, interest-free. Your lawyer should be able to negotiate on your behalf, as most people do not have the skills or objectivity and are too emotionally involved. Also, your lawyer should have experience in negotiating, and thus more credibility in the eyes of the creditor.

- Consider RRSPs with insurance companies. If you have an RRSP, RRIF, or non-registered investments with an insurance company, under certain circumstances, creditors are not able to collect on the RRSP. Check with your financial and tax adviser and lawyer.

- Sign business documents as authorized signatory of corporation. In order to get the full protection of your corporation, always make it clear that you are signing on behalf of your corporation. That way, no one can try to claim that you were signing in your personal capacity.

- Consider allocating Canadian Pension Plan (CPP) income to your spouse. Another income-splitting option, which also has the effect of putting more money in your spouse's hands, is to apportion a certain percentage of your CPP to your spouse. You are entitled to start taking out your CPP at age 60, at a reduced amount. This approach means that there is less money available for creditors from your personal income. Get tax advice on the appropriateness of this option.

- Lend money to your corporation and become a secured creditor. You could lend money as a creditor to the company and take back security, like any other creditor could. This could be in the form of registered general or specific security agreements, assignment of receivables, or mortgage filed against the property, and so on.

- If your company wants to borrow money from a lender, and the lender does not want its security against your company's assets to rank in claim priority after the security you have previously registered for any personal loans you have made, you do have an option. You can subordinate or postpone your claim; in other words, give priority to the lender's security. However, your security document remains registered against the property. You therefore remain a secured creditor for any claim you make against the corporate assets after the lender gets its money back.

- Consider creating a personal management company for your services. Rather than drawing a salary as an employee of your own company, you may wish to have a management-consulting agreement with your own company as an independent contractor. You might consider a separate corporation as your personal management corporation. There are various tax and other considerations for this approach.

- Make sure you have a will. The legal and financial nightmares your family will have to deal with if you don't have a will won't be the type of legacy for which you want to be remembered. (Refer to Chapter 12, "Understanding Financial and Estate Planning.")

If you are interested in a discussion on legal protections relating to small business, refer to *The Canadian Small Business Legal Advisor* by Douglas Gray and *The Complete Canadian Small Business Guide* by Douglas Gray and Diana Gray.

## Limiting Your Estate Liability Exposure

What if you are currently running your own small business as a real estate investor when you die? Your business could cease to function, as you are the key person. If the business goes under, creditors will start looking for assets. If you are liable under a personal guarantee or as a director, then creditors could make claims against your estate.

Here are some options to discuss with your professional advisers to minimize the risk to your estate:

- Make sure you have a will. A current will that has been drafted with your lawyer and accountant is the first step. (Refer to Chapter 12, "Understanding Financial and Estate Planning.")

- Make sure you have a shareholders' agreement with a buy-sell clause. This enables one owner to buy out the other's interest in certain situations while they are alive or from their estate.

- Designate beneficiaries of your insurance policies. By doing so, the money bypasses the will completely, is not part of your estate, and goes directly to your designated beneficiaries tax-free. Your personal creditors can claim only from assets in your estate.

- Designate beneficiaries for your registered investments, including TFSAs, RRSPs, and RRIFs. By designating a beneficiary for registered retirement plans, you bypass your will and your estate. The money goes directly to the beneficiary and is unavailable to creditors. You can also designate beneficiaries for your non-registered investments.

- Consider trusts. If you set up a living trust while you are alive, it bypasses your will and therefore your estate on your death. A testamentary trust is set up through your will and takes effect after your death. Both types divert assets out of your estate, away from creditors of your estate.

- For more information on will and estate planning, refer to the latest edition of *The Canadian Guide to Will and Estate Planning* by Douglas Gray and John Budd, and visit www.estateplanning.ca.

## Keeping Peace in the Family When Money's at Stake

In a worst-case scenario, if you have a real estate–investment or small business and it goes under, ensure that your relationships with your friends, family, and relatives survive the ordeal. Here are some dos and don'ts.

- Secure loans from family and friends. If you borrow money from friends and family, consider securing them with security registered against property, such as a mortgage or general or specific security agreement. That way they are a secured creditor, like any other.

- Consider loans plus equity. You could structure your loans from family and friends to include an equity (share) feature in your business or real estate investment as a value-added incentive.

- Consider a convertible option from loans to equity. You could give an option to your family or friends who are lending money to convert those loans in part or in full to share equity if they wanted to do so later; that is, after the company has proven itself to be viable.

- Don't ask family or friends to sign personal guarantees or co-sign. If the loan is called, you will regret it. The relationship may not survive the financial loss, depending on the amount and related circumstances.

- Don't ask family or friends to act as directors. Directorship carries a lot of potential liability to a lot of different categories of creditors. Depending on the business, the risk could be very high. Directors don't generally appreciate being sued personally and having all their personal assets at risk. That process does not bode well for the continuation of a meaningful relationship.

- Don't ask your spouse or partner to consent to a collateral mortgage on your house, no matter how immune you think you might be to the statistical reality of business failure. Ask yourself how your marriage will be affected in a business downside situation if the bank starts action to foreclose on the house.

- Don't assign life insurance proceeds. If you do so to secure a loan and you die, your creditor could get all the money, leaving nothing for your family. If a creditor insists on insurance and you have tried all alternatives, most banks will offer special loan insurance. A monthly insurance premium is added to your loan, and if you die, the loan is paid off in full.

## *Avoiding the Pitfalls of Litigation*

At some point in your business or real estate investment career, you might be faced with a litigation issue as the plaintiff or defendant. As in any game, litigation is inherently an adversarial process; if you don't know how to play it well, or retain a lawyer who does, the odds of winning are not in your favour. No matter what debt, breach of contract, or negligence is causing you to consider suing, keep the following pitfalls and street-smart suggestions foremost in mind.

## Avoid Lawsuits Based on Emotion

You might feel that you have been wronged and you are naturally very upset. Your decision to sue, however, should be based on hard-nosed business realities. Maybe there is not much money involved, but it is a matter of principle. Give yourself some time, maybe several months, to see if the intensity of your emotions subsides. The litigation process itself has enough negative emotion associated with it.

## Have Realistic Expectations

Many people assume that if they are right, they will win at the end of the day; however, very few issues in law are black and white. The litigation process is inherently unpredictable. In addition, when you factor in legal fees, even if you win, the court costs you are awarded amount to only about 15 to 35 per cent of your legal fees, so you still lose financially. And then you still have the challenge of attempting to collect on the judgment.

## Assess the Defendant's Assets

You could win at trial, but still be a big-time loser. The defendant could have no assets in his or her name or have all the assets leveraged up with debt at the time you commence an action or by the time you get a judgment. A corporate entity could be a hollow shell without any net worth.

Do an objective risk assessment of the realistic potential of collecting on a judgment. You could be throwing good money after bad. The negative learning experience could be seen as a cost of doing business, and you could then commit to changing your business practices to pre-empt a recurrence.

## Weighing Potential Gains versus Losses

Realistically assess the relative pros and cons of litigation in terms of money and lost productivity. Can you afford the fight to the end? Have you obtained three written quotes as to the cost of the complete pretrial and trial process? Will it cost more than the amount you are claiming? What if you lose? You will be out not only legal fees, but court costs as well. What if the defendant counter-claims against you and wins?

## Consider a Settlement

Settlements occur all the time. Only about 5 per cent of lawsuits ever end up at trial, with the exception of small claims court. Even small claims court has a settlement-hearing process before trial in many provinces. Settlements allow both parties to strike a deal and get on with life, saving a lot of court time. Because of the uncertainty of the trial process outcome, settling for 20, 30, 50, or 70 per cent of the original claim is better than the risk of getting nothing and being out legal fees as well.

## Don't Sue Too Early

Don't commence your action before you have all the facts. Ideally, you want to have all your arguments included in your claim to show your opponent that you have done your homework.

## Don't Sue Too Late

If you wait too long, you could miss a statutory time limit to commence your action. Different actions and different provinces have different time limits.

## Get Expert Legal Advice

This is not a time to use your family lawyer whom you've known for a number of years. Instead, select a lawyer who specializes in the specific area of law or litigation if it will proceed to court. Before you make any decisions, have at least three lawyers give you objective feedback on your chances at trial, how long it will take, and how much it will cost. You need a benchmark for comparison and to make sure that the advice is consistent and, if not, why not. (Refer to Chapter 4, "Selecting Your Advisory Team.") A few legal consultations will enhance your knowledge and increase your confidence in your final decision. Then, sleep on your dilemma for a few weeks or a month. See if you have the same opinion at the end of that time.

## Alternative Dispute Resolution

Using the legal process to resolve a conflict should be a last resort. Apart from the time and costs involved, the relationship will probably be damaged beyond repair. If the parties get to the point where they communicate only through their respective lawyers, it is inevitable that there will be at best a winner and loser, or more likely two losers. It is doubtful that it will be a win-win situation, which is obviously the best outcome.

The first step to resolving a dispute is obviously for both parties to sit down together and attempt to work out a solution that is mutually acceptable. If a dispute cannot be resolved at this level, the alternative dispute-resolution (ADR) approach is gaining favour in many types of business conflicts. Trained professionals can provide mediation and arbitration services for business disputes, including mediating contract interpretation, disputes, or negotiations, or provide a written opinion proposing a pragmatic, equitable, and reasonable resolution to the conflict.

Mediation is an informal resolution facilitation service. Arbitration is more formal and is generally governed by the provincial arbitration legislation that sets out procedures and protocols. Many lawyers are also accredited mediators and arbitrators.

As mentioned earlier, for a detailed discussion of legal matters relating to small business, refer to the most current editions of *The Canadian Small Business Legal Advisor,* by Douglas Gray, and *The Complete Canadian Small Business Guide,* by Douglas Gray and Diana Gray.

## Summary

As you can clearly see from reading this chapter, there are many legal issues, options, and implications to consider when buying, selling, or investing in real estate. Topics covered included the different kinds of property ownership, what types of legal documentation are involved when buying or selling real estate, and what services are provided by a lawyer. Also covered were the different types of listing agreements and legal structures to hold revenue or investment property.

Part of prudent legal strategic planning is to anticipate and avoid legal problems and related financial risks. This chapter discussed how to limit your personal liability exposure and that of your estate in the event of your death. Tips were given on how to avoid the pitfalls of litigation if a dispute occurs. Finally, if you decide to borrow money or ask for investment funds from family or friends, suggestions were given on how to avoid estrangement or conflict with the people you care about the most.

Hand in hand with the financial and legal issues of purchasing a house are the tax issues, which are discussed next.

# Understanding the Tax Aspects

**Taxes are a key consideration**, whether you're buying a principal residence or investment property. The information and tips in this section will help you to understand the important issues, and even save you money. Since tax provisions can change at any time, contact a tax accountant to obtain current income tax advice before making any investment in real estate. (Guidelines on how to find a professional accountant are on page 116 in Chapter 4, "Selecting Your Advisory Team.")

The following discussion highlights the main categories of local, provincial, and federal government taxes that could affect you. It also includes tax-planning strategies, tax-saving tips, ways of maximizing your deductions, and ways to avoid pitfalls.

## Local and Regional Taxes

Canadian cities and towns raise revenues largely through property taxes. This leaves property owners in cash-hungry municipalities feeling like cash cows, while owners of valuable properties in municipalities that aren't so needy pay less than those getting milked. A condo owner in Vancouver, for example, might face a lower property tax bill than someone with a property of equal value in a small town where there are fewer properties to carry the burden of local services—even though that same Vancouver property owner may feel taxes are rising at a rapid rate.Some municipalities include assessments for utilities in the main property tax bill. Others separate out the taxes.

### Property Taxes

Property taxes are generally due on an annual basis, with assessment of value determined within six months prior to the property taxation year. For residential property, a "mill rate" is generally determined annually and multiplied by the assessed value of the property, including the building on the property, to determine the actual tax due. In many provinces there is a homeowner's grant that is subtracted from the gross taxes assessed for your property to determine the net payable tax you owe. This annual grant is for a principal residence only, not an investment property, and can vary depending on the age of the homeowner.

If you believe your property taxes are unfair because they are based on an artificially high assessment of property value, you can appeal the assessment notice. For example, when a real estate market has gone down, it is not uncommon for property assessment appeals to go up because of the lag time before the assessment reflects the reduction in value. Make sure you don't miss the appeal deadline, as the time window can be tight.

Property taxes are generally assessed for municipally supplied services such as schools, education, roads, and hospitals.

## Utility Taxes

Utility taxes pay for services such as water, sewer, and garbage pickup. A full list of the utilities for which property owners in a given area are assessed, and a breakdown of the local property tax bill are available from municipal staff in your area. The regional assessment authority or your lawyer will also be able to advise you on the specific taxes to which you're subject, and what kind of exemptions may be possible.

## Provincial Taxes

One of the most contentious taxes property owners face is the property transfer tax, which many provincial governments charge when a property is purchased. It isn't charged on the sale of the property, but rather on acquisition of real property by the buyer. It is the main form of property tax that provinces charge, though landlords also typically pay income tax (a subject discussed elsewhere in this chapter).

The property transfer tax is based on the purchase price of the property. The formula for determining the amount payable varies between provinces. To obtain further information about the tax, and other provincial taxes, contact your lawyer or the local branch of your provincial government land titles office.

## Federal Taxes

The federal government levies two main taxes of concern to property investors: sales tax and income tax.

## Sales Tax

Introduced on January 1, 1991, the goods and services tax (GST) applies to all "supply" of real property, both residential and commercial, except in certain, well-defined cases. Some provinces—Ontario, New Brunswick, Nova Scotia, and Newfoundland and Labrador—bundle it with their provincial sales taxes (PST) in the harmonized sales tax (HST). British Columbia harmonized its taxes on July 1, 2010, but it is now set to be phased out by March 31, 2013, and the PST and GST restored under the same terms in place prior to implementation of the HST.

The term *supply* has a broad meaning. It includes not only the sale and lease of real property but also any transfer via exchange, barter, and gifting. The tax is applicable to the various services related to the transfer, maintenance, and operation of properties, too. Originally set at 7 per cent, the GST (federal sales tax) rate is currently 5 per cent. An increase in the rate would not be unusual, however, given that most jurisdictions that have introduced so-called value-added taxes such as the GST have increased the rate over time.

The following overview discusses how certain types of real estate purchases are affected by or exempted from the GST/HST, and how the GST/HST rebate system operates. Check with your accountant to make sure that you are aware of any changes. Governments tend to modify legislation over time; in 2010, for instance, the rules governing "place of supply" changed, in some cases altering the tax rate on interprovincial transactions.

### Understanding the GST/HST

Purchasers pay the GST/HST to the vendor at the time of purchase. The vendor remits the tax to the CRA. Sometimes the vendor includes the GST/HST within the purchase price, and other times it may be added separately. It is a good idea to have it broken out in some manner on all records of sale.

There are also several categories of GST/HST exemptions relating to real estate, some of which are federally mandated and others, provincially mandated to address specific local conditions. For example, if you have to pay GST/HST on a property purchase, you may be able to receive a rebate or credit that reduces the tax paid against tax collected. Rebates and credits are linked to the property's use, whether as a principal residence, an investment, or a regular business of buying and selling properties.

### Resale Home or Other Residential Dwelling

A residential property purchased as a principal residence from the original or subsequent occupant is not subject to GST/HST. It is deemed exempt under

CRA rules, which define "used residential property" as an owner-occupied house, condominium, duplex, apartment building, vacation property, summer cottage, or non-commercial hobby farm offered for resale. The "used" property definition requires that the vendor was not a "builder," as defined in the legislation. A builder is someone who builds or substantially renovates the property as a business. A used property is also one that was recently built and is substantially complete, and which has been sold at least once (in this case, no occupancy is required for it to be deemed "used").

If you purchase a resale home that includes a room used as an office, and you are self-employed, the entire house still qualifies for the GST/HST exemption if you use it primarily as your residence. However, if you purchase a home that is used primarily for commercial business purposes, and it is zoned for that type of operation, at the time of purchase you would be GST/HST exempt only for the portion in which you plan to reside.

When purchasing a resale home, you can request that the vendor provide you with a certificate stating that the property qualifies as "used" for GST/HST purposes.

## New Home

When you purchase a newly constructed home from a builder as a principal residence for yourself or a relative, the entire purchase price, including land, is taxable. The word *home* refers to a residential dwelling and includes a single family house, condominium (apartment or townhouse format), or mobile home. If the home will be your principal residence, it may qualify for a partial GST/HST rebate, depending upon the sale price.

Purchasers across Canada of homes priced up to $350,000 will qualify for the maximum rebate of $8,750, or 36 per cent of the GST on the purchase price, whichever is less. Since $8,750 is 2.5 per cent of $350,000, the buyer is really paying the GST at a rate of 2.5 per cent on a $350,000 home instead of 5 per cent.

If you are purchasing a home priced at more than $350,000 but less than $450,000, the rebate is gradually reduced; in other words, it declines to zero on a proportional basis. On a home priced at $450,000, for example, the full GST of $31,500 is payable without rebate. There is no rebate available on homes selling for $450,000 or more.

If you are purchasing the home for investment purposes and you intend to rent out the property to tenants, the full GST/HST rate is charged on the purchase price and no rebate is available. If you are purchasing the home through a limited company, a rebate is not allowed.

Here are some examples of how the rebate is calculated if you are buying for a principal residence. The term *purchase price* refers to the price paid to the builder for the home and lot before the GST is calculated, and does not include any associated realty or legal fees.

*Example 1:* Formula used for homes selling for $350,000 or less

If you buy a new home for $150,000, you would calculate the rebate this way:

GST paid (5% of $150,000) = $7,500

Amount of GST rebate ($8,750 or 36% of $7,500; the smaller amount must be claimed) = $2,700

Net amount paid in GST (GST paid minus rebate) = $4,800

*Example 2:* Formula used for home selling for more than $350,000 but less than $450,000

If you buy a new home for $400,000 you would calculate the rebate this way:

GST paid (5% of $400,000) = $20,000

**Step 1** of rebate calculation ($7,200 is the amount because 36% of $20,000 is $10,080 and you must use the smaller amount)

**Step 2** of rebate calculation ($7,200 × [$450,000 − $400,000 purchase price] ÷ $100,000 = $3,600

Amount of GST rebate = $3,600

Net amount paid in GST (GST paid minus rebate) = $16,400

*Example 3:* Sample new home rebates

| Purchase Price | GST Paid | GST Rebate | Net GST Paid |
|---|---|---|---|
| $100,000 | $ 5,000 | $1,800 | $3,200 |
| $150,000 | $ 7,500 | $2,700 | $4,800 |
| $200,000 | $10,000 | $3,600 | $6,400 |
| $250,000 | $12,500 | $4,500 | $8,000 |
| $300,000 | $15,000 | $5,400 | $9,600 |
| $350,000 | $17,500 | $6,300 | $11,200 |
| $400,000 | $20,000 | $3,600 | $16,400 |
| $450,000 | $22,500 | no rebate | $22,500 |

When the home is purchased, the builder can either pay the rebate directly to you or deduct it from the GST you owe on the purchase price. You have to complete a form called GST New Housing Rebate (GST-191), which is available from your real estate agent, builder, or the CRA (www.cra-arc.gc.ca).

In addition, provincial rules allow for rebates of the provincial portion of the HST. Ontario allows a rebate to a maximum of $24,000 if you paid HST on the purchase a property including land, and $16,080 if the property consisted solely of buildings. Until it phases out the HST in March 2013, British Columbia allows a maximum rebate of $26,250 on purchases including land, and $17,588 when only buildings were part of the transaction. Nova Scotia allows for rebates in some parts of the province, but not others. For information regarding the rules governing your specific situation, speak with your real estate agent, builder, or the finance department of your province.

## Owner-Built Home

If you build your own home, or hire someone to build or substantially renovate a home for you as a principal residence for yourself or a relative, you will qualify for a federal GST rebate if you:

- paid the GST on construction materials and contracting services;
- or a relative are the first occupants of the home; or
- sell the home and ownership is transferred to the purchaser before it is occupied as a place of residence.

The amount of the rebate will depend on the fair market value (FMV) of the home and whether or not the GST was paid on the acquisition of the land. The FMV must be less than $450,000.

To determine FMV for the home you build, have it appraised or compare it to similar homes in your neighbourhood. A formal appraisal to substantiate your rebate application may be required if you claim a FMV that's close to or greater than $350,000 but less than $450,000.

If you paid GST when you acquired the land for your new home, the rebate is calculated on the land and the house in the same manner as if you had purchased the property from a builder. (This formula is discussed on page 204 under "New Home.")

If you did not pay GST when you acquired the land, the rebate is reduced for homes valued up to $350,000 to a maximum of $1,720 or 10 per cent of the GST paid, whichever is less. For homes valued at more than $350,000 but less than $450,000, the rebate is gradually reduced. There is no rebate for homes valued at $450,000 or more.

Here are some formulas to show how to calculate the rebate on an owner-built home when the GST has and has not been paid on the land.

### GST Paid on Land

*Example 1:* If the FMV of the home, including land, is $350,000 or less, the rebate calculation is $8,750 or 36% of the GST paid on the land, building, contracting services, and building materials, whichever is less. See Example 1 on page 205 for a similar calculation.

*Example 2:* If the FMV of the home, including land, is more than $350,000 but less than $450,000, the rebate calculation is based on the following formula:

$$A \times (\$450,000 - B) \div \$100,000$$

A = $8,750 or 36% of the GST paid on the land, building, contracting services, and building materials, whichever is less

B = the FMV of the home

See Example 2 on page 205 for a similar calculation.

### GST Not Paid on Land

*Example 1:* If the FMV of the home, including land, is $350,000 or less, the rebate calculation is $1,720 or 10% of the GST paid on the building, contracting services, and building materials, whichever is less.

*Example 2:* If the FMV of the home, including land, is more than $350,000 but less than $450,000, the rebate calculation is based on the following formula:

$$A \times (\$450,000 - B) \div \$100,000$$

A = $1,720 or 10% of the GST paid on the building, contracting services, and building materials, whichever is less

B = the fair market value of the home

## Renovated Home

Sales of substantially renovated homes are treated in the same way as sales of new housing when it comes to GST/HST. "Substantial renovations" mean that at least 90 per cent if not all of the house except the foundation, external walls, interior supporting walls, floor, roof, and staircases must be removed or replaced.

Here's an example: When a person in the renovation business buys an older home, GST/HST is not charged on the purchase price because GST/HST does not apply to resale homes. The person then completely guts the property, installing new walls, railings, flooring, wiring, and plumbing. The kitchen, bathroom, and other areas are totally reconstituted. This substantially renovated home, when sold, will be treated like a new home for GST/HST purposes. If you purchase this substantially renovated home, you will pay GST/HST on the purchase price and be entitled to claim the GST new-housing rebate if the price is less than $450,000. (Refer to the "New Home" section on page 204 in this chapter for information on this rebate and how it is calculated.)

Other renovations or improvements to a home, such as replacing a kitchen or building an addition, are not considered substantial renovations. If you buy an older home that has only been partially renovated, such as a remodelled bathroom, an additional bedroom, or a new roof, GST/HST is not applicable at the time of sale.

You can see the importance of making sure that any work done to a property does not constitute a substantial renovation. You will pay less for the house if you can avoid GST/HST, and boost your chances of a better return when your time comes to sell the property.

A substantially renovated home is considered a resale home if the renovator owns it and lives in it, even for a short time. That is an important point to keep in mind, especially if you are buying from another homeowner or renovating it yourself. You should be able to get more money on resale if the purchaser does not have to pay GST/HST.

## Land

There is no GST/HST on the sale of vacant land or recreational property, such as a hobby farm owned by an individual or by a trust for the benefit of individuals. Certain sales and uses of farmland are also exempt.

If you paid GST/HST on the land because the previous use of the land was such that GST/HST was applicable, the rebate would be the same as for a new home, as discussed in the "New Home" section on page 204.

If you build on the land and sell it, refer to the discussion of GST/HST in the "Owner-Built Home" section on page 206.

## Real Estate-Transaction Expenses

GST/HST is applicable to most of the services associated with completing a real estate transaction. For example, GST/HST is applied to the commission that a real estate agent charges for facilitating a sale. The tax is paid by the person responsible for paying the commission, usually the vendor. Real estate commissions are subject to GST/HST, even if the total tax owed is reduced by a rebate or the sale is exempt. For example, if you sell a used home, the sale price is exempt from GST/HST, but the real estate commission is still taxable.

Other real estate–related services on which GST/HST is levied include fees for surveys, inspections, appraisals, and legal and tax advice. GST/HST is charged on these fees regardless of whether the house you purchase is exempt from the tax. All moving charges are taxed.

There are several exemptions from GST/HST, however. Mortgage broker fees are not taxed if the fees are charged separately from any taxable real estate commissions. Also, mortgages and interest on mortgages are exempt from GST/HST.

## Rent

Most residential rents are exempt from GST/HST. A residential tenant is not required to pay GST/HST on rent paid to the landlord, provided the tenant occupies the premises for at least one month. Commercial leases are subject to GST/HST.

The landlord is required, of course, to pay GST/HST charges on all services necessary to keep the property in good repair. Rather than underwriting this additional cost, the landlord will generally increase rents. If you are the landlord, you will want to make sure you recover the additional cost.

If you employ a realtor or property-management company to find and arrange a tenant for your rental property, GST/HST applies to the fees and commissions charged for this service. All repair and maintenance services charge GST/HST.

## Condominium Maintenance Fees

If you own a condominium, the monthly fee charged by the condominium corporation is not subject to GST/HST; however, the condominium corporation will be charged GST/HST on all services employed to maintain the building and grounds. These additional GST/HST costs will obviously be passed on to the condominium owners in the form of increased monthly fees.

## Homeowner Expenses

Any service you employ around the house, such as gardening, plumbing, and carpentry, is subject to GST/HST, as are cable, hydro, and telephone bills.

# Income Tax

There are many tax considerations you should be aware of when buying real estate for personal use or for investment purposes. The following discussion highlights only the common areas to consider and is not complete or detailed. It is important that you get advice from a professional tax accountant familiar with real estate issues before you make a decision on real estate investment. The laws and regulations dealing with taxation matters are complex and constantly changing. Also, you need specific advice based on your personal circumstances. In addition, there are forms, guides, information criteria, and interpretation bulletins available on the CRA's website (www.cra-arc.gc.ca). The *Rental Income Guide* is especially important with respect to further tax details.

## *Principal Residence*

Most people start their first real estate investment by purchasing their own home to live in. Your principal residence may be a house, apartment, condominium, duplex, trailer, mobile home, or a houseboat.

A property will qualify as a principal residence if it meets various conditions:

- It is a housing unit, a leasehold interest in a housing unit, or a share of the capital stock of a co-operative housing corporation.
- You must own the property solely or jointly with another person.
- You, your spouse, your former spouse, or one of your children ordinarily inhabit it at some point during the year.
- You consider the property your principal residence.

## Tax Benefits of a Principal Residence

One of the key benefits is that the gain you will realize on the sale of your principal residence is not usually subject to tax. For example, if you bought the property originally for $50,000 and sell it for $250,000, you would not pay tax on this increase in value of $200,000.

## Renting out Part of the Principal Residence

It is not uncommon for people to rent out part of their principal residence as an income source or mortgage helper. Sometimes these rental suites are referred to as "illegal suites," which refers to the fact that the suite or room rented to someone who is not a relative may contravene existing municipal zoning bylaws in the community in which you reside. The zoning for your home might be single family, so renting to a tenant, in effect, means that you are arbitrarily converting your home into a multi-family dwelling. The important point to keep in mind is that the federal government does not care whether your rental space contravenes municipal zoning bylaws or not. Municipal bylaws and federal tax regulations are not related. The federal tax authorities don't care what your zoning is; they just want you to be honest about reporting all your income on your tax return.

In practical terms, many municipalities do not enforce the bylaw regulations relating to illegal suites if there is a shortage of rental accommodation in the community unless a neighbour complains. In most cases you have a right to appeal if your municipality requests that the tenant vacate your premises. Each situation can vary. Canada Post will occasionally refuse to deliver mail to a secondary address if it is not legally registered. Contact your lawyer for advice if you face challenges regarding the legitimacy of a rental unit.

If you are renting out one or two rooms of your house to a boarder, it will not interfere with its principal residence status as long as you do not claim capital cost allowance (CCA) on the rental portion. Essentially, CCA means depreciating a portion of the value of the home, excluding land, and deducting that portion as an expense from your income. (CCA is described in more detail in the next section, "Real Estate Investment Property" on page 219.) In addition, the rental portion is supposed to be minor in relation to the whole house, although in some cases this can be up to 50 per cent or more. You are not supposed to make major structural changes to your house to accommodate tenants. In normal circumstances, you should have nothing to concern yourself about. For peace of mind, speak to your tax accountant if you have any doubts.

If you do claim CCA, a change in use occurs. That rental portion will no longer qualify as a principal residence, and you might have a taxable capital gain on that rental portion. The change-in-use aspect is discussed shortly, and an explanation of capital gains is discussed on page 219 in "Real Estate Investment Property."

If you do rent out part of your principal residence, you can deduct many types of expenses from your income. The net effect might be that your expenses (excluding CCA, of course) exceed or equal the income, meaning that you have no tax payable. The normal expenses would be for things such as interest on your mortgage, property taxes, maintenance and repairs, insurance premiums, utilities, and advertising. Expenses specifically related to the rented part of the building may be claimed in full; however, expenses that relate to the whole property must be apportioned between rental and personal use. You may base the apportionment on square feet/metres or the number of rooms rented in the building, as long as it is done on a reasonable basis. For example, if you rent 4 rooms of your 10-room house, you may deduct the following:

- 100 per cent of expenses specifically related to the rented rooms, such as repairs and maintenance;
- 40 per cent (4 out of 10 rooms) of expenses that cannot be attributed specifically to the 4 rented rooms, such as mortgage interest, property taxes, insurance, utilities, and maintenance.

You are supposed to fill out a Statement of Real Estate Rentals and include it with your personal income tax. This form, along with examples, is included in the *Rental Income Guide* referred to on page 210. Rental expenses are also discussed on pages 223–6.

## Change in Use to or from a Rental Operation

If you were living in your home as a principal residence and then decided to leave and rent it out, the day you begin to use your residence as a rental property you are deemed to have:

- disposed of it for proceeds equal to its fair market value at that time; and
- immediately reacquired it for the same amount.

If your property had qualified as your principal residence every year since you acquired it, any gain you realized on the deemed disposition would be exempt from tax. For example, if you bought the property originally for $75,000 and lived in it and then subsequently decided to rent it out (and not reside in any part of it), and at that time the value was $275,000, you would not have to pay any tax on the capital gain of $200,000. If you sold the property a few years later for $325,000, you would have a taxable capital gain on $50,000—the difference between $275,000 and $325,000—minus any appropriate deductions, of course.

There are several ways that you could avoid paying tax on this capital gain, however. First, a provision in Canada's income tax legislation allows you to claim that you have not converted your principal residence to a rental property if you report your rental income, in certain circumstances. You may deduct any allowable expenses incurred, but not claim any CCA on the residence. The effect is that you don't pay any tax when the property is eventually sold.

Generally, the above provision is for a four-year maximum period and due to your leaving for various reasons, such as job relocation. Your intention should be to eventually return to the house. There are special provisions where you can extend that four-year limitation period indefinitely, such as:

- Your absence results from a relocation required by your or your spouse's employer.
- You and your spouse are not related to the employer.
- You return to the original house while still with the same employer or within one taxation year after leaving that employer.
- The original house is located at least 40 kilometres (25 miles) farther from your (or your spouse's) new place of employment than your temporary residence.

Check with your tax accountant to make sure that you make decisions that comply with CRA regulations. You don't want the government to disallow your claim to retain your principal residence status. Tax laws and regulations are always in a state of flux.

If you acquire a property for rental purposes and later begin to use it as your principal residence, you are deemed to have disposed of the property for an amount equal to its fair market value at the time you ceased to use it for rental purposes. However, you may elect to postpone the recognition of any capital gain until you actually dispose of the property. This is assuming you have not claimed CCA. Speak to your tax accountant to get proper advice in advance.

## Operating a Business Out of Your Home

Many people, at some point, start full- or part-time businesses out of their homes for various reasons: to eliminate the daily commute, to raise a family, to supplement salaried income, to test a business idea, to ease into retirement, or to save on business overhead and thereby reduce financial risk by writing off house-related expenses. There are many different types of home-based businesses, including managing your real estate investment property.

Remember that you need competent tax and legal advice before you start up. Also, you may want to obtain a GST/HST number if you have more than $30,000 in income in your business, or are paying GST/HST on items you purchase and want to set off against GST/HST you are charging. Check with your accountant and the closest CRA office.

A home business will not affect the tax status of your principal residence under federal rules as long as you don't claim a CCA on your home as part of your business operation. You can claim CCA on other non-home business capital expenditures, according to the CCA class. The percentages range from 4 to 100 per cent depreciation in a year. This is explained shortly.

There are numerous categories of expenses that can be deducted depending on the nature of your business. An expense is deductible if its purpose is to earn income, it is not a capital nature (that is, depreciated over time by using CCA), and is reasonable in the circumstances. Your accountant will advise you as to which are deductible and which are not. Also, if some of the expenses are related to personal use, you are required to deduct that portion from the business expense. Reasonable salaries paid to a spouse and/or children for services rendered to the business are also deductible. The Statement of Business or Professional Activities (T2125) from the CRA outlines some of the expenses that you may wish to consider. This form is available online as well as in Revenue Canada's *Business and Professional Income Tax Guide.* Your accountant may suggest other expenses for which you could be eligible.

You may only claim expenses for the business use of a workspace in your home if either of the following applies:

- The workspace is your principal place of business for the full- or part-time self-employed aspect of your career (you could have a salaried job elsewhere; it is not required that you meet people at your home).

- You use the workspace only to earn income from your business, and it is used on a regular basis for meeting clients, customers, or patients. In this case you could also deduct expenses from an office outside the home.

Also, the expenses you may deduct for the business use of your home cannot exceed the income from the business for which you use the workspace. This means that you must not use these expenses to create or increase your business loss. You may carry forward any expenses that are not deductible in the year and deduct them, subject to the same limitation, in the following year.

To deduct expenses, you take the portion relating to the space used for a home office. For example, you can divide the total number of rooms in the house by the number of rooms used for business to find the percentage of square feet used for business. So if you were using 20 per cent of your home for business purposes, including the basement for storage of inventory, then you would deduct 20 per cent of all your related expenses from your business income.

There are direct and indirect expenses relating to your home business that are deductible in part or in full. (Checklist 4 [page 370] outlines the home-business tax-deductible expenses with which you should be familiar and discuss with your accountant.) Remember that tax law changes can and do occur from time to time, which could affect any of the following common deductions.

## Maximizing Expense Deductions

A legitimate expense is worth using to reduce your taxable income. While you don't want to overspend, a smart investor will spend what's necessary to boost overall revenue and make the most of those expenses at tax time by claiming them against income. This section outlines some of the common opportunities for deductions.

### What Constitutes a Tax-Deductible Expense?

An expense is tax deductible if its purpose is to earn income; it is not of a capital nature; and it is reasonable in the circumstances. A capital expense means an asset that is depreciated over a period of time according to the CCA-class interest deduction. The allowance must not exceed the maximum rate allowable in any year. The percentages range from 4 to 100 per cent depreciation in a year. Obtain a copy of these CCA categories from the CRA.

Your accountant can advise you regarding the expenses you are eligible to deduct and those you cannot. If some of the expenses are related to personal use, you are supposed to deduct that portion from the business expense. Reasonable remuneration paid to spouses or partners for service rendered to the business is also deductible. The Statement of Business or Professional Activities (T2125) from the CRA and the associated guide, *Business and Professional Income Tax Guide*, outlines some of the expenses to consider. Your accountant can suggest other expenses you may be eligible to claim.

## Direct Business Expenses

Direct business expenses benefit only the business part of the home. Some of these costs are depreciated through a CCA and others are deducted:

- Room furnishings. Office furniture and equipment worth more than $250 have to be depreciated (use the CCA schedule from the CRA). Other items such as office supplies and materials can be deducted as part of your annual expenses.
- Remodelling or decorating costs. These include repairs or renovations done to a room to turn it into an office. These may include painting, carpentry, floor covering, plumbing, or electrical work, or even an extension to your house. This should be listed as an improvement and should be depreciated.

## Combined Business and Personal Expenses

These are expenses attributable to both the personal and the business use of a home. Only the business part is deductible as a business expense. Expenses should be apportioned on a reasonable basis between business and non-business use according to a reasonable formula, such as the percentage of the floor space used.

## Rent

If you rent a house or apartment and use part of it for business purposes, you may deduct the portion of your rent attributable to business use. For example, you may decide to claim 20 per cent of your apartment or 20 per cent of your home costs as rent. Common ranges for an apartment would be from 10 to 25 per cent, and for a house between 5 and 25 per cent. It could be more, of course, depending on use.

## Mortgage Interest

You can deduct the percentage of interest expense related to use of your home for business. For example, if your monthly mortgage payments are $2,000, generally about 99 per cent of that payment is interest and 1 per cent goes toward the principal. This would be the case especially in the first three years of the mortgage (assuming it is a 20-year amortization period). Therefore, for practical purposes, let's assume the interest portion is $2,000. If you were claiming 20 per cent of your house as business-use related, you would claim $400 per month × 12 months, which equals $4,800 a year, as a business expense.

## Insurance Premiums

You can deduct that portion of insurance expense which relates to your business (e.g., fire, theft, liability coverage). If you were claiming 20 per cent usage of your house or apartment, you would claim that portion of the premium as a business expense.

## Depreciation of Your Home

You can claim depreciation on the building portion (but not the land portion) of your home through a CCA, as explained earlier. A house is normally depreciated at 4 per cent, which means you could claim up to 4 per cent of the depreciated balance each year. A house that's worth $100,000 would let you claim depreciation of up to $4,000 in the first year. The second year, the value of the house would be $96,000 ($100,000 less $4,000) and your maximum claim for depreciation would be $3,840. Since you claim just the business-use portion, perhaps 20 per cent of the property, you would claim $800 in year one and $768 in year two, for example.

In practical terms, most home-business owners do not claim CCA. The reason is that if you later dispose of the property, a taxable capital gain could arise on the portion of the property that you used for business purposes. You could also be subject to recapture of the CCA previously claimed (that is, recording a portion of the CCA as income on the following year's tax return). If you are interested in claiming depreciation, speak to your accountant and have these concepts explained in further detail, and determine whether there is any advantage to making the claim.

## Utilities

You can deduct the portion of home utility expenses—oil, gas, electrical, and water costs, for example—related to business.

## Home Maintenance

You can deduct a portion of your expenses for labour and material for house maintenance and repairs for business use, such as furnace and roof repairs. You cannot claim your own labour; however, if you pay other family members to perform the work and issue receipts to them for the same, then you can claim the cost of their labour.

## Services

You can deduct a portion of municipal or private services such as snow and trash removal, yard maintenance, and the like for business use.

## Automobile

If your auto is used for personal and business travel, you need to take a portion of the expenses and depreciation relating to business use. CRA rules impose a ceiling of $30,000 plus GST plus PST (or HST where applicable) on the value of your car, regardless of its market value (check with your accountant for the current rules). In addition to depreciation, you can claim a portion of all other car-related expenses, such as oil, gas, repairs, insurance, maintenance, and interest relating to financing costs.

## Telephone

A separate business line may be deducted in full. A residential phone line that also serves as your business line would have its cost deducted in relation to the use that is business related. All long-distance charges that are business related are, of course, totally deductible. Other phone-related costs that you could deduct (in full or in part) would be installation costs, telephone equipment, answering machine, or answering service.

## Entertainment and Meals

Generally, you may deduct the cost of meals with business colleagues and associates if these expenses are incurred in the ordinary course of business. Documentation regarding the purpose of the meal and who it was with may also be required. You may claim only half the entertainment and meal expenses in your home city, but the full amount of such expenses incurred in the regular course of a business trip.

## Travel

Travel expenses—such as airfare and accommodation—incurred to attend conferences, conventions, trade shows, and other events as part of your activities as a landlord or real estate investor are eligible for deduction. If the trip combined personal and business activities, you would deduct the proportion related to the business portion of the trip.

## Child-Care Expenses

If you are self-employed and need to pay someone to care for your child so you can work, it may be possible to claim an expense deduction for a portion or all of the cost.

The expenses discussed are just some of the many tax deductions that may be available to you. As recommended earlier, refer to Checklist 4 for a detailed list of possible expense deductions. Remember, you may be able to claim 100 per cent of the cost of the expense or a depreciated amount over time, depending on the item.

To clarify what you can deduct and how to do it, as well as other home-business tax issues, speak to your accountant. It is also very important that you talk to your lawyer about the various types of legal issues when starting a business. (Chapter 6, "Understanding the Legal Aspects," provides an overview of the three main types of legal structures.)

## Keeping Records

If you are renting out part of your principal residence to a tenant, or intend to have a home-based business, make sure that you keep detailed records of all money collected and paid out. Purchases and operating expenses must be supported by invoices, receipts, contracts, or other documents.

You do not need to submit these records when you file your return. If you do not keep receipts or other vouchers to support your expenses, all or part of the expenses claimed may be disallowed. (For more information on record-keeping, see page 272 in Chapter 10, "Managing Your Property.")

## *Real Estate Investment Property*

It is important to understand the concepts and options outlined in this section. It will save you time when discussing the issues with your accountant and enhance your decision making. The following is only an overview to highlight some of the key areas. By the time you finish reading this section, you will appreciate the need and benefit of using professional advisers to maximize your tax savings and net after-tax profit.

### Capital Gains or Income

Many investors assume that when property is sold for a profit, the profit will be treated as a capital gain for income-tax purposes. This would result in a lower tax rate than other types of income. You have to be very careful, though, as Revenue Canada could consider the profit as regular income at regular tax rates.

Capital gains are usually taxed at 50 per cent of the capital gain. In other words, if you bought a property for $100,000 and sold it for $225,000, but after all expenses were taken into account you net $200,000, the net profit (gain) would be approximately $100,000. You would normally have to pay tax on 50 per cent of the net gain—in this case, $50,000. If the profit were deemed to be income instead of a capital gain, you would have to pay tax on 100 per cent of the amount; that is, on the full $100,000.

Revenue Canada applies various types of criteria to determine whether the profit is deemed to be a capital gain from a real estate investment, or income from a business of speculating in real estate without any investment intent. Each situation depends on the individual circumstances, so make sure you get tax advice from a professional accountant in advance.

For example, if you purchased a property with the intention of selling it as soon as possible in a hot real estate market, the profit from that could be deemed to be income. In other words, you "flipped" the property or sold your rights under an agreement of purchase and sale. Another example would be a situation in which a person bought vacant land with the intention of selling it quickly. The key tests are what your original intent was when you purchased the property, the facts and the circumstances, and how quickly you sold it. There are many credible and logical reasons to refute the income theory and argue that it should be considered a capital gain. It would be very frustrating to plan on specific after-tax money from a sale, and then find that you owe more in taxes than you had planned. That is why you need good tax planning and advice from a professional accountant, a point that is reinforced throughout this chapter.

## Business Income or Property Income?

Depending on the circumstances, rental income may be income from either a business or property. There are certain factors to be considered in determining if a rental operation is a source of business or property income. Revenue Canada recognizes as businesses very few rental operations carried on by individuals. One notable exception is when renting real property is incidental to, or part of, your business. In such cases, the rental activity is regarded as forming part of your business income or loss.

If your rental operation is not part of, or incidental to, an existing business, the number and kinds of services that you provide for your tenants will determine if you are earning income from a business or from property. Generally you are considered to be earning income from property if you merely rent space and provide basic services such as:

- heat;
- light;
- water;
- elevators;
- parking;
- laundry facilities; and
- general maintenance of the property.

However, if you provide services to tenants in addition to those basic services that have come to be considered part of property rental, you may be carrying on a business rather than merely renting property. For example, as the landlord of a building, your rental operation would be considered a rental business in the following situation:

- You rent apartments and, in addition to providing your tenants with the basic services listed above, you supply meals and drinks, operate a restaurant or lounge on the premises, or provide maid or linen services.

The more services you provide, the greater the likelihood that your rental operation is a business. However, the following factors are *not* to be taken into account when determining whether a rental operation is a business:

- the size or number of properties you are renting;
- the amount of time you spend on managing or supervising the properties; and
- whether the accommodation is rented furnished or unfurnished.

If two or more individuals participate in a rental operation, the same factors must be considered in determining whether the rental operation is a source of business income or property income. In the case of a legal partnership, if all factors indicate that your rental operation is not a business, your income from the operation is treated as property income, even though partnership income usually relates to a business operation.

## Capital Expenses

These expenses are usually outlays that provide a lasting benefit beyond the current year. This would include expenses such as purchasing or improving your property. Generally, capital expenditures are not fully deductible in the year they are incurred. Instead, you may deduct a portion of their cost each year as CCA. This percentage may vary between 4 and 100 per cent each year. In effect, you are depreciating the value of the item according to the CCA classification table, and writing off the depreciated amount against your rental income.

You cannot claim CCA on the cost of land, as it is not a depreciable property. On the contrary, as an investor, it is your hope and intention that the property will appreciate!

CRA rules deem the following types of expenses as capital in nature:

- the purchase of rental property;
- legal fees and other costs in connection with the purchase of property;
- the cost of furniture and equipment rented with the property;
- major repairs and expenditures that extend the useful life of your property, or improve it beyond its original condition.

Here are some of the guidelines the CRA uses in determining whether an expense is capital or current in nature. A discussion of current expenses follows shortly.

## Maintenance or Betterment

An expense that merely restores a property to its original condition is usually a current expense; however, an expenditure that materially improves a property beyond its original condition is likely a capital outlay. For example, the cost of reinforcing wooden steps would be a current expense. If you replaced the wooden steps with concrete steps, the expenditure would be capital in nature.

## Integral Part or Separate Asset

The cost of repairing an integral part of a property is a current expense; however, the cost of replacing the whole property or even a considerable part of it is a capital outlay. For instance, since electrical wiring is an integral part of a building, an amount spent to rewire would normally be considered a current expense, if it were not a betterment. The purchase and installation of air-conditioning units in the windows of a building that was not previously air conditioned, however, is a capital expenditure because the units are separate assets and not integral parts of the building.

## Enduring Benefit

A capital expenditure generally provides a lasting benefit or advantage. On the other hand, a current expense is one that usually recurs after a relatively short period. The installation of a central air-conditioning system in a building is an example of a capital expenditure.

## Relative Value

An additional factor that you may have to consider is the cost of the expenditure in relation to the value of the property. For example, while a filter for a furnace could be considered a separate asset, it is logical to treat its cost as a current expense. If you replace the furnace itself, you acquire a separate asset of substantial value in relation to the building where the furnace is installed. The cost of the furnace is therefore a capital expenditure. On the other hand, you might spend a substantial amount for normal maintenance and repair work to your property all at one time. If this expenditure was for normal maintenance that for some reason was not done on an ongoing basis, it is nevertheless a maintenance expense and, as such, would be deductible as a current expense.

Obtain professional tax advice on the issue of capital expenses before making decisions.

## Current Expenses

These types of outlays are usually ones that benefit the current year only, such as repairs made to maintain the rental property in the same condition it was in when you originally bought it. You may deduct current expenses from your gross rental income in the year you incur them. Current expenses are also referred to as operating expenses.

The following is a list of typical costs associated with renting a property. These are general guidelines only. You may deduct these expenses from your gross rental income in the year they are incurred unless otherwise stated. As mentioned many times, tax rules can change, so obtain current tax advice. In addition, your accountant may be able to advise you regarding various tax-planning options.

- Accounting fees. Amounts paid for bookkeeping services, auditing books and records, and preparing financial statements.
- Advertising. Amounts paid for advertising that you have space available to rent.

- Capital expenditures. Capital expenditures are not fully deductible in the year they are incurred.

- Commissions. Amounts paid or payable to agents for collecting rents or finding new tenants.

- Computer-related expenses. All your computer activity directly or indirectly related to managing should be deductible costs, including: Internet service provider (for e-mail and web access), paper, toner, computer repairs, printer, and fax machine.

- Condominium expenses. If you earn rental income from a condominium unit, you are entitled to deduct any expenses that are normally deductible from rental income. These may include condominium fees representing your share of the upkeep and maintenance of the common property, and other rental expenses you incur for the upkeep and maintenance of the unit.

- Education. If you are spending money to keep current with your landlord, investment, or business activities, you would be able to write off that legitimate expense to keep informed on issues of interest and to protect your investment and risk, for example, seminars or courses; conferences, conventions, and trade shows in or out of town; subscriptions; books and CDs related directly or indirectly to your business or investment activities; cable for your TV, which you are using as a medium for education, and so on.

- Finder's Fee. This is an expense incurred for arranging a mortgage or loan for the purpose of purchasing or improving the rental property. The expense is deductible in equal portions over five years. However, if you repay the mortgage or loan before the end of the five-year period, you can deduct any undeducted balance in the year of repayment.

- Insurance. Premiums for current insurance coverage on your rental property are deductible in the year. If your policy provides coverage for more than one year, you may deduct only the current-year premiums.

- Interest. Interest on money borrowed to purchase or improve your rental property is deductible. You may also deduct interest paid to tenants on rental deposits. However, if you refinance your rental property to obtain funds for purposes other than the acquisition or improvement of your rental property, you may not deduct the interest against your rental income.

- Landscaping. The cost of landscaping the grounds around your rental property is deductible in the year of payment.

- Lease cancellation payments. These are amounts paid or payable to tenants to obtain cancellation of their leases. You must amortize the payments over the remaining life of the lease, including renewals, to a maximum of 40 years. If you dispose of the property, the tax treatment will vary, depending on the particular circumstances.

- Legal expenses. Fees incurred for legal services such as lease preparation or collection of overdue rents are deductible. However, legal fees incurred for the purchase or sale of your rental property are not deductible against your gross rental income. Instead, legal fees you incurred to acquire your rental property are treated as part of your cost of the property. When you sell the rental property, any legal fees you incurred in connection with the sale may be deducted from the proceeds of disposition when calculating your gain or loss.

- Maintenance and repairs. If you do the repairs yourself, you can deduct the cost of the materials. The value of your own labour is not generally deductible unless you structure your services with the advice of a professional accountant. There are various creative and legitimate ways of getting paid for your services.

- Mortgage payments. Repayments of the principal portion of your mortgage or loan to purchase or improve your rental property are not deductible. See "Mortgage Interest" on page 216 regarding the interest portion of your mortgage.

- Motor vehicle expenses. Travel expenses you incur to collect rents are considered personal expenses and are usually not deductible. However, reasonable travelling expenses may be deductible if incurred in certain circumstances. For example, if you receive income from only one rental property that is located in the general area where you live, you may deduct motor vehicle expenses to the extent you personally do part or all of the necessary repairs and maintenance on the property, and incur the expenses transporting tools and materials to the rental property.

  If you own two or more rental properties, you may deduct reasonable motor vehicle expenses incurred for the purpose of collecting rents, supervising repairs, or generally providing management of the properties. This is the case whether your rental properties are located in or outside the general area where you live. However, technically the properties must be located in at least two different sites away from your residence for these expenses to be deductible.

- Office expenses. Expenses for items of stationery, such as journals, receipt books, photocopying, pens, paper, toner, and stamps, are deductible.

- Penalties. Amounts paid for early retirement of your mortgage (even on its renewal) are not deductible. Penalties for the late filing of your income tax return are also not deductible.

- Property taxes. They are deductible if assessed by a province, territory, or municipality and relate to your rental property.

- Salaries and wages. Amounts paid or payable to superintendents, maintenance personnel, and others employed by you for the operation or supervision of your rental property are deductible. Your professional accountant should be able to suggest creative and legitimate ways of structuring your contribution so that your services would be legitimately deductible as an expense—if you incorporate a management company, for example, and your company bills for services that you are providing to it.

- Tax-return preparation. Fees and expenses for advice and assistance in preparing and filing tax returns are deductible when the nature of your rental operation is such that it is a normal part of operations to obtain legal and accounting services.

- Travelling expenses. Costs of travel related to your landlord and investment activities are deductible, for example, if you are checking out other potential properties or land to buy, and need to fly to the location. Possibly you want to attend a trade show, conference, or convention out of town, which is related directly or indirectly to your real estate investment and management activities.

- Utilities. Utilities are deductible if your rental arrangement specifies that you will pay for the lights, heat, water, or cable used by your tenants.

## Tax Implications of the Purchase Structure When Buying an Apartment Building

There are several important tax implications to the way you structure the purchase of a revenue property, such as an apartment building. Here are some examples to illustrate the point and to discuss with your accountant.

### Allocating Purchase Price Value

If you are purchasing an apartment building for $800,000, for example, you may want to allocate as high a value for the land as realistically possible in the circumstances, say, $600,000. That would mean you have less of a capital gain on your eventual sale than if you valued the land on purchase at \$300,000. If you did not agree in writing at the time of the original purchase and eventual sale as to the value of the land portion, you could have problems in convincing Revenue Canada as to the capital gain portion if you were ever audited.

Another example is the value allocated for the building and for chattels. These two main categories can be depreciated over time, the amount of depreciation depending on the CCA classification of the building or land. The higher the value allocated for the building or chattels, the greater the amount of depreciation you could claim after you have purchased the property. These three examples—land, building, and chattels—are only a few of the issues you need to discuss with your tax accountant before making an offer. Basically you want to agree to a purchase allocation price package that benefits your interests. Conversely, if you are selling the revenue property, you want to negotiate quite a different allocation-of-value package. It all comes down to the tax implications, in terms of taxes saved or deferred.

There are tax implications to the way you structure the purchase price. In other words, the purchase price could consist of several components such as land, building chattels (e.g., appliances), inventory (e.g., supplies), and possibly goodwill. Goodwill is an intangible concept; essentially it is the value of the positive image or reputation that the investment property (e.g., an apartment building) enjoys. This has implications for keeping vacancy low and tenancy high. Negotiations relating to the purchase should include how you are going to apportion the purchase price, considering the above points. That is why you want to make sure you receive tax advice before you submit your offer. Once you have negotiated the terms of the offer, it is more difficult to revise them to your benefit.

## Purchasing the Shares or Assets of a Corporate Vendor

If you are buying an apartment building, for example, the vendor could be an individual or a corporation (limited liability company). If you are buying the shares or assets of the corporation, there are tax implications:

- You would be assuming any liability that the company has, such as debts owing or pending lawsuits. If you bought the assets (land, building, and chattels), you would not have this liability.

- If the company has losses from previous years that have not yet been used up to set off against future revenue property income, you could have a bonus in that regard, depending on the nature and amount of unclaimed losses. If you bought the assets, you would not have this loss available to you.

- You would probably be able to avoid paying the property purchase tax applicable in several provinces. The tax is normally triggered and payable upon transfer of title of the property. If you buy the shares of the corporation, that does not change the title on the property. The same corporation shows up as owner. If you bought the assets, you would have to pay the tax.

- You could end up losing money in terms of depreciation available. The corporation could have depreciated most of its depreciable assets such as building and chattels. Therefore, you would not have that depreciation benefit. If you bought the assets, as described earlier, you could negotiate the value of the building and chattels when allocating the purchase price. You could then start depreciating them at that higher values, thereby having more tax deductions.

- You could end up losing money in terms of the value of the land if the corporation's valuation of it is artificially low. You could therefore have a higher capital gain tax to pay if a future purchaser wanted to buy the apartment building assets from you and wanted to have a current market value on the land at that time.

## Purchasing in a Personal or Corporate Name

There are different—and considerable—tax implications if you purchase an apartment building in your own name or with others, or through a corporation. You could purchase the shares or assets of the apartment owner personally or with your own corporation. (Chapter 6, "Understanding the Legal Aspects," provides an explanation of the available options.)

## Soft Costs

Certain outlays made in connection with the construction, renovation, or alteration of a building to make it rentable are referred to as "soft costs," which include interest, legal fees, accounting fees, and property taxes.

Soft costs may be incurred during construction, renovation, or alteration of a building, or outside that period, as long as the outlays are attributable to that period. You must treat soft costs as capital expenditures until the work is completed, or until all or substantially all of the building is rented, whichever comes first.

If you are going to renovate a building, you should ask your tax accountant which costs during the period of renovation you can claim as expenses and which are considered capital expenditures.

## Vacant Land

If you are holding vacant land for investment purposes, there are various tax rules that may restrict the deduction of interest on borrowed money used to buy the land, and of property taxes paid on the land. If you are not earning rental income from the vacant land, Revenue Canada will probably consider your costs as capital expenditures and therefore they would be added on to the original cost of the property on sale. Because of this approach, when the property is sold, the cost for tax purposes is higher than it otherwise would be and therefore the capital gain is lower.

On the other hand, you may decide to rent or lease out the vacant property—say, to a farmer—in order to generate revenue. If you earn rental income from the vacant land, there are limitations to the amount you may deduct for interest on money borrowed to acquire the land, as well as property taxes and related land assessments. Your deduction is restricted to the amount of rental income remaining after you have deducted all other expenses from your rental income. You cannot create or increase a rental loss, nor can you reduce other sources of income by claiming a deduction for the above expenses. However, if you are unable to deduct a portion of the expenses because of the limitation, you may add the undeducted portion to the cost of the land.

The above are general guidelines. Check with your tax accountant for specific and current advice.

## *Investing in Real Estate in the United States*

Tax issues can be very confusing to many Canadians. If you own property or other investments in the United States, it can become quite complex. That is because the tax laws of both countries could affect you. In the United States, for example, you could be liable under certain circumstances for income tax, capital gains tax, estate tax, and gift tax.

## Rental Income from U.S. Real Estate

You may be renting out your U.S. property part- or full-time. As a non-resident "alien," you are subject to U.S. income tax on the rental income.

## Tax on Gross Rental Income

The rents you receive are subject to a 30 per cent non-resident withholding tax, which your tenant or property management agent is required to deduct and remit to the Internal Revenue Service (IRS). It doesn't matter if the tenants are Canadians or other non-residents of the United States, or if the rent was paid to you while you were in Canada. The Canada-U.S. Tax Treaty allows the United States to tax income from real estate with no reduction in the general withholding rate. Rental income is subject to a flat 30 per cent tax on gross income, with no expenses or deductions allowed. The 30 per cent withholding tax therefore equals the flat tax rate.

## Tax on Net Rental Income

Since a tax rate of 30 per cent of gross income is high, you may prefer to pay tax on net income after taking all deductible expenses. This step results in reduced tax and possibly no tax. IRS regulations permit this option if you choose to permanently treat rental income as income that is effectively connected with the conduct of a U.S. trade or business. You are then able to claim expenses related to owning and operating a rental property during the rental period, for example, mortgage interest, property tax, utilities, insurance, and maintenance. You can also deduct an amount for depreciation of the building. However, the IRS permits only individuals (rather than corporations) to deduct the mortgage or loan interest relating to the rental property if the debt is secured by the rental property or other business property. If you borrow the funds in Canada, secured by your Canadian assets, you would not technically be able to deduct that interest on your U.S. tax return. Obtain strategic tax-planning advice on this issue.

## Selling U.S. Real Estate

If you are a non-resident alien, any gain or loss that results from a sale or disposition of your U.S. real estate has tax-reporting implications. The purchaser or agent of the purchaser is generally required to withhold 10 per cent of the gross sale price at the time the sale transaction is completed and the balance of payment is made. The 10 per cent holdback is to be forwarded to the IRS as a non-resident withholding tax credit.

## Waiver of Withholding Tax

If you anticipate that the U.S. tax payable would be less than the 10 per cent withheld, you can apply to the IRS in advance to have the withholding tax reduced or eliminated by completing a withholding certificate. If the 10 per cent had already been paid, you would still be entitled to a refund after you filed your U.S. tax return if the 10 per cent was greater than the amount due.

You may be exempt from withholding tax if the purchase price of your property is less than US$300,000 and the buyer intends to use the property as a residence at least half of the time it is used over the subsequent two-year period. The buyer does not have to be a U.S. citizen or resident or use the property as a principal residence. To obtain this type of exemption, the buyer must sign an affidavit setting out the facts related above. If the purchase price is more than US$300,000 or the buyer is unwilling or unable to sign the affidavit, you can request the waiver from withholding discussed in the previous paragraph.

## Reporting to the Canada Revenue Agency

Under the Income Tax Act, you are required to report all your income and capital gains from your worldwide activities to the Canada Revenue Agency. Tax is levied on all financial activities, no matter where those activities occurred. However, Canada has tax treaties with many countries throughout the world, including the United States. The implication for a Canadian taxpayer is that there would be a foreign tax credit, so that you are not paying tax in both countries. For example, if you paid $10,000 tax in the United States on the sale of a property there, you would receive that as a credit for whatever tax you owed in Canada for the taxable capital gains on the sale of the property.

## Information Sharing

The American and Canadian tax departments exchange data on taxpayers by computer, an exchange that's increased dramatically with the IRS's requirement for certain Canadians to have an individual taxpayer identification number (ITIN).

When you apply for your ITIN, you must provide some brief but personal information to the IRS. In addition to your name, and your name at birth (if different), you must provide your Canadian address. Post office boxes and care-of addresses are not allowed. Your date and place of birth are also required, along with your sex, your father's complete name, your mother's maiden name, your passport number, and your U.S. visa number, if applicable.

You are also asked for your Canadian social insurance number. You can imagine the potential co-operation between the IRS and CRA this facilitates. The IRS has a fast, sophisticated, computerized cross-referencing capability between your U.S and Canadian taxpayer numbers. For example, information on certain U.S. tax-related activities in which you are involved—such as the sale or rental of U.S. real estate, or your claim for a U.S. tax refund on U.S. investment or pension income—can be transmitted to Revenue Canada.

## Need to Obtain Expert Tax Advice

Obtain professional tax advice on IRS filing requirements from an accountant who specializes in U.S. and cross-border tax and financial planning issues and strategies. Dealing with Canadian and American tax matters is complex, and the laws and regulations are always changing. There is an excellent cross-border financial planning and tax newsletter for Canadians written by Richard Brunton, CPA, whose firm provides services to Canadians. For more information, visit his site at www.taxintl.com.

## *Tax Effects on Different Legal Structures*

If you are the sole proprietor of your business, your salary is included as an expense. The profits that you earn in your business constitute your personal income and are taxable as such in that taxation year. When you file your personal income tax return with the CRA, you have to complete the Statement of Business or Professional Activities (T2125). It outlines the basic sources of income and types of expenses and allowances.

If your business is a partnership, all partners are taxed on their salaries and their share of the profits, whether withdrawn or not. The same Statement of Income and Expenses form is used for a partnership, although you must also provide the percentage share of profit or loss that is being declared.

A corporation files a corporate tax return, which is separate and distinct from the individuals involved in the company. It is therefore not filed with the personal income tax return, as with a proprietorship or partnership.

A corporation in Canada is entitled to a small-business tax deduction, assuming various conditions are met, such as generating an active business income. This deduction, which is approximately one-half the regular tax rate, is designed to help Canadian-controlled private companies accumulate capital for business expansion. Many provinces also allow a provincial tax rate reduction as well as other incentives. An active business, as the name implies, is one in which people are actively generating income, rather than passively receiving income.

For more detail on these three business structure options, refer to Chapter 6, "Understanding the Legal Aspects."

## Keeping Records

If you are investing in real estate or are generating revenue from your investment, keeping detailed records is essential. Make sure that you have all the documents necessary to verify money collected and paid out. This includes all receipts, invoices, and contracts. You do not need to submit these records when you file your return; however, the CRA may disallow your claim if you cannot provide them upon request. Regulations require you to report rental income using the accrual method. This means that:

- rents are included in income for the year in which they are due, whether or not you received them in that year; and
- allowable expenses are deducted in the year they are incurred, regardless of when you actually made the payments.

Refer to Chapter 10, "Managing Your Property," for more information.

## Summary

This chapter discussed the wide range of taxes of which you need to be aware. Topics covered also included practical ways of saving on taxes, maximizing your deductions, pitfalls to avoid, tax-planning strategies, and money-saving tips. The need to select the right professional accountant and obtain expert tax advice is critical to reaching your short- and long-term financial goals and minimizing risks.

Insurance is another key aspect to owning property. It is discussed next.

# CHAPTER 8

# Understanding the Insurance Aspects

**Although it is** possible to buy too much insurance, many people don't purchase enough or the right type of insurance. Considering the time, energy, commitment, and resources that you are putting into your business venture as a real estate investor, you want to minimize the inherent risk by making sure you have adequate insurance protection. There will be references to business-related insurance. If you are investing in, and possibly managing, residential real estate, you are operating a business.

This chapter will cover a wide range of types of insurance to enhance your awareness and the quality of your decision making. The discussion will include organizing your insurance program for all your needs, including property and general insurance. Then the different types of property insurance coverage will be explained, followed by the different types of general insurance that are important to consider for your total protection, as well as life and disability insurance. You need to look at your complete insurance picture. Tips to follow and pitfalls to avoid will also be discussed.

## Organizing Your Insurance Program

It is important to consider all criteria to determine the best type of insurance for you and your business. Your goal should be adequate coverage. That can be achieved by periodic review of the risk you are insuring for and by keeping your insurance representative informed of any changes in your business that could affect the adequacy or enforceability of your coverage. Such changes could include additional equipment purchases, extensions to your property, the business use of your personal car, or starting a home-based business.

The following advice will help you plan an insurance program.

### Assess Your Business and Identify the Likely Risk Exposure:

- Cover your largest risk(s) first.

- Determine the magnitude of loss that the business can bear without financial difficulty, and use your premium dollar where the protection need is greatest.

- Insure the correct risk.

Decide which of these three kinds of protection will work best for each risk:

- absorbing the risk (that is, budgeting to cover loss or expense without getting insurance);

- minimizing the risk (that is, reducing the factor that could contribute to the risks, rather than getting insurance); or

- insuring against the risk with commercial insurance.

## Reducing the Cost of Insurance

Use every means possible to reduce the cost of insurance:

- Negotiate for lower premiums if your loss experience is low or if you have had no claims.

- Increase deductibles as much as you can if you need the protection but can't afford a low deductible premium.

- Shop around for comparable rates and analyze insurance terms and provisions offered by different insurance companies. Try to get a minimum of three comparative quotes.

- Avoid duplication of insurance; have one agent handle all your business insurance if possible and practical. However, the variety of insurance available—property, general, life, and health—means you will most likely have two different brokers.

- Ask about the types of discounts available—say, for age, monitored fire alarm system, security alarm system.

- Check out group insurance coverage at lower rates from various membership organizations such as the chamber of commerce or board of trade.

- If you have a financial planner, ask him or her about different types of life, health, and disability insurance coverage. Generally, financial planners do not deal with property insurance, but could recommend some brokers they know.

- Incorporate if necessary to further reduce personal liability.

## *Selecting an Insurance Broker*

Chapter 4, "Selecting Your Advisory Team," includes an overview of how to select an insurance broker on page 126. Specific assistance related to your area of need may be found online through the following organizations:

- The Insurance Brokers Association of Canada (www.ibac.ca) maintains a list of members from whom you can obtain comparative quotes on business and property insurance.
- For life and health insurance, visit the Canadian Life and Health Insurance Association (www.clhia.ca) for a list of members and helpful consumer information.
- Advocis, the Financial Advisors Association of Canada (www. advocis.ca), provides advice on insurance and the financial planning aspects of insurance policies.

Regular reviews of risk exposure can help avoid overlaps and gaps in coverage, and thereby keep your risk and premiums lower. This is especially important if your real estate investment and management business are growing. Reviews can also help you keep current with inflation.

# Types of Property Coverage

When you are buying real estate for personal use, investment, or rental purposes, it is important to understand the jargon of the property insurance trade, and how premiums are determined and risk assessed. This will enhance the quality of your decision making, improve your negotiating skills, and save you money. It will also protect you from having inadequate insurance coverage or running the risk that a claim could be denied. Here is an overview of the key concepts.

## *Inflation Allowance*

This coverage protects you against inflation by automatically increasing the amount of your insurance during the term of your policy without increasing your premium. On renewal, the insurance company will automatically adjust the amount of your insurance to reflect the annual inflation rate. The premium you pay for your renewal will be based on those adjusted amounts of insurance.

Inflation allowance coverage will not fully protect you if you make an addition to your building or if you acquire additional personal property. This is why you need to review the amount of your insurance every year to make sure it is adequate.

## Special Limits of Insurance

The contents of your dwelling are referred to as "personal property." Some types of personal-property insurance such as jewellery, furs, and money have "special limits of insurance." This is the maximum the insurer will pay for those types of property. If these limits are insufficient for your needs, you can purchase additional insurance.

Your policy automatically includes some additional coverage to provide you with more complete protection.

## Insured Perils

A peril is something negative that can happen, such as a fire or theft. Some policies protect you against only those perils that are listed in your policy. Other policies protect you against "all risks" (*risk* is another word for peril). This means you are protected against most perils.

All insurance policies have exclusions. Even if you have selected all-risks coverage, this does not mean that everything is covered. It is important that you read the exclusions carefully in order to understand the types of losses that are not covered by your policy. For example, floods and earthquakes may not be covered if you reside in a high-risk location for these types of perils. Ask your broker what the specific exclusions on your policy are, and if there are alternative policies that provide coverage.

## Loss or Damage Not Insured

This is the fine print, the section that tells you what is not covered. They are also known as "exclusions." Exclusions are necessary to make sure that the insurance company does not pay for the types of losses that are inevitable (e.g., wear and tear), uninsurable (e.g., civil unrest or war), or for which other specific policy forms are available to provide coverage (e.g., automobiles).

## Basis of Claim Settlement

This section describes how the insurer will settle your loss. It's the real test of the value of your policy and the reason why you purchased insurance.

## Replacement Cost

You should purchase replacement-cost coverage for your property. This is particularly important for your personal property (the contents of your dwelling and personal effects). Otherwise the basis of settlement will be "actual cash value," which means that depreciation is applied to the damaged property when establishing the values. You therefore would get less money, possibly considerably less.

"New for old" coverage is available. All you have to do is ask for replacement-cost coverage and then make sure that your amounts of insurance are sufficient to replace your property at today's prices.

## Guaranteed Replacement Cost

This is one of the most important types of coverage available to a homeowner. You can qualify for this coverage by insuring your home to 100 per cent of its full replacement value. If you do, then the insurance company will pay the full claim, even if it is more than the amount of insurance on the building. Make sure this is shown on your policy.

The guaranteed replacement-cost coverage applies only to your building, not your personal property.

There is usually an important exclusion. Many insurance companies won't pay more than the amount of insurance if the reason the claim exceeds that amount is the result of any law regulating the construction of buildings. Check this out.

## Bylaws

Some municipalities have laws that govern the height of a house, what materials you have to use, or even where you can build it. These are known as bylaws. If the insurance company has to rebuild your house to different standards, this can increase the amount of your claim significantly.

Your policy doesn't cover this increased cost because the insurance company has no way of knowing which laws may apply in your municipality, but you can find out. Then make sure that your amounts of insurance are high enough to cover the increased cost, or increase them if necessary, and ask for a bylaws-coverage endorsement. It'll cost a bit more now, but it can save you a lot later.

## Deductible

There is a deductible and the amount is shown on the coverage summary page of your policy. It means that you pay that amount for most claims, for example, $250 or $500. The insurance company pays the rest.

As you can imagine, the cost to investigate and settle a claim can be considerable, often out of proportion when the size of the claim is relatively small. These expenses are reflected in the premiums you pay. By using deductibles to eliminate small claims, the insurance company can save on expenses and therefore offer insurance at lower premiums.

## Conditions

This is a very important part of your policy. It sets out the mutual rights and obligations of the insurer and the insured. This section governs how and when a policy may be cancelled, as well as your obligations after a loss has occurred.

## Purchasing Adequate Amounts of Insurance

Purchasing adequate amounts of insurance that reflect the full replacement value of everything you own is without a doubt the single most important thing you can do to protect yourself. The penalty is that insurance companies will not pay more than the amounts of insurance you have purchased, so it is up to you to make sure the coverage is adequate and realistic. Review it annually.

Establish how much it would cost to rebuild the home from scratch. This is the amount for which you should insure the house, in order to make sure that you are fully protected.

If you put an addition onto the house or carry out major renovations, you should recalculate the replacement value, as your current amount of insurance doesn't take this into consideration. Notify your insurance company representative. The inflation allowance feature of your policy does protect you against normal inflation, but is not sufficient to cover major changes.

You may also want to check with municipal authorities to see whether there are any bylaws that govern the construction of houses in your area, as you may need a higher amount of insurance so that the reconstruction of your home will be fully covered.

## Contents Coverage

If you are using the home personally, the following discussion relates to personal use. Your policy provides coverage for your contents. You should make sure that this amount is enough to replace all your possessions at today's prices. If the home is rented to a tenant, they are responsible for obtaining tenant's insurance. You should make that a condition of any rental agreement.

If you have a claim, the insurance company will ask you to compile a complete list of everything that you have lost. Ideally, you should maintain an inventory of everything: furniture, appliances, clothes, and other possessions. Estimating what it would cost you to replace them is a good way to check if the amount of insurance you carry is enough.

At the very least you should keep the receipts for all major purchases in a safe place. Another good idea is to take pictures of your contents or make a video of everything by walking from room to room. In addition, most insurance companies will provide you with a checklist, so you can compile a list of your contents. This may seem like a chore right now, but it can really save time and aggravation if you do have a claim.

As you could lose your inventory checklist or photographic evidence in a major loss, you should store your records away from your house. The best place is a safety deposit box. Since most documents and photos can be saved as digital files, these should be able to fit onto a flash drive that fits within the safe deposit box; alternatively, the files may be stored on a remote server through one of the many providers offering this service, including Google. The online option allows you to access the evidence from anywhere, and easily e-mail materials as needed. Whatever method you use, remember that you should update it periodically (ideally annually) to make sure that it remains accurate.

## How Insurance Companies Calculate the Premium

The insurance pricing is governed by a principle known as the "spread of risk," which means that the premiums paid by many people pay for the losses of the few. When more dollars in claims are paid out than taken in as premiums, then the premium paid by everyone goes up. The premium you pay therefore represents the amount of money needed by the insurance company to pay for all losses, plus their expenses in providing the service, plus a profit factor divided by the number of policyholders.

The potential for loss assessment is based upon a number of risk factors. Most of these risk factors are based upon where you live. Here are the four most important ones:

## Fire

Although theft losses occur more often, fire still accounts for most of the dollars insurance companies pay out in claims. The potential damage due to fire is therefore based upon a municipality's ability to respond to, and put out, a fire.

If you own property in an area with fire hydrants, your premium will be lower because the fire department will have access to a large water supply. Fires in hydrant-protected areas can be extinguished at an earlier stage than those in less well-protected areas.

If you own property in an area without hydrants or even a fire department close by, the premium will be higher.

## Theft

Statistics show that theft is narrowing the gap with fire for dollars paid out. Generally, there are more break-ins in cities than in rural areas. Insurance companies track the loss experience caused by theft by area, which is reflected in the premium you pay.

## Weather

If your geographic area has a history of severe weather storms, such as wind storms, snowstorms, hail, or flooding, insurance companies obviously look at these risks as well.

## Earthquake

The mere thought of an earthquake, especially on Canada's West Coast, immediately conjures up the worst-case scenario. The Big One has been expected for years, and when it hits, the damage is expected to be severe and devastating. Your investment property? Well, if you have insurance, you may get some compensation, but the terms are typically strict, limiting coverage to actual quake-related damage as opposed to fires that start as a result of the quake or water damage as a result of shake damage. Premiums may also be expensive, depending on your location. Sophisticated actuarial tools help insurers determine the premium for your location, with properties farthest away from seismically active or otherwise vulnerable areas being the least costly to insure.

## *Ways to Reduce Your Premiums*
### Higher Deductible

Many people don't realize there are ways to reduce the premium payment significantly. What exactly do you want protection for? What you are really concerned with is the possibility of a catastrophe or a total loss. If so, you can save money by increasing your deductible. By doing so, you save the insurance company the expense of investigating and settling small claims. That saving is passed back to you in the form of a reduced premium.

### Discounts

You can reduce your premium if you qualify for any of the discounts insurance companies offer. Generally, discounts recognize a lower category of risk, for example, buying a new home, installing an approved burglar alarm system, non-smoking policyholders, or seniors. Always ask what discounts are available and see if you are eligible.

### Claims-Free Discount

This is a discount you don't have to request. Most insurance companies will reduce your premium automatically if you have been claim-free for three or more years.

You should never reduce your amount of insurance so that you pay a lower premium. If you ever do have a claim, it could cost you a lot more than any amount you might save.

### Personal Liability Protection

This is the part of the policy that protects you if you are sued. If someone injures himself or herself on your property by falling on your stairs, slipping on your driveway, or some other mishap, and a court determines that you are responsible, your insurance company should defend you in court and pay all legal expenses and the amount up to the limit of the policy. The normal minimum limit is $1 million; however, you can increase this amount if you want.

There are specific exclusions that apply to this section of the policy. They are listed under the heading "Loss or Damage Not Insured." Make sure you read this carefully.

## How to Avoid Being Sued

Every year, many people are injured while visiting the premises of others. The last thing you want is to be sued; it's stressful, time-consuming, negative, protracted, and uncertain. Here are some suggestions to avoid problems. If you are renting to a tenant, your contract should cover hazard reduction and require the tenants to have tenant insurance coverage as a condition of your tenancy agreement. You should receive a copy of the policy.

### Maintain Your Premises

Most injuries are caused by slipping and falling, which is usually the result of a lack of maintenance. In winter, clear ice and snow from all walkways on your premises and the stretch of sidewalk in front of your house. Exterior steps should be kept in good repair and a handrail provided.

Inside your house, carpets should be secured to stairs and floors and kept free of toys or objects that could trip a visitor.

### Alcohol

If you serve alcohol to guests, you could be found responsible, to some extent, for their subsequent actions. Some courts have gone to extraordinary lengths to assign responsibility to a host. Use good judgment, and never allow an intoxicated guest to drive a car.

### Other Hazards

You are potentially responsible for everything that happens on your premises, such as the safe use of your swimming pool, the actions of your dog, and so on. If you have a tenant, pass on as much responsibility and liability as possible to that person. As mentioned earlier, you should make it a condition of tenancy that the renter obtain tenant insurance prior to moving in and provide you with a copy of the policy.

The good news is that most injuries can be avoided by using common sense. All you have to do is be alert to the potential hazards on your own premises.

## Types of General Insurance

The following brief overview is intended to alert you to the main types of coverage you may wish to consider, depending on the nature of your business needs. After you review them, you will see the wide range of coverage that you might require for your peace of mind. It includes a discussion of life, health, and disability insurance.

## General Liability

This type of policy covers losses that you would be liable to pay for causing bodily injury to someone (e.g., in an accident) or damage to the property of others. Make sure that your policy covers all legal fees for your defence and related costs. This policy generally covers negligence on your part that accidentally causes injury to clients, employees, or the public.

## Business Property

If you are operating a business out of your home, your current basic home-owners' or apartment owners' policy may void any coverage of business-related assets. Request that coverage be added to include the business assets, or purchase a separate policy. If you own a computer, you may wish to get a special floater policy covering risks unique to computer owners, including power-surge and fire damage and theft of hardware and software.

## Fire

This coverage enables you to replace or rebuild your office or home as well as replace inventory and equipment. Make sure your policy is a replacement policy. (This was covered in the previous section on property insurance.)

## Automobile

Automobile coverage insures physical damage to the car and bodily injury to the passengers, as well as damage to other people's property, car, or passengers. It also includes theft of your car. Make sure that your car is insured for business use; otherwise, if the facts came out on a claim that it was being used for that purpose, your policy would be void and your claim disallowed.

## Mortgage

If you owe money on your mortgage and die, the bank insurance offered by your lender will pay off the outstanding mortgage. However, there are drawbacks and other options available to this type of insurance. The good news is that almost everyone is considered insurable. The drawbacks are that the premiums are high and the insurance is not portable. In other words, it is only for the purpose of paying off your mortgage. A better alternative is to get your own private term life insurance coverage. The premiums will be lower, and you can keep the insurance coverage long after the mortgage has been paid off. It gives you that flexibility. Also, if you become uninsurable in the future due to health reasons, at least you will have your own portable life insurance protection.

## Life

Term life insurance insures a person for a specific period of time or term, and then stops. Term life does not have a cash-surrender value or loan value as with a whole-life plan. Term premiums are less expensive than whole-life premiums. If you have a bank loan or personal or business obligations, consider term life coverage. Whole-life insurance costs more as it includes a "term" component plus an investment savings component—you obtain interest on the investment part of your premium.

## Home Office

It is important to recognize the potential risks of working from home and the policies available for protection against them. If you don't have insurance protection, you could be personally liable for all financial losses. Always advise your insurance agent that you are operating a business from your home. You will need extra coverage for any risk areas involved directly or indirectly with your business operation. The home-office coverage is normally an extension endorsement of your regular homeowner insurance policy coverage.

Almost all homeowner policies exclude home businesses. However, the increased premium on your current home insurance policies will still be a saving compared to the higher insurance premium you would pay if your business were located in commercial premises. Use the same insurance broker for all your policies if possible, as you should be able to negotiate better rates. Ask for copies of the extra policy coverage for your file.

## Disability

Good health is by far our greatest asset. With it, we can improve our financial net worth; without it, we have only liabilities.

Statistics show that the chance of becoming disabled between 45 and 65 years of age for a minimum of three months is almost 40 per cent. Almost one-half of those still disabled after six months will still be disabled at the end of five years.

Depending on the disability, you might be covered by Workers' Compensation benefits, CPP benefits, or Employment Insurance (EI) disability benefits. You may have group or personal disability insurance benefits. Group and individual plans will cover only a portion of your gross earnings before you were disabled by injury or illness.

Definitions of disability vary. Whether or not you receive benefits may well depend on how the company defines disability. Carefully read the wording of your contract, as some are so restrictive that it might be almost impossible to be eligible for a claim. Most contracts define disability according to one of four types, from the least to the most restrictive.

## Own Occupation

Disability is defined as the inability to work in your own occupation only. If you can prove that you are disabled from doing your own job and are under the care of a doctor, you will qualify for benefits. Even if you went to work in another occupation, you may still qualify for benefits. Individual insurance contracts may offer an own-occupation clause to age 65.

## Regular Occupation

This type provides coverage in the event that you are disabled and unable to work in your own occupation, provided that you choose not to work in an alternative occupation.

## Any Occupation

This covers disability from any suitable occupation, based on your education, training, and/or experience. Most, but not all, group insurance contracts specify an any-occupation disability after the first two years of disability.

## Total and Permanent

Some insurance contracts require that you not only be totally disabled from working, but also that your disability must be permanent. Naturally, this insurance is high risk for you due to the severe nature of disability required before coverage commences. The insurance premium is lower as the risk is lower to the insurance company.

## Summary

With insurance, it is important to be realistic. Weigh the risks and potential business and personal financial exposure if you have no insurance or inadequate coverage. You need to look at your total insurance picture to make sure that you have adequate and integrated coverage. Always comparison shop, and make sure you understand the jargon of the trade. Speak to accredited insurance brokers and financial planners.

With the fine points out of the way, we're going to enter the world of negotiations.

# CHAPTER 9

# Buying Your Property

**Understanding the art** and science of negotiating is important if you want to make money in real estate. Whether you are a first-time homebuyer or an experienced real estate investor, you will benefit from the practical tips and street-smart strategies explained in this chapter.

A large part of the purchase process comes down to negotiations; indeed, most interactions involve some form of negotiation, even something as simple as setting up a coffee date. If you are attempting to sell, persuade, convince, or influence another person's thinking or feeling to match your own wants and needs, you are negotiating. If, at the same time, you have defined and satisfied the other person's needs, you have attained an optimal or win-win type of negotiation. Real estate negotiations may not satisfy all of the seller's or buyer's needs, as his or her needs and expectations may be unrealistic—or simply not in your interests.

This chapter covers key points geared to giving you an edge in negotiations. Tips include selecting an agent who will help you identify an appropriate property, evaluating the property for investment purposes, and actually making an offer. You will learn how to get the best price and terms, and how to buy low and sell high. This information will help you invest wisely and therefore make more money on any type of real estate purchase or sale.

## Selecting the Right Real Estate Agent

The real estate agent you select should have your interests at heart and be both an adviser and an advocate for your property dealings. An agent will know where the properties best suited to your portfolio lie. He or she can also secure your position in dealings with vendors, particularly in hotly contested negotiations and bidding wars. For these reasons, it's better to work with an agent than without one. (See page 106 in Chapter 4, "Selecting Your Advisory Team," for tips on selecting a real estate agent.)

Discuss your investment strategy with the agents you consider to ensure the one you select shares your goals and vision, or at least understands what you're trying to achieve. For example, you may have a clear timeline for your investments—say, 10 years—and believe yourself capable of handling two small residential properties in addition to your own. Or, you might have a longer time frame and be seeking a more ambitious portfolio that includes two or more multi-unit complexes. These will be criteria you'll apply to your selection, and points the prospective real estate agent will want to know before getting involved.

## What You Bring to the Table

A few key points you'll want to share with the real estate agents you approach include:

- Resources. The amount you have to invest will determine the starting point for the portfolio, and potentially how quickly you'll be able to grow it. A real estate agent suitable for a smaller investor may not be the same one you'll pick if you have a larger stash of funds to invest.

- Portfolio. The kind and size of portfolio you want to develop is a key point to share. Depending on the growth plan, you may start off with one real estate agent, but require an agent with different skills and contacts than your original broker. Some agents will be stronger in some neighbourhoods and property types than others (say, condos versus single-family homes). Match the agent with your interests.

- Objectives. An agent will want to know how you see your portfolio evolving. A time frame will help the agent assess potential properties for your investment, determine whether you'll need additional help in future, and potentially help you craft an exit strategy from the moment you start investing.

- Weaknesses. Being able to share your weaknesses with prospective advisers shows not only your self-awareness but also flags areas where you might come into conflict. While agents should challenge you and help you broaden your horizons, an agent who's ignorant of your sore points or limits will run you the wrong way. It's best if they're forewarned, because it will help them know what to do, what not to do, and potentially help you find an alternative if all signs point to the relationship not working out.

- Strengths. Your strengths may shine when everything's going well, but they'll shine a lot brighter (and you'll feel good about it, too) if the agent you select appreciates those strengths. On the other hand, an agent who doesn't make those strengths work to your advantage will weaken and frustrate you.

## What the Agent Brings to the Table

A real estate agent should provide the assistance and advice you need to invest wisely and effectively. The qualities they bring should include:

- Knowledge. A real estate agent's knowledge, whether from personal experience, the brokerage with which he or she is connected, or an ability to use technology efficiently, should supplement and broaden your own research. A real estate agent who knows less about the market than you do may be a good yes-person who respects your opinion, but not terribly useful in introducing you to new opportunities. An agent should be able to make you aware of properties, neighbourhoods, and alternatives you might want to consider as you develop your portfolio.

- Connections. The connections a real estate agent brings, both in terms of his or her brokerage and the industry generally, will help you tap into the experience you need to develop your portfolio. An insular agent may be effective, but you'll have to find those second opinions on your own—which may be arduous (after all, you may be an independent operator of sorts yourself). The connections an agent enjoys may also smooth the transition if you seek a new agent to handle your portfolio as it grows. Ideally, the agent that got you started will know an agent suited to continuing the work.

- Personality. The agent's personality is important. He or she should understand your needs (and make you feel understood) as well as show a willingness to aggressively defend your interests during negotiations such that you can feel confident leaving your business in their hands.

- Flexibility. An agent should be responsive to your objectives, and be as willing to adapt as you are (maybe even more so). You may have one objective starting out, but a realtor should be willing to advise you differently—as well as be willing to change course mid-market if it serves your best interests. Chances are you will find it annoying if you give one instruction and the agent obeys without informing you that there is another, better option to be had.

- Vision. As an investor you will have a vision for your portfolio. The agent you choose should also have a vision—of the market. An agent with a keen sense of how the market is developing, where it is heading, and what the impacts are for your portfolio can make an important difference in the decisions you make. An agent who lacks vision, or the ability to grasp the vision you have, will probably frustrate you.

Selecting the right broker will not only help you develop a portfolio with a lot less worry than you might otherwise experience, but you also stand to see some cost savings. The properties may not only be profitable, but establishing a relationship with a broker may hand you a break when it comes to transaction costs because you've proven yourself a loyal customer who's willing to give the agent the business of both investing and reinvesting your wealth.

## Determining a Property's Value

There are many methods for determining a property's value. Appraisers spend years learning the business. Chances are you'll want to spend just enough time learning the methods to know what constitutes a reasonable offer. There are two ways to assess a property's value: research and intuition.

### Just the Facts, Please

A fact-based appraisal is the starting point for the valuation process. The two key tools for measuring a property's value are assessment records and recent sales of similar properties, known as comparables, ideally in the same area as the property you're considering.

Assessment records aim for fair market value based on the highest and best use of a property. Typically, the published assessment record states the value of the land and any improvements such as buildings. The land may have a far greater value than the improvements in areas where land is in short supply because the highest and best use for that land may change, especially where multiple uses are allowed under the applicable zoning. The assessment record will generally indicate how the value of the property has changed since the previous assessment, giving you an idea of whether or not to value the property higher or lower. The assessment record often provides the most recent sale price for the property.

The listing and sale prices for similar properties in the area around the property (comparables) will indicate what people hope to sell properties for, what buyers are willing to pay, and where the property you're considering might rank. Your realtor's opinion, coupled with recent sales reports from the local real estate board, should confirm the amateur valuation you make.

## Considering Other Factors

When considering a property for purchase, a variety of non-factual elements may play into the value you assign to a property. These will be integral to your bid and inform the subsequent negotiations.

During a rising market, where competition for properties is tight and every deal seems to set a new benchmark price, you may wish to value a property more aggressively (maybe 5 per cent more) just to secure it. This works well in a market where prices have been depressed for a significant period and there's significant potential for appreciation over the long term, but it's probably not the best strategy in a market where you suspect values are about to peak.

Similarly, in a market where values are under some downward pressure, you may get away with valuing a property at slightly less than existing market prices because that's where values are heading. Sure, you may contribute to a self-fulfilling prophecy of where the market's heading, but it's far better to lead the trend than suffer by it.

To value a property accurately will require knowing something of the prevailing market cycle (see the section on market cycles on page 10 in Chapter 1, "Understanding Real Estate Investment"). Some of the common factors to consider include whether the owner(s):

- is in ill health, or has died recently;
- has lost money and needs to sell the property in order to pay debts;
- has not made payments on the mortgage due to personal or financial problems, resulting in court proceedings by the lender that lead to a court-ordered sale of the property at fair market value;
- wants to take advantage of a seller's market, when demand is strong and prices are high;
- is concerned that the market is changing and could become a buyer's market, resulting in lower demand and downward pressure on prices;
- is adjusting his or her portfolio and seeks to sell the property to purchase another; or
- is testing the market to see what the market will pay, without any serious attempt to actually sell the property in question.

Any one of these reasons might justify a negotiating strategy that would put downward pressure on the price of the property, potentially yielding a bargain. This might be true even during a seller's market, unless competition is so great that buyers compromise on negotiating strategies in the rush to acquire a property at any price whatsoever. On the other hand, the vendor's advisers may drive as hard a deal as you're seeking, meaning that market forces will yield a fair price for the property.

A number of other reasons may prompt the sale of an investment property. In many cases, an astute investor could turn the property into an attractive investment by determining the roots of the problems and identifying opportunities for correcting them. The troubled state of the property would justify an offer at below market value, but the purchase would only make sense if the purchaser could make the property profitable.

Some of the common challenges prompting owners to consider selling a rental property include:

- Inexperienced owner. Possibly the owner was a first-time investor who feels intimidated by the responsibilities, time, and risk involved in managing the property and would prefer to sell.

- Partnership disputes. About 75 per cent of business partnerships eventually break up, prompting the sale of a property or portfolio.

- Run-down properties. Due to poor management or financial difficulties, the property may have deteriorated to a point where the owner would prefer to sell than invest in improvements.

- Poor management. Whether through inexperience, a poor choice of manager, or other reason, a rental property may be suffering and seem like a good property to sell. It may in fact be an opportunity for a savvy buyer, but the vendor has made the decision to sell in order to cut losses or trim an apparently money-losing asset from his or her portfolio.

- Excessive vacancies. High or persistent vacancies may prompt an owner to sell in the belief that the problems are a function of the market. Sound management policies may be able to turn the property around, making it a good bet for an investor with an eye for making improvements.

- Tax benefits. Maybe the owner has depreciated the building as much as possible and wants to sell because the land value has increased. The owner wants to minimize exposure to taxes on capital gains by selling in the current market.

# Preparing the Offer

Preparing an offer is the first step in negotiating the purchase of a property. Your offer should consider the value of the property as well as what you're willing to do to secure it as an investment. Having a negotiating strategy is therefore important before you make the offer—not when you receive the vendor's counter-offer and have to figure out what you're going to do. In a hot market, where many buyers are competing for the same property, the lack of a strategy may cost you the deal.

## Negotiating Strategies

There are various preliminary steps you should go through to maximize your chance of success before you make an offer:

- Know what you're willing to stake on the property, and have a sense of how important the deal is to the vendor.

- Determine the amount of mortgage that you are entitled to, the maximum price that you are prepared to pay, and the terms you prefer.

- Know what alternative properties you might target if the original deal falls through; knowing your alternatives should also give you a better idea of how valuable the property you plan to make an offer on really is.

- Have your realtor thoroughly check out the property, including the length of time it has been on the market, why it is for sale, how the vendor determined the asking price (including recent market comparables in the area), and any vendor deadline pressure.

- Use a realtor as a negotiating buffer between you and the vendor.

- Obtain legal and tax advice on the implications of your purchase.

- Don't get emotionally involved with the property. Be totally objective and realistic; otherwise it could taint your judgment.

- Train yourself to appear patient and unemotional to the vendor or vendor's agent.

- Look for negative features of the property to increase your bargaining leverage. All properties have flaws. For example, its large lot could be subject to property taxes above what you might wish to pay. Or, you might not want the maintenance responsibilities. Drafting a list of the positive and negative features will help you know what points you're willing to pay for and what drawbacks you can use to bring down the price.

- Establish a relationship with a building inspector and contractor in advance; you might need their services on short notice.

# Presenting the Offer

After you have done the preparation, the next negotiating step is to present your offer to the vendor. A number of factors will feature in the offer, and all provide some leeway for you to exercise the strategy you've developed in preparing the terms of the offer.

## Purchaser's Name

Depending on the nature of your purchase, you may want to put your name and the words "or assignee" if it is your intent to sign over the agreement to someone else. Alternatively, if you are purchasing an investment or speculative property with a degree of risk, you may want to incorporate a company and put the offer in the corporate name. If you back out of the deal before closing, your company could be sued for breach of contract and damages (losses) by the vendor, but not you personally. Presumably your new company does not have any assets at that stage.

## Deposit

Try to put the smallest deposit down. You don't want to tie up any more money than you have to. Also, if you back out prior to closing, your deposit funds could be at risk of being kept by the vendor. Whatever deposit money you put down, never pay it directly to the vendor. Always have it paid to a realtor's or lawyer's trust account. Make sure you write in the offer that your deposit funds are to accrue interest to your credit pending the closing date.

## Price

Attempt to offer the lowest possible price the market and circumstances allow. Always start with your ideal price and terms. You never know what the vendor will find to be acceptable or not, so don't anticipate disfavour. Think positive. If the vendor counter-offers, you may want to extract concessions from the vendor due to the variation of your original offer.

By the same token, ensure your offer is reasonable. A low-ball offer may turn off the vendor, and make you seem less knowledgeable than you are about the market.

## Closing Date

Depending on your objectives, you may want to have a long closing date such as three or four months. Maybe you will be receiving funds by then. Maybe the market will have gone up in an escalating market, and you would be entitled to a higher mortgage on closing.

## Financing Terms

You may want to ask the vendor for vendor-back financing for a first or second mortgage. Depending on your objectives, you may want to ask for a long-term open mortgage (say, five years) with an attractive interest rate and assumable without qualifications. This latter provision would make it easier for resale. The vendor may be willing to provide such favourable terms because the market is slow and he or she is anxious to sell.

## Conditions

Conditions are sometimes referred to as "subject" clauses, because the deal is subject to the satisfaction of the conditions outlined in the clauses. Often, they are an integral part of the negotiating strategy on both the vendor's part (through the counter-offer) as well as the buyer's.

Setting conditions on the deal ensures you get the property you want, and can give you extra negotiating room. The clauses should state a specific date by which they must be met (or satisfied), as well as the person whom the clause benefits (this allows the party in question to waive the condition if it is either no longer desired or if it becomes unnecessary).

Some of the common clauses included in the offer to purchase include:

- Confirmation of financing. You may need time to arrange a mortgage, or may plan to use proceeds from the sale of another property or investments to finance your new purchase. This clause gives you time to make sure you have the funds required, and reduces the risk to the deal should you not be able to secure the needed financing. It registers your willingness to buy with the vendor, but also acknowledges that all may not work out.

- Deposit funds. The offer to purchase should state what happens to the deposit paid to secure your interest in the property. Similar to a clause regarding financing, the deposit clause might also detail what the conditions are for payment of the deposits—to whom it is being paid, how, and how it will be treated during the conditional phase of the deal. Ideally, your deposit should got into an interest-bearing account where interest accrues to you in trust (the trustee being someone other than the vendor) until the deal closes. Should the deal fail to complete, you should receive the deposit back with interest.

- Conveyance of free title. Being able to secure and receive clear title to a property is the *sine qua non* of a real estate deal. Unless you can hold actual ownership of the property (or a long-term lease that expires well after your ownership term does), why proceed? You want to be sure title to the property you're buying is free of any outstanding legal claims. It's typically the responsibility of the vendor to make sure that's the case. This condition should state what the vendor has to do to provide and assure you of clear title, and establish the deadline for clearing the title. Securing clear title may require more time than you expect, so you'll want to set a time limit in case you are considering other, equally favourable properties that are less hassle to acquire.

  Being unable to secure clear title has killed many deals. An owner who lacks clear title may not have the rights a standard purchase grants, and may face great cost to rectify title before it can be sold (thereby cutting into the return a property yields). While title insurance can be had to cover the cost of clearing title, why court the trouble in the first place?

- Resolution of site conditions. Depending on the type of property being purchased, some purchasers require time to verify the condition of the lands and buildings. A clause could be in order requesting the time for adequate inspection of the site and the condition of the premises, and perhaps a request that the vendor indemnify the purchaser for any remediation work that is required or found to be required.

  A site adjacent to a former gas station might require testing for soil contamination. The site of a former marijuana grow operation or drug lab would bear inspection for mould or noxious residues that might compromise the value of the property as an investment or living quarters for tenants. Similarly, clauses regarding an older property could require the vendor to provide assurances that no asbestos or UFFI is on site (some of these scenarios are covered by specific disclosure statements in individual provinces).

- Satisfactory inspections. A second opinion from a building inspector is always helpful. This is especially important when it comes to an investment property, and you may even wish to stipulate that the deal is subject to the approval of key advisors: a lawyer, a financial planner, an appraiser, and others. Any one of these people may have expertise and insights to make you wary of buying the property. A structural engineer may notice weaknesses in the building that could save you headaches as a manager, for instance. Whatever the reason, make sure you secure enough time to get the opinions you need to make an informed decision.

The purchase of a condo (strata) unit or an apartment building may require special clauses. For instance, you might want to stipulate that the deal is subject to examination of the building owner's books to be sure that the cash flow is as stated in the disclosure documents. You might want to subject the deal to a review of the condominium council's minutes, not to mention engineers' reports on the integrity of the unit and building. This information could strengthen your bargaining position by supporting a lower price than the vendor is asking. The minutes could alert you to potential structural problems that may need repairs, something that could significantly impact your investment.

The vendor may also stipulate certain conditions in a counter-offer that you'll want to take into account, as these may affect the timing of the deal. The vendor's conditions primarily aim at determining your authenticity as a purchaser and the quality of the deal the vendor is achieving through the transaction. The clauses may include:

- Removal of conditions in the event of a back-up offer. An attractive property may draw more than one offer, giving the vendor more choice in terms of buyers. To expedite the processing of your offer, and to give the vendor a free hand in other negotiations, he or she may ask that you remove your conditions within a set period of time (usually 72 hours). Such a clause, especially for more complex deals, will require that you have your advisers willing to step in and get the deal done swiftly.

- Confirmation of vendor-take-back mortgage. The property you're considering may have been previously purchased with the assistance of a mortgage broker. To ensure the financing can be paid off through the proceeds from the deal you are trying to achieve, the vendor may ask for time to negotiate the specifics with the mortgage broker that arranged the previous financing.

- Deposit funds. The vendor will want to ensure that the funds you have deposited will go toward the purchase price of the property once the deal completes. Many vendors stipulate that deposits are nonrefundable once all conditions for the purchase of a property are met.

- Credit check. Depending on the financing arrangements for the property, the vendor may want to ensure you have a good credit rating and won't default on payment for the property. This sort of clause may be of particular interest in the case of a deal in which the vendor hopes to use the proceeds to pay off debts or secure another investment. A vendor may also want to see confirmation of your financing sources for the property. Whatever is required, providing the time to confirm your creditworthiness will boost their confidence that you're the best investor for the property.

- Legal review. Just as you will want your lawyer to review the deal you're hoping to close, the vendor will also want to make sure you're offering legitimate terms and that there are no complications. Provide the vendor as much time as you need yourself to ensure the deal is clear to go firm, and that you haven't included legal loopholes or traps that could compromise the vendor's interests.

- Expiry date. Barring a clause that provides for the consideration of back-up offers, a time limit for completing the deal should be noted in the offer to purchase. The buyer may stipulate one date, but the vendor could require a different date depending on the nature of the conditions involved and the requirement to do the deal. The broker representing the vendor should be aware of the vendor's interests and make it clear what kind of a time frame would be suitable.

  If you're considering purchasing urban land or a commercial property, it's not unusual for it to sit under contract for months while due diligence proceeds. Make sure all parties have enough time to satisfy all concerns and close the deal properly. Too short a time frame and the buyer may not be able to satisfy questions about the property's prospects; too long, and the vendor may question the buyer's motives.

- Closing date. The closing date may be requested by the buyer, but the vendor also has the power to name a closing date that suits his or her interests. Regardless of when the deal closes, possession and occupancy of the property could be at a mutually agreeable date after the closing. The closing date should give both parties enough time to complete any outstanding paperwork, and respect both the buyer's desire to take possession as well as the needs of the vendor to leave the property in the condition promised in the deal.

Since the various elements in the offer to purchase will become the basis for the purchase contract if your offer is accepted, make sure that they give the negotiations the momentum needed to complete a deal that's satisfactory to both vendor and purchaser as soon as possible.

## Giving a Deposit

A deposit serves various purposes. It is a partial payment on the purchase price, a good-faith indication of seriousness, and an assurance of performance if all the conditions in the offer to purchase have been fulfilled. The deposit is generally no more than 10 per cent of the purchase price. If there were conditions in the offer, and these conditions were not met, then the purchaser is entitled to receive the full amount of the deposit back. This is one reason why it is important to have conditions in the offer to protect one's interests fully. Most agreements for purchase and sale have a provision that gives the vendor the option of keeping the deposit as "liquidated damages," in the event that the purchaser fails to complete the terms of the agreement and pay the balance of money on the closing date.

When making a deposit, it is very important to be careful about to whom you pay the funds. If you are purchasing on a private sale and no realtor is involved, never pay the funds directly to the vendor; pay them to your own lawyer in trust. If a realtor is involved, the funds can be paid to the realtor's trust account or your own lawyer's trust account, as the situation dictates. If you are purchasing a new property from the builder, do not pay a deposit directly to the builder. The money should go to your lawyer's trust account, or some other system should be set up for your protection ensuring that your funds cannot be used except under certain conditions based on those that are clearly set out in the agreement. The risk is high in paying your money directly to a builder, because if the builder does not complete the project and goes into bankruptcy, you could lose all your money, and in practical terms could have great difficulty getting it back. Although several provincial governments have brought in legislation dealing with new property projects to protect the public on the issue of deposits—as well as many other property risk areas—legislation provides only partial protection.

Another matter you have to consider is interest. If you are paying a deposit, you want to ensure that interest at the appropriate rate or based on the appropriate formula is paid to your credit. In many cases, deposit monies can be tied up for many months, and that could represent considerable interest.

## Making a Deal

Striking a deal may seem simple, but only on the surface. While negotiations typically involve three basic steps—the bid, the counter-offer, and the decision (sometimes repeated a few times)—the negotiations themselves are a healthy challenge for those who like to reconcile the various sides of an issue.

### The Bid

The purchaser submits an offer to purchase, and the vendor evaluates it and eventually responds. Unless there's an outright rejection of the offer, the response typically takes the form of a counter-offer that agrees to some aspects of the purchase offer, but offers suggestions to make the deal more suitable. The purchaser may continue to perform due diligence on the property in order to achieve a stronger negotiating position. Work to fulfill the subject clauses will typically strengthen any response to a counter-offer from the vendor.

As a prospective purchaser, make the best possible offer you can under the conditions. A hot market may require a slightly richer bid; a market where there's downward pressure on prices may benefit from an approach that makes the vendor feel you're doing them a favour.

### The Counter-offer

Waiting for the vendor's answer is a time of anticipation. An offer that's accepted will allow you to get on with closing the transaction and becoming an owner. But if your offer is rejected, you may want to consider submitting an amended offer that addresses the vendor's concerns. Similarly, if the vendor thinks there is a prospect of a deal, they will counter-offer and set a deadline for acceptance, rather than simply reject your offer and walk away.

The counter-offer may focus on the price, what's included in the deal in terms of chattels and improvements, or may include additional terms and clauses that make the offer better for all parties to the agreement.

### The Decision

A counter-offer will test your negotiating skills. Ask your realtor exactly why your initial offer was rejected. Perhaps the vendor knows a better offer than yours is in the offing and wants to see how far you're willing to go to secure the property. It helps to be able to provide an argument for the competitiveness of your offer. And whatever the circumstances of the counter-offer, be candid but professional as you hammer out a deal that satisfies both yourself and the vendor.

## Using a Lawyer

A lawyer can be a fount of sound advice regarding your purchase. Due to the variety of clauses in the agreement to purchase, it is important that a lawyer review the offer before you sign it. While some people don't see the value, and others perceive it as more costly than it's worth, it would be false economy to go without it. The cost of legal advice is very reasonable relative to the risk involved in signing a bad contract, and many lawyers will be more than willing to provide the review at a reasonable rate. Alternatively, rather than seeing a lawyer before submitting an offer to purchase, you may wish to insert a condition that states the offer is "subject to approval as to form and contents by the purchaser's solicitor, such approval to be communicated to the vendor within X days of acceptance, or be considered withheld." (See page 110 in Chapter 4, "Selecting Your Advisory Team," for tips on selecting a lawyer.)

## Insuring Gain

It is important that the parties agree to an exact date when the responsibilities and risks associated with property ownership will pass from the vendor to the new owner. The purchase agreement may state that the risk of ownership will pass at such time as a firm, binding, unconditional purchase and sale agreement is in place. Alternatively, the contract may state that the risk passes on the completion date or the possession date. In any event, make sure that you have adequate insurance coverage taking effect as of and including the date that you assume the risk. The vendor should wait until one day after the new owner assumes responsibility for the property before terminating the property's existing insurance coverage.

Don't forget to investigate title insurance. It may even be required in areas where there's a high rate of title fraud, not to mention other complications associated with obtaining clear title to a property. Many mortgage providers require it in order to protect their interest in your property, too. Title insurance protects you against any losses or costs incurred in the course of securing title to a property.

Chapter 8, "Understanding the Insurance Aspects," provides further information on insurance and its importance to your investment property.

# Closing the Deal

Once a deal has been reached and the purchase offer has been accepted, there are a number of financial considerations that need to be addressed. The cost of closing a deal will take into account not just the legal work, but also figuring out what value to assign to chattels as well as paying the several taxes and fees owing to advisers. This section provides an overview of what to consider as you approach closing.

## Finalizing the Price

An agreement over price comes before a decision to close—no one buys something without knowing how much they're going to pay for it; however, there is some wiggle room when it comes to chattels and goodwill. The due diligence and satisfaction of subject clauses may have brought issues to light that require a little consideration for various aspects of the property, either to support the asking price on the part of the vendor or to get a better deal on the part of the buyer.

The two key areas for negotiation are the chattels—moveable elements of a property that are part and parcel of the property itself—as well as goodwill, a more intangible attribute.

## Assessing Chattels

Chattels are considered separate from the property itself, but an integral part of what the buyer receives. A typical example of chattels associated with a rental property, for example, might be landscaping or maintenance equipment. A retail property might have items such as tables and chairs or display cases that would be great for the next purchaser, but which aren't necessarily part of the property itself. The final sales agreement should identify the chattels included with a property and assign a value to them. Since there are tax implications associated with the value attributed to the land, buildings, and chattels, it is important to state clearly and accurately what the chattels include. This will affect how much sales tax is payable on chattels, as well as taxes and fees owing on the transfer of the property itself. A fixture that isn't specifically designated a chattel in the agreement will be considered part of the purchase price of the building (rather than as a chattel). To avoid future legal difficulties, it is often worth stating that all fixtures are included except those specifically excluded in the agreement.

Assign a fair market value to the chattels, but be ready to negotiate. A greater value may be appropriate in cases where the chattels are unique or antique, and may justify a higher asking price. The chattels may also hold a value in themselves that the building itself doesn't have.

## Assessing Goodwill

Some properties have a history, a location, or a reputation that deserves a value in its own right. This component is known as goodwill and should feature in the offer to purchase. The goodwill inherent in the property may allow you to ask (or offer, depending which side of the table you're on) for a property than is otherwise deemed fair, resulting in a lower material value, but a value that flatters the vendor. In some cases, goodwill is a good means of sidestepping the standard market forces and executing a deal for an investment property for reasons of rejigging portfolios between investors and any number of other reasons.

Consult an appraiser and accountant to determine an appropriate value of goodwill for a given property.

## *Rewarding Advisers*

Closing a sale not only requires paying the vendor; it requires paying the various advisers and professionals who've helped you make the investment. To help you keep track of the various payments required, consult the checklist of Real Estate Purchase Expenses on page 368 in the Appendix.

The fees and commissions owing on the sale of the property, usually a percentage of the purchase price, should appear in the sale agreement along with the name of the party receiving the commission.

The most significant fee will be the commission to the real estate agent who assisted in brokering the deal. Though this is negotiable, it often amounts to about 5 per cent of the purchase price. The standard fee for legal services is less, usually between 0.75 and 1 per cent of the purchase price, though this will vary in proportion to the documentation required for the purchase. Other fees are relative to the amount of advice provided.

There are also several taxes to take into account:

- sales taxes, including the GST and the HST, apply to newly built properties and renovations affecting more than 90 per cent of the property, as well as chattels;
- provincial property purchase tax, which varies from province to province; and

- non-resident withholding tax, a special charge applicable on properties purchased from non-residents of Canada that's equivalent to a quarter of the purchase price.

For more information regarding the taxes applicable on real estate transactions, see page 202 in Chapter 7, "Understanding the Tax Aspects."

## Summary

This chapter provides an overview of the steps necessary to negotiate for and purchase an investment property, and to understand the dynamics at play. Advance research knowledge is critical to ensure a profitable purchase.

Once you have purchased a property, you will need to ensure it is managed well in all respects. The next chapter discusses property management.

# CHAPTER 10

# Managing Your Property

**Property management has** many objectives, the primary ones being to attain the highest possible cash flow, net income, and, ultimately, property value. The trick is achieving successful management and minimizing risk with the least amount of stress. Other objectives, which are fundamental to achieving the primary objectives of managing a rental property, include selecting the best possible tenants for a property, minimizing vacancies, maximizing revenues, and limiting expenses. In addition, routine maintenance of the property will ensure the property retains its appeal to tenants and potential purchasers—which translates into value for you, as the owner.

Many novice landlords decide to put their properties up for sale, frequently at a loss, when it isn't necessary. A lack of property management skills and the resulting waves of frustration, stress, and time spent dealing with the effects of poor management such as disruptive and late-paying tenants, vacancies, vandalism, and negative cash flow as well as high repair and maintenance costs drive many property owners quite literally out of the business.

There's plenty to be said about being a landlord; indeed, my book with Peter Mitham, *The Canadian Landlord's Guide* (Wiley, 2009) is devoted to the topic. This chapter will help you develop a strategy for stress-free property management, and avoid the common pitfalls. It covers the types of management possible, record-keeping options, tenant selection, and tenant documentation. It also addresses strategies to limit expenses and increase the income from your revenue property. Common home-maintenance problems and avoiding common fire hazards will also be discussed.

## Types of Management

The initial decision that you make regarding the form of management will be largely determined by the size of the property, the type and number of investments, the number of tenants, your interest and experience in management, and the time you have available. If you are purchasing a condominium, the same considerations are taken into account by the condominium corporation on behalf of and under instructions from the condominium owners.

There are essentially three forms of property management: self-management, resident management, and professional management. A combination of these may also be used.

## Self-Management

In the case of small revenue properties, such as a duplex or single-family house, it is often more practical for the owner to be responsible for managing the investment directly. It is not necessary in a self-management situation that the owners themselves clean the grounds, cut the grass, do the gardening, and sweep the driveways. It does mean, though, that the owners, or a representative of the owners, would have to be directly involved in supervising the performance of these types of services. Frequently the jobs are done by firms under contract or by the tenants themselves.

There are cost savings to managing the property yourself, but not everyone is suited for it. Ask yourself how much free time you have, and if you're prepared to spend that time managing a property. Real estate is not a passive investment, especially if you expect the property to have tenants! Still, you don't have to be retired or working part-time at a day job to have time to manage a property. By managing your time well, you may be capable of managing several properties successfully.

To decide whether or not you should manage a property, determine your likes and dislikes, and your responses to various situations landlords encounter, such as:

- disruptive tenants;
- high vacancies;
- steady turnover;
- vandalism;
- regular complaints, both real and surreal; and
- predictable and unpredictable maintenance costs.

Remember, in terms of real estate management, you can involve yourself as little or as much as you want. It comes down to personal choice, circumstances, and desire for profit. Although it is easier to have someone else assume the management responsibilities, there will be a cost factor. You may wish to work at it on a part-time basis and have the right tenant assist on matters such as minor cleanup, cutting the lawn, and watering the plants.

Having the interest and the abilities to get involved in property management still doesn't mean you'll do a good job. Some properties are simply more complex than you expect, or your life circumstances may prevent you from managing them even if this was your original plan. Typically, small portfolios of no more than eight or a dozen units are suitable for self-management. A larger number of units under management might benefit from professional attention or a team of on-site managers who can attend to the needs of each property.

Here are a few considerations that might determine how great the demands of a property or portfolio might be on you:

- Size of the portfolio. One property is usually easier to manage than many, and properties that are scattered throughout a city or region will take time to visit if you're managing them personally. Knowing your limits is important. By the same token, some properties may require you to manage them simply because they're in areas where no other manager is available.

- Scope of the responsibilities. Not every unit of property is the same. That newly built condo unit you bought as an investment is likely to require less attention than an older, single-detached home you bought with plans to lease it out. Knowing how much time a property requires to manage may help determine whether you're the right person to handle management.

- Other responsibilities. One or two units might be easy to manage at first, but if you're suddenly put on the fast-track for a promotion at work or if there's a family crisis, you may have to relinquish management of your property for a period of time. Appointing a manager can provide you the extra time and freedom you need.

Don't forget that self-management doesn't mean doing everything yourself! While you are the manager, you also can manage the delegation of responsibilities to others. The regular chores of maintenance and landscaping, for example, can be farmed out to contractors. You may even wish to assign the job to a tenant in exchange for a break on the rent. If you ultimately decide to maintain the properties yourself, you may wish to take a residential-property-manager course offered through a local college or apartment owners' association.

## Resident Management

In this situation, the owner employs one or more people directly to perform the daily management requirements. These people would normally operate out of an office on the property and would be paid a full- or part-time salary, or have a partial rent or rent-free apartment in exchange for services. It is important to be very careful in selecting the resident manager and to check their references thoroughly beforehand. Generally only apartment buildings with more than eight suites can financially justify employing a full-time resident manager, but this can vary.

The prospective resident manager could already be a tenant living in the building, rather than someone new. It is not uncommon to have a husband-and-wife team share the responsibilities. Frequently this is an excellent arrangement. The chief qualities and qualifications to look for in a resident manager include:

- a pleasant personality;
- honesty and integrity;
- conscientiousness;
- knowledge of the job to be done, and a willingness to do it;
- pride in a job well done, whether or not it's enjoyable;
- familiarity with the service industry in some form.

Moreover, a resident manager should command the respect of other people. A resident manager who isn't respected by tenants or who easily aggravates others isn't the best person for the job. You may be better off contracting out management, or selecting someone who will represent your interests and manner far better to tenants and neighbours. One measure of the manager's abilities is the certified property manager (CPM) designation, which is awarded to managers who have completed a program established by the Real Estate Institute of Canada (www.reic.ca).

The resident manager's responsibilities may include any number of the following jobs:

- collecting rent;
- making deposits;
- keeping the grounds neat and clean;
- making minor repairs and maintenance;

- showing vacant suites and signing up new tenants;

- keeping records; and

- advising you of any problems and serving as your representative to other tenants.

It's important to define the scope of duties and responsibilities you expect a manager to fulfill. This gives the manager an idea of what is expected, and a basis for accountability. A small rooming house, for instance, will have different requirements than an apartment block with a couple dozen units; a property tenanted by university students will be different than one tenanted by professionals and senior citizens.

A manager should receive fair and competitive compensation that reflects the duties you assign and the time commitment required to perform them. A full-time manager should receive a living wage, while a part-time manager might receive free rent in lieu of pay or some other arrangement. Be sure to speak with your accountant regarding the most tax-effective way of structuring the remuneration.

## Professional Management

Many landlords who own apartment buildings with more than 12 units, several single-family dwellings, or who are absent or inactive use professional management companies. These experienced companies have many systems and procedures for the efficient operation of their support function. The types of services and benefits provided could include:

- staffing;

- accounting and management systems;

- accessing suppliers who can provide volume discounts and good service;

- selecting and contracting out competent tradespeople for repair or general maintenance service, subject to a limit beyond which any expenditure would require your written authorization;

- finding and selecting tenants, showing apartments, and negotiating tenancy agreements or leases, and using forms supplied or approved by you and your lawyer;

- monitoring tenant problems and evicting, if necessary;

- collecting rents;

- paying all bills and mortgage payments on your behalf;
- maintaining all necessary records;
- sending you a monthly statement on the operation of the building;
- maintaining the grounds and buildings; and
- hiring and supervising the resident manager.

One of the key benefits is that a professional management company will provide a consistent level of quality. Fees can range from 2 to 5 per cent or more of the gross monthly revenue from the property. Like any business activity, fees are negotiable. It is important to give the company written guidelines that are also incorporated in the overall management contract. Have your lawyer review the contract before you sign it. Check out the company thoroughly and ask for references from owners of other properties being managed. Also, as with a resident manager, check to see if the company's employees have the CPM designation or have completed relevant courses offered by the Real Estate Institute of Canada. Remember, before making your final decision, attempt to shortlist at least three desirable candidates for resident manager or professional management company.

# Keeping Records

Records are essential and unavoidable no matter how small your real estate investment is. Beginning with the documents associated with the purchase of the property, a continual stream of information is generated that helps you to track, assess, and analyze the cash flow of your business as well as pay taxes on and eventually market and sell your property. Bank statements, invoices, receipts, sales slips, and contracts have to be managed for your and the government's best interests, requiring you to develop reliable and effective systems for managing the myriad data you'll accumulate.

## *Reasons to Keep Records*

Prompt and efficient storage of business records is essential for several reasons. The most fundamental one is because the government requires it. Government departments have established rules and regulations related to record keeping by the private sector. Statistics Canada, for example, may request information. A response is required to such a request. CRA rules require you to pay income tax on net revenue income and to remit deductions at source from any employee taxes, Employment Insurance (EI), and CPP contributions. You may not need to supply full documentation with your tax return, but you're required to maintain documentation to substantiate the information provided on your return in the event the government chooses to audit you.

There are additional reasons to maintain accurate records that you can retrieve at a moment's notice. Should your business suffer damage or a loss for which you're covered under insurance, the adjuster may require documentation to support your claim for compensation. And, when it comes time to sell the property, being able to demonstrate solid cash flow and significant upgrades will strengthen your case for a higher price from potential purchasers.

The same information that informs buyers of your property's track record is also important when it comes to your understanding of how the property is performing. Records, especially several years' worth, can reveal trends in tenancies, expenses, and income. Accurate records can also help you plan ongoing maintenance, and demonstrate if a particular task was completed or not completed in the event someone claims for an injury allegedly caused by the "worn and loose shingling" that, according to your records, was installed six months earlier. Here are a few more reasons for keeping accurate records:

- An orderly collection of expense receipts makes it easier to prepare an accurate income tax return and Statement of Business or Professional Activities (T2125).

- Records of income and expenses establish a basis for cash flow, income, and expense projections, as well as break-even analyses that enable you to make decisions that enhance revenue and management of cash flow.

- Detailed financial records create opportunities for comparing budget goals with historical records and future projections.

- A payment schedule reminds you when obligations to creditors and other payments are due, either to others or to yourself.

- Regular maintenance records provide a basis for evaluating the condition, efficiency, and operation of the revenue property.

- Tenant records allow you to be more responsive to tenant concerns, and to document past issues with tenants in the event problems arise that require documentation (such as eviction, or a need to contact next of kin).

Canada's Income Tax Act requires that business owners keep their records and books in an orderly manner at their place of business or ordinary residence. CRA officials may request this material at any time for review or audit purposes. While you typically receive notice of an impending audit, your stress level will be lower if you aren't scrambling to find the records you know you have. By law, you're required to maintain business records and supporting documents for at least six years from the end of the last taxation year to which they relate or from the date of filing (should you file a late return). Revenue Canada permits computer storage of records, as long as those records provide adequate information to verify taxable income.

## Record-Keeping Systems and Equipment

Some of the typical financial records and associated documents you'll keep as the owner of a revenue-generating property include:

- purchase contract and documents associated with the acquisition of the property;
- mortgage agreement and payment statements;
- property tax assessments and remittances;
- bank statements for your business account;
- tenant applications and schedule of rents;
- journal of expenses and accounts payable;
- employee records, including payroll journal;
- record of tax filings and associated documentation, including notice of assessment;
- record of GST/HST filings, including a ledger of GST/HST paid and, if applicable, received; and
- general synoptic ledger.

Some examples of non-financial records include documents relating to the hiring of personnel, operation and maintenance of equipment, inventory of supplies, and landlord-tenant documentation.

Copies of receipts may either be kept in paper format or scanned for electronic preservation. Keeping records in an old-style manual ledger may be simple for a small rental property, such as a secondary suite in your home, but larger properties will tend to be better managed using a formal accounting program. As your real estate investment expands in terms of numbers and types of properties, you will likely want and need to use one of the excellent software programs available, some of which are geared specifically for real estate investors. Your bookkeeper or accountant will be able to recommend the most efficient record-keeping system for your operation. Still, even if you lease just one suite for a while, you may benefit from entering some financial information in a basic spreadsheet to see if there are patterns or insights that may be gleaned from the data.

# Finding the Right Tenant

A vacant property costs you money on a daily basis; therefore, to minimize your losses, you should be prepared to find tenants. It is important to draft a marketing plan when preparing to lease a property. Whether you're seeking tenants for a single unit, several units in a residential apartment block, or non-residential tenants for commercial space, a solid marketing plan will help you address the specific needs of your situation.

Marketing rental properties may look easy in a strong market, but it requires a mix of skills that can be put to the test in a tough market. Getting the word out about the space you've got for rent is a first step; making sure the information reaches the people you want to have as tenants is quite another.

Treat the marketing of the space you want to rent with the same rigour you applied to its purchase and that you'll apply to its sale. You may not be selling the property outright, but you are selling prospective tenants on its merits with a view to leasing them the rights to use the property for a period of time. In order to make them buy in, you have a marketing plan in place, a strategy for marketing the space to tenants through the right channels, and a backup plan in case the original strategy falls flat. While some landlords use banners and incentives for inducing tenants to occupy space (something that may be helpful), it is better when you don't have to resort to such measures. Attention is good; gaudy attention in the form of banners across the building's facade is less so.

## Drafting a Marketing Plan

Consider these key points as you develop a marketing plan for your property:

- Type of tenant. The type of tenant you seek will depend on the rent you hope to charge as well as determine the venues you choose for advertisements. A broad tenant base could be reached through newspapers and street-side signage, while a targeted tenant base may prompt you to contact special groups or organizations that can let specific people know the space is available.
- Rental rate. Advertising a low rental rate will typically attract many more queries than a high one; a higher rate may be necessary to make

the economics of the property work, but may demand that you advertise in a narrower, more targeted range of outlets.

- Term of tenancy. Space available for short periods of time—say, less than six months—may be worth advertising on an ongoing basis to ensure you have a waiting list of prospective tenants. Properties that enjoy long-term tenants don't need to worry as much about maintaining visibility in the market. A newspaper ad or street-side sign may be enough to attract tenants, especially if the property is well-maintained.

- Lease restrictions. Restrictions such as "no smoking" and "no pets" are worth a mention in advertisements because it will automatically limit the kind of inquiries you get. This will help maximize the time you have to consider the most likely tenants for your property.

## Advertising Your Property

Back in the day, all a landlord would have to do to attract a tenant was run a newspaper ad or post a sign on a lawn or the local community bulletin board and inquiries would come flooding in. A wealth of media and communications technology means that rental properties can be more widely advertised than ever before. Still, some methods of advertising are more effective than others; all have strengths and weaknesses.

Nevertheless, a few key elements are critical for the success of any ad:

- Location. An advertisement should at least name a neighbourhood or the closest main intersection.

- Description. Keep your description short and sweet and include the number of bedrooms, location, amenities, and price. Text on social-networking sites such as Facebook is usually read in small chunks, and Twitter limits messages to 140 characters.

- Price. The price of the premises you're offering is a standard element of most ads, but you may wish to withhold pricing information to broaden the number of enquiries you receive.

- Availability. Let tenants know when a suite is available, usually the first of the month following the appearance of the ad. Most people scouting space will assume a unit is available immediately if you don't let them know. The date can make a difference if you're trying to lease space in advance of the current term ending, or to students trying to land space before term starts.

- Contact information. Give the phone number and e-mail you're most likely to answer promptly, and make sure to have a voicemail indicating whether or not you're likely to return calls.

Regardless of the information your ad contains, you'll need a place for it to appear. Some of the key avenues include:

- Print media. Newspapers remain the best option property hunters have for reviewing a large selection of properties in a single place, and thanks to a proliferation of market-specific publications a landlord can target specific segments of the rental market in more ways than ever before. Add in the fact that many print publications also offer online editions of their classifieds, and you can reach a very broad audience indeed.

- Online options. The most popular classified sites in Canada to post free listings for everything from comics to condos are Craigslist (www.craigslist.com) and Kijiji (www.kijiji.ca). Both allow landlords to target specific neighbourhoods, and have a popular following among landlords and tenants alike. However, dedicated services (charging a fee, of course) include ViewIt.ca and GottaRent.com. These sites are also community-specific, but offer the support and analytics Craigslist just doesn't provide. The analytics help improve the management and marketing of your property, especially if you've got a larger property with recurring vacancies. The key to using online listings effectively is choosing the right service for the market you're trying to reach. One service may be more popular in an area than another, so ask around and find out what people are using.

- Word of mouth and signage. Signage is a tried-and-true means of advertising properties. The widespread use of cellphones makes signage even more effective, because prospective tenants can see the sign and call you while standing in front of the property. If they don't like what they hear they can move on. Word of mouth is also effective. Happy tenants are often keen to tell others about the great place they've got, and put you in touch with tenants who are an equally good fit when they move out.

Should your own efforts not pan out, or if you're looking for a little extra support, don't hesitate to list your property with the local apartment owners association or with the local student union. Getting the word out via these organizations may help you fill gaps at odd times of the year or tap into tenants requiring premises for specific lengths of time.

## *Selecting the Tenant*

Experienced landlords and property managers are unanimous in their opinion that it is better to leave a suite vacant than to rent it to a bad tenant. Therefore, do not underestimate the importance of the application, screening, and interviewing process before making a selection. Most provinces have legislation relating to landlord-tenant relations. Before proceeding with your tenant selection, obtain a copy of the relevant provincial legislation and become familiar with it. Understand your rights and responsibilities as a landlord. You may wish to consider joining your local apartment owners' association or take a course on being a landlord through the apartment owners' association or a community college.

The screening process typically includes a few key points: interviewing and inviting potential tenants to view the space available for lease; soliciting applications; reviewing applications; following up with any questions you might have for the candidate, rejection, or acceptance and an offer to lease the property.

### The Invitation

The better your advertising strategy (discussed elsewhere in this chapter), the better the calibre of the potential tenants you'll have to consider. Some landlords advertise a specific viewing time and walk groups of candidates through the unit. Screening tenants before arranging a viewing can be useful, however. A brief conversation by phone can answer some basic questions regarding the suite that may make a viewing unnecessary for the tenant. This saves time for everyone. You may also discover information about the prospective tenant that will prompt you to invite the tenant or downplay the opportunity in an effort to discourage interest. Should the tenant have an interest in seeing the suite, and there are no apparent drawbacks to the tenant, you can arrange to view the unit at a mutually acceptable time.

### The Viewing

When showing a rental unit, proceed with caution. You want to make sure you have the current tenant's permission to enter the unit, and also to make sure that the people you invite for the viewing pose no danger to yourself or any belongings left in the suite.

Equally important, you want to ensure the timing will show the suite at its best.

Answer all questions candidly, highlighting the positive elements. A basic tour may suit someone with a mild interest in the suite, but those who have a deeper interest will warrant a full tour (including laundry and storage facilities).

Many observations will likely pass through your mind when you show the suite to each candidate. It pays to write these down so that you can judge between applicants if all reference checks come back equal. A positive gut feeling about one tenant rather than another may be the deciding factor if there's a tie for the tenancy.

## The Application

Candidates who view the suite should receive an application to lease, unless the viewing has turned them off the opportunity. The application form allows you to investigate the various candidates more fully, checking references, running a credit check, and, in some provinces, checking rental bureau records to see if previous landlords had difficulties with them. A note should alert the applicant that by signing the application form they consent to a check of their credit rating and other criteria. The application should not request information that violates the applicant's privacy or contravenes human rights legislation, of course. Questions regarding the candidate's race, ancestry, place of origin, colour, ethnic origin, citizenship, creed, sex, age, marital status, family status, handicap, or receipt of public assistance are not acceptable questions for determining suitability to rent.

## The Review

Reviewing the information you gather may take little or no time. Some of the information you discover may disqualify the applicant immediately; other information may confirm the applicant's quality beyond question. Regardless, the information requires careful consideration. While some landlords take just hours to evaluate a tenant, others will take a few days. It is important to be prompt but careful with your evaluation.

You may wish to conduct a follow-up interview if additional questions arise during your review of the applications. The more likely scenario will be that you let the applicant know that they've been selected or you are unable to offer them the unit. While you don't need to give a reason, it may be worthwhile assuring them when appropriate if there was no reason to disqualify them. At the very least, it's reassuring.

## *Tenancy Agreement*

Provincial landlord-tenant legislation and the standard forms available for tenancy agreements are not all-encompassing, so you want to reflect in writing your specific rental policies. Some issues you may wish to cover in the agreement include:

- smoking;
- pets;
- number of occupants;
- when the rental payment is due;
- penalty for late payment;
- penalty for cheques that do not clear the tenant's account;
- term of the tenancy (month to month or fixed period);
- proportionate share payment of utilities;
- amount of security deposit, typically 50% of the monthly rent, and deposit interest (if permitted by provincial legislation);
- tenant's obligations, such as care and maintenance of premises;
- landlord's access to premises;
- tenant's notice to landlord of extended absence; and
- no assignment or subletting of rental suite by tenant without the landlord's prior written permission and consent.

The candidate to whom you offer the suite will have to complete the formal lease agreement. A security (or damage) deposit and one month's rent should be collected at the time of signing, though the first month's rent doesn't need to be payable until the tenant takes occupancy. A cheque is acceptable.

The occupancy date will be when you deliver the keys to the new tenant, so additional communication will take place then to ensure the tenant gets a good start in the new premises and any outstanding issues regarding the rental of the space can be resolved. The date of occupancy is also when a property condition checklist should be completed, ensuring a standard for the return (or retention) of the damage deposit in the event the tenant damages the premises. For an example of a landlord-tenant suite-inspection checklist, see Checklist 5 on page 372 in the Appendix.

For your peace of mind, and to ensure that all aspects have been considered, you should have your lawyer review the additions you have made to the standard lease agreement. Additional information is available from your province's residential tenancy office:

- Alberta: www.servicealberta.gov.ab.ca/Landlords_Tenants.cfm
- British Columbia: www.rto.gov.bc.ca
- Manitoba: www.gov.mb.ca/fs/cca/rtb
- New Brunswick: www.gnb.ca/0062/Rentalsman/index-e.asp
- Newfoundland and Labrador: www.gs.gov.nl.ca/landlord/index.html
- Northwest Territories: www.justice.gov.nt.ca/RentalOffice/rentaloffice_information.shtml
- Nova Scotia: www.gov.ns.ca/snsmr/access/land/residential-tenancies.asp
- Ontario: www.ltb.gov.on.ca
- Prince Edward Island: www.irac.pe.ca/rental
- Quebec: www.rdl.gouv.qc.ca
- Saskatchewan: www.justice.gov.sk.ca/ORT
- Yukon: www.community.gov.yk.ca/consumer/landtact.html

## Dealing with Difficult Tenants

Despite your best efforts to be friendly, attentive, and responsive to the needs of tenants, it's not unusual to encounter the bad apple that ruins the barrel. Minor problems are often resolved by reiterating or clarifying the ground rules for the property. Other problems require stronger action and attention to appropriate legal protocols. This section discusses a few of the scenarios you may encounter.

### Resolving Minor Troubles

Tenants are individuals, and each has habits (good and bad) as well as desires that you may have to manage. Sometimes the baggage is quite tangible, because the tenant is trying to find space to store items such as barbecues and those places happen to be the common areas of the property you own.

### Bad habits

Some of the habits and desires tenants might bring with them to new accommodation include a penchant for gardening, composting, feeding the birds, hanging banners in or from windows, or any number of ostensibly harmless acts that may cause trouble or difficulties for a landlord. While gardening in itself isn't bad, a full-scale home garden may be difficult if it's located in common areas, causing inconvenience to neighbours because of watering practices or other elements, or is just plain unsightly. Similarly, bird feeders may be difficult because of the potential for mess and greater maintenance costs in terms of sweeping and potentially the control of insect pests.

You want to limit the incidence of these troubles, which may seem minor but could create greater difficulties in the future if they aren't limited or prohibited at the outset.

## Bad Behaviours

Tenants who keep odd hours or engage in unconventional behaviours may not be ones you would evict, but they could cause trouble in a building. While selecting an appropriate mix of tenants can help prevent confrontations between tenants, you may not discover a tenant's behaviours till after they move in.

Using the laundry facilities after a certain hour, dominating the common areas (and potentially disturbing the neighbours) on a regular basis, or storing personal items in the common areas could be problems.

Preventing the activities of one tenant from interfering with the lives of others makes good sense, but it's also important to accommodate the tenant's needs if, say, they can only do laundry in the morning just as the night-shift worker next door is going to bed.

## Making Good

When tenants act badly, it's a good idea to reiterate the ground rules for the leased premises. You may wish to post a notice in common areas outlining the troubles you've observed, reminding tenants that activities which contribute to the trouble should be avoided. Or, you may wish to distribute notices to tenants indicating that such-and-such is a problem, and that tenants should refrain from contributing to it.

When an issue is a minor annoyance, whether or not you can identify the tenant who is causing it, one of the best methods of handling the issue is to address specific tenants with a general warning. This ensures that the tenants know the policy is one for everyone, but also ensures that the tenant who is causing the problem recognizes that there is a problem and that it probably isn't wise to continue contributing to it. A tenant worth keeping will recognize the problem and amend his or her ways.

Confronting tenants with accusations or questions that aim to extract a confession doesn't help, and may even generate some resentment that they're being singled out. This could breed bad feelings that makes the tenant open to alternative arrangements should you, say, increase rents when the next opportunity arises.

## Resolving Major Troubles

Some minor troubles, if left alone, can evolve into major challenges for a landlord. A habitual use of common areas, which seemed innocuous at first, can become annoying to other tenants and the neighbours if it continues unchecked. Student houses, for example, may become more raucous through the academic year if a landlord doesn't respond to the neighbours' complaints that the occupants are becoming a tad rowdy.

Other issues are in a class of their own, major troubles from the start that demand immediate action and adherence to strict professional standards. While a professional approach is important at all times, some issues require a more casual approach to start before the formal manner kicks in; others, like non-payment of rent, require a landlord to take action and follow the protocols any other business would when a client defaults.

## Getting Payment

A tenant who doesn't pay the rent on time has immediately crossed a line. It's a basic condition of the landlord-tenant relationship that the tenant leases space and the landlord receives regular payments for the lease of said space. So the non-payment of rent amounts to a very serious dispute.

While a landlord can make provisions for tenants who may have encountered an unexpected bit of trouble (it's up to you to determine how much credit you're willing to extend), it's wise to follow-up immediately on tenants who haven't paid. Most provinces allow you to issue an eviction notice either as soon as the rent is late or after three days, but the important thing is to get the process rolling if you believe there could be trouble.

Getting the ball rolling in the right direction is also important; when notifying a tenant that rent hasn't been paid and that they should start looking for other accommodation, it's important to include the following details:

- the amount of rent outstanding;
- the eviction date; and
- a clause noting that the tenant can appeal the notice.

The inclusion of these points is critical when giving a tenant notice to move when rent hasn't been paid, as even a small mistake may be grounds for dismissing the eviction notice.

In the event of an appeal, the tenant may approach you with the rent. You are free to accept the payment and keep the tenant as an occupant of the premises. The legislation in some provinces allows tenants to seek a reduction in rent in cases where repairs or improvements don't justify the payment of rent (or an increased rent, if that is the root of the tenant's decision to not pay all or part of the rent).

A landlord may have recourse to the local rental authority if the tenant refuses to leave even after due notice has been given. When every other option available to you is exhausted, call the landlord-tenancy office or rental bureau in your area to see what help they can provide.

## Getting Peace and Quiet

When a tenant's behaviour transgresses local bylaws, you have a serious dispute on your hands. Warnings may work—a call by neighbours to the appropriate civic authorities (say, the police department or fire station) may yield a warning— but some matters require legal action.

Before taking legal action, however, take the following steps to address the matter:

- file a formal, written complaint or warning with the tenant, and keep a copy for your files;
- deliver copies of the appropriate municipal bylaws to the tenant, affected neighbours, and any agents you have who may be monitoring the property; several municipalities post bylaws online that you can print; and
- call the police, if needed (it helps to establish a benchmark for yourself of when this would be appropriate and even necessary).

Once you've taken these steps, pursue legal options for addressing the situation and ensure that any legal action you take complies with the pertinent landlord-tenant legislation for your area.

Your local rental authority or rental bureau may be able to offer support in your efforts to resolve the situation. Should the situation proceed to a hearing or court action, you may need to call upon neighbours (including tenants) who were impacted by the tenant's actions or behaviour. These witnesses would demonstrate the tenant's culpability and establish the grounds for any remedy—be it eviction, compensation, or other satisfaction.

## Getting Rid of Tenants

A bad tenant may cost you hundreds or thousands of dollars in lost rent, repairs, and other expenses, not to mention the lost time and stress of trying to resolve the issue at the heart of the dispute. A good real estate lawyer and staff at the tenancy office for your area will be able to provide support, but you must decide when enough is enough.

When you've made the decision to evict a tenant, there will be notices to give, forms to complete and the potential for an appeal by the tenant. While the process may take time, it is in your interest to get the process moving, keep it moving, and reach a resolution so that you can resume normal operations as soon as possible.

As in all your affairs, be sure to remain professional, sensitive to the tenant, and, if necessary, have someone with you to witness your dealings with the individual (and for your protection, if the person has a tendency to be aggressive), and any steps you take to remove their belongings from the rented space. Document all of your actions meticulously and consult the provisions of the appropriate tenancy act to ensure that you are complying with the legislation and avoid any counter-action by your former tenant.

## Maintaining Rental Properties

A property that falls into disrepair may have garnered you short-term savings, but the long-term value will have been eroded. There'll be few people who want to buy it, save as a renovation opportunity. Regular maintenance is therefore a necessary part of managing your property and building its value.

The current lifespan of many buildings constructed today is about 50 years. That is, the initial construction will usually need some sort of major overhaul within about 50 years of construction. What maintenance allows you to do is extend that lifespan, avoiding a single costly upgrade in favour of regular, ongoing improvements that should, ideally, make the building efficient to operate and attractive to users.

A maintenance schedule can help you plan regular upgrades, while regular property assessments will help you determine what to plan and whether some work should be a higher priority than others (for example, should you redo the landscaping this year as planned, or attend to the roof that's showing signs of weakness after last winter's heavy snows?). By encouraging tenants to take care of their units, you may be able to reduce the amount of work you do and make it easier to undertake more important work between tenancies that allows you to achieve higher rents from new tenants.

## Looking In

Some of the major interior facets of a building that will require regular attention include flooring, painting, heating and water systems, and matters associated with water and air flows. These elements will help the rental property look better, feel better for tenants, or perform better.

A tenant's departure is an ideal time to maintain and upgrade the unit. The work may allow you to rent the suite for a significantly higher rate. Undertaking general improvements between tenancies is also an important means of ensuring a property stays in good condition, and keeping on top of problems. The maintenance work between tenancies is typically aimed at addressing issues that may have cropped up in the previous tenancy, or that cannot be done while the suite is occupied.

### Flooring

Whether you have carpeting, tile, or hardwood floors, your flooring will need regular care. A weekly vacuuming of common areas is a start, but don't forget the importance of an annual waxing or shampooing. Scrubbing the tiles, waxing the wood or shampooing the carpet gives an extra lustre that tacitly adds to the experience of the property, as well as protect against wear and tear. In addition, reviewing the state of flooring on an annual basis will give you a sense of how often it might have to be renewed. While a durable flooring material can last several years, reducing your need to replace it, make sure you track what has to be done.

### Painting

Washing the walls and slapping on a fresh coat of paint can do wonders for the appearance. The walls of a highly trafficked building, or one in a busy urban environment, will become dirtier than you care to imagine within a very short time. Cleaning the walls on an annual basis will improve the appearance, and in some cases be as good as a new coat of paint.

Sooner or later, however, a fresh coat of paint will be needed. A neutral tone that helps reduce the visibility of dirt is helpful, but the choice is up to you.

The important message here is to not forget to spruce up your property with a fresh coat of paint once every five years or so.

## Heating Systems

An efficient heating system can make life more comfortable for tenants and more economical for you. An annual pre-winter check-up of the system makes sense, while regular checkups while in operation can ensure that the system is responding appropriately to weather conditions.

You may wish to have a thermostat in each apartment so that tenants can control the heat, which could save you money and help identify potential problems. This will prevent you from boosting temperatures overall to suit one tenant, while giving the tenant a reason to go to you if there's something wrong in his or her unit. Having an individual temperature control will allow you to determine if the problem is with the tenant's unit or in the main system, saving time and hassle.

## Hot-Water Systems

A hot-water boiler will operate more efficiently if it is the appropriate size for your building's the needs. Regardless of the size, schedule annual check-ups to make sure it is working smoothly. A boiler that cuts out in the middle of a tenant's shower or can't run a full bath will not win you friends. If your building is large enough, consider installing a small boiler in each residential unit to ensure that tenants have an adequate supply of hot water and that they bear the operating costs.

## Controlling water

Water is a significant threat for many property owners, whether it is seeping into the structure of the building from the inside or leaks are causing water ingress from the outside. The causes of interior leakage typically stem from poor maintenance of washrooms and kitchens, but may also require attention to basements.

- Washrooms. Cracked caulking and leaky pipes are primary culprits in the washroom. Keeping an eye on shower stalls and tubs is important, because lack of caulking could allow water to seep into interior spaces and rot the building from the inside out. It may also create a fertile breeding ground for damp-loving pests such as silverfish. Research indicates that 75 per cent of all homes lack adequate caulking in the bathroom, which can lead to costly repairs.

A leaky faucet or piping can be expensive not only in repairs, but through higher water bills (in locales that have water metering). Responding promptly to tenant complaints and conducting inspections between tenancies can help reduce the cost of poor or faulty plumbing.

- Kitchens. Caulking is as much a concern in the kitchen as in the washroom. The catch-all purpose of the kitchen sink means that you should have splash guards in place around the sink, and ensure that sinks themselves are caulked adequately. This creates both savings for you and a more pleasant environment for tenants cutting up veggies. Seeing the runoff from the salad greens you've just washed, or perhaps the juices from a chicken breast, heading under the sink leads to all sorts of speculation about what else has rolled under there to rot. Spare yourself and your tenants the trouble—clean up the kitchen area between tenancies, and ensure that you aren't giving water a way to cause damage.

- Basements. Shifting foundations can put stress on building foundations and eventually cause cracks. These can allow water to enter, creating problems for you, and reducing the space available for storage facilities. Water ingress may also threaten electrical systems. A regular inspection, particularly after the spring thaw, can ensure that you're on top of foundation cracks, and can take steps to stave off flooding in the future. Sometimes, a sump pump may be a good tool to have.

- Sprinkler systems. Sprinkler systems can help control fire when it happens, but when it isn't happening and the sprinkler goes off—it's more than inconvenient. Regularly check sprinkler systems and other fire-control systems in your property to ensure that they're working properly, and won't dampen the spirits of your tenants.

## Controlling Drafts

A drafty building may cut air-conditioning costs in summer, but in winter you may find yourself footing an expensive heating bill. Moreover, a building that exchanges air with the outside environment more frequently may potentially be collecting more dust, mould, and pollen that diminish indoor air quality. Reducing drafts not only saves money but creates a better environment for tenants.

The main areas to consider when it comes to maintenance aimed at reducing drafts include:

- Doors and windows. Weather-stripping around doors and windows can help block drafts, but if it isn't tight it may be no better than the loose frames it's trying to seal. An inspection of doors and windows is important between tenancies, but especially so in properties that are more than 10 years old. The placements for windows and doors in buildings more than 20 years old may need replacing to ensure current norms for performance are met.

- Kitchen and bathroom vents. The exhaust fans that clear the kitchen and remove moisture from the bathroom are important to inspect, as they can become easily clogged with foreign particles. Kitchen fans are prone to grease accumulation that can affect performance, while moisture from bathrooms can foster the growth of moulds. Install simple venting systems in kitchens and bathrooms to circulate the indoor and outside air. A secure system will help ensure tenants don't vent using windows, a rather unsophisticated means of venting that may boost heating costs.

- Attic vents. Preventing unwanted drafts is important but keeping a property completely airtight is unwise, too. Regular inspections can ensure that attic vents remain unblocked by insulation and secured against pests such as squirrels. A blocked vent leads to moisture accumulation, fostering mildew and rot that can destroy the fabric of your building.

## Looking Out

A good first impression is priceless, and a proper maintenance schedule can help your property stay attractive all year. Many aspects of outdoor maintenance can be contracted out, so don't feel everything that has to be done is your responsibility. Regular landscaping tasks, for instance, are something many landlords routinely contract out to others, while less-frequent tasks such as painting, roofing, and window cleaning may be handled by professional firms on an as-needed basis.

Keeping ahead of maintenance, expected and unexpected, requires a fairly intimate knowledge of your property. While you will collect a good deal of information in the course of the purchase process, each year brings new details to light. Some problems may also emerge as a function of the building's aging.

Recognize the signs that maintenance is needed in order to prevent small issues from becoming larger—and costlier—ones.

## Painting

Keeping the exterior of your building fresh and in good repair is probably more important than ensuring a cheery interior. A building's interior is what tenants make it, but a building's exterior is what you want tenants, current and prospective, to think it is!

Regularly painting the exterior—say, every 5 to 10 years, depending on the weather in your part of the country—is important. Many painting firms are available to do the job, from the ubiquitous student-run franchises to professional companies.

A greater challenge is cleaning the exterior of properties. While this will be part of the prep work for any painting work you have done, it is a key part of the maintenance for concrete and stucco-clad buildings. Such structures can easily become clad with more than the original building materials in milder parts of Canada, bearing unsightly crops of moss and moulds. When people speak about your building having a living wall, make sure they're referring to the ivy that clings to the facade.

## Roofing

The life expectancy of roofing materials can be anywhere from 10 to 20 years, depending on the climate in your region. Properties in parts of Canada that experience heavy snow in winter or steady freeze-thaw cycles should have their roofs inspected annually to ensure shingles are in good condition and that there is adequate protection against water ingress. A leaky roof can be one of the most costly forms of property damage because of the distance the water travels before it is noticed, and the potential for it to damage electrical wiring on the way down, increasing the risk of a fire. Clearing snow from your roof, when possible, will also help limit the chance of seepage through the roof, or a roof collapse.

## Windows

The regular inspection of windows, inside and out, will ensure that they're doing a good job of blocking drafts. A dirty window also makes for grim living conditions for tenants. Since you can't expect your tenants to erect a ladder and clean windows of accumulated grime, take the time to wash windows at your properties at least once a year.

## Gutters

An efficient gutter system helps manage rainwater, preventing it from causing damage to your property. Cleaning a clogged gutter or downspout regularly will prevent water from backing up and seeping into the roof or walls of your property.

Arranging downspouts in such a way that water doesn't pool along the foundation of your building is also important. Direct the spouts away from the property, preferably into a channel that runs toward the civic sewer or roadway. Should the water from downspouts begin pooling, try building up the area with dirt and either extend the spout or create a channel for the water to run off.

## Landscaping

Good landscaping is attractive, but it can also invite problems. An ivy-covered wall, for instance, may be an attractive feature that lends an air of the ancient to your property. The ivy can also damage mortar and remove siding, making it a noxious weed. Similarly, poorly sited trees may risk damaging your property or the water pipes that run to it. Trees crowding your property may also facilitate access to the roof and vents by squirrels and other pests, not to mention clogging drains. By locating trees away from your property and civic water pipes, you minimize the risk of damage and inconvenience.

# Avoiding Common Fire Hazards

Fire, whether minor or major, is a traumatizing experience. Even if no one is injured, there can be the loss of treasured family photos, memorabilia, and memories. However, with some advance planning, you can go a long way in avoiding accidental fires. Here are some tips.

## *Overloaded Fuses*

Fuses are the safety valves in your electrical circuits. They prevent wires from overheating, which can cause a fire. If a fuse keeps on blowing, then the circuit is overloaded. Never try to circumvent blown fuses by the use of pennies or foil. Call a qualified electrician.

## *Permanent Wiring*

All additions or alterations to permanent wiring should be done by a qualified electrician and must be inspected and approved by your local municipal electrical inspector.

## Careless Smoking

This is possibly the only cause of fire that is 100 per cent preventable. If you have a no-smoking policy with your tenants, that should include any guests as well, so that your policy is 100 per cent non-smoking. Make this provision in writing in your tenancy agreement. This will also have the added advantage of making your home more saleable when the time comes to resell. Many people are allergic to smoke and can detect the odour in a dwelling, no matter how hard one tries to conceal or mask it.

## Wood Stoves

All types of auxiliary heating appliances, such as wood stoves or portable heaters, require extra precaution. To avoid problems, you should note the following guidelines:

- Always look for an Underwriters Laboratories of Canada (ULC) or Canadian Standards Association (CSA) label on the unit, which means it meets the minimum safety standards and has been approved for use in Canada.
- If you install the unit yourself, follow the installation instructions precisely. In particular, pay close attention to the clearances required between the unit and any combustible material. It is better to have it installed by a professional.
- Use the unit strictly in accordance with the instructions.
- Call your local fire department or fire-prevention bureau for information and advice on any fire-safety-related topic, including wood stoves.

## Fireplaces and Chimneys

Always use a fireplace screen and dispose of the ashes in a closed metal container. Chimneys (for wood stoves as well as fireplaces) require cleaning by a chimney sweep service at least every two years to remove and prevent the buildup of creosote deposits. Creosote is flammable and can be ignited by the hot gases from your fireplace. This can spread to any combustible material, such as your roof.

## Fire Extinguishers

Buy at least one portable fire extinguisher and keep it in an easily accessible place in the kitchen. Ideally, you should have one extinguisher for every level of your house. Try to select an extinguisher with chemical contents to deal with A (paper and wood), B (flammable liquids, such as oil), and C (electrical) types of fire.

## Smoke, Fire, and Gas Alarms

These are absolute necessities. They are inexpensive and effective. Smoke alarms should be placed outside bedroom doors, kitchens, workshops, and other key areas. When you are researching which units to buy, refer to the recommended home sites on the box. Some alarms are heat sensitive, rather than detecting smoke or other by-products of a fire. A dwelling that uses natural gas should have a system that can detect carbon monoxide. And don't forget to replace the batteries twice a year on a memorable date, such as when you change your clocks forward for daylight saving time or back for standard time.

## Other Safety Measures You Can Take

- Have proper locks and be sure that all doors and windows can be secured.
- Keep entrances well-lit and trim all shrubbery so that it does not obscure entries.
- Lock away all ladders so that they cannot be used by an intruder.
- Review your property periodically to check for potential access points for burglars.

# Improving the Bottom Line

Any investment depends on savings; whether it's what you originally put away in the hope it would earn more, or what you've got now that you don't want to lose. The trouble with an investment property, however, is that you're always spending—whether on operating costs, maintenance, or taxes.

There are ways to improve the bottom line. Many businesses start at the top—with income. A landlord can raise rents annually, in line with the rate of inflation, or they can charge extra for specific amenities the property provides. In addition, current expenses can be watched carefully and pared back without reducing the quality of space you've got to lease. The ongoing improvements you make in both operations and profit will go a long way to making the property a solid deal for some future investor.

## Raising Rents

Annual increases are one means of raising rents within tenancies. Regardless of whether the lease you sign with a tenant is for a set term or goes month-to-month after a year, with appropriate notice you can ratchet up the rents to keep your income in line with the broader market. This is as true in competitive urban markets as in smaller markets outside the major centres, though it is important to consider local rental market reports. Visit the CMCH website (www.cmhc.ca) for information to help you gauge just what the market might bear.

Assess the average stay of tenants, gauge where rents and operating costs are going for your area, and charge new tenants a rate that reflects the future rental environment. This is effective if you're providing top-quality space because the tenants will enjoy what you're offering, and you will have less incentive to raise the rents on an annual basis. That's good news for tenants, and the above-average rate is good news for you. While this tactic may sound aggressive, it also has the advantage of ensuring that tenants know how much they'll be paying while assuring you of a reputation as a landlord disinclined to raise rents.

Regardless of how you go about raising rents, check to make sure the increases are in line with what provincial landlord-tenancy legislation allows.

## Tenant Fees

Rent isn't the only fee you can charge tenants. A variety of charges can be applied to paperwork associated with tenancies. While this may sound petty, and would be a burden for some tenants, for the landlord it can be a few extra dollars against reasonable expenses.

### Application Fee

It takes time to process tenancy applications, and credit checks aren't free. You may want to charge a non-refundable processing fee of $25 or more, depending on the expenses you face checking an applicant's references, creditworthiness, and so on.

### Penalties

Penalties such as late-payment fees and key charges should appear in the written tenancy agreement signed by the tenant. It will help ensure rent payments are delivered promptly, or garner you fees for past-due payments.

Charges such as fees for replacing keys will cover the cost and hassle of getting new keys cut for a unit.

## Additional Tenants

A lease agreement typically states that a unit will be occupied by a certain number of people on a regular basis. You may wish to limit the number of tenants allowed for a base rent. Any tenants over and above the limit would result in a set monthly extra rent for each extra tenant. Of course, the wording of the limit would have to respect landlord-tenancy legislation for your province. A standard exception would include allowing children if the tenants are a couple, for example.

## Pet Fees

Many landlords do not allow pets. To cover the extra cost of maintenance to restore a suite after a pet's occupancy—such as a thorough cleaning to ensure subsequent tenants are not subject to the pet's dander that may continue to lurk in the suite—you may wish to allow pets for a set fee above the base rent. A clause in the written tenancy agreement might outline the restrictions on the kind, size, and number of pets that are permitted, and the amount of the monthly surcharge for keeping a pet on the premises—say, $25.

## *Amenity Fees*

Many properties offer a variety of amenities, including common areas, parking, and storage facilities. Depending on the type of property, you may be able to expand these facilities or otherwise open them up to users besides residents of the building. Access could be controlled through fees, which would allow the property to generate extra income.

## Recreational Facilities

A property that offers recreational amenities such as a community room, fitness centre, pool, and tennis courts might have value to some tenants, but not others. To support the operation and permit access, consider charging tenants for the use of the facilities, either including it within the monthly rent or through a separate system that allows access by pass card or some other means.

You may also wish to allow outsiders to use the amenities on a selective basis and charge a higher fee than for tenants. Your lawyer can best advise you on the appropriate content and approach.

## Parking Fees

A rental property typically includes more than just rental units. Most apartments and commercial developments come with parking areas that can be lucrative sources of revenues. In large urban centres where parking is in short supply, you can charge tenants for the privilege of having a parking spot. The rate you charge will naturally be a premium because the spot is on private property and guaranteed. Should the building offer secure access, you may be able to charge even more.

Should tenants not require the parking spots available, you may be able to lease the spot to other users. You can advertise the spot in the same way you advertise a rental unit, posting an ad on a local notice board (online or otherwise) or in the classified ads section of the local paper.

## Storage fees

Many apartments include storage space, but you may also decide to provide extra storage space to tenants for a charge, either in the same building or at a secure, adjacent location. Conversely, you may want to charge extra for the privilege of having a storage locker, over and above the base rent. After all, not everyone requires storage space.

Alternatively, you may strike an arrangement with another provider, such as a local mini-storage facility, to give a discount to your tenants. In return, you would seek a referral fee or monthly commission from the mini-warehouse company.

## Furniture

A furnished apartment typically commands a higher rent than a non-furnished suite, sometimes as much as 10 per cent more. An apartment building that attracts younger tenants in a college or university town is an ideal opportunity for providing this kind of accommodation, at a higher fee. Rather than buying your own furniture and having that capital cost and inventory, you may want to rent the furniture directly from a furniture rental company for a discount, or refer your tenants to a specific furniture rental company. As with the example of storage space, you may wish to ask for a referral fee that would generate income for you, even though you are not renting the furniture yourself.

## *Other options*

A number of additional opportunities exist for generating extra income from your rental property. Many of the options relate to business opportunities or partnerships, but on-site opportunities include charging for laundry facilities and installing vending machines. While the machines invite greater maintenance responsibilities, the extra revenue may prove worthwhile.

Coin-operated washers and dryers are among the best of the extra coin-operated revenue streams. You may buy or lease the equipment and pay for a service contract, or contract with a company that supplies and services the equipment and returns to you a percentage of the gross revenue (sometimes as much as 75 per cent). Make sure the equipment used is energy-efficient, or the extra revenue may barely cover the operating costs.

While vending machines are temptations to tenants, these can be useful money-makers in larger properties. Typically stocked with candies, snacks, juices, soft drinks, and soap powder, they are particularly appropriate in common areas such as activity rooms and laundry areas. To reduce maintenance, provide garbage cans for litter.

## Saving on Expenses

Cutting costs is a logical place to look when you're considering improving the financial performance of your rental property. You may not be able to control how many tenants you have at a given time, but you can take steps to control expenses. While some costs can be passed on to tenants, a smart landlord will focus on reducing a property's overall operating costs. Then, everyone benefits.

Here are some of the common methods for reducing costs:

- appealing a high property-tax increase to the property assessment authority;
- hiring tenants who will handle maintenance, such as snow removal, gardening, and minor painting;
- utilizing government-subsidy programs for upgrades that improve the building's energy use;
- enforcing warranties and contracts to ensure quality service or operation.

Organizations such as Toronto's Evergreen (www.evergreen.ca) and Vancouver's Lighthouse Sustainable Building Centre (www.sustainablebuildingcentre. com) advise property owners on upgrades that will make their properties more sustainable. In addition, several local and national organizations offer relevant resources, including the federal Office of Energy Efficiency (oee.nrcan.gc.ca). The CMHC (www.cmhc.ca) offers incentives to homeowners that may be helpful in developing secondary suites within primary residences.

Don't underestimate the importance of shopping around for deals on services and supplies. Buying maintenance supplies and other items for your property (or properties) in bulk could give you the leverage needed to secure a discount on the order. Ask what discounts are available for what quantity of items, and see if you can schedule your purchases to take advantage of the discounts. You may be able to partner with other landlords to make the purchases together. When hiring a contractor, make sure you get at least three bids, and references, before making a final decision. The process could save you significant money on landscaping, painting, renovating, and other services, or at the very least allow you to make a more informed decision that will serve your interests.

## Summary

The property-management tips discussed in this chapter cover a range of issues including property-management options, keeping good records, locating the right tenant, and understanding the tenant documentation required. Practical suggestions were given for saving on expenses and increasing income from your revenue property. Finally, tips were offered on avoiding common home-maintenance problems and fire hazards.

How to prepare a property for sale is discussed in the next chapter, because owners and investors eventually want to dispose of their property—either to buy a new property or enjoy the fruits of their real estate investment.

# CHAPTER 11

**Selling Your Property**

**Selling is an integral** part of the real estate business. Whether you own a home or an investment property, sooner or later the time comes to sell. While the glitz of the business is in acquiring property and building a portfolio, selling seldom gets as much attention. Shrinking a portfolio isn't as appealing, until you understand that it means recouping the equity that's accumulated in the property—wealth you can reinvest in additional properties or some other investment.

Selling requires a distinct set of skills. Unlike purchasing a property, where you try to pay the lowest possible price, a sale requires you to extract the best price from the market (which, of course, is also going to be as low as the purchaser can negotiate for the property). Many people take the selling process casually without a full appreciation of the skills and techniques that should be used. They rely on luck or their realtor to get the top price. If you don't know how to maximize the selling price, you will probably make the wrong decisions and reduce your profit. This chapter gives you the foundation to make the right decisions.

There are many questions you should ask yourself before deciding to sell, including the reasons for selling, the timing, the price, the terms, and the benefits. You should also consider how you will sell, including selecting a realtor, a lawyer, and how you'll negotiate with interested buyers.

This chapter covers the key topics such as determining when to sell, preparing the property for sale, selecting a real estate agent, and the potential disadvantages of selling the property yourself. Practical home-selling tips will also be discussed.

## Determining When to Sell

One of the critical decisions of any real estate investor is deciding when to sell. Trying to time the market probably isn't the best strategy, as you may end up second-guessing yourself several times over. Nor do you want to come to market so eager to sell that buyers see the offering as a distress sale and try to grind you down on the price. By analyzing the facts of the market, the facts of your property, and the objectives of your portfolio, you will likely come to a more satisfying decision and be able to address buyers with confidence. The following factors could justify a decision to sell:

- the market is reaching its peak, with values high and buyers still willing to purchase;
- the property is near its peak value in the current market;
- income from the property shows little chance of increasing;
- capital expenditures are set to increase;
- the return on your investment is decreasing;
- the neighbourhood is entering a period of decline; or
- management of the property is frustrating.

Any of these factors could also drive one of the three key reasons investors large and small sell properties: equity is needed to fund retirement, the portfolio needs to be rebalanced, or other investments have become more attractive.

## Retirement Planning

A real estate portfolio is often the recipe for a comfortable retirement. While some investors see being a landlord as a retirement project, many others consider retirement a time to begin selling off their portfolio and enjoying the equity it's accumulated. Retirement planning should be part of your investment strategy, and you may have a timeline to help guide your plans to sell your portfolio in preparation for your golden years. The typical real estate cycle is five to eight years in duration, so you may consider selling properties and banking the proceeds a decade before you intend to retire. Should the perfect market conditions for a sale occur during that period, you'll be ready to sell, rather than selling into a poor market once you've retired and are counting on the cash.

## Balancing Act

Many investors make a point of routinely buying and selling investment properties in order to grow and renew their portfolios. Depending on the type of property you have, this may happen more frequently than not. A modest portfolio of two or three apartments may have built up enough equity to allow you to move into another neighbourhood with better potential, or even into a different class of investment altogether. Whatever the reason for the sale, there's no shame in capitalizing on the gains. Timing will be important as you strive to balance or diversify your portfolio. A good time to sell one asset may be a poor time to buy a new one. Selling when the market is at its height may require you to hold the proceeds from your sale until the market dips sufficiently to reinvest the funds. While every market holds opportunities for the savvy investor, it will help to run your plans by your accountant or financial planner. Advisers can provide the analysis required to help you determine when to sell, and what to do with the proceeds.

## Seeking Alternatives

Real estate is not the only investment in the world. An interest-bearing deposit could be a convenient cache for your wealth while you reorient your investment strategy or await an opportune time to jump back into the market. Consider gaining exposure to the real estate market through an indirect investment such as a real estate–investment trust or syndicate. Your accountant or financial planner can advise you on alternative investment options that will continue to meet your financial goals.

# Determining How to Sell

One of the hot topics in real estate circles across Canada in recent years has been the role of real estate agents in the market. An agent is a key adviser when you're buying properties (see page 109 in Chapter 4, "Selecting Your Advisory Team"), but many people wonder why they can't sell a property themselves and save on the commission. The rise of online marketing, some designed expressly for sale-by-owner properties, has also prompted people to question the value of exposure through the MLS. The system itself has come under fire for being exclusive, with court challenges seeking to open it up and break the effective monopoly real estate boards have over MLS listings. The result would be a more level playing field, more power to the people, and less influence in the hands of boards and agents.

This section aims to provide the information you need to assess your options. By selling a property yourself, you may indeed save money. On the other hand, the savings could be false economy. For example, various factors—the nature of the property, the market at the time, the specific realtor you are considering, and the real estate company involved—may enable you to negotiate a lower commission to facilitate the sale. But a reduced commission structure may discourage realtors who see the listing on the MLS to ignore your offering in favour of others offering a higher, standard-rate commission.

Key points when considering whether to use a real estate agent or sell a property yourself follow. The comments apply whether you are selling your principal residence or an investment property. The remarks are not intended to dissuade you from attempting to sell your own property, but to give you a realistic perspective. In the end, you will have to balance the benefits and pitfalls and decide for yourself.

## Professional Advice

Professional advice from people familiar with the local market and sales process can both complement and balance your own experience and emotions. Real estate agents, lawyers, and accountants are all vital to the success of an investment property from its selection and acquisition through to its operation and eventual sale. You wouldn't remit your taxes without talking to your accountant or bookkeeper, would you? Real estate agents can provide equally important advice when it comes to selling a property. (The benefits of selecting and using a realtor were discussed on page 109 in Chapter 4, "Selecting Your Advisory Team.")

An agent who knows the local market will help you make the correct decisions regarding the pricing and promotion of the property, as well as negotiating a price fit for the market even with the most hard-nosed buyers. This is particularly important in a down market, or other circumstances where emotions may play a role (such as the sale of a property following a partner's death, a separation, or some other family dispute).

In addition, frustration levels can rise if you list the house yourself and you aren't prepared for the one-on-one dynamics of particular realtors or buyers. You may be prone to take some comments personally, prompting you to accept a lower price than is necessary. If you use a real estate agent, you rarely (if ever) meet the prospective purchaser directly, either before the agreement of purchase and sale is signed, or before or after closing. The agent acts as a buffer, and an advocate for your interests.

## Professional Management

Professional management doesn't just apply to the operation of an investment property. The same factors that prompt you to hand management to a professional property manager may also factor into whether or not you sell a property yourself or list it with a real estate agent. The time commitment required to prepare the property, handle inquiries, and meet with potential purchasers are all details a real estate agent can handle. It's what their commission covers.

A realtor will save you time because you won't have to prepare the listing, arrange open houses, or be around when the property is shown. You won't have to field phone calls and e-mails. All inquiries go directly to the realtor, who will also screen potential purchasers. Screening is important because it weeds out people who are not seriously considering your property. They may be seeing what's on the market, or worse, casing your property for a break-in. Screening purchasers also reduces the risk you'll receive an offer from someone with no realistic chance of financing the purchase, or who will seek to include unrealistic subject clauses in the purchase agreement that will slow down the sales process.

## Market Smarts

When offering a property to the market, you want to have a clear idea of what similar properties in the market are fetching, the kind of interest they're seeing, the time it takes them to sell, and other factors. Current market conditions will place your property at an advantage or disadvantage, as will your understanding of those factors. You may be unrealistic in your price expectations and price yourself out of the market. Prospective purchasers may not even look at your property, let alone make an offer. You may eventually sell your property, but only after several price reductions and after a long period.

A savvy real estate agent can reduce the risk of your property sitting on the market too long, or undergoing repeated price reductions (which will be on record, and may increase a buyer's expectation of getting a deal). The pricing and overall marketing strategies a realtor familiar with your area recommends should be tailored to market conditions and expedite the process (after all, realtors want to get paid, too).

## Market Exposure

The amount of effort you're willing to put into marketing a property will also determine whether or not you use a real estate agent or go the sale-by-owner route. While moves are afoot to make the MLS more open, the exposure it offers both to the market and to other realtors whose clients may be interested in your property is the top reason for listing your property with a realtor. While there are sites that facilitate the sale-by-owner approach (PropertyGuys.com is one example), an MLS listing gives unparalleled exposure. And it beats an ad on Craigslist, in the local paper, or a sign in the yard. Unless you're a marketing wizard, self-advertising typically means limited exposure. And there's a direct correlation between the nature and degree of market exposure and the end price. Advertising really does pay for itself.

By listing with a realtor, all advertising costs are covered by the agent's commission. The nature and amount of advertising is negotiated at the time the listing agreement is signed. Depending on the kind of property you're offering, it will not only be included in the MLS but be advertised in local newspapers, weekly real estate publications, and in other marketing material the agent's office produces. An agent also has the discretion to show your property at special open houses specifically for local agents once the property is listed, giving interested realtors a chance to familiarize themselves with the property on behalf of clients. (More often, however, they'll be scanning the MLS for hot new listings and contacting your realtor within hours of the listing's appearance.) An experienced realtor will know how to write an ad that accentuates the key selling features of your property.

## Pricing Savvy

Pricing a property for the market is a challenge. Knowing whether a potential purchaser is just bluffing when they try to negotiate you down is also unsettling. You may have the smarts—and stomach—to handle this or you may wish to delegate it to a realtor.

A realtor normally researches the history of the property, comparable listings, and establishes the original asking (list) price of the property. An experienced agent will recognize a low-ball offer as a tactical ploy, and advocate on your behalf in favour of the list price. Some attempt may be made to determine the reasons for the original offer and provide advice on the negotiating tactics to use.

Having a realtor on your side is especially important if you lack negotiating and sales skills, and may well get you a higher price on better terms than you initially expected. This is especially important in a buyer's market, when purchasers are aggressively seeking the lowest possible price. Buyers negotiate aggressively because they feel they have an advantage, regardless of the merits of the property you're offering. They also have time to be selective because there is usually a large selection of properties available on the market.

You are at a disadvantage if you don't get all the exposure possible and use all the negotiating and selling skills available.

## Keeping It Legal

The prospective purchaser may supply you with his own agreement of purchase and sale. This contract may have clauses and other terms in it that could be legally risky, unenforceable, unfair, or otherwise not beneficial to you. You may not recognize these potential problems or risks. In addition, you could end up agreeing to take back a mortgage (vendor-take-back mortgage) when it would be unnecessary or unwise, or accepting a risky long-term option or other legal arrangement.

A real estate agent will recognize aspects of an agreement that are unfair, unenforceable, or unclear—or simply non-standard—and advise you accordingly. In addition, the lawyer you've engaged as part of your advisory team will be able to review whatever agreement the buyer offers and recommend amendments that will protect your interests. A lawyer is an inexpensive investment for peace of mind, especially if the advice makes you money.

## Negotiating Commissions

A real estate agent's commission is always contentious. If you undertake to sell a property yourself, a prospective purchaser may determine what the fair market value is, and then ask for an additional discount equal to the real estate commission you're saving. But the primary reason you're selling the property yourself is to save the commission owing to a realtor for listing and promoting the property, and dealing with potential purchasers. The purchaser will want a cut of those savings. But since you're doing the work a realtor would, you deserve to get paid for your efforts, and it makes sense to hold the line with purchasers.

Using a real estate agent will avoid the extra pressure a purchaser might try to exert to get a better price for your property. A realtor's knowledge of the market may also result in a higher selling price for your property. Statistically, if you had listed it and had greater market exposure, better pricing, and a realtor who had applied more experienced real estate negotiating and selling skills than you possess, a higher sale price would be achieved. The commission you pay to a realtor may be money well spent rather than money left on the table.

Regardless of all these factors, there are exceptions and certain situations in which you may choose to sell a property yourself. The information above will help you to gauge your situation. You must be keenly aware of the disadvantages and pitfalls. Most real estate investors realize the benefits of using a realtor and do so as a business decision, whether for buying or selling.

# Preparing to Sell

The sales process is slightly different from the vendor's perspective than it is from the buyer's. While certain key steps of the transaction remain the same—the negotiations, for instance—the vendor's considerations include determining an appropriate sales strategy; timing and pricing; preparing appropriate documentation for prospective purchasers; priming the appropriate advisers; establishing your terms for the transaction; and calculating closing costs.

## Determining Your Strategy

The decision to sell, and the research you've put into market conditions that prompt you to list your property, should yield a good foundation for the sales strategy you adopt. As the vendor, you are largely in control of key points such as the closing date and the price you're willing to accept. A strategy that meets your requirements will help you to enter the market with confidence and find a buyer that's right for the property—and meets your objectives in selling it.

Striking a realistic balance between your needs and the state of the market will improve your chances of securing a return that satisfies you. Here's how a sale might proceed in the market, based on some of the key reasons an owner might opt to sell:

- Retirement. A vendor who is selling a property with a view to recouping wealth to put toward retirement typically wants the best possible price. Ideally, the vendor will plan ahead to take advantage of peak market conditions, thereby ensuring plenty of potential purchasers and strong pricing. A vendor who comes to market when it's less than perfect may have fewer buyers stepping forward. The sales strategy may require a lower list price to attract purchasers, or extra patience.

- Balancing the portfolio. An owner who wants to sell one property and reinvest the proceeds in another property will strive for a good return, but also know that there's greater opportunity elsewhere. This may foster a willingness to compromise on the sale price in order to get the cash needed to reinvest, even if achieving the maximum possible value from a property is the ultimate goal. The market timing will also target the best possible return, with the property likely being listed at a time of high buyer demand and good prices.

By contrast, if the owner just wants to get rid of an underperforming property and scuttle into something better, pricing will be aggressive in the interests of a fast sale. An eager buyer lured by the thought of a bargain could be willing to pledge future gains against the current purchase price—giving you more than you might expect.

- New investment. Selling a property in order to invest in a new opportunity separate from real estate may see a vendor sell when the going is good for real estate, or when the opportunity to buy into the other investment arises. Depending on the requirements of the new investment, you may be able to reach an agreement that sees the buyer purchase the property gradually, giving you only as much as you need to finance the new venture. You may also choose to sell quickly, extracting what gains are possible to reinvest in another investment with even greater potential gains.

## Timing and Pricing

The timing and pricing of the deal are important factors in any real estate transaction.

Just as buyers are likely to be scouting the markets for potential investment properties in the spring (any time of the year, really, but especially spring), so you should be tracking market activity to know when would be a good time to list. While the fluctuations of market cycles may moderate or exaggerate seasonal trends, the winter months would not likely be a good time to list a property unless the sale is of immediate importance.

When you first start considering a sale, you will likely have some sense of your property's worth. Making sure it lists at somewhere close to the expected value, but in line with similar properties in the market, is important. A vendor should ballpark a target price for the property by comparing its value to others in the market, then factor in a 5 per cent margin for negotiating purposes.

## Preparing Documentation

Buyers need to prepare purchase offers, but vendors need to prepare the documentation buyers (and property brokers) will request. These include statements of cash flow, both income and expenses, as well as assessment notices detailing property taxes.

To assist the real estate broker managing the sale, identify features of your property that appealed to you or that may appeal to future owners. A list of talking points will help the realtor frame the property for potential buyers. Mention features such as recent improvements and any major renovations or upgrades that support the asking price. Achievements such as the improvement of a property's financial performance will also help highlight its value. Listing the local amenities such as transportation links, shopping centres, schools, parks, and playgrounds will also help make a case for the property.

Among other documentation, verify the repayment terms of existing mortgages. Some mortgages have a prepayment penalty that you need to factor into your closing costs. Alternatively, an assumable mortgage at an attractive rate may interest a prospective purchaser. Whatever the case, your lender will want to know that you're planning to sell and that you plan to discharge your obligations under your current mortgage (whether it's assumable or not).

## Priming Advisers

Your advisers will likely have played a role in your decision to sell any given property, but you will also want to make sure they're ready when the time comes to move forward with the deal. Your lawyer should be ready to handle the documentation associated with the sale, while your real estate broker will need time to gather the information required for marketing the property and presenting it to the market.

## Setting Limits

Regardless of your reasons for selling, chances are you will have limits to what you're willing to accept for a property, the closing date, and other elements of the purchase agreement. Determine what your best deal and bottom-line positions are going to be, and why. The purchaser will be attempting to negotiate the best deal, so be prepared. Draft potential counter-offers and subject clauses that would be applicable to the property, and make sure your broker is aware of these considerations. Keeping your broker informed of your desires will help you to be represented well in the course of the transaction.

## Calculating Costs

Determine what you are going to net after all commissions and fees, and before taxes. This may depend on the type of listing agreement you have with your realtor. (Chapter 6, "Understanding the Legal Aspects," discusses these.) A three- or six-month penalty clause may exist in your fixed-term mortgage for prepayment (unless the mortgage is assumed by the purchaser), a cost that you need to factor into your proceeds. Similarly, commissions will affect the total amount of proceeds. Determining how much remains will help you plan your next steps once the deal closes.

## Preparing the Property

Making your property as attractive as possible is essential, whether you are selling it yourself or through a real estate agent. Realtors will give sellers a package that includes tips on improvements to assist in selling a property. Both the inside and outside of the home must evoke a positive feeling with the prospective buyer in order to obtain the quickest sale at the highest price. Ask yourself objectively what you perceive a prospective buyer's first impression would be of your home, exterior and interior. If you feel you cannot be objective or want a second opinion, have a relative or friend look at your home with a critical eye and ask him or her to tell you all the negative aspects.

Part of preparing a property for sale means getting rid of unnecessary possessions that detract from a sale. Give yourself plenty of time to remove items that could detract from the property's appeal. You may have to allocate three or four months of weekends before you have cleaned out the excess. Many people are packrats and have difficulty in letting go of possessions accumulated over time. They feel more comfortable about being surrounded by familiar items, no matter how unattractive, junky, or impractical. Ask yourself about each item if you are having difficulty about whether to keep it or not. For example, ask yourself if you have used the item over the past year. If so, consider keeping it as long as it is still usable. If not, then ask yourself if it has any real value to you, or considerable sentimental value. If not, then get rid of it by selling it at a garage sale or donating it to charity.

Another important step, once you have completed all the home-improvement procedures, is to prepare a list of special features about your house that you like, such as a workshop, solarium, or garden. Make a list of the key selling points about the house, in your view. For example, if you have repainted, replaced the carpets, or had new landscaping done, those are things that make your home attractive. Finally, list the main points that you like about the neighbourhood, such as convenient shopping, transportation, schools, parks, or playgrounds. In addition, factors such as a quiet neighbourhood, friendly and helpful neighbours, lots of babysitters nearby, and a community spirit are important points to note. If you are using a realtor, give this list to your agent.

## Boosting Curb Appeal

A property's appearance to potential buyers should be a key focus of efforts to prepare the property for sale. Getting rid of elements that are likely to detract from the appearance of the property (such as dead flies in the hall light fixture) can do much to improve the impression a property makes, especially if the decor is otherwise unappealing.

Both the interior and exterior of properties will offer room for improvement, and the premium you capture on the sale may be well worth the extra maintenance bills run up in the weeks prior to listing.

## Polishing the Interior

Sprucing up the interior of a property may be as simple as a good spring cleaning: removing clutter, adjusting the decor, and polishing the places that need it. The following points are worth bearing in mind:

- Keep things clean. Wash the windows, wipe down walls, and shampoo the carpets throughout the building. Consider replacing carpeting that's especially worn. Keep front and back entrances clear, clean, and inviting. Remove clutter from corridors, halls, and storage areas.

- Refine the decor. Most apartment buildings have a bare minimum of artwork, but updating what graphics do exist may help update the look of the property. A new paint job may add extra verve to the interior. Washable latex paint is ideal; lighter colours will make the property appear larger and brighter. A condominium apartment unit owned as an investment may benefit from the attention of a staging company, which can make the property look comfortable for residential or rental use.

- Undertake needed repairs. A broken window latch, a sticking or squeaky door, broken switch covers, and loose doorknobs may be elements tenants have lived with, but they'll be viewed as liabilities to potential buyers. This could give them grounds for offering a lower price than what you're asking for. A proper maintenance schedule (see page 285 in Chapter 10, "Managing Your Property") should ensure that the repairs are minimal, but a review of the property prior to listing is important.

- Maintain a comfortable environment. The interior of the building should be pleasant, but not unnaturally sterile. Choose a time for the showing when tenants are likely to be quiet, and when the building is at a comfortable temperature. Aiming for a fresh and airy feel on a hot summer day or a cozy environment on cold days is the ideal, though not always possible. Consider replacing light bulbs with a stronger variety in order to create a brighter environment. Take steps to eliminate odours, such as smoking or cooking, that may turn off potential purchasers. While you can't control what tenants are preparing, a good cross draft or a dose of an air freshener may help create a better impression.

## Making Kitchens and Bathrooms Appealing

The two most important rooms for many buyers are the kitchen and the bathroom, so make those areas appealing. Keep both rooms spotlessly clean and tidy. You want to create the impression that the home is easy to maintain.

## Keeping Pets Out of the Way

Buyers may not enjoy being welcomed by a cat or dog; indeed, they may be allergic. Many people could be turned off by knowing that various animals have lived in the home, so remove the pets, their cages, and litter boxes before the showing and use a deodorant spray to minimize any odour.

## Removing Ashtrays and Odour of Smoke

Many people do not smoke and are allergic or otherwise negatively affected by the odour of cigarettes. Therefore, if you or anyone else who occupies the house or condominium for sale smokes, make sure you remove all ashtrays, dry clean the drapes, and shampoo the carpets. Also consider washing or painting the walls to remove any evidence of smoke, which might discourage a prospective purchaser.

## Shining the Exterior

First impressions begin with the property's exterior. The interior may look grubby, but a pleasant exterior can inspire hope that the property could have potential. Key elements of the exterior that deserve attention include:

- The landscaping. Cut the lawn and prune shrubs and hedges. Plant flowers in the garden and any planters you might have. Sweep the sidewalk and parking area, removing debris to create a tidy impression.

- Buy a doormat. One of the first items a buyer will see will be your front door. A doormat or other sign of welcome will help the entrance look attractive, and a door that's in good repair with shiny street numbers or other flourishes will boost the appeal.

- Maintenance requirements. Just before a property hits the market is a good time to catch up on overdue maintenance. While a proper maintenance schedule will limit the number of repairs that you need to accomplish, the exterior of the property may benefit from a paint job, and small elements you might otherwise ignore might benefit from attention. The entrance doors, for example, should be in good repair and work smoothly.

## Advising Tenants

Tenants will be sure to notice the maintenance work taking place and will very likely suspect the property is for sale. Be sure to inform tenants before listing the property that the sale you are planning is not intended to displace them (if that's the case), and that you will take every step possible to ensure that they are not inconvenienced by the transaction. Keep them up to date regarding your progress at key points. You may wish to announce when a tentative deal is reached, and especially when the deal has gone firm (that is, when conditions have been removed) and when the closing date is.

## Closing the Sale

When the buyer submits an offer to purchase, you will, as the vendor, have an option to make a counter-offer. The counter-offer will effectively be your negotiation to steer the deal in the direction you want. Buyers negotiate to get the best deal possible at the lowest reasonable price. While you will have listed the property at a reasonable price, the buyer may want to pay something less.

You can up the ante by stipulating that certain conditions be met before the deal closes, or put forward for consideration various facets of the property that the buyer may want to take into account in their own response to your counter-offer. You may offer something more in exchange for securing the price you want. Ultimately, you want a satisfactory deal, just like the purchaser.

## Setting Conditions

Determine what your best deal and bottom-line positions are and why. The purchaser will attempt to negotiate the best deal, so be prepared. A buyer's offer to purchase may include various subject clauses, which need to be resolved before the deal goes firm and closes. Asking for a few conditions of your own will give you some leverage of your own. These may include:

- Accommodating backup offers. You may want to keep your hands free in case a more attractive competing bid emerges following receipt of an initial purchase offer (usually 72 hours), stipulating removal of conditions from the initial bid in the event of a more favourable one.

- Legal review. Your lawyer should review any real estate deal you enter, whether it's a purchase or sale. Ask for enough time to thoroughly review the purchaser's offer, and then some in case you need to follow up any specific concerns.

- Timeline. Set a time limit for the evaluation of the deal, usually a minimum of 24 hours but sometimes as much as three or four months. You want to be able to satisfy any outstanding issues and be able to close the deal properly. Once you accept a purchase offer, you need to set a closing date. Requesting more time may give you greater opportunity to ensure the deal is the best one possible.

While the subject clauses shouldn't be frivolous, there is room to use them to negotiate a deal that satisfies your requirements as well as those of the purchaser. Part of the consultation with your lawyer should include a consideration of what you could request.

## Counting the Benefits

When a prospective buyer makes an offer you consider too low, you may wish to argue in favour of a higher value because of what the property has to offer. Writing some additional features into the offer to purchase as part of your counter-offer may provide a means of boosting the offered price without giving up too much value. Property features that may be worth citing include:

- The chattels. Goods that are ancillary to the property itself, chattels are often assigned a value that is negotiable aside from any buildings and lands included in the deal. The greater the perceived value of these, the greater the price you can ask for the property.

- Recent upgrades. The improvements you make to a property over the course of your ownership may have a greater value than the potential purchaser recognizes. Tout these as reasons why the property is worth the amount you've requested, perhaps including a subject-to clause that offers verification of the true value.

- Goodwill. A property with a reliable income may be doing well because it's a well-known property on a prime corner of town. Assigning a value to the goodwill the property enjoys can help support your request for a higher price. Document the established goodwill through your intimate knowledge of the property's history and importance to the surrounding community, highlighting why it is also a good investment for the potential purchaser.

Keep your insistence on the higher price you believe the property's worth in line with what the market demands, however. You may wish to review your assessment of the market value of the property in light of what a potential purchaser offers.

## Advising Tenants

When the deal closes, be sure to inform tenants of when the new ownership arrangement takes effect. Tenants will have to know where to deliver rent cheques, and will also want some assurance that the new owner won't be turfing them out to conduct a major renovation or to demolish the property for some other use. Being able to pave the way for the new owner is important, and will do much to set your tenants at ease as well as to preserve your reputation.

# Moving On

Being able to recoup the wealth you've accumulated in a property over several years is a great feeling, but more than one property investor has been plagued by efforts to find a place for the cash. Reinvesting the proceeds of a sale can be difficult, and requires a plan.

The government is all too eager to take a share; however, it's your duty, and being aware of the taxes owing on the sale of a property is an integral part of being an investor.

## Reinvesting Proceeds

A common destination for the proceeds of a successful sale is a successful purchase! Reinvesting the proceeds of one sale in another property could further the goals of your investment portfolio.

On the other hand, you may wish to retire. Consulting your financial planner will yield some suggestions of where to bank the money while you sort through options. You may wish to place the funds into a trust fund or annuity to support you.

Alternatively, you may choose to invest the funds in a new business venture or favourite pastime (a hobby farm or a yacht, for example) and enjoy the proceeds of your investment property.

Your advisers will be able to guide you as you prepare for the future.

## Paying Taxes

Before you spend too much of the proceeds, give a thought to the government. Review the various taxes owing on sale and discuss your options for managing taxes with both an accountant and financial planner. With a bit of planning, you may be able to mitigate the tax burden, ensuring that you get to enjoy as great a proportion of the proceeds from your properties as possible.

## Summary

The topics in this chapter are critical to obtaining an optimal sale price. The key strategies and tips discussed include determining when to sell, preparing to sell your property, and selecting the real estate agent. Also explained are the potential disadvantages of selling the property yourself, and practical tips on making your home more attractive to a buyer.

The final chapter in the book is about your future—and that of your family. We now turn to financial and estate planning.

# CHAPTER 12

# Understanding Financial and Estate Planning

**If you are investing** or thinking of investing in real estate, it is particularly important to make sure that you have a financial and estate plan in place. This chapter provides an overview of the financial- and estate-planning issues that you need to consider and update regularly as your needs change.

## An Introduction to Financial Planning

As part of your overall financial housekeeping, you need to have a detailed written plan of your financial needs and goals that includes your short- and long-term investment objectives. As the saying goes, "How do you know if you have arrived unless you know where you are going?" A realistic and objective plan, prepared with the support of your professional advisers, will provide you with peace of mind, a sense of control, and financial security.

You will need the right advisers to assist you in attaining your goals of maximizing your profits and minimizing risks. (See Chapter 4, "Selecting Your Advisory Team" for guidelines and tips on how to carefully select the right advisers.) This includes an integrated professional approach to all your personal and investment needs, utilizing a financial planner, insurance broker, accountant, and lawyer to protect your interests and accomplish your objectives.

There are five basic steps involved in financial planning: selecting the right financial planner and other professionals, assessing your current and future financial situation, establishing your goals and priorities, developing a realistic and attainable plan, and monitoring and evaluating the results on an ongoing basis. The plan should cover all the aspects of your financial life, including insurance, investments, loans, tax, retirement, and estate planning.

## An Introduction to Estate Planning

Your will is the most important document you will ever draw up. With very few exceptions, everybody should have a will. It is the only legal document that can ensure that your assets will be distributed to your beneficiaries according to your wishes, instead of by a government formula, in a timely manner and with effective estate planning. Your will takes effect only after your death and is kept strictly confidential until that time.

There are no estate taxes or succession duties in Canada, but estate planning can minimize the amount that is taxed in other ways. Part of estate planning includes having a power of attorney and possibly a living will. For a more detailed discussion, see *The Canadian Guide to Will and Estate Planning* by Douglas Gray and John Budd, and visit www.estateplanning.ca.

## Why You Need a Will

Many people die suddenly, and while there is growing awareness of the importance of wills and estate planning, many don't have a will, or if they do it isn't up-to-date. Those who die without a will oblige the government to become involved in winding up their estate. Some people just procrastinate or have busy lives and simply do not put a priority on preparing a will. Others do not appreciate the full implications of dying without a will or even think about it. And some people simply resist the reality that they are mortal. Preparing a will and dealing with estate-planning issues certainly faces the issue of mortality in a direct way.

Many of those who do have a will do not modify it based on changing circumstances. People first think of preparing a will when they marry, have children, fly for the first time without their children, or when they hear news of a sudden death of a friend or relative. Once they complete a will, they forget about it. Not updating your will can be as bad as not having one and could cause your beneficiaries much grief, stress, time, and expense. Your marital status may have changed, assets increased or decreased, or you may have started or ended a business, moved to a new province, or a new government tax or other legislation could be introduced that should prompt you to revisit your estate plan. For those who consider writing their own will, there is a risk of serious mistakes and oversight.

## What Is Estate Planning?

Estate planning refers to the process of preserving and transferring your wealth in an effective manner. From a tax perspective, your estate objectives, including a properly drafted will, include:

- minimizing and deferring taxes; and
- moving any tax burden to your heirs to be paid only upon future sale of the assets.

There are techniques to attain these objectives, including:

- arranging for assets to be transferred to family members in a lower tax bracket;

- establishing trusts for your children and/or spouse;

- setting up estate freezes, generally for your children, which reduce the future tax they pay on assets of increased value;

- making optimal use of the benefits of charitable donations, tax shelters, holding companies, or dividend tax credits;

- taking advantage of gifting during your lifetime;

- minimizing the risk of business creditors encroaching on personal estate assets;

- having sufficient insurance to cover anticipated tax on death; and

- avoiding probate fees by having assets in joint names or with a designated beneficiary.

## What Is in a Will?

Depending on the complexity of your estate, your will could be either simple or complex. A basic will contains:

- name and address of the person who is making the will (the testator);

- declaration that the document is your last will and testament and that it revokes all former wills and codicils (a supplementary document that may change, add, or subtract from the original will);

- appointment of an executor (person or organization who will administer your estate) and possibly a trustee (required where you have included trust provisions in your will);

- authorization to pay outstanding debts, including funeral expenses, taxes, fees, and other administrative expenses before any gift of property can be made;

- disposition of property and cash legacies to beneficiaries, or a gift of part or the entire residue of your estate (what is left after all debts, funeral and administrative expenses, taxes, and fees have been paid and specific property gifts and cash legacies distributed);

- attestation clause that states that the will was properly signed in the presence of at least two witnesses who were both present at the same time, and who both signed in your presence and the presence of each other; and

- appointment of a guardian for infant children.

## Special Provisions

Consult a lawyer who specializes in wills and estates to assist you in identifying and preparing special provisions for your situation. A few of the many special provisions include:

- Alternative beneficiaries and 30-day survivorship clause. When spouses die together or within a very short time of each other, if they have wills leaving everything to each other without naming alternate beneficiaries, the situation is similar to not having a will at all. Although uncommon, you still should provide for the possibility that your spouse may not be able to benefit from the estate. A 30-day clause provides that in order for your beneficiaries to benefit from the estate, they have to survive you by 30 days. If it is impossible to determine which of a married couple died first, it is presumed that the younger spouse survived the older spouse.

- Trusts. If you want to give someone a gift, but do not want him or her to have direct control of the property, you can set up a trust provision in your will to manage the gift. Trusts are discussed in more detail later.

## Funeral Instructions

Some people leave instructions regarding funeral arrangements and the disposition of the body their will; however, these instructions are not legally binding on the executor for various legal reasons. Inform your executor and immediate family of your wishes, because your will is generally not located and read until *after* the funeral has already occurred. Your comments in the will should simply reinforce what you have stated verbally.

## What Happens If You Don't Have a Will?

If you don't have a will or a valid one, it could result in legal, financial, and emotional ordeals for your loved ones. This is compounded greatly if you have a business. Not having a will at the time of death is called being intestate. Under provincial legislation, the court will appoint an administrator. If no family member applies to act as administrator, the state appoints the public trustee or official administrator. Your estate will be distributed in accordance with the legal formulas of your province, which are inflexible, and many may not reflect either your personal wishes or the needs of your family or loved ones.

While the law attempts to be fair, it does not provide for special needs. A home or other assets could be sold under unfavourable market conditions in order to distribute the assets. Your heirs may pay taxes that might easily have been deferred or reduced. There may insufficient worth in the estate to pay the taxes. Your family could be left without money for an extended period, and your assets may be lost or destroyed. There may be a delay in the administration of your estate and added costs such as an administrator bond. This is similar to an insurance policy if the administrator makes a mistake.

If you die without a will appointing a guardian for your children defined as minors under provincial or territorial law (either 18 or 19 years old), and there is no surviving parent who has legal custody, provincial laws come into effect. The public trustee becomes the guardian and manager of the assets to which your children are entitled. The provincial child welfare services assume responsibility for their care, upbringing, education, and health. A relative or other person can apply to the court for guardianship, but it is up to the court's discretion.

## Is Your Will Valid in the United States for U.S. Assets?

In general terms, if you have a valid will that is legally enforceable in your province, it would probably also be valid in the American state in which you have assets. Perhaps you own recreational property or are thinking of buying property in the United States for business purposes.

There could be a serious problem if you have two wills, one Canadian, one American. Because they are different legal jurisdictions, a beneficiary (or someone who would like to be one) might challenge the contents of the will in one jurisdiction but not in the other one. Standard boilerplate clauses often state that the most recent will automatically revoke any and all previous wills. If you inadvertently included that clause in a U.S. will, it could automatically nullify your Canadian will!

You could instruct your Canadian lawyer to include specific terms in your Canadian will relating to your U.S. assets and have affidavit attestation of the witnesses of your will at the same time. All this must be done in conjunction with feedback from a U.S. lawyer who has expertise in will matters in the state in which you own assets. Another option is to have a U.S. lawyer transfer your U.S. assets into joint names, with right of survivorship, so that those assets would automatically go to your surviving spouse. Consider having your U.S. property in a living trust or revocable trust. This bypasses your estate, and therefore probate procedures, as the trust is not in the deceased's name, but a trustee's name. Your lawyer will help you assess the options in your situation.

## Preparing a Will

There are two ways to prepare a will: writing it yourself or having a lawyer prepare one. The advantages and disadvantages of each are outlined in the following:

### Preparing Your Own Will

This is not a good choice because the inadequacies of a writing a will yourself could result in myriad problems for your family and beneficiaries. How you expressed your wishes may be legally interpreted differently than what you intended. Worse still, a clause or the whole will could be deemed void for technical reasons. Some people draft a will from scratch or use a "standard form" purchased in a bookshop or stationery store. The risk is very high and it is false economy as, depending on your situation, you could have a lot to lose.

## Having a Lawyer Prepare Your Will

In most cases, wills should be prepared by an experienced lawyer who is qualified to provide advice on such matters and is knowledgeable on how to complete the work. For more information, see *The Canadian Guide to Will and Estate Planning* by Douglas Gray and John Budd, and the website www.estateplanning.ca. Your lawyer will customize your will to your specific facts and circumstances, your personal wishes for your family and preferred beneficiaries, build in legal protections, and apply the correct wording to avoid hassles down the road.

Depending on the complexity of the estate, you may also need to enlist the expertise of the other specialists, including a professionally qualified tax accountant or a financial planner. (Refer to page 114 in Chapter 4, "Selecting Your Advisory Team" to assist you in finding professional assistance.)

The fee for preparing a basic will is modest, ranging from $200 to $300 or more per person. If your affairs are complex, the fee could be higher due to the additional time and expertise required. A "back-to-back" will is a duplicate reverse will for each partner, and is generally done at a reduced price.

## Key Reasons for Consulting a Lawyer

To reinforce the necessity of obtaining a legal consultation before completing or updating a will, just look at some of the many reasons why legal advice may be specifically required because of the complex legal issues and options involved:

- You own or plan to own investment real estate.
- You currently jointly own investment real estate with others or plan to do so.
- You own or plan to own foreign real estate on your own or jointly with others.
- You own or plan to own your own business.
- You own or plan to own a business with partners.
- You are separated from your spouse but not divorced.
- You are planning to separate from your spouse or partner.
- You are divorced and paying support.
- You are living in, entering, or leaving a common-law relationship.
- You are in a blended family relationship.
- Your estate is large and you need assistance with estate planning to reduce or eliminate taxes for your beneficiaries.
- You anticipate being a beneficiary of a substantial inheritance.
- You have a history of emotional or mental problems such that someone could attack the validity of your will on the basis that you did not understand the implications of your actions.
- You want to have unbiased, professional advice rather than being influenced by or under duress from relatives.
- You want to live outside of Canada for extended periods of time, for example, retire and travel south in the winter. Your permanent residence at the time of your death has legal and tax implications. For more information, see *The Canadian Snowbird Guide (Everything You Need to Know about Living Part-Time in the USA and Mexico)* by Douglas Gray.
- You have a will that was signed outside Canada or plan to have one.
- You want to forgive certain debts, or make arrangements for the repayment of debts to your estate should you die before the debt is paid.

- You want events to occur that have to carefully worded, such as having a spouse have income or use of a home until he or she remarries or dies, at which time the balance goes elsewhere.

- You want to set up a trust for your family, business, or investment real estate.

- You want to donate money to a charitable organization.

- You want to make special arrangements to care for someone who is incapable of looking after himself or herself or unable to apply sound financial judgement, for example, a child, an immature adolescent, a gambler, an alcoholic, a spendthrift, or someone with special needs or who is ill.

- You wish to disinherit a spouse, relative, or child because of a serious estrangement or the fact that all your children are now independently wealthy and don't need your money.

- You have several children and you want to provide one specific child with the opportunity to buy, have an option to buy, or receive in the will a specific possession of your estate.

As you can see, there are many reasons to consult with a legal expert for a will that is customized for your needs. The general factors to look for when selecting a lawyer are discussed on page 110 in Chapter 4, "Selecting Your Advisory Team."

## Other Key Factors to Consider

### Selecting a Trust Company

A trust company can offer extensive services in terms of will and estate planning, generally in conjunction with a lawyer of your choice, or they could recommend one. Always obtain independent legal advice. A trust company is invaluable when a trust is set up as part of your estate planning, as well as to act as your executor, for example, if you don't have anyone who has the time, ability, skill, temperament, or desire to be the executor or trustee of your estate. Needs vary and, after obtaining advice, you may not require a trust company.

### Selecting an Executor

Your executor acts as your personal representative and deals with all the financial, tax, administrative, and other aspects of your estate. You grant your executor the power to convert any part of your estate into money as he or she thinks best in order to wind up the estate. It is difficult to find a layperson or family member who could adequately fulfill all the qualifications that might be required. Not only can the process be time-consuming and complicated, it can also expose the executor to personal legal liability if errors are made. The executor is accountable to all beneficiaries.

There are two kinds of executors: a lawyer, accountant, or trust company staff; and an inexperienced layperson, generally a relative or family friend. Many people consider being asked to be an executor an honour, a reflection of the trust in the relationship; however, conflicts can and do arise between executors and beneficiaries. The executor may be perceived as overzealous or indifferent, authoritarian or showing favouritism, lacking necessary knowledge or making decisions too hastily. An executor can retain a lawyer or a trust company as an agent. You can also name more than one person to administer the estate, referred to as co-executors. For example, you could consider having a spouse and a trust company as co-executors. If you are naming an individual, make sure you have an alternate executor in case the first one is unwilling or unable to act.

## Selecting a Trustee

Trusts that operate during your lifetime are called *inter vivos* trusts. A trust that is operable upon your death as outlined in your will is a testamentary trust. You would need to have a trustee manage for either type; both are discussed later in this chapter.

You may wish to appoint a trustee to manage a portion of your assets for an extended period. If you are selecting a layperson to be the executor, you may not want the same person to be the trustee to prevent a potential conflict of interest. Trustees are normally responsible for taking in and investing money, selling assets, and distributing the estate proceeds in accordance with the trust terms. The trustee must maintain a balance between the interests of income beneficiaries and beneficiaries subsequently entitled to the capital. In addition, a trustee should maintain accounts and regularly issue accounting statements and income tax receipts to beneficiaries, make income payments, and exercise discretion or early withdrawal of capital to meet special needs.

Finally, the trustee makes the final distribution of the trust fund in accordance with the will. You can see why trust companies perform a vital role. An individual may not have the long-term continuity required due to death or lack of interest or ability. Selecting the right executor and trustee will enhance the smooth disposition of your assets and reduce your family's stress. Use professionals to act as an executor or trustee, or appoint a family member to be a co-executor or co-trustee if the circumstances warrant. Remember to shortlist three prospects and/or trust companies before you decide whom to select as your executor and/or trustee.

## Selecting a Guardian

If you have children, it is in your children's best interests to thoroughly plan for their upbringing and care in the event of your death. When you appoint a guardian, you are really just making a request; your wishes are not legally binding as children are not property and therefore cannot be willed. If the guardian is willing and able to perform the responsibilities, the courts will generally uphold your wishes. Make sure you name an alternate guardian in case the first one is unwilling or unable to assume the responsibility or predeceases you.

Talk with, and obtain the consent of, the main and alternate guardians before naming them in your will. Leave with your will, in your safety deposit box, a letter detailing your wishes with regard to raising your children. This would include fundamental issues such as religion, education, values, and general upbringing. Discuss these issues with the guardian.

Appointing different people to be the trustee and guardian of a child should eliminate any potential conflict of interest. The trustee is responsible for protecting the child's inheritance. A guardian frequently attempts to obtain more funds for the child's upbringing, health, and education. One way of making sure there is sufficient money for the trust is to purchase life insurance.

## *Understanding Trusts*

Trusts are a very common way of dealing with a range of personal, family, or business considerations. A trust is a legal structure in which management of property or assets—cash, stocks, bonds—rests with a trustee, who manages the property and assets for the benefit of beneficiaries. The trustee may also be one of the beneficiaries. Although the trustee has legal title to the trust property, beneficial ownership rests with the beneficiaries.

A trustee derives only certain limited powers by provincial statute. Your will should therefore specify what powers you want to give your trustee in carrying out the provisions of the trust. For example, if you do not want the trustee to be restricted in the kinds of investments made with trust funds, you must provide your trustee with expanded investment powers in your will.

## Living Trusts

There are a number of creative ways that you can use a living trust, including the following examples.

### Family Trust

This involves having some of the shares in a company owned by a spouse held in the name of a family trust. These shares could be non-voting shares. The family trust could comprise your spouse and children. The monies that go to the trust by means of dividends could then be distributed as dividends to each of the trust members. If the members of the trust were not receiving any other income, they could each take out up to $50,000 (indexed for inflation) of dividend income each year, tax-free. As the tax legislation can change at any time, check with your accountant. If the family members are minors and if the trust is formed properly, the standard practice of attributing a minor's income to the parents for tax purposes (the attribution rule) would not be applicable.

Unfortunately, several years ago, the federal government clamped down on income-splitting arrangements by introducing a special income-splitting tax. This tax will apply at the marginal income tax rate to individuals under 18 years of age who directly or indirectly receive taxable dividends on shares of Canadian private corporations and foreign corporations. This special tax will also apply to some business income allocated to a minor from a partnership or a trust. Seek advice from your tax accountant.

### Estate Freeze

If your company or other assets have shown a consistent pattern of growth over time, which you anticipate will continue, an estate freeze using a corporation set up for the purpose, along with a living trust agreement, could be an effective strategy. This technique freezes the value of your assets as of the effective date of the agreement. All future capital gains will accrue to the benefit of your beneficiaries, such as a spouse or children.

### Providing for Family Members with Special Needs

If you have family members who are unable to handle their own affairs due to mental or physical incapacity or other reasons, a living trust can be established to provide for their financial needs for their lifetime. On the recipient's death, the remaining funds can be left to a charity or put to some other use.

## Giving to Charity

You may wish to set up a charitable remainder trust. In this situation, you could assist your charity of choice by donating a residual interest in a trust—the capital available at the time of your death, also known as the remainder—to the charity. Such trusts usually designate a charity to receive the remaining capital on your death; in the meantime, you receive the income earned from the trust's assets. It is possible that the trust could be structured so that you receive a non-refundable tax credit when the trust is established, representing the projected fair market value of the residual interest. This is a convenient option if the trust's capital won't be eroded during your lifetime.

# Managing Retirement Needs

With the advances in medical science and people leading healthier lives, the average life span has increased greatly over the years. It is not uncommon for people to live into their 80s and 90s.

However, many people do not feel comfortable managing their own affairs. Possibly their children do not have money-management skills, are very busy, or live out of town. For these reasons, many people consider the benefits of a living trust, managed by a trust company and a responsible family member as co-trustees. Assets are set aside and put into the trust. Normally it is structured so that the parents receive income for life, with the capital distributed to the children and/or grandchildren on the death of the surviving parent.

The trust could also have a provision stating that the capital of the trust could be used under certain conditions, such as greater financial needs dictated by health, for example, paying for long-term care in a retirement home.

# Testamentary Trusts

Testamentary trusts, created in your will, provide for spouses, minor children or grandchildren, family members with special needs, children who are spendthrifts, and charities. Here are some examples:

## Spousal Trust

In this situation, you set up a trust to provide income for the life of your spouse, with the capital remaining at death to go to the children or grandchildren. This type of trust is common when a spouse is ill or incapacitated or lacks financial expertise. A variation of this format, if there are no children or grandchildren, is to leave the capital to charity on the death of the surviving spouse.

### Trusts for Minor Children or Grandchildren

This is probably an obvious one for most people. You may already have it stated in your will that in the event that both parents die at the same time, or when the surviving parent dies, a portion of your estate shall be held in trust for minor children or grandchildren until they reach a certain age. In the meantime, the trustee can encroach on the capital for specific needs of the children. Many people then arrange to have the money disbursed over various time periods as the children mature, for example, one-third at 19, one-third at 25, and one-third at 30.

### Spendthrift Trust

Perhaps you have a child who has a history of financial irresponsibility. One solution is to set up a trust to control the funds or assets that the child would otherwise receive.

### Special Needs Trust

If you have a family member with special needs of any nature, a trust can be established to provide financial comfort and legal structure to facilitate meeting those needs.

### Trust for Charities

You may wish to set up a trust that provides family members with income for life, but on their death the remaining capital in the trust is distributed to a charity of your choice.

## Living Will

A living will is designed for those who are concerned about their quality of life when they are near death. It is a written statement of your intentions to the people who are most likely to have control over your care, such as your family and your doctor. Have a copy of the living will where it can be readily obtained, such as in your wallet. Give a copy to your spouse and family doctor. You should also review your living will from time to time.

The purpose of a living will is to convey your wishes if there is no reasonable expectation of recovery from physical or mental disability. Such a will requests that you be allowed to die naturally, with dignity, and not be kept alive by "heroic medical measures." In some provinces, a living will is merely an expression of your wishes and is not legally binding on your doctor or the hospital. Other provinces have officially endorsed the concept through legislation if your written instructions are correctly done. For further information, visit the University of Toronto Joint Centre for Bioethics at www.jointcentreforbioethics.ca.

## Power of Attorney (PA)

Many lawyers recommend a power of attorney (PA), sometimes referred to as an enduring PA, at the same time that they prepare a will. The purpose of a PA is to designate a person or a trust company to take over your affairs if you can no longer handle them due to illness or incapacitation, for example. Another reason is that you may be away for extended periods on personal or business matters. A power of attorney is important if you have substantial assets that require active management. You can grant a general PA over all your affairs, or a limited one specific to a certain task or time period. You can revoke the power of attorney at any time in writing. A PA is valid only in your province. You would need to have a separate PA if you own assets in the United States or elsewhere.

If you do not have a power of attorney and become incapacitated, an application has to be made to the court by the party who wishes permission to manage your affairs. This person would be called a committee. If another family member does not wish to perform this responsibility, a trust company can be appointed, with court approval. Committee duties include filing with the court a summary of assets, liabilities, and income sources, with a description of the person's needs and an outline of how the committee proposes to manage the accounts and/or structure the estate to serve those needs.

## Personal Information Record

If you died suddenly, or had a serious head injury or stroke, would anyone have an accurate and current knowledge of your personal, business, and investment matters? For most people, the answer is no. That is why you need to prepare a personal information record, and keep it updated annually and when any financial matters change. Your family, executor, and trustee will think of you fondly for having the foresight to make the administration of your estate so much easier. This personal information record should be kept with your will in your safety deposit box, with a copy at your home.

You can download a personal-information-record template from www.estateplanning.ca/forms. The types of matters covered in a typical personal information record include:

- names of partners, children, and dependants;
- key documents and their locations;
- names of professionals or advisers who handle your affairs;
- bank accounts;
- investments;
- personal property;
- real estate holdings;
- business ownership;
- mortgages and other debts;
- insurance; and
- funeral arrangements.

## Summary

Proper and professional financial planning is an integral part of your short- and long-term personal and investment strategy. It encompasses an integral range of matters, such as personal, business, insurance, tax, retirement, and estate planning.

A will is part of your estate planning, and should be customized for your specific needs and updated on a regular basis. As a will is a legal document, the wording and necessary clauses to reflect your wishes should be approved by your lawyer. Most people would not choose to inflict the consequences of not having a will on their family. There is no logical reason not to have a will, an enduring power of attorney, and a living will—all necessary components of a prudent estate plan.

# Appendix

## FORM 1: Personal Cost-of-Living Budget (Monthly)
### (See Chapter 1)

I. Income (Average monthly income, actual or estimated)

| | |
|---|---|
| Salary, bonuses, and commissions | $_____ |
| Dividends | $_____ |
| Interest income | $_____ |
| Pension income | $_____ |
| Other: | $_____ |
| | $_____ |
| TOTAL MONTHLY INCOME | $_____(A) |

II. Expenses

Regular Monthly Payments:

| | |
|---|---|
| Rent or mortgage payments | $_____ |
| Automobile(s) | $_____ |
| Appliances/TV/cable | $_____ |
| Internet charges | $_____ |
| Home improvement loan | $_____ |
| Credit-card payments (not covered elsewhere) | $_____ |
| Personal loan | $_____ |
| Medical plan | $_____ |
| Installment and other loans | $_____ |
| Life insurance premiums | $_____ |
| House insurance | $_____ |

(Continued)

Other insurance premiums (auto, extended medical, etc.)    $_____

RRSP deductions    $_____

Pension fund (employer)    $_____

Investment plan(s)    $_____

Miscellaneous    $_____

Other:    $_____

   $_____

TOTAL REGULAR MONTHLY PAYMENTS    $_____

Household Operating Expenses:

Telephone    $_____

Gas and electricity    $_____

Heat    $_____

Water and garbage    $_____

Other household expenses (repairs, maintenance, etc.)    $_____

Other:    $_____

   $_____

TOTAL HOUSEHOLD OPERATING EXPENSES    $_____

Food Expenses:

At home    $_____

Away from home    $_____

TOTAL FOOD EXPENSES    $_____

Personal Expenses:

Clothing, cleaning, laundry    $_____

Drugs    $_____

Transportation (other than auto)    $_____

Medical and dental    $_____

Daycare    $_____

Education (self)    $_____

Education (children)    $_____

Dues    $_____

Gifts and donations    $_____

Travel    $_____

Recreation $_____

Newspapers, magazines, and books $_____

Automobile maintenance, gas, and parking $_____

Spending money, allowances $_____

Other: $_____

$_____

TOTAL PERSONAL EXPENSES $_____

Tax Expenses:

Federal and provincial income taxes $_____

Home property taxes $_____

Other: $_____

$_____

TOTAL TAX EXPENSES $_____

III. Summary of Expenses

Regular monthly payments $_____

Household operating expenses $_____

Food expenses $_____

Personal expenses $_____

Tax expenses $_____

TOTAL MONTHLY EXPENSES $_____(B)

TOTAL MONTHLY DISPOSABLE INCOME AVAILABLE $_____(A – B)

(subtract total monthly expenses from total monthly income)

# FORM 2: Personal Net-Worth Statement
## (Format Commonly Requested by Lenders)
### (See Chapter 1)

Name:_____

Date of birth: MM____/DD____/YR____     Social Insurance No.: _____

Street Address: _____

City: _____     Province: _____     Postal code: _____

Home phone: _____     Residence: ❑ Own   ❑ Rent   ❑ Other

How long at address?  _____Years  _____Months

❑ Married   ❑ Single   ❑ Separated     Number of dependants: _____

Occupation: _____     Employer's Phone: _____

Currently employed with:_____

How long with employer? _____Years _____Months

Your principal financial institution and address: _____

_____

**Personal Data on Your Spouse**

Under the federal and some provincial laws, your spouse may have a legal interest or
obligation arising from your business dealings and may also have an interest in your
personal assets.

Spouse's name:_____

Spouse's occupation: _____

Spouse currently employed by: _____

Spouse's work phone: _____

How long with employer? _____Years  _____Months

**Financial Information**

As at _____ day of _____month, 20_____

| Assets | Value |
|---|---|
| (List and describe all assets) | |
| Total of chequing accounts | $_____ |
| Total of savings accounts | $_____ |
| Life insurance cash surrender value | $_____ |

Automobile: Make _____ Year _____          $_____

Stocks and bonds (see Schedule A attached)          $_____

Accounts/notes receivable (please itemize):

_____          $_____

_____          $_____

_____          $_____

Term deposits (cashable)          $_____

Real estate (see Schedule B attached)          $_____

Retirement plans:

  RRSP          $_____

  Employment pension plan          $_____

  Other          $_____

Other assets (household goods, etc.):

  Art          $_____

  Jewellery          $_____

  Antiques          $_____

  Other          $_____

TOTAL ASSETS (A)          $_____ (A)

**Liabilities**

(List credit cards, open lines of credit, and other liabilities including alimony and child support.)

| | Balance Owing | Monthly Payment |
| --- | --- | --- |
| Bank loans | $_____ | $_____ |
| Mortgages on real estate owned (see Schedule B attached) | $_____ | $_____ |
| Monthly rent payment | $_____ | $_____ |
| Credit cards (please itemize): | | |
| _____ | $_____ | $_____ |
| _____ | $_____ | $_____ |
| _____ | $_____ | $_____ |
| _____ | $_____ | $_____ |
| Money borrowed from life insurance policy | $_____ | $_____ |

*(Continued)*

| | | |
|---|---|---|
| Margin accounts | $_____ | $_____ |
| Current income tax owing | $_____ | $_____ |

Other obligations (please itemize):

| | | |
|---|---|---|
| _____ | $_____ | $_____ |
| _____ | $_____ | $_____ |
| _____ | $_____ | $_____ |
| TOTAL MONTHLY PAYMENTS | | $_____ |
| TOTAL LIABILITIES (B) | | $_____ (B) |
| NET WORTH (A − B) | | $_____ (A − B) |

## Income Sources

Income from alimony, child support, or separate maintenance does not have to be stated unless you want it considered.

| | |
|---|---|
| Your gross monthly salary | $_____ |
| Your spouse's gross monthly salary | $_____ |
| Net monthly rental (from Schedule B attached) | $_____ |

Other income (please itemize):

| | |
|---|---|
| _____ | $_____ |
| _____ | $_____ |
| _____ | $_____ |
| TOTAL | $_____ |

## Sundry Personal Obligations

Please provide details below if you answer yes to the following question: Are you providing your personal support for obligations not listed above (i.e., co-signer, endorser, guarantor)? _____ Yes _____ No

Details of any of the above: _____

## Schedule A: Stocks, Bonds, and Other Investments

| Quantity | Description | Where Quoted | Market Value | Pledged as collateral? | |
|---|---|---|---|---|---|
| | | | | Yes | No |
| | | | | | |
| | | | | | |

TOTAL _____

**Schedule B: Real Estate Owned**

Please provide information on your share only of real estate owned.

Property address (primary residence): _____

Legal description: _____

Street _____

City: _____ Province: _____

Type of property: _____

Present market value: $ _____

Amount of mortgage liens: 1st $ _____ 2nd $ _____

Gross monthly rental income: _____

Monthly mortgage payments: 1st $ _____ 2nd $ _____

Monthly taxes, insurance, maintenance, and miscellaneous: _____

Net monthly rental income: $ _____ $ _____

Name of mortgage holder(s)

First mortgage: _____

Second mortgage: _____

Percentage ownership: _____% Month/year acquired: _____

Purchase price: $ _____

**General Information**

Please provide details if you answer yes to any of the following questions:

Have you ever had an asset repossessed? Yes _____ No _____

Are you party to any claims or lawsuits? Yes _____ No _____

Have you ever declared bankruptcy? Yes _____ No _____

Do you owe any taxes prior to the current year? Yes _____ No _____

Details:

_____

_____

_____

_____

_____

_____

_____

_____

*(Continued)*

_____

_____

_____

The undersigned declare(s) that the statements made herein are for the purpose of obtaining business financing and are to the best of my/our knowledge true and correct. The applicant(s) consent(s) to the Bank making any enquiries it deems necessary to reach a decision on this application, and consent(s) to the disclosure at any time of any credit information about me/us to any credit reporting agency or to anyone with whom I/we have financial relations.

Date: _____ Signature of applicant(s) above: _____

# FORM 3: Calculating Your
# Gross Debt-Service (GDS) Ratio
## (See Chapter 5)

Your GDS ratio is calculated by adding the total of your monthly mortgage principal, interest, and taxes (PIT) together and dividing that figure by your monthly income. Guidelines have been set that generally allow a maximum of 27 to 30% or more, depending on the financial institution, of your gross income to be used for the mortgage PIT.

$$\text{GDS ratio} = \frac{\text{Monthly Principal} + \text{Interest} + \text{Taxes (PIT)}}{\text{Monthly income}}$$

Gross (pre-tax) *monthly* income of purchaser(s)                              $_____

Other forms of income (e.g., annual) averaged to monthly                     $_____

TOTAL MONTHLY INCOME                                                         $_____

Estimate monthly property tax on home (net after any provincial homeowners' grant is taken into consideration, if applicable)                              $_____

1. To estimate the *maximum* monthly mortgage payment plus property taxes you could carry (monthly PIT), calculate 30% of the total monthly income:

30% of $ _____                                                      $_____

2. To estimate the *maximum* monthly mortgage payment, not including taxes (PI), that you could carry, subtract the monthly tax amount from the monthly PIT:

Monthly PIT                                                                  $_____

Less: Monthly property tax                                                   $_____

MAXIMUM MONTHLY MORTGAGE PAYMENT                                             $_____

(not including taxes) = Monthly PI

Use Chart 7 to determine the maximum mortgage (not including taxes) for which you qualify under your GDS ratio guidelines. Simply look up your maximum monthly mortgage payment under the current interest rate.

Maximum mortgage available under GDS Ratio guidelines                        $_____

# FORM 4: Calculating Your Total Debt-Service (TDS)·Ratio
## (See Chapter 5)

Most lenders require that an applicant meet a TDS ratio, in addition to looking at the GDS ratio. The TDS ratio is generally a maximum of 35 to 40% or more of gross income—actual rules may vary between financial institutions. The TDS ratio is calculated in much the same way as the GDS ratio, but takes into consideration all other debts and loans you may have.

$$\text{GDS ratio} = \frac{\text{Monthly Principal} + \text{Interest} + \text{Taxes (PIT)} + \text{Other monthly payments}}{\text{Monthly income}}$$

Gross (pre-tax) monthly income of purchaser(s)          $_____

Other forms of income (e.g., annual) averaged to monthly          $_____

TOTAL MONTHLY INCOME          $_____


Other monthly payments:

Credit cards          $_____

Other mortgages          $_____

Car loan          $_____

Other loans          $_____

Alimony/child support          $_____

Charge accounts          $_____

Other debts (list):          $_____

_____          $_____

_____          $_____

_____          $_____

TOTAL OTHER MONTHLY PAYMENTS          $_____

To calculate your TDS ratio, take 40% of $_____ (total monthly income) = $ _____ available for monthly principal + interest + taxes + other payments (PIT + Other).

To estimate the *maximum monthly mortgage payment* you could carry within your allowable TDS ratio:

| | |
|---|---|
| Monthly PIT + Other | $_____ |
| Less: Other monthly payments | $_____ |
| SUBTOTAL | $_____ |
| Less: Estimated property taxes | $_____ |
| MAXIMUM MONTHLY MORTGAGE PAYMENT | $_____ |

Use Chart 7 to determine the maximum mortgage for which you qualify under the TDS Ratio guidelines. Simply look up your maximum monthly mortgage payment under the current interest rate.

Maximum mortgage available under TDS Ratio guidelines                    $_____

# FORM 5: Projected Cash Flow (Three Months)

## (See Chapter 3)

| | Month 1 | | Month 2 | | Month 3 | | Quarterly Summary | |
|---|---|---|---|---|---|---|---|---|
| | Projected | Actual | Projected | Actual | Projected | Actual | Projected | Actual |
| **INCOME:** | | | | | | | | |
| Contributed capital | | | | | | | | |
| Loans | | | | | | | | |
| Miscellaneous | | | | | | | | |
| Rent received | | | | | | | | |
| Other: _____ | | | | | | | | |
| **TOTAL INCOME (A)** | | | | | | | | |
| **EXPENSES** | | | | | | | | |
| Accounting fees | | | | | | | | |
| Advertising | | | | | | | | |
| Bank interest and charges | | | | | | | | |
| Equipment purchase (appliances) | | | | | | | | |
| Insurance | | | | | | | | |
| Interests on rent deposits | | | | | | | | |
| Legal fees | | | | | | | | |
| Loan repayments | | | | | | | | |
| Maintenance services | | | | | | | | |
| Major repairs | | | | | | | | |
| Management fees | | | | | | | | |
| Minor repairs and maintenance | | | | | | | | |
| Miscellaneous expenses | | | | | | | | |
| Mortgage payments | | | | | | | | |
| Property taxes | | | | | | | | |
| Renovations | | | | | | | | |

| | | | | | | | | | |
|---|---|---|---|---|---|---|---|---|---|
| Utilities | | | | | | | | | |
| Other: _____ | | | | | | | | | |
| TOTAL EXPENSES (B) | | | | | | | | | |
| OPENING CASH BALANCE | | | | | | | | | |
| PLUS TOTAL INCOME (A) | | | | | | | | | |
| LESS TOTAL EXPENSES (B) | | | | | | | | | |
| CLOSING CASH BALANCE | | | | | | | | | |

# FORM 6: Projected Income and Expense Statement (as of _____)

## (See Chapter 3)

INCOME:

   Rental income ......................................... $_____

   Other sources of income ......................... $_____

   TOTAL INCOME ....................................... $_____ (A)

OPERATING EXPENSES:

   Accounting fees ...................................... $_____

   Advertising ............................................. $_____

   Bank interest and charges ...................... $_____

   Equipment purchase (appliances) .......... $_____

   Insurance ............................................... $_____

   Interest on rent deposits ....................... $_____

   Legal fees ............................................... $_____

   Loan repayments .................................... $_____

   Maintenance services ............................. $_____

   Major repairs ......................................... $_____

   Management fees .................................... $_____

   Minor repairs and maintenance ............. $_____

   Miscellaneous expenses ......................... $_____

   Mortgage payments ............................... $_____

   Property taxes ........................................ $_____

   Renovations ........................................... $_____

   Utilities .................................................. $_____

   Other ..................................................... $_____

  TOTAL OPERATING EXPENSES .............. $_____ (B)

  NET INCOME .......................................... $_____ (A − B)

# FORM 7: Projected Balance Sheet
# (as of _____)
### (See Chapter 3)

ASSETS

CURRENT ASSETS:

Cash                                    $ _____ (a)

Rent receivables                        $ _____ (b)

Prepaid expenses                        $ _____ (c)

TOTAL CURRENT ASSETS                              $ _____ = (A) [a + b + c]

FIXED ASSETS:

Land                                    $ _____ (d)

Buildings                               $ _____ (e)

Less accumulated depreciation           $ _____ (f)

Chattels                                $ _____ (g)

Less accumulated depreciation           $ _____ (h)

TOTAL FIXED ASSETS                               $ _____ = (B) [d + e + g − f − h]

TOTAL ASSETS                                     $ _____ (C) [A + B]

LIABILITIES

CURRENT LIABILITIES:

Accounts receivable                     $ _____ (i)

Accrued expenses                        $ _____ (j)

Rent deposits                           $ _____ (k)

Interest on rent deposits               $ _____ (l)

Interest on mortgage                    $ _____ (m)

Due in next 12 months                   $ _____ (n)

TOTAL CURRENT LIABILITIES                        $ _____
                                                 = (D) [i + j + k + l + m + n]

LONG-TERM LIABILITIES:

Mortgage principal payable              $ _____ (o)

TOTAL LONG-TERM LIABILITIES                      $ _____ = (E) [o]

TOTAL LIABILITIES                                $ _____ = (F) [D + E]

NET WORTH                                        $ _____ (C − F)

# FORM 8: Income Approach Worksheet
## (See Chapter 3)

Date: _____

Name of apartment building: _____

Address: _____

City: _____

Type of property: _____

Number of suites: _____

Asking price: _____

Cost per suite: _____

Cost per building sq. ft: _____

Zoning: _____

Age of building: _____

|    |                                                    | % | Amount | Comments |
|----|----------------------------------------------------|---|--------|----------|
| 1  | MAXIMUM POTENTIAL RENTAL INCOME (assuming no vacancies) |   |        |          |
| 2  | Less: Vacancy/bad debt losses                      |   |        |          |
| 3  | EFFECTIVE RENTAL INCOME (A)                         |   |        |          |
| 4  | Plus: Other income (B)                             |   |        |          |
| 5  | GROSS OPERATING INCOME (C) [A + B]                 |   |        |          |
| 6  | Less: OPERATING EXPENSES                            |   |        |          |
| 7  | Advertising, licences                              |   |        |          |
| 8  | Accounting and legal fees                          |   |        |          |
| 9  | Resident manager                                   |   |        |          |
| 10 | Property management company                        |   |        |          |
| 11 | Government payments (EI, CPP, WCB)                 |   |        |          |
| 12 | Property insurance                                 |   |        |          |
| 13 | Other                                              |   |        |          |
| 14 | Property taxes                                     |   |        |          |
| 15 | Repairs and maintenance                            |   |        |          |

| 16 | Services: Elevator | | | |
|----|--------------------|---|---|---|
| 17 | Janitorial | | | |
| 18 | Lawn | | | |
| 19 | Pool | | | |
| 20 | Rubbish | | | |
| 21 | Other | | | |
| 22 | Supplies | | | |
| 23 | Utilities: Electricity | | | |
| 24 | Gas and oil | | | |
| 25 | Sewer and water | | | |
| 26 | Telephone | | | |
| 27 | Other | | | |
| 28 | Miscellaneous | | | |
| 29 | GROSS OPERATING EXPENSES (D) | | | |
| 30 | NET OPERATING INCOME (E) [C − D] | | | |
| 31 | Less: Annual debt service (F) (mortgage and loan payments) | | | |
| 32 | CASH FLOW BEFORE TAX (E − F) (positive or negative) | | | |

CAP RATE _____ GIM _____ NIM _____

RATING OF PROPERTY    1    2    3    4    5    6    7    8    9    10
(circle)

              Low                                High

# FORM 9: Investment Property Analysis Checklist
## (See Chapter 3)

Date of analysis: _____

**Property:** _____

Present use: _____

Year built: _____

Type of construction: _____

Architectural style: _____

Summary of physical condition: _____

Square footage of building: _____

Square footage of land: _____

**Assessed Value for Property Tax Calculation Purposes**

Date of assessment: _____

Land                                               $_____

Building                                           $_____

Total                                              $_____

Total annual tax bill                              $_____

Tax rate per $1,000 assessed value                 $_____

Cost per square foot (building)                    $_____

**Restrictions on Property Use**

Most feasible use(s): _____

Building code restrictions: _____

Zoning restrictions: _____

Other restrictions: _____

**Calculations of Value**

**MARKET COMPARISON**

Estimate value range                        _____ to _____

Estimate of value                                  $_____

Terms: Down payment                                $_____

First mortgage rate                                $_____%

Total amount of first mortgage                     $_____

Annual total payment of first mortgage             $_____

**COST METHOD**

New building cost                                        $_____

Minus:

  Physical depreciation                          $_____

  Functional depreciation                        $_____

  Economic depreciation                          $_____

  Depreciated cost of building                   $_____ (A)

Add:

  Land value                                     $_____ (B)

Total cost value                                        $_____ (A + B)

**INCOME CAPITALIZATION METHOD**

Gross income                                            $_____

Total expenses                                          $_____

Net income (before taxes)                               $_____

Expenses represent what % of gross income?              $_____ %

Gross operating income × multiplier                     $_____

Net operating income × multiplier                       $_____

Estimate of value using NOI and CAP rate                $_____

**Summary of Value Calculations**

Using market comparisons                                $_____

Using cost (minus depreciation)                         $_____

Using income capitalization                             $_____

Most probable value (average of above)                  $_____

**Property Feasibility Summary**

Feasible use(s) recommended: _____

Feasible use(s) considered: _____

Major benefits: _____

Minor benefits: _____

Major costs: _____

Minor costs: _____

Major disadvantages: _____

Minor disadvantages: _____

# CHART 1: Criteria for Determining Real Estate Cycle
(See Chapter 1)

|  | A | B | C | D |
|---|---|---|---|---|
| Values | Depressed | Increasing | Increasing | Declining |
| Rents | Low | Increasing | Increasing | Declining |
| Vacancy level | High | Decreasing | Low | Increasing |
| Occupancy level | Low | Increasing | High | Decreasing |
| New construction | Very little | Increasing | Booming | Slowing |
| Profit margins | Low | Improving | Widest | Declining |
| Investor confidence | Low | Negative to neutral | Positive | Slightly negative |
| Media coverage | Negative and pessimistic | Positive and optimistic | Positive and optimistic | Negative and pessimistic |
| Action | Buy | Second-best time to buy | Sell | Be cautious |

# CHART 2: Recovery on Renovation Costs
(See Chapter 2)

| Renovation project | Recovery on resale (%) |
|---|---|
| Adding a full bath | 96 |
| Adding a fireplace | 94 |
| Remodelling kitchen (minor) | 79 |
| Remodelling kitchen (major) | 70 |
| Remodelling bathroom | 69 |
| Adding a skylight | 68 |
| Adding new siding | 67 |

| Renovation project | Recovery on resale (%) |
|---|---|
| Adding insulation | 65 |
| Adding a room | 62 |
| Re-roofing | 61 |
| Adding a wood deck | 60 |
| Adding a greenhouse | 56 |
| Replacing windows, doors | 55 |
| Adding a swimming pool | 39 |

# CHART 3: Amortization Period in Year
## (See Chapter 5)

The following examples assume a $50,000 mortgage loan and an interest rate* of 6% for the amortization period selected.

### Amortization period in years

| Payment | 10 | 15 | 20 | 25 |
|---|---|---|---|---|
| Monthly payment of principal and interest | $553.26 | $419.95 | $356.10 | $319.91 |
| Total of mortgage payments over the amortization period | $66,390.31 | $75,558.58 | $85,461.45 | $95,968.63 |

*Interest being compounded semi-annually.

# CHART 4: Interest Payments
## (See Chapter 5)

Interest* on each $1,000 of mortgage is based on payment period.

| Interest rate (%) | Weekly ($) | Every two weeks ($) | Twice a month ($) | Monthly ($) |
|---|---|---|---|---|
| 3.50 | $0.67 | $1.33 | $1.44 | $2.90 |
| 4.00 | $0.76 | $1.52 | $1.65 | $3.31 |
| 4.50 | $0.85 | $1.71 | $1.86 | $3.72 |
| 5.00 | $0.95 | $1.90 | $2.06 | $4.12 |
| 5.50 | $1.04 | $2.08 | $2.26 | $4.53 |
| 6.00 | $1.13 | $2.27 | $2.47 | $4.94 |
| 6.50 | $1.23 | $2.46 | $2.67 | $5.34 |
| 7.00 | $1.32 | $2.64 | $2.87 | $5.75 |
| 7.50 | $1.41 | $2.83 | $3.07 | $6.15 |
| 8.00 | $1.51 | $3.01 | $3.27 | $6.56 |

*Interest being compounded semi-annually.

# CHART 5: Prepayment or Increased Payment Savings
## (See Chapter 5)

Based on a $50,000 mortgage at a 6% interest rate.*

|  | Standard mortgage 25-year amortization | 10% annual increase in mortgage payment | 10% annual prepayment of principal |
|---|---|---|---|
| Mortgage repaid in months | 300 | 164 | 97 |
| Total interest charged | $45,968.63 | $29,504.54 | $14,060.22 |
| Interest savings vs. standard 25-year mortgage | N/A | $16,464.09 | $31,908.41 |

*Interest being compounded semi-annually.

# CHART 6: Mortgage Amortization Chart
## (See Chapter 5)

Follow the chart *down*, under the current interest rate, to the amount of your maximum monthly mortgage payment (not including taxes).

Follow that line *across* to determine the maximum mortgage, after down payment, for which you may qualify.

| Maximum Mortgage* | 4% | 5% | 6% | 7% | 8% |
|---|---|---|---|---|---|
| 30,000 | $157.81 | $174.49 | $191.95 | $210.13 | $228.97 |
| 40,000 | $210.41 | $232.65 | $255.93 | $280.17 | $305.29 |
| 50,000 | $263.02 | $290.81 | $319.91 | $350.21 | $381.61 |
| 60,000 | $315.62 | $348.97 | $383.89 | $420.25 | $457.93 |
| 70,000 | $368.22 | $407.13 | $447.87 | $490.30 | $534.25 |
| 80,000 | $420.82 | $465.29 | $511.85 | $560.34 | $610.58 |
| 90,000 | $473.42 | $523.45 | $575.83 | $630.38 | $686.90 |
| 100,000 | $526.03 | $581.61 | $639.81 | $700.42 | $763.22 |

| Maximum Mortgage* | 4% | 5% | 6% | 7% | 8% |
|---|---|---|---|---|---|
| 110,000 | $578.63 | $639.77 | $703.79 | $770.46 | $839.54 |
| 120,000 | $631.23 | $697.93 | $767.77 | $840.50 | $915.86 |
| 130,000 | $683.83 | $756.09 | $831.75 | $910.55 | $992.18 |
| 140,000 | $736.43 | $814.25 | $895.73 | $980.59 | $1,068.50 |
| 150,000 | $789.04 | $872.41 | $959.71 | $1,050.63 | $1,144.83 |
| 160,000 | $841.64 | $930.57 | $1,023.70 | $1,120.67 | $1,221.15 |
| 170,000 | $894.24 | $988.73 | $1,087.68 | $1,190.71 | $1,297.47 |
| 180,000 | $946.84 | $1,046.89 | $1,151.66 | $1,260.75 | $1,373.79 |
| 190,000 | $999.44 | $1,105.05 | $1,215.64 | $1,330.79 | $1,450.11 |
| 200,000 | $1,052.05 | $1,163.21 | $1,279.62 | $1,400.84 | $1,526.43 |

*Based on 25-year amortization period. Amounts are approximate. Interest compounded semi-annually.

## CHART 7: Monthly Mortgage Payments for Principal Plus Interest
### (See Chapter 5)

The table gives the monthly payments for principal and interest* (not including taxes) for each $1,000 of the amount of the mortgage.

| Interest rate (%) | 5 years ($) | 10 years ($) | 15 years ($) | 20 years ($) | 25 years ($) |
|---|---|---|---|---|---|
| 3.50 | $18.19 | $9.88 | $7.14 | $5.79 | $5.00 |
| 4.00 | $18.41 | $10.11 | $7.39 | $6.05 | $5.27 |
| 4.50 | $18.63 | $10.35 | $7.63 | $6.31 | $5.54 |
| 5.00 | $18.85 | $10.59 | $7.89 | $6.58 | $5.82 |
| 5.50 | $19.08 | $10.83 | $8.14 | $6.85 | $6.11 |
| 6.00 | $19.30 | $11.07 | $8.40 | $7.13 | $6.40 |
| 6.50 | $19.53 | $11.32 | $8.67 | $7.41 | $6.70 |
| 7.00 | $19.76 | $11.56 | $8.94 | $7.70 | $7.01 |
| 7.50 | $19.99 | $11.82 | $9.21 | $7.79 | $7.32 |
| 8.00 | $20.22 | $12.07 | $9.49 | $8.29 | $7.64 |

*Interest being compounded semi-annually.

# CHECKLIST 1: Real Estate Assessment
# Checklist
## (See Chapter 2)

1. This assessment checklist has most of the essential features to look for in a house, condominium, or apartment building.
2. Not all the categories are necessarily applicable in your individual case. Terminology in some instances can vary from province to province.
3. On the line provided, indicate your rating of the listed factor as: excellent, good, poor, available, not available, not applicable, further information required, etc.

### A. General Information

Location of property                          _____

Condition of neighbourhood                    _____

Zoning of surrounding areas                   _____

Prospect for future increase in value         _____

Prospect for future change of zoning          _____

Proximity of

- Schools                                     _____
- Places of worship                           _____
- Shopping                                    _____
- Recreation                                  _____
- Entertainment                               _____
- Parks                                       _____
- Playgrounds                                 _____
- Public transportation                       _____
- Highways                                    _____
- Hospital                                    _____
- Police department                           _____
- Fire department                             _____
- Ambulance                                   _____

Traffic density                               _____

Garbage removal                               _____

Sewage system                                 _____

Quality of water                              _____

Taxes:

- Provincial                                  _____
- Municipal                                   _____

Maintenance fees/assessments (if condominium) _____

Maintenance fees/management fees (if apartment building) _____

Easements _____

Quietness of

- Neighbourhood _____
- Condo or apartment complex _____
- Individual condominium unit _____
- Individual apartment unit _____
- House _____

Percentage of units that are owner-occupied (if condominium) _____

If next to commercial centre, is access to residential
section well controlled? _____

Is adjacent commercial development being planned? _____

Size of development related to your needs
(small, medium, large) _____

Does project seem to be compatible with your lifestyle? _____

Style of development (adult-oriented, children, retirees, etc.) _____

Age of development (new, moderate, old) _____

**B. Exterior Factors**

Privacy _____

Roadway (public street, private street, safety for children) _____

Sidewalks (adequacy of drainage) _____

Driveway (public, private, semi-private) _____

Garage _____

- Reserved space (one or two cars) _____
- Automatic garage doors _____
- Security _____
- Adequate visitor parking _____

Construction material (brick, wood, stone) _____

Siding (aluminum, other) _____

Condition of paint _____

Roof:

- Type of material _____
- Age _____
- Condition _____

Balcony or patios:

- Location (view, etc.) _____
- Privacy _____

- Size                                                                    _____
- Open or enclosed                                                        _____

Landscaping:

- Trees                                                                   _____
- Shrubbery, flowers                                                      _____
- Lawns                                                                   _____
- Automatic sprinklers                                                    _____

Condition and upkeep of exterior                                          _____

## C. Interior Factors

Intercom system                                                          _____

Medical alert system                                                     _____

Fire safety system (fire alarms, smoke detectors, sprinklers)            _____

Burglar alarm system                                                    _____

General safety:

- TV surveillance                                                        _____
- Controlled access                                                      _____

Pre-wired for television and telephone cable                             _____

Lobby:

- Cleanliness                                                            _____
- Decor                                                                  _____
- Security guard                                                         _____

Public corridors:

- Material used                                                          _____
- Condition                                                              _____
- Plaster (free of cracks, stains)                                       _____
- Decor                                                                  _____

Stairs:

- General accessibility                                                  _____
- Number of stairwells                                                   _____

Elevators                                                                _____

Wheelchair accessibility                                                 _____

Storage facilities:

- Location                                                               _____
- Size                                                                   _____

Insulation: (The R factor is the measure of heating and
cooling efficiency; the higher the R factor, the more efficient)

- R rating in walls (minimum of R-19; depends
  on geographic location)                                               _____

- R rating in ceiling (minimum of R-30; depends on geographic location)   _____
- Heat pumps   _____
- Windows (insulated, storm, screen)   _____

Temperature controls:
- Individually controlled   _____
- Convenient location   _____

Plumbing:
- Functions well   _____
- Convenient fixtures   _____
- Quietness of plumbing   _____

Suitable water pressure   _____

Heating and air conditioning (gas, electric, hot water, oil)   _____

Utility costs:
- Gas   _____
- Electric   _____
- Other   _____

Laundry facilities   _____

Soundproofing features   _____

### D. Management

Apartment management company   _____

Condominium management company   _____

Owner-managed   _____

Resident manager   _____

Management personnel:
- Front desk   _____
- Maintenance   _____
- Gardener   _____
- Trash removal   _____
- Snow removal   _____
- Security (number of guards, hours, location, patrol)   _____

### E. Condominium Corporation

Experience of directors of corporation   _____

Average age of other owners   _____

### F. Recreation Facilities (if condominium or apartment building)

Clubhouse   _____

Club membership fees (included, not included)   _____

Sports:
- Courts (tennis, squash, racquetball, handball, basketball)    _____
- Games room (ping-pong, billiards)    _____
- Exercise room    _____
- Bicycle path/jogging track    _____
- Organized sports and activities    _____

Children's playground:
- Location (accessibility)    _____
- Noise factor    _____
- Organized sports and activities (supervised)    _____

Swimming pool:
- Location (outdoor, indoor)    _____
- Children's pool    _____
- Noise factor    _____

Visitors' accommodation    _____

## G. Individual Unit (if condominium or apartment building)

Location in complex    _____

Size of unit    _____

Is the floor plan and layout suitable?    _____

Will your furnishings fit in?    _____

Is the unit exposed to the sunlight?    _____

Does the unit have a scenic view?    _____

Is the unit in a quiet location (away from
garbage unit, elevator noise, playgrounds, etc.)?    _____

Accessibility (stairs, elevators, fire exits)    _____

Closets:
- Number    _____
- Location    _____

Carpet:
- Colour    _____
- Quality/texture    _____

Hardwood floors    _____

Living room:
- Size/shape    _____
- Windows/view    _____
- Sunlight (morning, afternoon)    _____
- Fireplace    _____
- Privacy (from outside, from rest of condo)    _____

Dining room:
- Size      _____
- Accessibility to kitchen      _____
- Windows/view      _____

Den or family room:
- Size/shape      _____
- Windows/view (morning or afternoon sunlight)      _____
- Fireplace      _____
- Privacy (from outside, from rest of condo)      _____

Laundry room:
- Workspace available      _____
- Washer and dryer      _____
- Size/capacity      _____
- Warranty coverage      _____

Kitchen:
- Size      _____
- Eating facility (table, nook, no seating)      _____
- Floors (linoleum, tile, wood)      _____
- Exhaust system      _____
- Countertop built in      _____
- Countertop material      _____
- Workspace      _____
- Kitchen cabinets (number, accessibility)      _____
- Cabinet material      _____
- Sink (size, single, double)      _____
- Sink material      _____
- Built-in cutting boards      _____
- Oven (single, double, self-cleaning)      _____
- Gas or electric oven      _____
- Age of oven      _____
- Microwave (size)      _____
- Age of microwave      _____
- Refrigerator/freezer (size/capacity)      _____
- Refrigerator (frost-free, ice maker, single/double door)      _____
- Age of refrigerator      _____
- Dishwasher (age)      _____
- Trash compactor/garbage disposal      _____
- Pantry or storage area      _____
- Is there warranty coverage on all appliances?      _____

Number of bedrooms                                           _____

Master bedroom:

- Size/shape                                               _____

- Privacy (from outside, from rest of condo)              _____

- Closets/storage space                                   _____

- Fireplace                                               _____

- Floor and wall covering                                 _____

Master bathroom (en suite):

- Size                                                    _____

- Bathtub                                                 _____

- Whirlpool tub/jacuzzi                                   _____

- Shower                                                  _____

- Steam room                                              _____

- Vanity                                                  _____

- Sink (single, double, integrated sink bowls)           _____

- Medicine cabinet                                        _____

Number of bathrooms                                          _____

Complete, or sink and toilet only?                           _____

Overall condition of condo, apartment, or house              _____

Overall appearance and decor of condo,
apartment, or house                                          _____

### H. Legal and Financial Matters

Project documents (e.g., disclosure/declaration)
received and read (if new condominium)                       _____

Bylaws received and read (if condominium)                    _____

Rules and regulations received and read
(if condominium or apartment)                                _____

Financial statements received and read
(if condominium or revenue-generating property)              _____

Condo council minutes, and annual general meeting and
special general meeting minutes over past two years received
and read (if condominium or revenue-generating property)     _____

No litigation or pending litigation                          _____

No outstanding or pending special assessments                _____

No pending repairs, or leaky condo problems                  _____

Other documents (list):

- _____              _____

- _____              _____

- _____              _____

- _____              _____

All above documentation (as applicable) reviewed by
your lawyer and legal advice on investment obtained     _____

Financial statements reviewed by your accountant
and tax advice on investment obtained     _____

All assessments, maintenance fees, and taxes detailed     _____

Condominium corporation insurance coverage adequate     _____

Restrictions acceptable (e.g., pets, renting of unit,
number of people living in suite, children, etc.)
for rental property     _____

All verbal promises or representations of sales representative
or vendor's agent that you are relying on written into
the offer to purchase     _____

Other

- _____     _____
- _____     _____
- _____     _____
- _____     _____

# CHECKLIST 2: Mortgage Checklist
## (See Chapter 5)

### A. Ask Yourself These Questions

1.  Is your income secure?                                                   _____

2.  Will your income increase or decrease in the future?                     _____

3.  Are you planning on increasing the size of your family
    (e.g., children, relatives) and therefore your living expenses?          _____

4.  Will you be able to put aside a financial buffer for unexpected
    expenses or emergencies?                                                 _____

5.  Are you planning to purchase the property with someone else?             _____

6.  If you answered yes, will you be able to depend on your
    partner's financial contribution without interruption?                  _____

7.  If you rely on an income from renting out all or part of your
    purchase, have you determined:

    • If city zoning and use bylaws permit it?                               _____

    • If the condominium corporation bylaws permit it?                       _____

    • If the mortgage company policies permit it?                            _____

8.  Have you thoroughly compared mortgage rates and features
    so that you know what type of mortgage and mortgage company
    you want?                                                                _____

9.  Have you determined the amount of mortgage for which you will
    be eligible?                                                             _____

10. Have you considered the benefits of a pre-approved mortgage?            _____

11. Have you considered talking to a mortgage broker?                        _____

12. Have you considered assuming an existing mortgage?                       _____

13. Have you considered the benefits of a portable mortgage?                 _____

14. Have you considered having the vendor give you a mortgage?               _____

15. Have you determined all the expenses you will incur relating
    to the purchase transaction? (See Checklist 3.)                         _____

16. Have you completed your present and projected financial needs
    analysis (income and expenses)? (See Form 1.)                          _____

17. Have you completed the mortgage application form, including
    net-worth statement (assets and liabilities)? (See Form 2.)            _____

### B. Ask the Lender These Questions

Interest Rates

18. What is the current interest rate?                                       _____

19. How frequently is the interest calculated? (Semi-annually, monthly, etc.) _____

20. What is the effective interest rate on an annual basis? _____

21. How long will the lender guarantee a quoted interest rate? _____

22. Will the lender put the above guarantee in writing? _____

23. Will you receive a lower rate of interest if the rates fall before you finalize your mortgage? _____

24. Will the lender put the above reduction assurance in writing? _____

25. Will the lender show you the total amount of interest you will have to pay over the lifetime of the mortgage? _____

## Amortization

26. What options do you have for amortization periods (10, 15 years, etc.)? _____

27. Will the lender provide you with an amortization schedule for your loan showing your monthly payments apportioned into principal and interest? _____

28. Have you calculated what your monthly payments will be based on each amortization rate? _____

29. Are you required to maintain the amortized monthly payment schedule if annual pre-payments are made, or will they be adjusted accordingly? _____

## Term of the Mortgage

30. What different terms are available (six months, one, two, three, five years, etc.)? _____

31. What is the best term for your personal circumstances? _____

32. What are the different interest rates available relating to the different terms? _____

## Payments

33. What is the amount of your monthly payments (based on amortization period)? _____

34. Are you permitted to increase the amount of your monthly payments if you want to without penalty? _____

35. Does the lender have a range of payment periods available, such as weekly, biweekly, monthly, etc.? _____

36. What is the best payment period in your personal circumstances? _____

Prepayment

37. What are your prepayment privileges?

   • Completely open?　　　　　　　　　　　　_____

   • Open with a fixed penalty or notice requirement?　_____

   • Limited open with no penalty or notice requirement?　_____

   • Limited open with fixed penalty or notice requirement?　_____

   • Completely closed?　　　　　　　　　　　　_____

   • Some combination of the above?　　　　　　_____

38. What amount can be prepaid and what is the penalty or notice required, if applicable?　　_____

39. How long does the privilege apply in each of the above categories, if applicable?　　_____

40. When does the prepayment privilege commence (six months, one year, anytime, etc.)?　　_____

41. Is there a minimum amount that has to be prepaid?　_____

42. What form does your prepayment privilege take—increase in payments or lump sum?　　_____

43. Is your prepayment privilege cumulative (e.g., make last year's lump sum prepayment next year)?　　_____

Taxes

44. How much are the property taxes?　　_____

45. Does the lender require a property tax payment monthly (based on projected annual tax), or is it optional?　　_____

46. Does the lender pay interest on the property tax account? If yes, what is the interest rate?　　_____

Mortgage Transaction Fees and Expenses

47. What is the appraisal fee? Is an appraisal necessary?　_____

48. What is the survey fee? Is a survey necessary?　　_____

49. Will you be able to select a lawyer of your choice to do the mortgage work?　　_____

50. Does the lender charge a processing or administrative fee?　_____

51. Does the lender arrange for a lawyer to do the mortgage documentation work at a flat fee, regardless of the amount of the mortgage?　　_____

52. Does the lender know what the out-of-pocket disbursements for the mortgage transaction will be?　　_____

53. Does the mortgage have a renewal administration fee?
    How much is it? _____

## Mortgage Assumption Privileges

54. Can the mortgage be assumed if the property is sold? _____

55. Is the mortgage assumable with or without the lender's approval? _____

56. What are the assumption administrative fees, if any? _____

57. Will the lender release the vendor of all personal obligations
    under the terms of the mortgage if it is assumed? _____

## Portability

58. Is the mortgage portable (can you transfer it to another property
    that you may buy)? _____

# CHECKLIST 3: Real Estate Purchase Expenses Checklist
## (See Chapter 4)

In addition to the actual purchase price of your investment, there are other expenses to be paid on or prior to closing. Not all of these expenses will be applicable. Some provinces may have additional expenses.

| Type of Expense | When Paid | Estimated Amount |
|---|---|---|
| Deposits | At time of offer | _____ |
| Mortgage application fee | At time of application | _____ |
| Property appraisal | At time of mortgage application | _____ |
| Property inspection | At inspection | _____ |
| Balance of purchase price | On closing | _____ |
| Legal fees for property transfer | On closing | _____ |
| Legal fees for mortgage preparation | On closing | _____ |
| Legal disbursements for property transfer | On closing | _____ |
| Legal disbursements for mortgage preparation | On closing | _____ |
| Mortgage broker commission | On closing | _____ |
| Property survey | On closing | _____ |
| Property tax holdback (by mortgage company) | On closing | _____ |
| Land transfer or deed tax (provincial) | On closing | _____ |
| Property purchase tax (provincial) | On closing | _____ |
| Property tax (local/municipal) adjustment | On closing | _____ |
| GST/HST | On closing | _____ |
| New Home Warranty Program fee | On closing | _____ |
| Mortgage interest adjustment (by mortgage company) | On closing | _____ |
| Sales tax on chattels purchased from vendor (provincial) | On closing | _____ |
| Adjustments for fuel, taxes, etc. | On closing | _____ |
| Mortgage lender insurance premium (CMHC or Genworth) | On closing | _____ |
| Condominium maintenance fee adjustment | On closing | _____ |

| | | |
|---|---|---|
| Building insurance | On closing | _____ |
| Life insurance premium on amount of outstanding mortgage | On closing | _____ |
| Moving expenses | At time of move | _____ |
| Utility connection charges | At time of move | _____ |
| Redecorating and refurbishing costs | Shortly after purchase | _____ |
| Immediate repair and maintenance costs | Shortly after purchase | _____ |
| House and garden improvements | Shortly after purchase | _____ |
| Other expenses (list): | | |
| _____ | _____ | _____ |
| _____ | _____ | _____ |
| _____ | _____ | _____ |
| TOTAL CASH REQUIRED | | $ _____ |

# CHECKLIST 4: Business Deductions Checklist
## (See Chapter 7)

*Note:* The tax laws are constantly changing, so be sure to verify annually the following deductible items with a professionally qualified accountant or other tax authority. Some exceptions to the following deductions may apply.

- Accounting or bookkeeping services
- Advertising expenses
- Automobile expenses
- Bad debts/bounced cheques
- Books related to business
- Business development expenses
- Business gifts
- Cable charges (TV, Internet)
- Cleaning services (supplies, equipment, service)
- Commissions (sales representatives, agents, others)
- Computer hardware and software (depreciated)
- Consulting fees
- Delivery charges
- Donations (charitable or business-related)
- Dues to professional organizations
- Educational expenses (business seminars, workshops, classes, handbooks, manuals)
- Entertainment (e.g., meals), business-related (50% deductible; must be carefully documented)
- Equipment purchases (may be depreciated or expensed)
- Freight and shipping charges
- House-related expenses (mortgage interest, depreciation, utilities, services, repairs)
- Internet charges
- Insurance premiums (special riders on homeowner's policy, e.g., computer insurance, etc.)
- Interest on business loans or charge cards, bank charges
- Labour costs (independent contractors or employees)
- Lease payments (equipment, etc.)
- Legal and professional fees
- Licences and permits
- Maintenance contracts on office equipment and other repairs
- Membership fees in business-related organizations

- Office furnishings (depreciated)
- Office supplies
- Postage
- Rent (apartment or house)
- Safety deposit box (if it holds documents related to business)
- Salaries (including those paid to spouse or children)
- Salary expense (employer's contributions to CPP, EI, WCB, etc.)
- Stationery and printing
- Subscriptions to business magazines and periodicals
- Supplies and materials
- Tax preparer's fee
- Telephone (equipment, monthly service charges, long-distance calls, etc.)
- Telephone-answering service/machine
- Travel expenses connected with business (meals and lodging for overnight stays, airfare, train, bus, taxi, auto expenses, tips, tolls)
- Other (itemize)

## CHECKLIST 5:  Landlord and Tenant Suite-Inspection Checklist
### (See Chapter 10)

Apartment number: _____  Apartment address: _____
Modify this checklist as necessary.

| ITEM | Poor = 1 | 2 | 3 | 4 | 5 = Excellent | Landlord/Tenant |
|------|----------|---|---|---|---------------|-----------------|
| | | | CONDITION | | | INITIALS |
| **Kitchen** | | | | | | |
| Drawers | 1 | 2 | 3 | 4 | 5 | _____ _____ |
| Countertop | 1 | 2 | 3 | 4 | 5 | _____ _____ |
| Table (built-in or nook) | 1 | 2 | 3 | 4 | 5 | _____ _____ |
| Sink | 1 | 2 | 3 | 4 | 5 | _____ _____ |
| Windows | 1 | 2 | 3 | 4 | 5 | _____ _____ |
| Screens | 1 | 2 | 3 | 4 | 5 | _____ _____ |
| Cupboards | 1 | 2 | 3 | 4 | 5 | _____ _____ |
| Doors | 1 | 2 | 3 | 4 | 5 | _____ _____ |
| Floor | 1 | 2 | 3 | 4 | 5 | _____ _____ |
| Ceiling | 1 | 2 | 3 | 4 | 5 | _____ _____ |
| Walls | 1 | 2 | 3 | 4 | 5 | _____ _____ |
| **Dining Room** | | | | | | |
| Floor | 1 | 2 | 3 | 4 | 5 | _____ _____ |
| Ceiling | 1 | 2 | 3 | 4 | 5 | _____ _____ |
| Walls | 1 | 2 | 3 | 4 | 5 | _____ _____ |
| Carpet | 1 | 2 | 3 | 4 | 5 | _____ _____ |
| Doors | 1 | 2 | 3 | 4 | 5 | _____ _____ |
| Hanging light | 1 | 2 | 3 | 4 | 5 | _____ _____ |
| **Living Room** | | | | | | |
| Bookcase | 1 | 2 | 3 | 4 | 5 | _____ _____ |
| Fireplace | 1 | 2 | 3 | 4 | 5 | _____ _____ |
| Windows | 1 | 2 | 3 | 4 | 5 | _____ _____ |
| Screens | 1 | 2 | 3 | 4 | 5 | _____ _____ |
| Doors | 1 | 2 | 3 | 4 | 5 | _____ _____ |
| Ceilings | 1 | 2 | 3 | 4 | 5 | _____ _____ |
| Walls | 1 | 2 | 3 | 4 | 5 | _____ _____ |
| Carpet | 1 | 2 | 3 | 4 | 5 | _____ _____ |

| ITEM | Poor = 1 | 2 | 3 | 4 | 5 = Excellent | Landlord/Tenant | |
|---|---|---|---|---|---|---|---|
| **CONDITION** | | | | | | **INITIALS** | |
| Bedroom #1 | | | | | | | |
| Closet | 1 | 2 | 3 | 4 | 5 | ____ | ____ |
| Drapes | 1 | 2 | 3 | 4 | 5 | ____ | ____ |
| Lights | 1 | 2 | 3 | 4 | 5 | ____ | ____ |
| Floor | 1 | 2 | 3 | 4 | 5 | ____ | ____ |
| Ceiling | 1 | 2 | 3 | 4 | 5 | ____ | ____ |
| Walls | 1 | 2 | 3 | 4 | 5 | ____ | ____ |
| Windows | 1 | 2 | 3 | 4 | 5 | ____ | ____ |
| Screens | 1 | 2 | 3 | 4 | 5 | ____ | ____ |
| Doors | 1 | 2 | 3 | 4 | 5 | ____ | ____ |
| Carpet | 1 | 2 | 3 | 4 | 5 | ____ | ____ |
| Thermostat | 1 | 2 | 3 | 4 | 5 | ____ | ____ |
| Bedroom #2 | | | | | | | |
| Closet | 1 | 2 | 3 | 4 | 5 | ____ | ____ |
| Drapes | 1 | 2 | 3 | 4 | 5 | ____ | ____ |
| Lights | 1 | 2 | 3 | 4 | 5 | ____ | ____ |
| Floor | 1 | 2 | 3 | 4 | 5 | ____ | ____ |
| Ceiling | 1 | 2 | 3 | 4 | 5 | ____ | ____ |
| Walls | 1 | 2 | 3 | 4 | 5 | ____ | ____ |
| Windows | 1 | 2 | 3 | 4 | 5 | ____ | ____ |
| Screens | 1 | 2 | 3 | 4 | 5 | ____ | ____ |
| Doors | 1 | 2 | 3 | 4 | 5 | ____ | ____ |
| Carpet | 1 | 2 | 3 | 4 | 5 | ____ | ____ |
| Thermostat | 1 | 2 | 3 | 4 | 5 | ____ | ____ |
| Bedroom #3 | | | | | | | |
| Closet | 1 | 2 | 3 | 4 | 5 | ____ | ____ |
| Drapes | 1 | 2 | 3 | 4 | 5 | ____ | ____ |
| Lights | 1 | 2 | 3 | 4 | 5 | ____ | ____ |
| Floor | 1 | 2 | 3 | 4 | 5 | ____ | ____ |
| Ceiling | 1 | 2 | 3 | 4 | 5 | ____ | ____ |
| Walls | 1 | 2 | 3 | 4 | 5 | ____ | ____ |
| Windows | 1 | 2 | 3 | 4 | 5 | ____ | ____ |
| Screens | 1 | 2 | 3 | 4 | 5 | ____ | ____ |
| Doors | 1 | 2 | 3 | 4 | 5 | ____ | ____ |
| Carpet | 1 | 2 | 3 | 4 | 5 | ____ | ____ |
| Thermostat | 1 | 2 | 3 | 4 | 5 | ____ | ____ |

| ITEM | CONDITION Poor = 1 | 2 | 3 | 4 | 5 = Excellent | INITIALS Landlord/Tenant |
|---|---|---|---|---|---|---|
| **Bathroom** | | | | | | |
| Sink | 1 | 2 | 3 | 4 | 5 | _____  _____ |
| Toilet tank | 1 | 2 | 3 | 4 | 5 | _____  _____ |
| Toilet seat | 1 | 2 | 3 | 4 | 5 | _____  _____ |
| Shower (door, curtain) | 1 | 2 | 3 | 4 | 5 | _____  _____ |
| Bathtub | 1 | 2 | 3 | 4 | 5 | _____  _____ |
| Shower head | 1 | 2 | 3 | 4 | 5 | _____  _____ |
| Door | 1 | 2 | 3 | 4 | 5 | _____  _____ |
| Walls | 1 | 2 | 3 | 4 | 5 | _____  _____ |
| Ceiling | 1 | 2 | 3 | 4 | 5 | _____  _____ |
| Floor | 1 | 2 | 3 | 4 | 5 | _____  _____ |
| Windows | 1 | 2 | 3 | 4 | 5 | _____  _____ |
| Screens | 1 | 2 | 3 | 4 | 5 | _____  _____ |
| Towel racks | 1 | 2 | 3 | 4 | 5 | _____  _____ |
| Cabinet | 1 | 2 | 3 | 4 | 5 | _____  _____ |
| Tissue holder | 1 | 2 | 3 | 4 | 5 | _____  _____ |
| Countertop | 1 | 2 | 3 | 4 | 5 | _____  _____ |
| Mirror | 1 | 2 | 3 | 4 | 5 | _____  _____ |
| **Common Areas** | | | | | | |
| Front hallway | 1 | 2 | 3 | 4 | 5 | _____  _____ |
| Floor | 1 | 2 | 3 | 4 | 5 | _____  _____ |
| Ceiling | 1 | 2 | 3 | 4 | 5 | _____  _____ |
| Walls | 1 | 2 | 3 | 4 | 5 | _____  _____ |
| Lights | 1 | 2 | 3 | 4 | 5 | _____  _____ |
| Carpet | 1 | 2 | 3 | 4 | 5 | _____  _____ |
| Stairwells | 1 | 2 | 3 | 4 | 5 | _____  _____ |
| **Upper** | | | | | | |
| • floor | 1 | 2 | 3 | 4 | 5 | _____  _____ |
| • ceiling | 1 | 2 | 3 | 4 | 5 | _____  _____ |
| • walls | 1 | 2 | 3 | 4 | 5 | _____  _____ |
| **Lower** | | | | | | |
| • floor | 1 | 2 | 3 | 4 | 5 | _____  _____ |
| • ceiling | 1 | 2 | 3 | 4 | 5 | _____  _____ |
| • walls | 1 | 2 | 3 | 4 | 5 | _____  _____ |

| ITEM | | CONDITION | | | | | INITIALS |
|------|---------|---|---|---|---------------|--------------|
| | Poor = 1 | 2 | 3 | 4 | 5 = Excellent | Landlord/Tenant |
| Thermostat | 1 | 2 | 3 | 4 | 5 | ____  ____ |
| Front door | 1 | 2 | 3 | 4 | 5 | ____  ____ |
| Rear door | 1 | 2 | 3 | 4 | 5 | ____  ____ |
| Basement | | | | | | |
| Washer | 1 | 2 | 3 | 4 | 5 | ____  ____ |
| Dryer | 1 | 2 | 3 | 4 | 5 | ____  ____ |
| Freezer | 1 | 2 | 3 | 4 | 5 | ____  ____ |
| Furnace | 1 | 2 | 3 | 4 | 5 | ____  ____ |
| Sink | 1 | 2 | 3 | 4 | 5 | ____  ____ |
| Floor | 1 | 2 | 3 | 4 | 5 | ____  ____ |
| Ceiling | 1 | 2 | 3 | 4 | 5 | ____  ____ |
| Walls | 1 | 2 | 3 | 4 | 5 | ____  ____ |
| Windows | 1 | 2 | 3 | 4 | 5 | ____  ____ |
| Screens | 1 | 2 | 3 | 4 | 5 | ____  ____ |
| Doors | 1 | 2 | 3 | 4 | 5 | ____  ____ |
| Other items | 1 | 2 | 3 | 4 | 5 | ____  ____ |

The apartment conditions are confirmed as of the date noted by our signatures below.

Date: _____ Tenant _____

Date: _____ Landlord _____

# CHECKLIST 6: Master Checklist for Successful Real Estate Investing
## (See Chapter 1)

1. Understand why real estate could be a good investment for you.
   - Learn the advantages and potential disadvantages of real estate investing.
   - Make a list of the advantages of investing in real estate.
   - Make a list of the disadvantages of investing in real estate.
2. Learn how the real estate market works.
   - Understand the cycles involved in the real estate market and how they work.
   - Understand what factors affect the real estate market and prices.
   - Understand when the best time is to buy and sell.
3. Educate yourself about real estate.
   - Take courses or seminars offered locally through school boards, colleges, institutes, universities, or private seminar companies.
   - Read books on real estate and real estate investment.
   - Familiarize yourself with mortgage tables, mortgage calculations, accounting, management, and real estate investment computer software and spreadsheets.
   - Familiarize yourself with on line mortgage calculators.
   - Search online for property opportunities, e.g., www.mls.ca.
   - Subscribe to newspapers, magazines, and newsletters that cover real estate issues.
   - Subscribe to free publications such as the *Royal LePage Canadian House Prices Survey* and the various Canada Mortgage and Housing Corporation (CMHC) surveys and forecasts.
   - Receive free weekly real estate publications possibly available in your community.
4. Analyze your present financial situation.
   - Determine your personal cost-of-living budget (income and expenses). Calculate your personal net worth (assets and liabilities).
   - Calculate your gross debt-service ratio (GDS).
   - Calculate your total debt-service ratio (TDS).
   - Determine the maximum amount of mortgage for which you are eligible.
   - Determine the maximum amount of mortgage with which you would feel comfortable.
   - Utilize online mortgage calculators.
5. Establish your investment goals.
   - Determine your real estate investment needs and goals in the short, medium, and long term.
   - Determine your personal and family needs and goals in the short, medium, and long term.

- Do a detailed and candid self-assessment. Prepare an objective analysis of your personal strengths, weaknesses, skills, talents, and goals, and compare them to the attributes required to invest in and manage real estate. If you assess that certain skills, etc., are needed, determine how you will acquire them.
- Determine what time and talent involvement you expect or require from your family.
- Do a SWOT (strengths, weaknesses, opportunities, and threats) analysis of your investment plans on a periodic basis.
- Develop a written investment strategic plan.
- Prepare a projected personal cash-flow statement over the next five years (monthly).
- Prepare a projected personal income and expense statement over the five next years (annually).
- Prepare a projected personal balance sheet (assets and liabilities) over the next five years (annually).
- Determine how much money you believe you will need to maintain your desired standard of living after retirement.
- Make sure you take into account the value of your money in real terms, in terms of buying power, after inflation is taken into account. Allow a factor of 3 per cent inflation each year. Of course, inflation might be less or more than 3 per cent at any given time.
- Determine the degree of financial risk you are prepared to take, if any.

6. Understand the basic real estate guidelines.
   - Learn the common rules of thumb used to quickly analyze a potential real estate investment. Recognize which methods are more or less reliable in determining the value of a property.
   - Always perform a thorough property analysis before deciding to seriously consider a property purchase.
   - Know how appraisers determine the value of property. Learn the various formulas that experts use to determine value.

7. Determine your desired degree of involvement in property management.
   - Determine if you want to do all the management yourself.
   - Determine if you want to employ a resident manager who lives in the building and deals with common problems that can occur or tasks that have to be performed. This may include collecting rents, renting apartments, cleaning apartments, and general building cleaning and maintenance.
   - Determine if you want to employ a professional property-management company to handle the investment. This may include finding tenants, collecting rent, paying bills, bookkeeping, maintenance, and overall management.

8. Select the type of investment ideal for your needs.
   - Review the various types of real estate investments that fit within your investment goals and needs.

- Look for the availability of the type of real estate investment that you are considering.
- Do your research and compare and contrast alternative properties.
- Determine if you will purchase the property yourself or with others.

9. Select your professional and business advisers carefully.
   - Lawyer
   - Accountant
   - Financial planner
   - Building inspector
   - Realtor
   - Insurance broker
   - Lender/mortgage broker

10. Determine the form of legal ownership of property.
    - Proprietorship
    - Partnership
    - Limited partnership
    - Limited company (corporation)
    - Joint tenancy
    - Tenants in common
    - Freehold
    - Leasehold

11. Locate your investment property.
    - Review the amount of money you have available for purchase purposes.
    - Review the maximum amount you are willing to pay for the property.
    - Review your real estate investment criteria.
    - Select the geographic area or areas in which you want to have your investment.
    - Obtain copies of all municipal zoning maps in the selected investment area, as well as any municipal zoning regulations that may affect your purchase. Find out future policy plans for the specific street area that you intend to purchase in, e.g., rezoning from existing single- to multi-family.
    - Obtain a municipal street map showing the geographic area in detail.
    - Contact your realtors and provide them with the guidelines of what you are looking for. Have them utilize the MLS, if they are on it, to search for properties within your guidelines.
    - Review all real estate newspapers in your area to become aware of what is available in your areas of interest, as not all listings are on MLS.
    - Read the real estate section of local newspapers under the types of property you are looking for, such as houses, condominiums, apartment buildings, etc.
    - Research the market thoroughly in every way, using the guidelines and checklists in this book.

- Shortlist three potential purchases that fall within your investment criteria, then negotiate for the best overall price and package. Make sure that you put in conditions to give yourself room to get out of the deal if need be, and to satisfy all your needs.

- Consult with your lawyer and tax accountant to make sure that you have covered everything necessary in the offer, either before making the offer or after making the offer, but with the condition that the offer is subject to your lawyer's and accountant's approval.

12. Analyze your prospective investment property.

- Have all details, essential information, and representations verified in writing. Make sure that the financial information is accurate, especially the income and expense statement.

- Make sure you have compared your prospective investment with other alternative choices.

- Complete an initial property analysis using a system that you understand and that works for you. Develop a prepared form that will have all the critical factors for comparative and evaluative purposes that you need to know. This would include factors such as lot size, age of property, price, rent breakdown per unit, vacancy history, financing, expenses, income, tax benefits, rezoning potential, etc.

- Make sure that the property makes financial sense or don't buy it.

- Make sure that you obtain your accountant's and lawyer's opinions before finally committing yourself to a purchase.

13. Utilize the most effective financing techniques.

- Familiarize yourself with the many conventional and creative financing techniques.

- Determine the amount of financing with which you feel comfortable. Some people, especially with principal residences, want to put in as much down payment as possible because the interest on the mortgage is not deductible (unless you are writing off a portion as a home office). Others want to have high-ratio financing of 90 per cent and put down just 10 per cent, so that they have cash available for other purposes. Some people worry about mortgage debt and feel uncomfortable having more than their threshold level.

- Determine which financing technique meets your investment objectives, e.g., 30-year amortization period because of lower monthly payments, vendor-take-back financing to save on bank financing, or assuming an existing mortgage because of lower interest rates.

- Prepare your reasons for requesting the financing package to sell the vendor and/or lender.

- Be aware of the benefits and pitfalls of leveraging your real estate investment, e.g., borrowing on increasing equity.

14. Consider the tax implications.

- Obtain all the documentation and information you can about the financial aspects of the investment for review and analysis.

- Analyze your investment from a tax perspective. The important thing is not the amount of money you make but the amount you can keep after taxes.

- Analyze your investment from the perspective of how you should structure the initial purchase. For example, if you are buying a small apartment building, you would want to structure the allocation of value given for leasehold improvements, building, land, chattels, and goodwill (if any) to be to your benefit. This is part of your initial negotiating.

- Analyze your investment from the tax perspective of the legal ownership and nature of ownership. For example, principal residence with or without rental suite, revenue property, single or joint ownership, capital gains exemption implications, etc.

- Make sure that you obtain the advice of a professional accountant (CA or CGA) who is knowledgeable on the tax aspects of real estate investment before you commit yourself to a purchase.

15. Consider the legal implications.

- Analyze your purchase in terms of issues such as ownership, control, and management.

- Decide if you want to purchase through a limited liability company or in your personal name.

- Determine if you want to purchase the property with partners and, if so, make sure the arrangement is clearly documented in writing in advance.

- Make sure that you insert appropriate conditions in the agreement of purchase and sale to protect your interests.

- Make sure that you obtain the advice of a lawyer who specializes in real estate before you submit an offer of purchase and sale. An alternative is to put a condition in the offer that the agreement has to meet the approval of the purchaser's lawyer. The advantage of the first approach is that it is easier to make the terms of the first offer the best terms, rather than attempting to change the terms later after speaking with a lawyer.

16. Negotiate the purchase.

- Determine your best terms for an agreement and your bottom-line fallback position in advance, after advance consultation with your lawyer and, if you are intending to generate revenue from your investment, after speaking with your accountant.

- Determine your persuasive reasons for your negotiating position, so that you can convince the vendor through the realtor.

- Make sure that you feel comfortable with the terms of the offer with regard to the overall package.

- Insert all the necessary conditions in the agreement for your protection, e.g., receipt and verification by your accountant of income and expense statements.

- Make sure you understand the real estate market and the value to you of the property, and make sure you have alternative property options so that you can make realistic decisions comparatively.

- Make sure that you have assessed the property objectively, using the checklists in this book.

- Offer less than the listing price. How much less depends on each individual situation? Look for reasons why the property is worth less to you than the asking price.

- Determine the factors that are motivating the vendor to sell.

- Make sure that you have listed all items that are part of the purchase price and all documents that you want from the vendor.

- Never buy a property without viewing it thoroughly inside and outside, and on several occasions beforehand. Be very cautious about buying a property that is more than a three-hour drive from where you live.

- Make sure that you are satisfied with the overall deal before removing the conditions in the agreement and thereby having a firm legal commitment.

17. Take necessary steps before and after closing the purchase.

   - Make sure you have selected a lawyer who is experienced in the type of real estate purchase you are making; e.g., new or resale house, condominium, duplex, apartment building, raw land, renovation, property development, etc. Never attempt to close your own real estate transaction.

   - Ask your lawyer in advance what the anticipated fees and disbursement costs will be for the property transfer and mortgage.

   - Calculate realistically all your closing costs. See Checklist 3 on page 368.

   - Make an itemized list of all the documents or items you want to receive from the vendor at the time of closing. All these matters should have been referred to in the agreement of purchase and sale, so there is no misunderstanding.

   - Visit your property on the day of closing. Make sure that it is in the same condition as when you last inspected it.

   - Make a point of meeting your tenants, if it is a revenue property, as soon as convenient after you have purchased the property.

18. Set up a record-keeping system.

   - Keep your personal bank accounts separate from your revenue property accounts in order to simplify your bookkeeping.

   - Before closing the purchase, open up two separate bank accounts so you can order cheques and have the accounts ready for operation. One account is a chequing account for operational and management expenses relating to your revenue property, in other words for income and expenses. The second account is a savings account to hold the tenants' security deposits. In most provinces you have to pay interest on the security deposits of residential tenants.

   - Set up a bookkeeping and accounting system that is simple to understand and operate. You can use a manual or computerized system, depending on the number of tenants. Speak to your accountant. The key point is to set up a system that works for you. This will provide a convenient record for the purpose of completing your tax returns. There are excellent accounting and management software programs available.

19. Monitor your investment.

   - Monitor your investment on a regular basis, at least semi-annually.

   - Make sure that your real estate investment continues to meet the investment goals that you have set for yourself. If you are not getting the return on your investment you anticipated, or if you can anticipate that there will be unacceptable future expenses, or if you no longer enjoy dealing with the property, then consider selling it.

- Have your professional accountant advise you on the performance of your revenue investment, ideally every six months, to make sure that you are keeping your expenses as low as possible, keeping your income as high as possible, and minimizing personal and investment tax payable. For example, you may want to renew your mortgage if the interest rate is low for a longer period of time, e.g., three or five years or longer, rather than one year, depending on your long-term plans.

20. Structure the sale to meet your needs.

- Determine the basis on which you would like to sell before you buy. This is part of your advance planning.

- Make a decision to sell your property and set a price based on objective assessment of market reality rather than emotion.

- Don't be influenced to sell your property unless you believe, based on the facts, that the timing is right for you to sell.

- Consider the benefits of listing your property with a realtor on the MLS to maximize sale price and market exposure.

- Consider the advantages and disadvantages of vendor-back financing.

- Insert appropriate conditions to protect your interests, such as a 72-hour clause for the purchaser to remove conditions if another offer comes in.

- Attempt to negotiate as large a deposit as possible and attempt to negotiate that the deposit is non-refundable and goes directly to the vendor after all the purchaser's conditions are removed.

- Obtain your lawyer's and tax accountant's advice before accepting an offer.

21. Continue implementing your real estate investment goal plans.

- Remember to reassess your investment plans on a regular basis, based on your tax accountant's advice and your own evolving and changing needs, goals, and comfort zone.

- Refer back to the sequence of steps in this checklist for your next purchase.

- Be prudent about leveraging and pyramiding your real estate investments.

- Make sure that your property produces net positive income; that it is a viable investment as a revenue business.

- Make sure that you yourself verify the income and expenses and that you have control over your investment.

- Avoid high-risk, get-rich-quick schemes. Concentrate on sound real estate investment techniques.

# Glossary

## A

**Acceleration clause:** A clause written into a mortgage agreement to allow the lender to accelerate or call the entire principal balance of the mortgage, plus accrued interest, when the borrower is delinquent with payments.

**Adjusted cost base (ACB):** The value of real property established for tax purposes. It is the original cost plus any allowable capital improvements, certain acquisition costs and any mortgage interest costs, less any depreciation.

**Agreement of purchase and sale:** A written agreement between the owner and a purchaser for the purchase of real estate for a predetermined price and terms.

**Amenities:** Generally, those parts of the condominium or apartment building that are intended to beautify the premises and that are for the enjoyment of occupants rather than for utility.

**Amortization period:** The actual number of years it will take to repay a mortgage loan in full. This can be well in excess of the loan's term. For example, mortgages often have 5-year terms but 25-year amortization periods.

**Amortization:** The reduction of a loan through periodic payments in which interest is charged only on the unpaid balance.

**Analysis of property:** The systematic method of determining the performance of investment real estate using a property analysis form.

**Appraised value:** An estimate of the property's fair market value, usually performed by an appraiser.

**Arbitrator:** A person chosen to settle a dispute between the landlord and tenant, or a landlord and any other party.

**Arrears:** The overdue payments owing on either a mortgage or a lease; it also refers to the state of being late in fulfilling the obligations of the mortgage or lease agreement.

**Assessment fee:** A monthly fee that condominium owners must pay, usually including management fees, costs of common property upkeep, heating costs, garbage-removal costs, the owner's contribution to the contingency reserve fund, and so on. In the case of time-shares, the fee is normally levied annually. Also referred to as the maintenance fee.

**Assign:** The act of transferring ownership of or responsibility for a property to a purchaser or tenant; usually a step that occurs prior to the original owner or tenant completing the purchase or lease term. The assignee assumes the right to purchase a property, or becomes the subtenant of the original tenant.

**Assumption agreement:** A legal document signed by a home buyer that requires the buyer to assume responsibility for the obligations of a mortgage made by the previous owner.

# B

**Balance sheet:** A statement that indicates the financial status of a condominium corporation or apartment building, or other revenue property, at a specific point in time by listing its assets and liabilities.

**Base rent:** The fixed rent paid by a tenant. This is separate from any rent paid as a result of extra charges or percentage rents.

**Blended payments:** Equal payments consisting of both a principal and an interest component, paid each month during the term of the mortgage. The principal portion increases each month, while the interest portion decreases, but the total monthly payment does not change.

**Breach:** The violation of a law, contract, or obligation.

**Budget:** An annual estimate of a condominium corporation or apartment building's expenses and the revenues needed to balance those expenses. There are operating budgets and capital budgets. (See also **Capital budget**.)

# C

**Canada Mortgage and Housing Corporation (CMHC):** The federal Crown corporation that administers the National Housing Act. The CMHC services include providing housing information and assistance, financing, and insuring home-purchase loans for lenders.

**Canada Revenue Agency (CRA):** The federal agency responsible for collecting taxes on behalf of the federal government; formerly known as Revenue Canada, a name many people (and even some agency staff) continue to use when referring to it.

**Canadian Real Estate Association (CREA):** An association of members of the real estate industry, principally real estate agents and brokers.

**Capital budget:** An estimate of costs to cover replacements and improvements, and the corresponding revenues needed to balance them, usually for a 12-month period. Different from an operating budget.

**Capital gain:** Profit on the sale of an asset that is subject to taxation.

**Capital improvements:** Major improvements made to a property that are written off over several years rather than expensed off in the year in which they are made.

**Capitalization rate (cap rate):** The percentage of return on an investment when purchased on a free-and-clear or all-cash basis.

**Charge:** A document registered against a property, stating that someone has or believes he or she has a claim on the property.

**Closing costs:** The expenses over and above the purchase price of buying and selling real estate.

**Closing date:** The date on which the sale of a property becomes final and the new owner takes possession.

**Closing:** The actual completion of the transaction acknowledging satisfaction of all legal and financial obligations between buyer and seller, and acknowledging the deed or transfer of title and disbursement of funds to appropriate parties.

**Collateral mortgage:** A loan backed up by a promissory note and the security of a mortgage on a property. The money borrowed may be used for the purchase of a property or for another purpose, such as home renovations or a vacation.

**Common area:** The area in a condominium project that is shared by all of the condominium owners, such as elevators, hallways, and parking lots.

**Common-area maintenance fee:** The charge to owners to maintain the common areas, normally due on a monthly basis.

**Condominium corporation:** The condominium association of unit owners incorporated under some provincial condominium legislation, automatically at the time of registration of the project. It is called a strata corporation in British Columbia. Under each of the provincial statutes, it will differ from an ordinary corporation in many respects. The condominium corporation, unlike a private business corporation, usually does not enjoy limited liability, and any judgment against the corporation for the payment of money is usually a judgment against each owner. The objects of the corporation are to manage the property and any assets of the corporation, and its duties include effecting compliance by the owners with the requirements of the Act, the declaration, the bylaws, and the rules.

**Condominium:** A housing unit to which the owner has title and of which the owner also owns a share in the common area (such as elevators, hallways, swimming pool and land).

**Condominium council:** The governing body of the condominium corporation, elected at the annual general meeting of the corporation.

**Conventional mortgage:** A mortgage loan that does not exceed 75 per centof the appraised value or of the purchase price of the property, whichever is the less. Mortgages that exceed this limit generally must be insured by mortgage insurance, such as that provided by CMHC and Genworth Financial Canada.

**Conversion:** The changing of a structure from some other use, such as a rental apartment to a condominium apartment.

**Conveyancing:** The transfer of property, or title to property, from one party to another.

**Credit bureau:** An agency that maintains credit files, such as Equifax and others.

**Credit check:** A report typically run to review the credit history of an individual to assist in determining whether or not the individual is worthy of receiving credit.

**Credit file:** A history of past credit granted, debts owed, and the manner in which those debts were repaid. The file may also include information on a party's places of residence and employment history.

**Credit rating:** The score—usually expressed as a number—calculated using information in an individual's credit file. The credit rating is typically used to determine credit worthiness. The better the score, the more worthy of credit an individual is.

# D

**Damage deposit:** Also known as a tenant's or security deposit, the damage deposit is the amount of money given to a landlord when a tenancy begins to cover the expense of any damages to a property over the course of the tenancy. It is returned to the tenant on departure if the property has been left in good condition. Quebec is the only province where landlords cannot collect a damage deposit.

**Debt service:** Cost of paying interest for use of mortgage money.

**Deductions:** The expenses that the Canada Revenue Agency (CRA) allows one to deduct from gross income.

**Deed:** This document conveys the title of the property to the purchaser. Different terminology may be used in different provincial jurisdictions.

**Depreciation:** The amount by which a property owner writes off the value of a real estate investment over the life of the investment. Depreciation is not applicable to the value of land.

**Down payment:** An initial amount of money (in the form of cash) put forward by the purchaser. Usually it represents the difference between the purchase price and the amount of the mortgage loan.

# E

**Encumbrance:** See Charge.

**Equity return:** The percentage ratio between an owner's equity in a property and the total of cash flow plus mortgage principal reduction.

**Equity:** The difference between the price for which a property could be sold and the total debts registered against it.

**Escrow:** The holding of a deed or contract by a third party until fulfillment of certain stipulated conditions between the contracting parties.

**Estate:** The title or interest one has in property such as real estate and personal property that can, if desired, be passed on to survivors at the time of one's death.

**Eviction:** The removal, by force, of a tenant and his or her effects. The due legal process provided for this in each province must be followed.

# F

**Fair market value (FMV):** The value established on real property that is determined to be one that a buyer is willing to pay and for which a vendor is willing to sell.

**Fee simple:** A manner of owning land, in one's own name and free of any conditions, limitations, or restrictions.

**Financial statements:** Documents that show the financial status of the condominium corporation, apartment building, or other revenue property at a given point in time. Generally includes an income-and-expense statement and a balance sheet.

**Fiscal year:** The 12-month period in which financial affairs are calculated.

**Floating-rate mortgage:** Another term for variable-rate mortgage.

**Foreclosure:** A legal procedure whereby the lender obtains ownership of, or the right to sell, the property following default by the borrower.

**Freehold:** The outright ownership of land, or land and buildings; differs from leasehold.

# G

**Genworth Financial Canada:** A private company providing mortgage insurance in Canada.

**Goods and services tax (GST):** A value-added tax charged on goods and services, including all supply of "real property" (except residential rents and in other well-defined circumstances), in Canada. Sometimes harmonized with provincial sales taxes (see **harmonized sales tax**).

**Guarantor:** A party that guarantees to pay the debts of an individual in the event the individual is unable to pay the debts.

**Guarantor's letter:** A legal document by which the guarantor agrees to assume the debt of another party.

# H

**Harmonized sales tax (HST):** A value-added tax combining both federal and provincial sales taxes in Ontario, New Brunswick, Nova Scotia, and Newfoundland and Labrador. Charged on goods and services, including all supply of "real property" (except residential rents, and in other well-defined circumstances). See also **goods and services tax**.

**High-ratio mortgage:** A conventional mortgage loan that exceeds 75 per cent of the appraised value or purchase price of the property. Such a mortgage must be insured.

**Highrise:** Any multi-unit residential building of six or more stories.

**Human Rights Code:** The federal and provincial laws that define the basic rights of citizens. The code most commonly protects individuals to freedom from discrimination.

# I

**Income, gross:** Income or cash flow before expenses.

**Income, net:** Income or cash flow after expenses (but generally before income tax).

**Interest averaging:** The method of determining the overall average interest rate being paid when more than one mortgage is involved.

**Interim financing:** The temporary financing by a lender during the construction of real property for resale, or while awaiting other funds.

# J

**Judgment:** The official outcome of a lawsuit or other legal proceeding. The judgment may be financial or otherwise.

# K

**Key money:** Typically, the fee charged to secure or cut the keys at the start of a tenancy, or to replace the keys in the event of loss. It may also refer to a fee required to secure a spot on a waiting list for accommodation.

# L

**Landlord:** The party that rents or leases a premises to another party, called the tenant.

**Lease:** The agreement between a landlord and a tenant. Also, the act of securing rights to use a property for a given term under such an agreement. A sublease is the assignment of rights under the lease agreement to another party.

**Legal description:** Identification of a property that is recognized by law that identifies that property from all others.

**Lessee:** The tenant in rental space.

**Lessor:** The owner of the rental space.

**Letter of intent:** Used in place of a formal written contract with a deposit. The prospective purchaser informs the seller, in writing, that he or she is willing to enter into a formal purchase contract upon certain terms and conditions if they are acceptable to the seller.

**Leverage:** The use of financing or other people's money to control large pieces of real property with a small amount of invested capital.

**Limited partnership:** An investment group in which one partner serves as the general partner and the others as limited partners. The general partner bears all of the financial responsibility and management of the investment. The limited partners are obligated only to the extent of their original investment plus possible personal guarantees.

**Listings, exclusive agency:** A signed agreement by a seller in which he or she agrees to co-operate with one broker. All other brokers must go through the listing broker.

**Listings, multiple:** A system of agency amd subagency relationships. If broker A lists the property for sale, A is the vendor's agent. If broker B sees the MLS listing and offers it for sale, B is the vendor's subagent. See also **multiple listing service**.

**Listings, open:** A listing given to one or more brokers, none of whom have any exclusive rights or control over the sale, by other brokers or the owner of the property.

## M

**Marginal tax rate:** That point in income at which any additional income will be taxed at a higher tax rate.

**MLS:** See multiple listing service.

**Month-to-month:** A tenancy that renews each month, often under a commonly understood agreement between the landlord and tenant. Typically exists when tenancies continue after the term of a formal lease agreement.

**Mortgage wraparound:** Sometimes called an all-inclusive mortgage. A mortgage that includes any existing mortgages on the property. The buyer makes one large payment on the wraparound and the seller continues making the existing mortgage payments out of that payment.

**Mortgage, balloon:** A mortgage amortized over a number of years, but that requires the entire principal balance to be paid at a certain time, short of the full amortization period.

**Mortgage, constant:** The interest rate charged on a mortgage consisting of both the rate being charged by the lender and the rate that represents the amount of principal reduction each period.

**Mortgage, deferred payment:** A mortgage allowing for payments to be made on a deferred or delayed basis. Usually used where present income is insufficient to make the payments.

**Mortgage, discounted:** The selling of a mortgage to another party at a discount or an amount less than the face value of the mortgage.

**Mortgage, first:** A mortgage placed on a property in first position.

**Mortgage, fixed:** A conventional mortgage, with payments of interest and principal. Fixed terms with a fixed rate can vary from 6 months to 10 years or more.

**Mortgage, insurance:** Insurance provided by the lender as an option for the borrower. It would pay out the balance outstanding on the mortgage, in the event of the borrower's death.

**Mortgage, interest only:** Payments are made only of interest; the payment does not reduce the principal of the debt.

**Mortgage, points:** The interest rate charged by the lender.

**Mortgage, second:** A mortgage placed on a property in second position to an already existing first mortgage.

**Mortgage, variable:** A mortgage with an interest rate that fluctuates with the Bank of Canada interest rate. The mortgagee just pays the interest, with optional pay-down on the principal. Different from a fixed-rate mortgage (see **mortgage, fixed**).

**Mortgage:** The document that pledges real property as collateral for a debt.

**Mortgagee:** The lender.

**Mortgagor:** The borrower.

**Multiple listing service (MLS):** A service licensed to member real estate boards by the Canadian Real Estate Association. Used to compile and publish information in guides and online concerning a given property to a large number of agents and brokers.

# N

**National Housing Act (NHA) loan:** A mortgage loan that is insured by Canada Mortgage and Housing Corporation to certain maximums.

**Normal wear and tear:** The damage to a property that results from its normal use by tenants, and for which they cannot be held liable.

**Notice:** The written notification the landlord or tenant gives to the other announcing the end of a tenancy.

**NSF cheque:** A cheque for which there are not sufficient funds. The cheque is said to bounce because the bank returns the order for the transfer of funds, typically at a charge to the party trying to cash the cheque.

**Offer to purchase:** The document that sets forth all the terms and conditions under which a purchaser offers to purchase property. This offer, when accepted by the seller, becomes a binding agreement of purchase and sale once all conditions have been removed.

**Operating budget:** An estimate of costs to operate a building or condominium complex and corresponding revenues needed to balance them, usually for a 12-month period. Different from a capital budget.

**Operating costs:** Those expenses required to operate an investment property, generally excluding mortgage payments.

**Option agreement:** A contract, with consideration, presented to a purchaser of a property giving him or her the right to buy at a future date. If the individual chooses not to purchase, the deposit is forfeited to the seller.

## P

**Periodic tenancy:** A tenancy for a set period of time that's governed by the terms of a lease but for which the term of the tenancy is open-ended; that is, the tenancy continues on the same terms, week to week, or month to month, until such time as the parties give written notice to one another of the tenancy's end.

**Personal property:** Property in an investment property, such as carpeting, draperies and refrigerators, which depreciate over a shorter useful life than the structure itself.

**PI:** Principal and interest due on a mortgage.

**PIT:** Principal, interest, and taxes due on a mortgage.

**Post-dated cheque:** Any cheque written with a future date for the purposes of delivering payment on the date for which it is written.

**Prepayment penalty:** A penalty charge written into many mortgages that must be paid if the mortgage is paid off ahead of schedule.

**Principal:** The amount the purchaser actually borrowed, or the portion of it still owing on the original loan.

**Property manager:** A manager or management company hired to run an investment property for the owner.

**Purchase-and-sale agreement:** See agreement of purchase and sale.

**Pyramiding:** The process of building real estate wealth by allowing appreciation and mortgage principal reduction to increase the investors' equity in a series of ever larger properties.

## R

**Renew:** The act of entering a new lease or mortgage agreement following the end of a previous lease or agreement with the same party. A residential lease may renew automatically at the end of its term, whereas a mortgage is typically renegotiated.

**Rent assistance:** Assistance provided to tenants who cannot afford to pay rent. The type and range of assistance varies from organization to organization.

**Rent control:** Regulations that limit frequency with which a landlord can raise rent in a given period of time, and the amount by which the rent can be increased on each occasion.

**Rent:** The amount owing pursuant to a lease agreement for the use of a property; also the act of using a property under the terms of such an agreement.

**Rental agreement:** An agreement under which one party, the landlord, agrees to lease premises to another party, called the tenant.

**Rental application:** Filled out by a prospective tenant and often including an authorization to conduct a credit check, a landlord uses the application to determine the suitably of renting a unit to the individual. Questions on the rental application cannot violate the applicant's rights.

**Rental authority:** The organization, usually appointed by a province or territory, established to oversee landlord-tenant issues in the said province or territory.

**Resident manager:** An individual, usually living in the building, who handles all of the day-to-day problems therein.

**Roommate:** The co-occupant of the primary tenant of a rental apartment, who may or may not be listed on the rental agreement.

## S

**Sale/lease-back:** The tenant in a building sells it to an investor and leases it back for a period of years.

**Security deposit:** See damage deposit.

**Sublease:** Contract by which the lessee leases part of his or her premises to another user.

**Sublessee:** A party to whom a property is leased by an existing tenant.

**Sublet:** The act of renting property to another party while remaining fully responsible for the fulfillment of lease obligations to the primary landlord. Subletting differs from an assignment of a lease agreement, in which the responsibility for the fulfillment of the agreement falls to the new tenant. See **assign**.

## T

**Tax shelter:** The tax write-off possible through the depreciation benefits available on investment real estate ownership.

**Tenancy:** The term for which a tenant has agreed to lease and occupy property; also, the act of leasing the property.

**Tenant insurance:** The insurance a tenant purchases to protect property contained in a rental unit from loss.

**Tenant:** The party who rents an investment property from the landlord.

**Title insurance:** This insurance covers the purchaser or vendor in case of any defects in the property or title, that existed at the time of sale but which were not known until after completion of the sale.

**Title:** Generally, the evidence of right that a person has to the possession of property.

**Trust account:** The separate account in which a lawyer or real estate broker holds funds until the real estate closing takes place or other legal disbursement is made.

**Trust funds:** Funds held in trust, either as a deposit for the purchase of real property or to pay taxes and insurance.

# U

**Unit:** Normally refers to the rental suite or that part of a condominium owned and occupied or rented by the owner.

**Useful life:** The term during which an asset is expected to have useful value.

**Utilities:** Any one of the array of services that allow a property to function, and which typically deliver a basic social good, such as heat, water and electricity, or phone and television service. The landlord may provide access to utilities for a fee, or the tenant may be responsible for arranging a connection to the utilities.

# V

**Vacancy allowance:** A projected deduction from the scheduled gross income of a building to allow for loss of income due to vacant apartments or other rental units.

**Value, assessed:** The property value as determined by local, regional, or provincial assessment authority.

**Vendor take-back:** A procedure wherein the seller (vendor) of a property provides some or all of the mortgage financing in order to sell the property. Also referred to as vendor financing.

**Vendor:** A person selling a piece of property.

# W

**Week-to-week:** A tenancy that renews each week, typically under a commonly understood agreement between the landlord and tenant. It usually exists when tenancies continue after the term of a formal lease agreement.

# Z

**Zoning:** Rules for land use established by local governments.

# Further Education and Information

**For further information** about real estate investment in Canada, including seminars, books, software programs, and consulting, contact:

Canadian Real Estate Education Group
3665 Kingsway, Suite 300
Vancouver, B.C. V5R 5W2
Or visit them at www.homebuyer.ca.

# Index